Proslavery Priest

Also by B.W. Higman

Slave Population and Economy in Jamaica, 1807–1834

Slave Populations of the British Caribbean, 1807–1834

Jamaica Surveyed: Plantation Maps and Plans of the Eighteenth and Nineteenth Centuries

Montpelier, Jamaica: A Plantation Community in Slavery and Freedom, 1739–1912 (with George A. Aarons, Karlis Karklins and Elizabeth J. Reitz)

Writing West Indian Histories

Domestic Service in Australia

Plantation Jamaica, 1750–1850: Capital and Control in a Colonial Economy

Jamaican Food: History, Biology, Culture

Jamaican Place Names (with B.J. Hudson)

A Concise History of the Caribbean

How Food Made History

Proslavery Priest

The Atlantic World of John Lindsay, 1729–1788

B.W. Higman

University of the West Indies Press
Jamaica • Barbados • Trinidad and Tobago

University of the West Indies Press
7A Gibraltar Hall Road Mona
Kingston 7 Jamaica
www.uwipress.com

A catalogue record of this book is available from the
National Library of Jamaica.

ISBN: 978-976-640-255-6

Cover illustration: Flowering hedge plants, 1767. John Lindsay,
"Elegancies of Jamaica". Courtesy of the Bristol Museum and Art Gallery.

Book and jacket design by Robert Harris.
Set in Bembo 11/15 x 24
Printed in the United States of America.

IN MEMORY OF KEN INGRAM

Contents

Illustrations

Figures

Colour Plates

Between pages 144 and 145

Preface

PROBABLY IT IS AS IMPOSSIBLE to attempt a full account of a biographical subject as it is to live a coherent life. The effort is worthwhile but, like having a plan for one's life, rarely achieved. Only in the larger scheme of things, the great sweep of history, is it possible to get some sense of the significance of individual experience. This is without doubt true of the history of the so-called Atlantic world in the eighteenth century, a vast oceanic region connected and partially integrated, yet rarely a coherent concept for the people who lived in it. No wonder it is a hard task to reconnect the lives even of those who left behind substantial documentary traces. Many of them, including the Reverend John Lindsay, the subject of this book, remain elusive.

Lindsay did not publish a memoir of his own life in the manner of Olaudah Equiano, though the Atlantic journeys of these two men were as closely parallel as the contrast in their experience. Nor did Lindsay seem to keep journals of the sort that enabled the wonderfully detailed accounts of the life of Thomas Thistlewood, Lindsay's contemporary in Jamaica, published by Douglas Hall and Trevor Burnard, and provided in turn the foundations for James Walvin's recent comparison of "parallel lives" in *The Trader, the Owner, the Slave.* The truly spiritual transnational journey and interracial experience of Rebecca Protten, who was born in the Virgin Islands in 1718, recounted in Jon F. Sensbach's *Rebecca's Revival,* also contrasts strongly with that of Lindsay. And his was less obviously a global life than that of the extraordinary Elizabeth Marsh, born in Jamaica, whose travels and travails have been powerfully retold by Linda Colley in *The Ordeal of Elizabeth Marsh: A Woman in World History.* Yet, however starkly different in gender, colour and civil status, all these people had much in common, simply because they shared the same world.

What makes Lindsay important is that he left behind a substantial corpus of writing in a range of genres in which he is forthright in expressing his opinions and beliefs. It is in this way that he has something significant to contribute to understanding the world in which he lived and moved. He enables a history of thought and ideas. Believing that ideas can be more significant and influential than the details of individual existence – however much the opposite is proved true as soon as we are deprived of food and drink or break a limb – I intend in this book to centre attention on the intellectual world of Lindsay. I have attempted to create a "life and writings" rather than a "life and times". Although several aspects of the eighteenth-century life of John Lindsay have been reconnected in this book and although he has been distinguished from more than one namesake with whom he has previously been conflated, many details remain hazy and undiscovered. I have not been able to locate all of Lindsay's writings. Some of the gaps, such as those in the ecclesiastical records at Lambeth Palace, seem irreparable. Others simply require due diligence and a pinch of serendipity.

I have dedicated this book to the memory of Ken Ingram, former librarian of the University of the West Indies at Mona, because it was his wonderful guides to archival records which first brought John Lindsay to my attention. Entries in his *Sources of Jamaican History, 1655–1838* (1976) and *Manuscript Sources for the History of the West Indies* (2000) put me on the track to published and unpublished works in the United Kingdom. Once I got started on the project I quickly discovered that my interest was shared by James Robertson of the Department of History and Archaeology at the University of the West Indies, Mona, who had come to Lindsay from a different direction, namely the history of the city of Spanish Town. James's generosity in supplying me with transcripts, references and advice is much appreciated, and indeed was vital to making me aware of several aspects of Lindsay's life and writings, notably his authorship of the novel *Memoirs of Sir Thomas Hughson and Mr Joseph Williams*.

For their kind assistance in helping me obtain a copy of Lindsay's *Memoirs*, I thank Laurie Klein and Sandra Markham of the Beinecke Rare Book and Manuscript Library, Yale University, and Jillian Galle of Monticello. Dalea Bean collected a variety of materials for me from Jamaican libraries and archives, and Lawrence Niewojt assisted me similarly in Canberra. Issues of the *Columbian Magazine* in the Shoults Collection, Special Collections, University of Otago, New Zealand, were made accessible by Donald Kerr, with the assistance of Diana Brown and Rani Kerin. At the Bristol Museum and Art Gallery I had generous encouragement and assistance from Samantha Hallett and Rhian Rowson. There I made use of transcriptions of museum sources by Ann Brain, Ben Brown, Carole Gray, James Parsons and Libby

Houston and of determinations by Nick Wray of the University of Bristol Botanic Garden. From the University of Edinburgh I received valued advice from Stewart Brown, Nicholas Phillipson, M.A. Stewart and Nuala Zahedieh. Colleagues at the University of the West Indies who have assisted include Patrick Bryan and Verene Shepherd; Veront Satchell kindly provided me with images of one of Lindsay's Jamaican churches. Materials have also been made available to me by Trevor Burnard, Kirsty Douglas, Daive Dunkley, Jerome Handler, Mary Mill, Kenneth Morgan, Helen Rountree and April Shelford. Kenneth Morgan and Sue Thomas read chapters in draft, while Merle Higman, Shino Konishi, James Robertson and Margaret Steven read the entire manuscript. I am most grateful for the help and guidance I have received. I also thank Linda Speth and Shivaun Hearne of the University of the West Indies Press for their interest and enthusiasm.

Research for this book was carried out in association with a Discovery Project titled "A Creole Landscape: Jamaica in Time and Space", funded by the Australian Research Council. The writing was done in the History Program (now the School of History) of the Research School of Social Sciences at the Australian National University. Members of the School have encouraged my researches, and I particularly thank Margaret Steven for her advice on eighteenth-century Scotland and Susan Mary Withycombe for her help with Horace.

For permission to reproduce images, I thank the Beinecke Rare Book and Manuscript Library, Yale University; Bristol Museum and Art Gallery; the Syndics of Cambridge University Library; Ray Chen; the National Portrait Gallery, London; and the Victoria and Albert Museum, London.

In quotations from Lindsay's manuscripts I have retained the original spelling but modernized the use of capital letters and occasionally introduced and/or deleted punctuation. His underlined words have been italicized throughout.

CHAPTER ONE

A Curious Christian

THE GREAT EIGHTEENTH-CENTURY migration across the Atlantic saw millions of people moved to the Americas from Africa and Europe. Few of these people were able to return to their home places. Enslaved Africans, the majority of the migration, had no choice. Many died even before they reached the other side. Most of the Europeans lacked the resources to make return journeys and some had no desire to do so. Those who travelled to tropical America experienced heavy mortality. In the midst of this overwhelming pattern, a small number of Europeans and a tiny number of Africans managed to be peripatetic, shuttling back and forth across the ocean and around its rim. It was these exceptional people who were able to experience both the diversity and the connected character of the Atlantic world rather than simply a highly personal localized knowledge of two small places – the points that marked the beginning and end of their migration. Among the peripatetic minority were a few who struggled to make sense of this oceanic world and left behind evidence of their attempts to comprehend what they encountered. One such was John Lindsay.

Born in Scotland in 1729 and dying in Jamaica in 1788, John Lindsay crossed the Atlantic at least nine times. He also participated in voyages that took him to scattered points along the coasts of Europe and Africa. Brought up in a religious family and educated at Edinburgh University, he left Scotland as a young man to experience the wider world of Great Britain in its Atlantic dimensions. By the time he was twenty, Lindsay was on board a ship sailing off the banks of Newfoundland. He went next to Virginia, where he journeyed into the interior, well beyond the frontier of colonial settlement. Returning to Britain in 1753, he was ordained as a clergyman in the Church of England, not the Church of Scotland of his father. This affiliation enabled him to become a chaplain in the Royal Navy, and by 1755 he was again at sea, with fleets cruising into the brewing storm of the Seven Years' War.

In the midst of this Atlantic journeying and alongside his establishment as a clergyman, Lindsay found time for literary pursuits. In 1757, the year he was part of a British force against French Canada, he published a novel – *Memoirs of Sir Thomas Hughson and Mr Joseph Williams* – which blended his personal experience with fictitious geographies and classical mythologies. In 1758 he sailed to Senegal as chaplain with the British squadron that defeated the French at Gorée, an account of which he published the following year as *A Voyage to the Coast of Africa*. These two books were the most substantial of Lindsay's publications.

The second half of Lindsay's life was relatively settled. Towards the end of 1759, at the age of thirty, he travelled to Jamaica. Except for an occasional journey back to Britain, he remained there until his death in 1788. During his almost thirty years in Jamaica, Lindsay served as rector of several parishes, rising to become the island's most important representative of the established church. In 1773 he was made a doctor of divinity by Edinburgh University. As well as fulfilling his ecclesiastical duties, Lindsay made time to observe the flora and fauna of Jamaica. He produced a large number of watercolour paintings of plants and animals, accompanied by descriptive text, but failed to have this work published. The volumes eventually found their way into the collections of the Bristol Museum, sent there along with the papers of another amateur naturalist, Dr Arthur Broughton. Lindsay had better success with a series of papers on waterspouts that drew on his earlier experiences at sea. One of his sermons was published in his lifetime and another after his death, and in these Lindsay revealed something of his religious ideas.

Lindsay married into the Jamaican plantocracy and he became a slave-owner. He saw no conflict between his ownership of people and his Christianity. In the last years of his life, he set to writing justifications for slavery in order to defend his fellow planters against the attack on slavery and the slave trade that had begun to build after the American Revolution. In support of his proslavery arguments, Lindsay delved into the problem of the origin of human diversity, and this in turn led him to critical consideration of the status of Scripture as revealed truth. He also made proposals for improvement in the practice of slavery. However, the large manuscript on these subjects that Lindsay completed shortly before his death in 1788 was not published. It survives in the British Library among the papers of the planter-historian Edward Long, to whom Lindsay had entrusted it.

In Jamaica, Lindsay lived surrounded by enslaved black African people, but he inhabited a British intellectual milieu, a world of ideas nurtured by the Scottish Enlightenment yet English and Anglican in orientation. His was a truly British eighteenth-century life. He knew only two kings: George II, who reigned from 1727 to 1760, and his successor, George III. He witnessed the defeat of Scots' ambitions to have their own monarch and the bloody battles that accompanied that failure. He was an eager participant in the British imperial attack on his prime enemy, the popish French, and saw naval and imperial superiority placed in the hands of the British. He observed the American Revolution from afar, but died before the French Revolution and the revolution in Saint Domingue.

Although Lindsay lived through war and peace, revolution and reaction, and although he witnessed significant events, he was typically an onlooker, watching from the balcony rather than onstage as a leading character. He is more important for the record he created of his ideas and observations than for the information he supplies about eighteenth-century life. Little of the documentary record Lindsay left behind describes his daily experiences; the bulk of his quite substantial archive consists of texts intended for publication. Even what remained unpublished was written self-consciously, with a reading public in mind. He wished to inform and to entertain but sought also to closely observe the natural world and to locate it within a grander narrative of universal Christian history. Thus Lindsay's texts raise questions about the relationship between truth and fiction, reality and the world of the imagination.

A curious Christian, it was Lindsay's desire to understand the world around him not only in religious terms but also within the framework of eighteenth-century philosophy and science. He looked out for the unusual – the curious – in the natural world but attempted to account for what he observed through logic rather than measurement or experiment. What makes his texts significant is the way they help reveal how concepts of Christian theology could be accommodated to systems of social oppression and exploitation and applied to the explanation of human diversity and plurality. Lindsay lived in a time that saw both the invention of race theory and the emergence of antislavery movements. He struggled to come to terms with these new ideologies, seeking to reconcile them with the immediate self-interest of the colonial slave-owning class as well as with arguments surrounding the revelation of God's will in Scripture. It was an impossible task.

CHAPTER TWO

Atlantic Scotland

WHEN JOHN LINDSAY WAS born, Scotland had been united with England and Wales for more than twenty years as part of the kingdom of Great Britain (figure 2.1). The union of Parliaments in 1707 had ended the constitutional independence of Scotland, a process begun a century before, but many Scots refused to accept their subordinate status. The Jacobites – supporters of restoration of the Catholic James II and his successors – engaged in a series of abortive risings up to 1746, when their cause was finally defeated at the Battle of Culloden. The Presbyterian Church of Scotland was successful in maintaining its independence and its status as the established church of Scotland, but it fell to internal disputes over theology and governance.[1] Union opened access to the rapidly expanding British Empire, and Scots migrated in large numbers, becoming increasingly numerous among colonial administrators and military men. The imperial clergy were, however, compromised, forced to choose between identities and allegiances.[2]

Lindsay came to maturity when the religious and political turmoil of the previous hundred years had been resolved in favour of a binding alignment with England established alongside the emergence of a strong but paradoxical understanding of what it was to be separate, Scottish. His youth was spent surrounded by the parallel struggles of the church and debate over the content and character of Christian faith. These were questions that followed him throughout his life.

Bothkennar and Perth

John Lindsay was baptized at Bothkennar, Stirlingshire, on 13 June 1729. His parents were Henry Lindsay and Mary Simpson. Henry was a minister of

Figure 2.1 The British Isles, circa 1760

the Church of Scotland who preached at Bothkennar from 1722 to 1741 and then at Perth until his death in 1745. While at Bothkennar, he married Mary Simpson, or Macky, in 1727, the widow of an Edinburgh bookseller. John Lindsay was their second child and second son. Another seven children were born to them, the last in 1742.[3]

The village of Bothkennar is about four kilometres north-east of Falkirk, on the Forth River, roughly halfway between Edinburgh and Stirling (figure 2.2). Ships "of great burden" came there to load coal, which was traded to Scandinavia and the Baltic in return for timber, flax, hemp and iron, along with wine from Portugal, Spain and France. The Firth of Forth's trade was oriented eastwards, to Europe, unlike that of the Firth of Clyde to the west, where Glasgow's much larger trade was founded on tobacco from the Americas. Bothkennar was on the margins of modernity and pointed in a direction opposite to John Lindsay's Atlantic destiny. Described in 1723, the year after Henry Lindsay commenced preaching at Bothkennar, the kirk and manse were located at the centre of the parish. Settlement was sparse and dominated by tenant farmers. Close by the kirk was "Nun yeards, a nunerie in the time of popery", which in 1723 was replaced by a country house. Bothkennar, together with its larger surrounding region of Stirlingshire and Perth, had from the Reformation been known for its strong anti-Catholic sentiments. Henry Lindsay was the first Presbyterian minister to serve in the parish after the abolition in 1689 of the episcopacy – government of the church by bishops and archbishops – which saw the restoration of a separation between church and state and placed Catholics and Episcopalians under the control of a Presbyterian Church of Scotland, the established church.[4]

Henry Lindsay's years at Bothkennar were years of turmoil for the Church of Scotland. Old conflicts between Presbyterians and Episcopalians found new life in a struggle over church government and the role of patronage. In theory, the Presbyterian organization of the church placed government in the hands of an elected body of lay elders (of equal rank) and allowed parish congregations to elect their own leaders and ministers. This democratic theory came in conflict with the system of secular patronage whereby local lairds might inherit the right to make their own selections of ministers, a system given fresh life by the Patronage Act of 1712, which was passed by the English Tory government in contravention of the Act of Union and in the face of popular hostility. The act made clerical appointments the secular gift of the aristocracy and the Crown. The struggle over patronage proved a persistent problem for the church and came to represent a broader eighteenth-century rift between the Evangelical or Popular party and those who by the 1750s came to be known as Moderates. The difference extended beyond ecclesiastical government. The Popular party saw in the softened Calvinism of the Moderates signs of worldliness and a tepid spirituality.[5] This was a rift essential to the lives of the Lindsays, father and son. Henry Lindsay aligned himself with the Evangelicals, John with the Moderates.

The struggle over patronage came to a head in 1732 when Ebenezer Erskine (1680–1754), a minister at Stirling, opposed a decision of the General Assembly – the supreme ecclesiastical court of the Church of Scotland, which met once a year in Edinburgh – to require presbyteries to work with heritors (landowners who received a portion of the tithe) and elders in the appointment of ministers, and to give presbyteries the authority to overrule

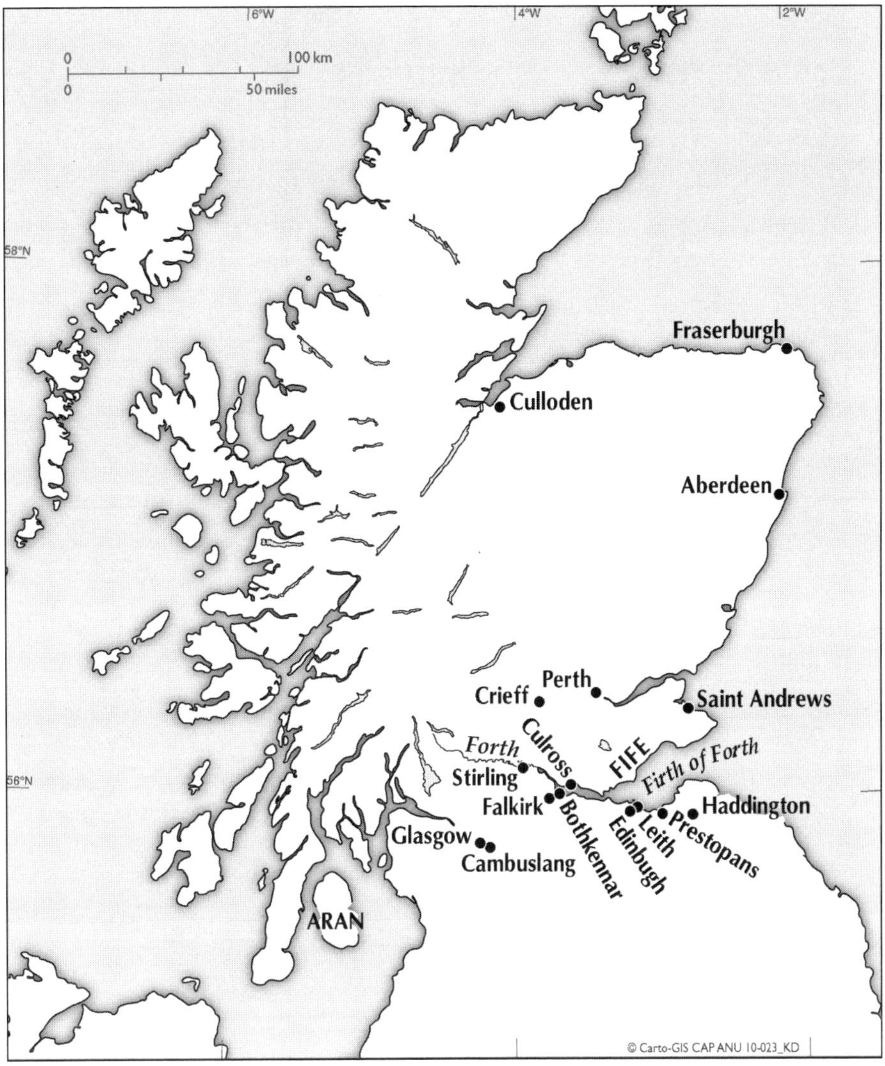

Figure 2.2 Scotland, circa 1760

congregations. (In the parish of Bothkennar there were twenty heritors, only half of whom lived in the parish, while its patronage was attributed to the family of Airth.) The Assembly's decision, said Erskine, denied "the divine right of the people in the choice of their pastors". Elected moderator of the synod of Perth and Stirling in October 1732, Erskine preached a sermon, later published as *The Stone Rejected by the Builders, Exalted as the Head-Stone of the Corner*, in which he denounced the decision and decried the erosion of church doctrine and government. Following heated debate in the synod, Erskine was formally rebuked.[6]

Henry Lindsay's Bothkennar parish was governed by the synod of Perth and Stirling. He entered the debate at the October 1733 synod, speaking from experience. The same year, the parish of Falkirk had fallen vacant and the congregation had called him as minister, but their choice had been overruled and the candidate of the heritors installed.[7] At the synod, Lindsay delivered a sermon, published before the end of the year as *The Present State of the Church of Scotland*, in which he spoke against patronage and advocated Evangelical beliefs but at the same time called for unity among his brethren. On church government, Lindsay found that "pastors have been intruded on congregations, contrary and in opposition to the good-will and choice of the bulk of the congregation; by which the Lord's people have been scattered like sheep upon the mountains without a shepherd". As "sons of Zion", he called on his reverend listeners to seek to repair the breach that had opened among them. They should think of themselves as "children of the family" and have "the concerns of our heavenly Father" at heart, Lindsay declared. It was necessary to follow the God of truth: "And more honourable it is to contend for his cause, and the *royalties* of his Crown and Kingdom, than to be the favourite of the great ones of the earth, or to sway a sceptre over an universal monarchy."[8]

When he came to offer advice, in his sermon of 1733 Henry Lindsay declared himself unfit because of his "younger years, and want of experience", in the presence of such an august assembly of "reverend fathers and brethren". However, he used a common device to get around his reluctance, declaring that he would do no more than bring forward examples from Scripture. He referred in particular to Nehemiah's role in "bringing back his people from Babylon, in building his temple, in repairing the breaches of Jerusalem". Without mentioning the case of Ebenezer Erskine, their moderator, Lindsay declared that all of those assembled needed to admit their errors, to mourn and to endure humiliation. He hoped for redress from the "Mother-Church" – the General Assembly – but proposed they take their grievances (meaning, above all, patronage) to King George, their gracious sovereign. Only thus could they expect blessing. Lindsay's approach was relatively temperate in the midst of so many hotheads; he moderated his dissent, saying that he had "used all dutiful respect to the authority of this Church" and revealed nothing of their internal troubles which was not already common knowledge.[9]

The synod to which Henry Lindsay delivered his sermon was held just two months before the founding of the Secession Church, in December 1733. When Erskine appealed against the rebuke he had received from the General Assembly the year before, he was admonished. When he and three other ministers were required to retract their protest and refused, their churches were taken from them. They established a separate communion and an "Associate Presbytery", which developed into a full-fledged church, drawing its initial adherents from the counties of Fife, Stirling and Perth.[10] In spite of his reputation as a "highly evangelical minister" and his heated remonstrations from the pulpit, Henry Lindsay did not join the Secessionists. He cooperated with Erskine and his associates but publicly testified against defection.[11]

Henry Lindsay's opposition to patronage was founded in his evangelical theology and his Presbyterian model of ecclesiastical government. He believed this was the best mechanism to ensure that ministers would be those who took their task seriously. Supporters of patronage, on the other hand, had a variety of motives. Members of the General Assembly with Episcopal leanings wished to preserve the hierarchical system of power and influence. Others held that patronage delivered a better-quality minister, arguing that congregations too often chose demagogic preachers, "men of little learning, sense, or moderation, or any other good qualities". They hoped for men of "learning and manners" and a clergy that was more moderate, tolerant and urbane – in fact, gentrified.[12] This argument was anathema to Henry Lindsay but welcome to his son John.

Yet another dispute over appointment engulfed Henry Lindsay when in 1737 the congregation at Perth called him to be their minister, in opposition to a separate call from the magistrates and patronal families. The General Assembly denied his appointment. The following year he was called to the parish of Culross – like Bothkennar, an old coal port on the Firth of Forth – but this too was set aside by the General Assembly and the patron's nominee was installed.[13] In spite of this series of rejections, Henry Lindsay clung to the Church of Scotland, his distaste for patronage outweighed by his love of unity. He did eventually go to Perth, in 1741, and died there on 2 May 1745.

In the last years of Henry Lindsay's life, when he was in Perth, the splinter congregations of the Church of Scotland were flourishing, bathed in an intense revivalist spirituality that spilled over from the enthusiastic evangelicalism associated with John Wesley (1703–91), the founder of Methodism, and George Whitefield (1714–70). Ebenezer Erskine and the Associate Presbytery invited the firebrand Whitefield to Scotland and he took part in a revival focused on Cambuslang, near Glasgow, which reached its climax of spiritual excitement in August 1742. Whitefield preached to tens of thousands, and in these vast outdoor communions many recognized the working of the Holy Spirit and entered ecstatic trances. However, the revival at Cambuslang – which had strong links with the Great Awakening in America and the Methodist revival in England – was denounced by the Associate Assembly and Whitefield's role declared the work of the devil.[14]

In 1742, when the revival at Cambuslang took place, John Lindsay was thirteen years old. The family had moved to Perth the year before. He had grown to adolescence in a household dominated by intense religious practice and persistent doctrinal dialogue. Faith and commitment were the core of life.

Edinburgh

Much of John Lindsay's early education must have come from his father, through his sermons and his library of classics and theology. At the Bothkennar parish school, John would have been taught English, writing, arithmetic and Greek. When Henry died, John was in his seventeenth year. By this time he was at Edinburgh University, most probably an arts student, but whether he took a degree is unclear. The absence of his name in the record is not surprising. As D.B. Horn observes, in both arts and medicine, "graduation was the exception – so much so in Arts that the Faculty was never very sure what the requirements were for an MA degree".[15]

Edinburgh University had gone through a dramatic reform of its curriculum and method of teaching in the first decades of the eighteenth century. It was transformed to match the model associated with Leyden, in Holland, where the application of a scientific approach to medicine made it the most celebrated European educational institution. Indeed, the establishment of the medical school marked the beginning of the Enlightenment in Edinburgh, promoting open, rational ways of thinking about the world, free of any religious test.[16] Edinburgh University became increasingly specialized, with the appointment of professors of mathematics, Greek, logic and metaphysics, ethics and natural philosophy, and moral philosophy, as well as ecclesiastical and civil history. There was for the first time, beginning in 1738, a professor of botany, and it may be that Lindsay attended his lectures and had his interest sparked. William Robertson (1721–93), principal from 1762 to 1793 and later a correspondent with Lindsay, introduced a chair of natural history in 1770. The medical school was a magnet for students from the British colonies, including the West Indies, and Lindsay may have encountered some of these creoles.[17]

In Lindsay's day, students were given a new freedom to choose their classes and the order in which they took them. What exactly Lindsay did with his time is uncertain. Students reading for an arts degree with an eye on a career in the church typically took a broad range of subjects, including Latin and Greek and classical texts in logic, metaphysics and ethics. They could also attend public lectures given by the professors and hear sermons, including those of the principal. In 1734 the professor of moral philosophy was ordered by the university "to prelect every Monday morning 'upon the truth of the Christian religion' and if any books used in his class 'shall contain anything contrary to the scriptures or the Confession of Faith or to good manners, he shall confute the same to prevent the youths' being corrupted with error or immorality' ". The (Westminster) Confession of Faith, ratified by the Scottish Parliament in 1647, was from the time of Union the foundation of doctrine for the Church of Scotland. Belief in the inspiration and infallibility of Scripture was fundamental.[18]

The city of Edinburgh was an important place in the middle of the eighteenth century. It had a population of about twenty-five thousand within its walls, and sixty thousand if its suburbs and port – Leith – are included. The "New Town" was just beginning to emerge. It was by far the richest city in Scotland. Its wealth derived not from business or finance but from the city's central role in the legal, religious, educational, administrative and governmental life of the country. In 1745 it also became the site of military activities, which were witnessed by the young Lindsay and incorporated into his fiction. The Glorious Revolution of 1688 had transformed the university from an Episcopalian college into a Presbyterian and Whig establishment. In the 1730s and 1740s the university made known its loyalty to Crown and Parliament and its abhorrence of "Popery" and Jacobitism. The declaration of war between Britain and France in 1744, followed by the arrival of Bonnie Prince Charlie in Edinburgh, elicited vocal support for the house of Hanover from many professors and students.[19]

In his novel, *Memoirs of Sir Thomas Hughson and Mr Joseph Williams*, published in 1757, Lindsay refers to the Battle of Prestonpans, where the Jacobites won a surprise victory against an English contingent on 21 September 1745. He claims to have fought in that battle. Charles Edward, the Young Pretender, had landed in Scotland on 23 July and an army of Highlanders had entered Edinburgh. In *Memoirs* Lindsay asks to be excused from "tedious narration" of the contest between "the King's army under Sir John Cope, and the forces under the Chevalier Stewart, in the field at Preston", declaring, "I was myself at the ensuing battle, a soldier under his majesty; volunteers and soldiers make insufferable historians." If this is true, Lindsay was sixteen years old and his father had been dead just four months. His account parallels the experience of twenty-four-year-old William Robertson, who similarly sided with the Hanoverians and volunteered his services to Cope; Robertson was not permitted to engage in combat but did collect intelligence before Prestonpans. Perhaps this was when Lindsay and Robertson first met.[20]

In his preface to *Memoirs* Lindsay says, "I wrote the following narrative, when but in my 17th year." He also claims that while "a young man on my studies at the University" one of his teachers had advised him privately "That in whatever sort of study I found the greatest entertainment, I should give myself a loose swing into its fields" in order to at first make it "an amusement and not a toil".[21] Lindsay felt he had perhaps gone too far in this direction, having got, "I am apt to think, too early into the acquaintance of the fair sex", for the entertainment of whom he found tales of Robin Hood and Little John more appealing than philosophy. In order to please such feminine tastes, he said, he had neglected his studies and given himself "a sort of loose to the reading of wretched *novels*". Thus "inchanted by magick softness", he drafted *Memoirs* "for the entertainment of a particular favourite".[22] This introduction to *Memoirs* was not written in 1746, however, but ten years later, by which time Lindsay was an ordained priest of the Church of England, anxious to promote his work as a contribution to moral improvement and a warning against the wretchedness and even indecency of the novel as a form.

Whatever the precise content of Lindsay's education and his degree of application to study, by the 1750s he was familiar with the theodolite, mathematical calculation and chart-making; he could draw and paint; he knew Latin, Greek and Hebrew and could read and speak French. He was well read in classical and theological literature, as well as contemporary histories and fictional entertainments. He was also acquainted with Lowlands geography, including the cities of Glasgow, Stirling and Edinburgh. He quickly came to have knowledge of a wider world, the Atlantic Empire.

Virginia

From 1749 to 1759 Lindsay was often at sea, spending brief periods at scattered colonial settlements on both sides of the Atlantic. He was in his twenties, the period between his youth and his settling in Jamaica. It was also the period of his greatest success in literary production, with the publication of *Memoirs* in 1757 and *A Voyage to the Coast of Africa* in 1759. Vital to the framing of his life during this time was the progress of imperial expansion and the growing conflict between Britain and France. In all the naval engagements observed by Lindsay, the enemy was the French.

Both the French and the English had established their first American – and Caribbean – colonies in the early seventeenth century, but they followed different models of settlement. Whereas the French preferred trade and religious conversion, the English sought to cultivate the landscape with their own agricultural technologies and their own varieties of private piety.[23] The English population grew rapidly on the North American eastern seaboard but the French extended a loose hegemony over vast stretches to the north and west. The struggle between the French and the English was broadly based, with its foundations in Europe and extending throughout the colonial world. Lindsay witnessed the balance shift firmly, though not definitively, towards the English, or rather, following union of England and Scotland in 1707, the British. He was one of those Scots who embraced Britishness enthusiastically. The patriotic hymn "Rule, Britannia", composed in 1740, with its proud claim that "Britons never will be slaves", was, after all, the work of a Scot, James Thomson.[24]

In the decades immediately before Lindsay's birth, one of the most significant political developments was the signing of the Treaty of Utrecht in 1713, marking the end of the War of Spanish Succession. Under the treaty, the French recognized the Protestant succession in Britain and agreed to expel the Jacobite "Old Pretender". The French gave up the island of St Kitts, making it exclusively a colony of Britain (figure 2.3). In North America, the French ceded to the British the territories of Newfoundland, Nova Scotia (Acadia) and Hudson Bay. These losses led them to establish a heavily fortified settlement at Louisbourg, on Cape Breton Island, in order to defend Quebec. Alliances continued to shift within Europe, however, and only in 1748 – the year before Lindsay commenced his Atlantic voyaging – did another decade-long struggle come to an end, with the Treaty of Aix-la-Chapelle. Beginning with the "War of Jenkins' Ear", which signified British attempts to break the trade monopoly of Spanish America, the conflict had developed into the War of Austrian Succession and finally hostilities with France. The British took Louisbourg in 1745 but returned it to the French under the treaty; the French destroyed the seaward fortifications they had built at Dunkirk, recognized the Hanoverian succession and agreed to exclude the Pretender from France.[25]

In 1749, the year after Aix-la-Chapelle and the year Lindsay turned twenty, he was sailing off the coast of North America. Writing in 1781, he recalled that he had first observed a waterspout while taking "a voyage to America in July 1749, about the banks of Newfoundland". This is the only evidence known of his taking ship in that year.[26] Later Lindsay referred more broadly to his personal experience of these regions, in the context of a critique of the credulity of contemporary commentators on the peopling of the polar regions who had not themselves faced the hardships of this harsh environment. Here he particularly had in mind Georges Louis Leclerc, Count de Buffon (1707–88), and Cornélius de Pauw (1739–99) and their respective works *Histoire naturelle* (1749) and *Recherches philosophiques sur les Américains* (1770–71). Unlike these "cabinet voyagers" to whom "every thing seems easy and possible – they dream o'er downy beds for northern seas: and as they wish for it, all is landed and happily over", Lindsay declared,

Figure 2.3 The Atlantic Ocean, circa 1760

“~~I~~We however who have shivered in the midst of this sea, when dismally thicken’d with huge and frightful tumbling islands of piercing ice, dare not to allow ~~myself~~ ourselves in such a mode of population.”[27]

A second visit to North America is known from a later casual reference, this time with more detail but less precise chronology. Writing in 1788, Lindsay recalled, “In 1752 or 3 I forget now which, I was of a party who went up from Virginia to meet a party of Indean chiefs (a temperate zone) in a renewal of peace, or brightening the hatchet betwixt us, and to distribute a number of royal presents amongst them, sent from England for them”. He mentioned this experience to establish his credentials as an observer of the indigenous peoples of North America. He was able to criticize other writers, he said, “from my own personal knowledge: not like a hasty [t]raveller or an ill inform’d voyager from a slight sample, but from interviews of numbers taken at leisure”. In the same document Lindsay referred to his “seasoning” – his initial exposure to the American environment – saying, “I was myself at time of the year, seized with a tertian fever and ague, in the neighbourhood of surrounding marishes (upon the side of the Potomack River, Stafford County Virginia) and was severely handled with it for some months: I was a stranger to the country – it was my seasoning – but far from being dangerous it never hindered me from visiting abroad.”[28] Again in 1788, discussing monster frogs claimed by M. Dumont to weigh as much as thirty-seven pounds – meaning Jean François Benjamin Dumont de Montigny (born 1696) in his *Memoires historiques sur la Louisiane* of 1753 – Lindsay said:

> I have seen the large bull frog (as they are call’d in Virginia) and so near this same Louisiana as the haunts of the Cherokee Indeans: but as far as my memory goes (for I did not weigh any of them) – but indeed I am so much ashamed of my frog, in the same company with M. Dumont – for upon my honour I dont think the largest frog, in all the swamps of Virginia, Carolina, or the hunting grounds of the Cherokees, did ever come near four or even three pounds weight – and *that*, no ill conditioned sort of frog neither![29]

In these disconnected references, Lindsay locates himself in Stafford County, Virginia, at the beginning of his time in North America; he mentions travelling to less precisely located places to the west (figure 2.4). He suggests that he travelled as far as the territory of the Cherokee, though he might also have met some of these people when they came to Williamsburg.[30] Lindsay attributes his journey from Virginia to the interior, with the purpose of “brightening the hatchet”, to either 1752 or 1753. He was back in London by December 1753. Contemporary documents have not revealed his presence in Virginia, but he does demonstrate detailed local knowledge, and the journey of 1752 or 1753 has good credentials.

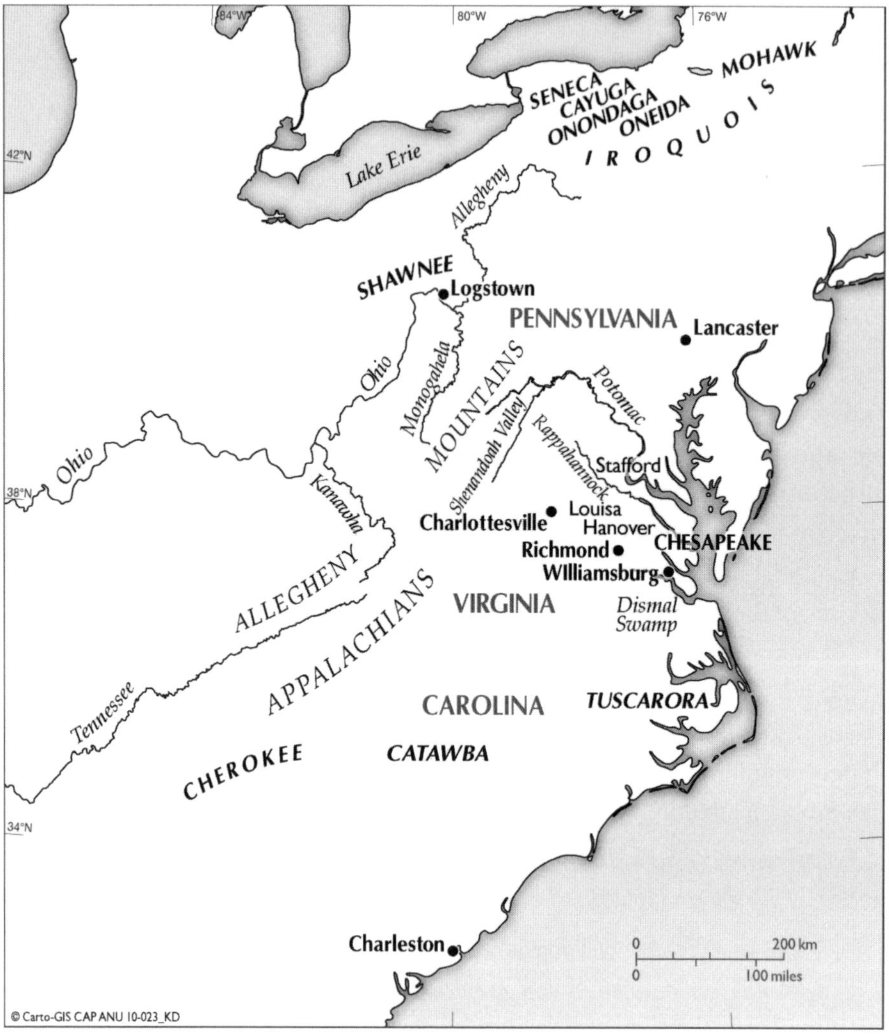

Figure 2.4 South-eastern North America, circa 1760

By Lindsay's time, the British colonization of Virginia had pushed the indigenous peoples towards the swamps and the mountains. Many sought the protection of the still powerful Iroquois, but Native Americans surviving within the zone of colonization were most likely to be servants or enslaved people.[31] A space opened up in the interior, between the Iroquois to the north and the Cherokees to the south, that was disputed between these two nations and settled by neither; it provided a setting for hunting and raiding parties. This zone proved highly attractive to European speculators and colonizers. One such speculative enterprise was the Ohio Company of Virginia, founded in 1748. It held its regular meetings at the Stafford courthouse, in the county where Lindsay had his "seasoning". At meetings held there in May and July 1751, the company determined to "cultivate a friendship and correspondence with the Ohio Indians" in order to confirm its rights to lands granted by the (British) king.[32] In December 1751, commissioners were appointed with the task of agreeing a treaty and to meet with the Indians the following May. The preamble to their commission stated: "his Majesty has been graciously pleased to make a Present of extraordinary Value to the northern Indians in Amity with us, and it has been agreed between this Government [Virginia] and those Indians to have the said Present delivered at Logg's Town in May next, and then and there to enter into a Treaty for polishing and strengthning the Chain of Friendship subsisting between us". The words are not exactly those of Lindsay but the essence is the same, and he was probably a party to this enterprise. To "brighten the hatchet", as Lindsay put it, meant renewing alliances and friendships, roughly equivalent to "polishing and strengthning the Chain of Friendship", whereas to "take up the hatchet" indicated the initiation of violent conflict.[33]

Appointment of the commissioners followed quickly with the arrival at Williamsburg of a new lieutenant-governor, Robert Dinwiddie (1692–1770), who had previously been a collector of customs in Bermuda and had travelled widely through the colonies as "Surveyor General of the Southern Part of the Continent of North America", a region stretching from Pennsylvania to Jamaica. The son of a Presbyterian Glasgow merchant, he married the daughter of the principal Anglican clergyman in Bermuda. He was "a champion, if not a communicant, of the Church of England" and had "acquired at least some of the habits and notions of an English gentleman".[34] In Virginia, Dinwiddie served as deputy to William Anne Keppel, second Earl of Albemarle (1702–54), an absentee governor who never visited the colony. In addition to his official duties, Dinwiddie was a shareholder in the Ohio Company and had a direct personal interest in preserving the territory's trade for the British and countering the French presence.[35]

Logstown, the site of the proposed meeting of May 1752, was on the Ohio River, close to the site of the modern city of Pittsburgh and somewhat beyond the settlements of Virginia's "back inhabitants". Settled first by the Shawnees, Logstown was now occupied by various peoples considered friendly to the British. It was a focal exchange point for the French as well as the British, and a central meeting place.[36] The council at Logstown commenced on 1 June 1752, the day after the arrival of three canoes full of gifts, and continued for two weeks. The British met with "the six united Nations of Indians on the River Ohio", namely the Mohawks, Oneidas, Onondagas, Cayugas, Senecas and Tuscaroras, who together made up the Iroquois league. When the formal proceedings began, the commissioners addressed first the

"Sachims and Warriors of the six united Nations, our Friends and Brethren", saying, "We are Glad to meet you at this place to enlarge the Council Fire already kindled here, by our Brethren of Pennsylvania, to brighten the Chain and to renew our Friendship, that it may last as long as the Sun, the Moon and the Stars shall give Light". They believed that "tho' at some times the Chain of friendship may have contracted some Rust, it has been easily rubbed off, and the Chain has been restored to its brightness".[37]

When the speeches had concluded, the commissioners presented the gifts sent by George II. The hard negotiations that followed revealed a wide open misunderstanding about the extent of land ceded by the Iroquois at an earlier conference held at Lancaster, Pennsylvania, in 1744. The Indians believed that the Lancaster treaty had not ceded territory beyond the Alleghenies. The commissioners claimed that if British settlement south of the Ohio were sanctioned, the Indians would gain cheaper goods and greater security against the French. The commissioners got what they wanted. The Treaty of Logstown gave Virginia the right to establish a trading post or fort at the Ohio River forks, plus two hundred thousand acres, but the Indians still did not want settlers on their territory.[38]

Although Lindsay is not listed among the important figures present at the Logstown conference, this is not surprising, in view of his youth. Descriptions of the event make clear that unnamed white men were indeed involved in one role or another.[39] Certainly Lindsay's later account of his time in Virginia points to the possibility, and even though he devotes few words to his experience, what he does say matches the events quite closely.[40] Lindsay also suggests that he had carefully observed the forests of the interior and was capable of recognizing differences between regions and types of trees. And he claims to have met Benjamin Franklin, though whether in the American colonies or in Europe he does not say.[41]

Further clues to Lindsay's claim to knowledge of the Virginia community and its customs are to be found in his *Memoirs* of 1757. A character in the novel, known only as Mr *****, is sent abroad from Scotland by his grandfather "in the *Virginia* trade: where he remained as a store-keeper to his parent in a town on the side of the *Rappohanock*: till his twentieth year, when he was allowed to trade for himself".[42] This places him close to the site of Lindsay's own "seasoning" on the Potomac. Although the colony of Virginia was stridently English and anti-Scots, the Scottish population of merchants and planters grew rapidly in the eighteenth century, particularly after 1740, through the role of Glasgow merchants in the tobacco trade. Scots clergy became equally common in spite of "general characterizations of them as uncouth, self-seeking, secret Presbyterians, or Jacobites".[43] Another character in Lindsay's novel, Syphax (in fact the father of Mr ***** but unknown to him), is transported to Virginia as a convict and sold to a master who "used him with a roughness the worst of his slaves were strangers to". Syphax flees and "got the distance of six counties away from his master's plantation, when the hue and cry laid hold on him". Following a series of lashings, "with a scourge of the toughest twigs", Syphax is returned to his master's plantation.[44]

These events take place "not many miles" from the residence of Mr *****, who learns the story of Syphax and, his paternity revealed, "pitied his unhappy father's condition". Although Mr ***** believes Syphax "merited his hard servitude for his cruelty to his mother" and although he was "ashamed to own his relation to so unworthy a man", he finally, "under the pretence of common humanity for the abused person, bought from the rugged planter the remaining years of his father's servitude". Since Syphax possesses "a kind of university education", Mr ***** sets him up in a school. He has few pupils but manages to teach "a shallow notion and knowledge of the languages" to a young man, Moncur,

> which without the smallest judgement, but mere strength of memory, enabled him to hobble through a verse or two in the New Testament, and to obtain thereby (as it was for the cure of a *Virginian* congregation) a power of repeating from the pulpit a group of common-place expressions, and [plagiarized] sentences. A mixture hideous to a critical ear: but being in a country where sermons are but rarely read, the theft passes as his own: And a popular cant being his principal qualification: he has had the good fortune, by taking upon himself a French expression of his name, to pass for a gentleman of family, and a scholar of great abilities.[45]

The story of Moncur presented by Lindsay in *Memoirs* matches closely the experience of Rev. John Moncure, a Huguenot born in Scotland 1709 and ordained as a deacon and a priest in 1737. Moncure was priest of Overwharton parish, in Stafford County, Virginia, from 1738 to 1764. He also worked as a physician and tutor. He was appointed a justice of the peace for Stafford County in 1752, around the time Lindsay lived there. Moncure had friends among the planter elite who were said to value the company of clergymen since they were "meant to be, after all, men of some learning", with some Latin and perhaps Greek, as well as "knowing something of the ancient philosophers and the Church Fathers, presumably interested in the political and religious controversies that had embroiled England since time immemorial, and curious about the natural history of religion".[46]

Lindsay's novel also suggests close observation of some indigenous social practices and their survival at a relatively late date. For example, he says:

> they have in America, amongst the Indians, towards the back parts of our settlements, a certain form of ceremonies in creating those persons who are to serve in

> any public employment, which they call Huskanawin; they confine the candidate to some particular part of the woods, where he may have the sun's full influence beating upon him for two days: after this, being an hungry, he is fed with herbs, poisonous of nature, which, with the sun's continued influence render the patient intirely distracted, and mad; having been a proper time in this state of madness, he is recovered by degrees, with the assistance of antidotes, and then invested into his office, in which he continues for life. They imagine, that by this means the patient is transformed into a new nature; and during this state of madness forgetting all worldly affairs past, and thereby losing all prejudice and partialities, is rendered the more proper to do justice between man and man.[47]

Lindsay's account suggests personal observation or direct hearsay evidence collected somewhere in America. This practice was, however, confined to Virginia, and Lindsay's reference to the "back part of our settlements" could point more precisely to the journey he may have made to Logstown. The *Oxford English Dictionary* defines *huskanaw* as a "ceremony or ordeal, formerly in use among the Indians of Virginia, of preparing young men for the duties of manhood by means of solitary confinement and the use of narcotics", and it gives as its earliest citation Robert Beverley's *History and Present State of Virginia*, first published in 1705. Lindsay's shorter account matches Beverley's description of *huskanawing* in content but not in composition. Nothing else in *Memoirs* seems to derive from Beverley; Lindsay was a close though limited observer of colonial Virginia.[48]

At the end of 1753, when Lindsay had left Virginia, Dinwiddie sent another mission to Logstown. As its leader he chose George Washington, aged twenty-one (two years younger than Lindsay), recently returned to Virginia from Barbados, and now engaged in making land surveys in the Shenandoah Valley.[49] Although this second mission to Logstown was not part of Lindsay's journey, the events surrounding Washington's negotiations were momentous, serving as triggers for the so-called French and Indian War and the Seven Years' War, which kept the British and French in conflict from 1756 to 1763.[50] Lindsay was well informed on all of these developments, and they formed the context for his later journeys to Nova Scotia, Senegal and Jamaica.

Naval Chaplain

In December 1753, soon after his return to Britain from Virginia, Lindsay was ordained as a deacon in the Church of England.[51] He took this step in spite of his Scottish birth, his father's allegiance to the Church of Scotland, his education in Edinburgh and his continuing links with Scotland, but the transition was less dramatic and difficult than might appear. Lindsay was one of many, and indeed the route he followed was the only way for Scots to find ecclesiastical places in the British imperial system, in both its colonies and its military. Further, there are many clues that Lindsay did not share the evangelical orientation of his father or his father's aversion to patronage. Rather, the younger Lindsay aligned himself with the opposite camp – the Moderates – and, like Dinwiddie and many other Scots, willingly enough came to think of himself as not only British but even "English". Anglicanism followed a path of religious moderation, regarding it as a cardinal Christian virtue much preferred to the clerical controversies that had persisted into the early eighteenth century. Toleration, even lukewarmness, seemed appropriate both as a strategy of the Hanoverian government and as an attitude attuned to the Enlightenment.[52]

The qualifications demanded of candidates for ordination in the Church of England were limited. To be admitted as a deacon, the candidate had to be male, at least twenty-three years of age, and able to offer evidence of a university education or its equivalent, and he must have a knowledge of the Scriptures and of the articles of faith. He had also to exhibit seriousness of purpose and be of good character. Lindsay had no difficulty in demonstrating these qualities, and he may have carried with him a recommendation from a sympathetic Dinwiddie. To advance to the next stage, that of priest, the candidate had only to be twenty-four years of age. Lindsay was just a few months older than that when he was ordained as a priest. Underlying the graduation from deacon to priest was a probationary model, but this was rarely followed in eighteenth-century practice, and the transition could occur in days rather than years.[53]

Lindsay's objective was not to become a parish priest in England or Scotland, as his father had been, but rather to seek appointment as chaplain in the Royal Navy, which he achieved in 1755. He was one of forty-four appointed that year, a relatively large recruitment, as the Seven Years' War was looming. It was an opportunity to join the fight against the French and popery, to be at the centre of the action and to enjoy life at sea. Indeed, this final desire may in itself explain Lindsay's decision to seek ordination in the Church of England. Ministers of the Church of Scotland, as well as those belonging to other Protestant denominations and Roman Catholics, were not included among the chaplaincy on a regular basis until much later. Not every ship had a chaplain, however, and it remained the practice that ship captains could select their favourites for the post.[54]

In the 1750s it was complained that because chaplainships could be obtained by "interest" it was possible for an appointee to choose to be excused from the associated duties, "for a cruise or an expedition cannot be supposed extremely agreeable to a person who has had a liberal land-education". Lindsay was perhaps unusual in combining a liberal education and a love of literature with an enthusiasm for life on the ocean wave and the sound of gunfire. His elder brother, William, was a soldier in the British army. Lindsay could come as close to the action as he wanted. As a naval chaplain he was expected to tend to the sick and dying, as well as to read divine service at least twice every day. This was the theory. In practice, even the reading of prayers was extremely rare until the 1770s.[55] The naval chaplain was left with a good slice of time available for reading and writing, an opportunity even greater than that enjoyed by the typical parish priest. Lindsay grasped at the chance.

He was appointed first to HMS *Newcastle*, a fourth-rate ship of fifty guns and about a thousand tons, which was launched at Portsmouth in 1750. It had a complement of 350 men and was commanded by John Lloyd. Together with his servant Thomas Levally (or Lovally), Lindsay joined the ship as chaplain on 10 May 1755. The *Newcastle* had been at Portsmouth since March, and it was there that Lindsay boarded.[56] Although Lindsay later recalled that he had been "chaplain of His Majesty's ship Newcastle" in 1755, he gave no indication of voyages made. The only other clue he left was that there was a prisoner on board, "a French Counsellor at Law (P.A.M. Lohier) a man of great probity, and learning", who had with him "an excellent and well chosen library" which he shared with Lindsay.[57]

Captain John Lloyd's log shows that the *Newcastle* left Spithead (Portsmouth) on 23 July 1755 and joined a fleet of about fifteen vessels (the numbers changed from time to time) in company with Vice-Admiral Hawke on board the *St George*.[58] Edward Hawke (1705–81) had risen slowly through the ranks of the navy; he was dependent for advancement on the patronage of his uncle, Colonel Bladen, a commissioner of trade and plantations. He cruised widely through the Atlantic, but it was a period in Jamaica in the early 1730s that proved vital to his promotion. Hawke engaged in many battles in the war with France and Spain and, together with George Rodney, took the *Fougueux*, the French vessel in which Lindsay would later serve as chaplain, at the Battle of Cape Finisterre in 1747, when the fleet escorting a convoy to the West Indies was defeated by the British.[59]

When Hawke left port in the middle of 1755, the Seven Years' War was brewing but still undeclared. The formal declaration of war did not come until 18 May 1756. The conflict had its roots in North America, as Lindsay observed during his time in Virginia: the French seemed to be blocking British colonial invasion of lands stretching from the St Lawrence River to Louisiana. Fearing invasion at home, the British stepped up patrols of the French coast and sought to inhibit trade and the movement of military forces

Figure 2.5 Europe, circa 1760

from France to Quebec. News of the French defeat of a Virginian force under Washington, in the Alleghany Valley, confirmed Britain's fears and encouraged its attempts to control the Atlantic. Hawke, appointed commander-in-chief at Portsmouth, was given responsibility for securing the Bay of Biscay, the great sweep of Spanish and French coastline from Ushant to Cape Finisterre, and the home of the major trading ports of Bordeaux and La Rochelle.[60]

Hawke ordered the *Newcastle* to cruise off Cape Finisterre and take any warships it could (figure 2.5). None were intercepted, but on 25 August 1755 the vessel chased and captured two French merchant ships – the *Mariana* and the *Sophia* – bound from Bordeaux for Martinique. The next day the *Newcastle* took a schooner from Bayonne, a smaller port south of Bordeaux, that was laden with flour destined for the French fortress at Louisbourg. Further chases followed but no fresh captures, until 10 September, when the *Newcastle* took the *Amiable Catherina*, which was sailing from the Newfoundland banks to Havre de Grace (Le Havre) with a cargo of saltfish. With greater significance for Lindsay's account, on 22 September his ship took the *Concord* and the *Expenditure*, French merchant vessels carrying sugar, coffee, indigo and cotton to Bordeaux, and the following day brought on board the *Newcastle* a number of French prisoners. Probably these included Lohier, who had been travelling from the French West Indian colonies. After six months at sea they returned to Portsmouth, arriving 29 September, together with Hawke's contingent and the prizes taken from the French. Whereas British opinion saw commerce raiding as good policy, sweeping aside trade and shipping before an official declaration of war, the French were less understanding about what verged on privateering.[61]

The Lords of the Navy were unimpressed by Hawke's premature return while French warships continued to cross the Atlantic. But it meant that Lindsay and his shipmates were in port, away from Cape Finisterre and the Portugal coast, when the great Lisbon earthquake struck on All Saints' Day, 1 November 1755, sending a tsunami across the Atlantic. Not only was this the strongest earthquake in European history, it sent shockwaves through religion and philosophy, dividing those who saw it as an act of divine retribution from others, such as Voltaire, who declared that the disaster demonstrated that undeserved suffering is a reality in the world.

Lindsay's second voyage on the *Newcastle* commenced on 13 March 1756. How he filled the intervening months is unknown but he must have spent at least some of his time rewriting his novel, *Memoirs*, incorporating nautical and military material learned on the first voyage, along with the character named Lohier. The *Newcastle* was now once more part of a fleet led by Hawke, and it returned to the fruitful hunting grounds off Cape Finisterre and nearby Cape Ortegal. The objectives were more obviously military, since the French were known to be massing troops at Brest – a major French naval port – for despatch across the Atlantic. While blockading Brest, the *Newcastle* was sent south, alone, for ten days. Cruising off Cape Ortegal, on 5 April 1756 the ship encountered the *Bon Amy*, a French schooner bound for Quebec from Bordeaux, laden with wine, brandy, iron bars, musket balls, small shot and oil. After firing three times, the *Newcastle* brought the *Bon Amy* to and captured the vessel. The next day they took a French troop ship, the *Ranson*, on its way from Port Louis (on the northern tip of the Bay of Biscay) to Cape Breton Island. The remainder of this short voyage saw no further incidents, however, and by the end of May the *Newcastle* was back at Portsmouth.[62]

This time the *Newcastle* spent only a few weeks in port, and by the end of July 1756 it was back at sea, venturing further into the Atlantic, cruising off the Azores and chasing but failing to capture a Portuguese ship on its way from Brazil to Lisbon. With no prizes to show, it returned to Portsmouth at the end of August. This time it spent only two weeks in port, dashing off again to the seas near the island of Ushant. Sweeping south, it had success on 10 October, when it took the *Elizabeth*, a French ship with a cargo of coffee and cotton on its way from Martinique to Le Havre. By the first day of December, the *Newcastle* was moored once more at Portsmouth.[63]

The *Newcastle* sailed next to India, leaving Portsmouth on 10 March 1757. By April 1758 it was engaged in action against the French off the coast of India. Severely damaged in battle in September 1759, the ship was lost in a storm in 1761.[64] Fortunately for Lindsay and his servant, Thomas Levally, they were no longer on board. They had left the *Newcastle* on 27 January 1757, before it set sail for the east.[65] Whether Lindsay was discouraged from remaining on the *Newcastle* or saw better opportunities elsewhere is unknown. His four voyages on the ship had kept him at sea for much of the time from May 1755 to November 1756, though he spent roughly eight of those nineteen months in port or on land. Perhaps he was daunted by the prospect of the long voyage to India and thought action in the North Atlantic more to his taste, now that the British had begun their aggressive attack on the French settlements of North America. His sphere had thus far been firmly located within the Atlantic world, and it remained his familiar territory and region of specialized knowledge. A more immediate reason for not wishing to sail for India in 1757 was simply that he wished to see his novel through the press and needed a longer breathing space in order to complete the task.

Lindsay's next voyage commenced three months after leaving the *Newcastle*, when he boarded the *Fougueux* on 26 April 1757 and headed west to Cork and across the Atlantic towards Newfoundland. In the meantime, he had busied himself with bringing to publication his novel, dating the preface 8 April and locating himself in London, in Leicester Square.[66] The fleet with which the *Fougueux* sailed did not leave Cork until May, the month in which the novel was first noticed in the London press. Perhaps Lindsay received a copy before he began his voyage across the Atlantic, but he was not in Britain to read the first reviews when they appeared later that year.

CHAPTER THREE

Fictive Kin

When Lindsay's novel was published in 1757, it appeared without his name on it. The title page trumpeted that its four volumes contained the *Memoirs of Sir Thomas Hughson and Mr Joseph Williams, with the remarkable history, travels, and distresses, of Telemachus Lovet: The whole calculated for the improvement of the mind and manners; and for a becoming and useful entertainment for the youth of both sexes*, but it merely noted that the work had been printed in London "for the author".

Lindsay is known to be the author of *Memoirs* because he later identified himself as such. He did so while in Jamaica, in his preface to an "oration" prepared to be delivered before the island's governor, William Henry Lyttleton, at a celebration of the peace of 1763. The preface was written later, either in 1766 or 1767, when the lieutenant-governor was Roger Hope Elletson. In it Lindsay explained that the oration closely followed a "discourse" he had prepared in September 1761, about two years after his arrival in the island, at the request of the then lieutenant-governor Sir Henry Moore, to be delivered at a ceremony to mark the coronation of George III. Given only a day's notice and quickly "ruminating on a subject proper for the coronation of a *young* prince", said Lindsay, "I recollected that I had some years before published a work called *Memoirs of Sir Thomas Hughson, &c.* in the forth volume of which I introduced a chapter containing some ideas concerning a patriot king". The text of the oration, together with the preface containing the admission of authorship, did not come to light until published by the Kingston *Columbian Magazine* in 1797, after Lindsay's death.[1]

Memoirs was never reprinted, so there was no opportunity for a new edition to carry Lindsay's name; rather than bringing him fame, his authorship seems not to have been known to those who wrote his obituary. In spite of his self-identification in 1766–67, the fact remained hidden until excavated at the beginning of the twenty-first century by James Robertson. Only two copies of *Memoirs* are known, one in the National Library of Scotland and the other in the Beinecke Collection of Yale University Library. If they know it at all, literary scholars have mined the novel only for its Shakespearean performance references.[2]

Anonymity was a common conceit among British novel-writers of the eighteenth century. Concealing the identity of the writer added yet another layer to the mystery of the fictional foundations of this new – "novel" – genre. Pseudonymity was equally popular. It was also common to reveal authorship soon after publication, as Lindsay sought to do, or to have it revealed. Some authors claimed that their reason for publishing anonymously was modesty, suggesting the privacy of authorship. In other cases there was a desire to see how the work would fare among critics and readers, denying authorship if it sank but being quick to accept the accolades if it was a success (and prevent some other person claiming the praise). Lindsay's contemporaries, including some of the more famous founders of the modern novel in English, did this often.[3]

Lindsay openly discussed the reasons for his decision not to put his name on the title page of *Memoirs*. He included in the book an "Apology" from "the author to the public" in which he reflected on the view that "the great means of an author's escaping the criticisms of the partial and malevolent, is to remain unknown". Anonymity might be possible for some, he said, "But with me, though extreamly desirable, I'm afraid 'tis impracticable", because his "method of publication" (by subscription) had already "given the secret to hundreds".[4] *Memoirs* did not include a list of these subscribers, and whoever they were – and however numerous they might have been – they seem not to have advertised his authorship.

Although quickly forgotten, Lindsay's *Memoirs* was significant for its appearance among the first flurry of works published in the 1740s and 1750s that firmly established the novel as a literary genre. Public acceptance was hard won; the terms *novel* and *fiction* were most often used in a pejorative sense, pointing to the grounding of these works in falsehood and lies. Few writers referred to their works as novels. Like Lindsay, most called them histories or memoirs.[5] Probably the reason why Lindsay thought it "extreamly desirable" to remain anonymous was that, as an ordained priest, he did not wish to be associated with the more salacious side of fiction writing. He said he was "heartily ashamed to appear in the character of a writer of modern entertainments" but declared that, compared to the "many contemptuous volumes" that were available to the public, he thought his own tale "at least decent". What might be accounted "decent" was very much a matter of current debate in the London of the 1750s. Lindsay did not venture into this debate, but he was correct in believing that the literature and popular art of his time permitted much – for example, the depiction of bodily functions – that would soon become less acceptable.[6]

Hundreds of "novels" were published in the 1740s and 1750s, but only a handful are remembered. From the 1740s, six works in English by three writers are recognized as worthy of study, and even fewer worthy of the modern reader's time: Samuel Richardson's *Pamela* (1740) and *Clarissa* (1747–48); Henry Fielding's *Joseph Andrews* (1742), *Jonathan Wild* (1743) and *Tom Jones* (1749); and Tobias Smollett's *Roderick Random* (1748). The 1750s, until the publication of Lindsay's *Memoirs*, saw also Fielding's *Amelia* (1751) and Richardson's *Sir Charles Grandison* (1753–54). Lindsay had read most of these books and referred to them explicitly in his text. For the modern reader, probably the least easily recognized is *Sir Charles Grandison*, a work that was highly influential into the nineteenth century and esteemed by both Jane Austen and George Eliot.[7] It is *Sir Charles Grandison* that comes closest in style and form to the narrative in Lindsay's *Memoirs*.

Lindsay's claim that he wrote *Memoirs* in his seventeenth year in order to impress a "favourite" would locate its composition in 1745 or 1746, before his time in Newfoundland and Virginia and his ordination and appointment as a naval chaplain, and immediately after publication in 1744 of *The Adventures of David Simple*, the work of Fielding's sister Sarah. However, the action of *Memoirs* continues up to 1750, and elements and events within the narrative point to a later date than 1746.[8] Lindsay quotes from Smollett's *Roderick Random* (1748) and refers to Richardson's *Clarissa* (1747–48). *Memoirs* also mentions Sophia Western and Blifil as characters of "Mr Fielding"; these appeared in Fielding's *Tom Jones*, first published in 1749. Even closer to 1757, *Memoirs* contains references to Richardson's *Sir Charles Grandison* (1753–54).[9] Thus, although some of the composition may have been completed by 1746, Lindsay must at least have returned to the manuscript and made additions and amendments at a later date up to about 1755, his original target date for publication and the year he became a naval chaplain.

Once his initial aim had been achieved, Lindsay claimed, "the manuscript was thrown by" and lost for the next five years amongst the books in his library. But the volumes eventually came to the notice of "a clergyman in town, the Rev[d] Mr L—d H—d, D.D. a man in esteem; known in the republic of letters, and employ'd at court", and he "insisted on my publishing them". Lindsay told him that "if he would be at the trouble of overlooking and correcting the stile; I should not only find credit for carrying on the work, and procure a subscription for its sale", but also give him half the profit.[10] However, his partner proved less than equal to the task. The proposed publication date in 1755–56 passed, and finally Lindsay "sent each volume to a different press" to meet his obligations to his subscribers. However, "even in this expedition, before I could get the whole compleated, the summer drew nigh; and the service of his Majesty called me abroad". Here Lindsay alludes to his abortive voyage to Louisbourg in 1757. The "Apology" at the front of *Memoirs*, dated 8 April 1757, locates him in Leicester Square. By the time *Memoirs* was first noticed – listed under "Poetry and Entertainment" in the May 1757 issue of the *Gentleman's Magazine*, and available for twelve shillings – Lindsay was on board the *Fougueux*.[11]

The four octavo volumes of Lindsay's *Memoirs* comprise 12 books in 195 chapters. There are 1,035 pages of text and an additional 69 preliminary, errata and blank pages. At about 290,000 words *Memoirs* is a large work, though shorter than Fielding's *Tom Jones*, which was published in six volumes containing approximately 410,000 words of text. The title page of *Memoirs* declares that the work was sold by L. Davis and T. Waller, booksellers in Fleet Street; T. Osborn and J. Shipton, Gray's Inn; W. Strahan, Cornhill; R. Griffiths and W. Fenner, Paternoster Row; J. Millan, Charing Cross; and Messrs Wilson and Durham, in the Strand. All of these were in London, the undisputed capital of publishing in English. Although there were active printing, publishing and bookselling industries in cities such as Glasgow, Aberdeen and particularly Edinburgh, and in spite of the Scottish orientation of the book itself, London offered Lindsay his greatest market. As well as having its own resources, London was a magnet that drew entrepreneurs from other towns and cities, including some of those whose origins were north of the border.[12]

Lockyer Davis, the first bookseller listed on the title page of *Memoirs*, had premises in both Fleet Street and Holborn, having commenced business in 1753. He also acted as a publisher, and in 1757, the year of Lindsay's *Memoirs*, he published the highly successful *Estimate of the Manners and Principles of the Times*, by Dr John Brown, which rapidly went through several editions. Davis's partner, T. Waller, had published Dr Dodd's *Beauties of Shakespeare* in 1752. Thomas Osborne, of Gray's Inn, was a bookseller, publisher and book auctioneer. Although sneered at in Pope's *Dunciad* and accused of overcharging, Osborne was also called "the most celebrated bookseller of his age". William Strahan was unusual in being known best as a printer; he apprenticed first in Edinburgh but came to London in 1737, and was a personal friend of Benjamin Franklin. Ralph Griffiths was a bookseller and publisher with several London premises. He was famous for founding in 1749 a critical magazine, the *Monthly Review, or Literary Journal*, and for employing Oliver Goldsmith as a reviewer. William Fenner was the son of a printer and operated in London from 1756 as bookseller and publisher. John Millan was a well-known publisher who dealt extensively in new and second-hand books.

D. Wilson and T. Durham were in partnership in the Strand as booksellers and publishers.[13] But these were not the only booksellers who were selling Lindsay's *Memoirs*, even within London. Thomas Lowndes, who claimed to have ten thousand books in his circulating library, included *Memoirs* in his 1758 catalogue, classifying it under "Romances and Novels, and other Books of Entertainment".[14]

"Neither Connection, Taste, nor Entertainment"

The first reviewer of Lindsay's *Memoirs* was Oliver Goldsmith; his brief notice appeared promptly in the May 1757 issue of the *Monthly Review*, the magazine published by Ralph Griffiths. Goldsmith (1728–74) was freshly embarked on his literary career, having arrived in London the year before to work as an apothecary's assistant, medical practitioner and teacher. Born in Ireland, the son of a clergyman of the established Protestant church, he had begun medical studies at Edinburgh University in 1752 but soon after travelled to Leyden and took his own version of the Grand Tour. The reviews he wrote in 1757 preceded his own multifarious work; his most famous novel, *The Vicar of Wakefield*, modelled on the rectory life of his father, did not appear until 1766.[15]

Goldsmith dealt with the thousand and more pages of *Memoirs* in just two sentences, beginning with Lindsay's wordy title:

> Fair promises! yet, like a Smithfield conjuror, who, to draw company, exhibits at the door his best shew for nothing, this author exhausts all his scanty funds on the title-page. When our memoir-mongers have once found a title to their intended romance, it is but writing a romance to their title, and *dash away* is the word, without looking behind or before, through three or four such sizeable volumes as the memoirs of Sir Thomas Hughson, and Mr. Joseph Williams.[16]

This was one of Goldsmith's first literary pieces, one of twenty-two short notices he contributed to the May issue of the *Monthly Review*. Most of these were in the same style: a paragraph long and directed at the book's title rather than its contents. It is not surprising that Goldsmith seems to have had little time to consider the contents of these tomes, though in the same issue he contributed longer, considered reviews of works such as Edmund Burke's (anonymous) *Philosophical Enquiry into the Origin of Our Ideas of the Sublime and Beautiful* and Smollett's *Complete History of England*, both of which Goldsmith approved of as virtuous searches for truth. He was on a treadmill, but it is hard to see how his assessment of Lindsay's novel could help the *Monthly Review*'s publisher, Ralph Griffiths, sell copies of the work.[17]

In November 1757 *Memoirs* was reviewed in another London journal, the *Critical Review*. Established only the year before, the *Critical Review* was a project of Archibald Hamilton, a Scottish printer, and edited by the "irascible" novelist Tobias Smollett. Although Smollett solicited reviews of Scottish works from friends in the circle of William Robertson, he wrote a great many of them himself and became well known for the harsh treatment he meted out to his contemporaries, his rivals. It is probable that Smollett reviewed Lindsay's *Memoirs* for the *Critical Review* but it is impossible to be certain.[18]

Smollett's career had some parallels with the life of Lindsay. Born in Scotland, Smollett (1721–71) attended classes at Glasgow University and joined the navy to gain medical experience. He sailed with a squadron for Jamaica, reaching Port Royal early in 1741, and took part in the failed British attempt to take Cartagena. He revisited Jamaica and in 1743 married Anne Lassells, the creole daughter of a Kingston merchant-planter family. Although only a few of its chapters are set in Jamaica, it was his experience there that provided raw material for substantial sections of Smollett's best-known novel, *The Adventures of Roderick Random* (first published anonymously in 1748).[19] His translation of *Don Quixote* was published in 1755 and his seven volumes of *Voyages* in 1756. In 1757, the year of Lindsay's *Memoirs*, Smollett published the first three volumes of his *Complete History of England*, which was reviewed by Goldsmith and highly regarded by contemporaries. Smollett, "Scotland's first novelist", was by then one of the leading lights of literary London.[20]

The *Critical Review* opened with sarcastic comments on the learning and literary skills of the anonymous author of *Memoirs*, saying:

> The manufacturer of this piece must certainly be a great scholard; he has his French and Latin *ad anguem*, as the saying is; and spouts Italian with the grace of a Bolognese lapdog. Indeed he sometimes mistakes the orthography and grammar; but these errors are as common to him in English. In his preface he begs the reader to attribute them to the press – terrible must have been the press indeed, for in the four volumes there is scarce one sentence correct; yet he pretends to great connections, and talks as familiarly about Horace, Ovid, Juvenal, Persius, Plautus, Cicero, Justinian, Grotius, and Puffendorf, &c. as if they were his bottle companions.

Extended specimens of the novel's style, helping to fill up the pages, were interspersed with political commentary. Thus the reviewer observed that the author "stamps the characteristic of valour upon Germany, and of perfidy upon England, out of complaisance to a certain royal personage, whose ear this vile sneer of flattery can never reach". The reviewer – probably Smollett – found in Lindsay's *Memoirs* "neither connection, taste, nor entertainment".[21]

Forty years later, in 1797, the review published in the *Critical Review* was brought to light in Jamaica and reprinted in full in the Kingston *Columbian Magazine*. An accompanying letter, maintaining the sarcasm, noticed that Lindsay, in connection with his oration of 1763, had acknowledged as his own "a publication, intituled, *Memoirs of Sir Thomas Hughson, &c.* which appeared originally without the magic of a name so justly celebrated in the walks of literature as Mr. L's". The letter writer continued: "The nature or character of these memoirs is not perhaps known to the generality of the reverend author's admirers; who have therefore much yet to add to the stock of veneration for abilities so manifold and material, as were manifested in his various literary labours both at home and abroad."[22] None of this offers much to suggest that Lindsay's literary output was held in high regard by his contemporaries. The *Memoirs* was not a popular success and sank rapidly, leaving few ripples.

Modern critical assessment of Lindsay's *Memoirs* as creative literature has barely begun. Brian Vickers in 1976 put the work in the category of "anonymous picaresque novel". He offered no detailed justification, but the assessment is well placed. The picaresque novel is characterized by speed of action and rapid changes of scene, a dazzling, shifting stage designed to suggest that the hero is at the mercy of events and often unable to moderate his behaviour through prudence and principle; it is impossible for him to function as a moral agent. The type example is *Don Quixote*, the work of Cervantes, first published in Spanish in 1605–15. Of Lindsay's contemporaries, argues Margaret Anne Doody, the most successful writers in the picaresque style were Fielding and Smollett, who followed the model developed by Cervantes, coloured their work with classical allusion and employed the classical theory of comedy.[23]

Both Fielding and Smollett were conscious of both the classical and contemporary sources of this "kind of writing". The title of Fielding's *The History of the Adventures of Joseph Andrews and of his friend Mr Abraham Adams* (1742) included a declaration that it was "written in imitation of the *manner* of Cervantes, author of *Don Quixote*". At the same time he saw *Joseph Andrews* as a "comic epic-poem in prose" with its roots in Homeric poetry, notably the *Odyssey*.[24] Smollett similarly paid tribute to Cervantes in the preface to *Roderick Random*. Lindsay linked the two in *Memoirs* when discussing the difficulty of describing emotions, saying, "to paint a tortured heart by displaying distorted features, would call, with the fancy of a Smollat for the knowledge of Cervantes". Both Lindsay and Smollett revelled in mixing intense realism and authenticity with the bizarre and the absurd.[25]

Certainly Lindsay's *Memoirs* contains elements of the picaresque. The novel is episodic but intricately interconnected through accident, coincidence and minor miracle. It is epic in its structure, the story forever moving forward, the characters carefully revived whenever they are introduced after a long absence. Although the multiple strands and subplots of Lindsay's novel, its twists and turns, place considerable demands on readers, it is no harder to get through than its closest model, Richardson's *Sir Charles Grandison*. The "chains of circumstance" essential to the stories often seem too contrived, too complete, but there is an inevitability about them that makes the surprises less surprising. Rather than the episodes narrated in *Memoirs* lacking coherence, the development of the novel is determined by its movement through time, with only the occasional well-signposted digression seeming to lack a by-route back to the mainstream. Lindsay was not alone in adopting this model; it underlay the fiction of many of his more illustrious contemporaries.[26]

None of the heroes and heroines in Lindsay's *Memoirs* is particularly pious or devout. Their journeys are not spiritual odysseys but rather, as in many eighteenth-century novels, simply chart the "progress" or "history" of a character.[27] This progress is not cast as sacred history or salvation history; it is not a pilgrim's progress, yet Lindsay's novel is strenuously didactic and political. Altogether, he hoped *Memoirs* would "strike the imagination so as to amuse and entertain my readers, to the improvement and regulation of the manners of mankind".[28] He seeks to do so through a series of oppositions: between the fine gentleman and the rake, between father and son, between brothers, between wastrels and gentlemen, between good and evil and between lust and moderation. The women of *Memoirs* are occasionally virtuous but more often debauched, easily seduced by the lusts of the flesh. Lindsay reels out a string of standard moral failures: adultery, incest, murder, fratricide, patricide, cruelty and theft. The worst of his characters possess failures in combination, their "lust and cruelty" making them "a reproach to human nature".[29] Lindsay did not talk about sin or salvation. The golden rule – "whatsoever ye would that men should do to you, do ye even so to them" (Matthew 7:12) – underpinned his ethical stand, as it did his theology in later writings. Doing well to others was a concept that crossed the boundaries of class, gender and race – at least in theory – and was something one should attempt, however oppressed one might be.

A Son's Odyssey

At the core of *Memoirs* is a search for identity and kin. The declared hero, Telemachus Lovet, born in 1724 and brought up in Virginia by a patron, is looking for his father. He believes he is of noble birth, perhaps the son of an

Indian prince. Accompanied by Sicco, an enslaved African man, Telemachus is sent to Scotland for his education. An accumulation of mistaken identities and confusions of paternity is unravelled – after a thousand pages of adventure – when it is finally revealed that Telemachus is in fact the son of Sir Thomas Hughson, who is in turn the brother of Mr Joseph Williams, all of whom appear in the novel's title (figure 3.1). Unknown and unsuspected, Telemachus discovers that a large part of his life has been spent in close association with his father, grandmother, brother, sister, uncle and cousins. The father imagined by him to be distant, mysterious, American, Indian and possibly unknowable turns out to be comfortably British and noble, staring him in the face.

Eighteenth-century readers of Lindsay's *Memoirs* recognized Telemachus from both classical and modern literature as a hero in search of his father. In classical Greek mythology, Telemachus, the son of Odysseus and Penelope,

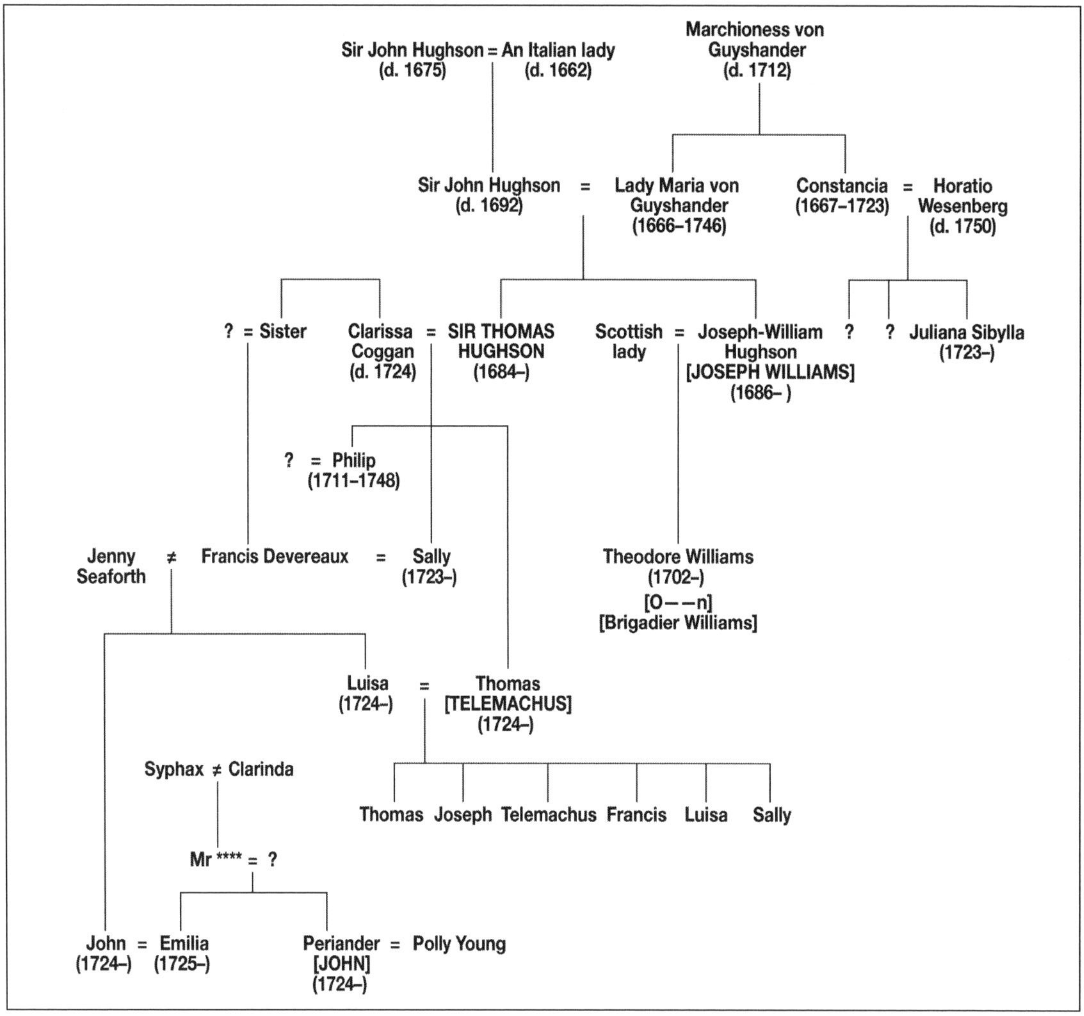

Figure 3.1 Family tree, Lindsay's *Memoirs*

was a dominant figure in the first four books of Homer's epic poem the *Odyssey*, which was constructed around 750 BCE but derived from an ancient tale. The Telemachus of myth is born the very day that Odysseus – king of the western Greek island of Ithaca – is commanded to join the Trojan War, around 1200 BCE. Penelope, waiting faithfully for the return of her husband, is pressed by suitors (local nobles) to remarry. Odysseus sets out for home, navigating between Scylla and Charybdis while strapped to the mast of his ship to save himself from the disastrous temptations of the sirens. He is shipwrecked and made captive by Calypso on her island. After Odysseus has been gone from home for close to twenty years, the goddess Athena comes to Telemachus in male disguise as Mentor, and the two travel widely. Eventually Telemachus finds Odysseus, who has been reduced to beggary. Father and son slaughter the suitors who beset Penelope and the family is reunited. In the course of the classical narrative, Telemachus grows to manhood, becoming increasingly resourceful and energetic.[30]

Homer's story has been vastly influential in the world of creative literature, poetry, opera, theatre and film. In Lindsay's time, the *Odyssey* provided the model for Daniel Defoe's contemporary *Robinson Crusoe* (1719), the prototypical desert islander but also a reborn Christian. A feminine version came from the hands of Mrs Mary Davys, in *The Reformed Coquet; or, Memoirs of Amoranda* (1724), in which the spoiled heroine is led by Mentor through a series of adventures that make her a better person. In modern times, Telemachus provides the model for Stephen Dedalus in James Joyce's *Ulysses* (1922), Ulysses being the Latin name for Odysseus. Derek Walcott's *Omeros* (1990) makes the story of Odysseus stand for the separation from Africa of the people taken across the Atlantic in slavery and exiled in America.[31]

Lindsay's version was one of many written when Telemachus served as a more attractive subject than the father Odysseus and was deployed in Europe as a pedagogical model. Lindsay's modern Telemachus differed from the classical character in several respects, most particularly in his not knowing either of his parents and needing first to identify them, rather than wishing simply to find or recognize his father.[32] Lindsay's Telemachus is also different in being explicitly declared the "hero" of the work, whereas although the Telemachus of the *Odyssey* is the "brilliant son" of Odysseus, he is outshone by his father.[33] In the *Odyssey* the story of Telemachus is presented as a relatively ordinary progress to (male) maturity and used to illuminate the status of Odysseus as the supreme hero of Troy.[34] The mother Penelope, marked by her fidelity, has no equivalent in Lindsay's tale. Lindsay's Mentor is also less constant.

The classical origins of the character are never suggested in *Memoirs*, though Telemachus does wonder once why he has a Greek name. When asked about his supposed nobility by Lady Maria von Guyshander – in fact his father's mother, but unknown to him – Telemachus reluctantly recalls his father's "gay retinue and magnificent mansion" but claims only a faint memory of his parents. He has been told, he says, that he "came from *New-England*" and that his father "was in these parts, or backward, a king". Telemachus is comfortable believing the first part, he says, because he remembers the voyage, but declares the latter – that he is the son of a king – "a puff, certainly too high". That he is an Indian (a Native American) seems never to preoccupy Telemachus. He has studied the history of the region, he says, and found that "A king in *New-England* there is not; and should I be the son of any of the neighbouring *Indians*, whence have I my Christian name, which is originally from *Greece*? or my sir-name [Lovet], which sounds nearly of *Scots* descent?"[35] Doubting his supposed high birth, Telemachus thinks himself probably no more than "illegitimate, unwelcome proof of some fatal intercourse". Near the end of the novel, Telemachus says: "I know not the reasons my parents had – but they have given me a name prophetick of my fortune – Telemachus".[36]

No doubt Lindsay expected his readers to know the story of Telemachus well enough from reading either the *Odyssey* or a contemporary gloss. Translations into English were available in good number before 1750, and Homer's *Odyssey* and *Iliad* provided key texts for classical language learning in eighteenth-century Britain.[37] Lindsay and his readers also knew the extended prose romance *Les aventures de Télémaque*, published in French in 1699 by the bishop of Cambrai, François Fénelon (1651–1715) and available in English the same year as *The Adventures of Telemachus, the Son of Ulysses*. Fénelon's work was, argues Edith Hall, "The most historically influential of all novels that develop one figure or episode in the *Odyssey*". With the exception of the Bible, it was the best-read work of literature in eighteenth-century France. Written for the education of the Duke of Burgundy, grandson of Louis XIV and heir apparent to the French throne, Fénelon's *Télémaque* was meant to teach good government but was often regarded as a satirical attack on court life. The work's central lessons – that monarchs exist to serve their subjects, that war is evil and nature wonderful – prefigured the rational world of the eighteenth century. Its message proved as popular in the American colonies as it was in France, and *The Adventures of Telemachus* became the best-read work of French authorship in British North America.[38]

Fénelon's Telemachus is identified explicitly only once in *Memoirs*. This occurs in 1745, according to the chronology of the novel, when after a long separation Lindsay's Telemachus is reunited in Edinburgh with his true love, Luisa, who lives in the household of Joseph Williams. Her blushes on his return lead Joseph to tell Telemachus, "it was long after your departure from my house, before the name of Ulysses, Penelope, or Mentor could be used in this family, without making my child colour like vermilion. Bishop Cambre's [Fénelon's] Telemachus was oftner in her hands than her bible; and particularly that part where Telemachus threw himself from the rock into the sea, to escape the danger of a woman's love".[39] Here Joseph refers to the time when Fénelon's Telemachus, shipwrecked on Calypso's island and his boat burned, is pushed into the sea by Mentor so they can escape in a passing vessel.

As well as these literary models, the origins and Atlantic odyssey of Lindsay's Telemachus had parallels in eighteenth-century experience. Several of the powerful indigenous nations of North America sent delegations to Britain to negotiate treaties directly with politicians and monarchs. In 1710 Mohawk representatives (called Iroquois "kings") were taken to England and had an audience with Queen Anne. In 1730, the year after Lindsay's birth, seven representatives of the Cherokee nation – including a "king" and "prince" – travelled from South Carolina to lodge at Windsor Castle, meet George II and sign a treaty.[40] The notion that Lindsay's Telemachus was the offspring of a princely Mohawk was not more than the fiction could bear.

Beyond these direct connections and the fundamental theme of the novel – the quest for the father – Lindsay's *Memoirs* relates to the classical *Odyssey* through its many set scenes such as confrontations, the intermixing of known and fictitious geographies, the Protean experience of shipwreck on a secluded island, the seductive role of debauched sirens and the rediscovery of lost souls.[41] But it is loading too much cultural cargo onto the *Odyssey* to make it responsible for every feature. Lindsay's world – post-Commonwealth, post-Catholic, post-Columbus, post-Union – offered its own examples and possibilities, as did his personal experience within the voyaging world of the island Atlantic. Unlike Fénelon's Telemachus, who inhabits an ancient (Mediterranean) world shared with gods, Lindsay's hero is firmly located in the secular modern (Atlantic) world and relates more loosely to Homer's *Odyssey*.[42]

Because the Telemachus of Lindsay's *Memoirs* knows nothing true about his father until the very end and because Sir Thomas believes Telemachus died in infancy, there can be no long-term development of the relationship between father and son. However, the theme is important to Lindsay and he devotes much attention to proper filial and paternal behaviour. Several of his examples involve unknown or mistaken identity, but always in a more partial sense than the ignorance of one another experienced by Telemachus and Sir Thomas, even when in the same scene.

A prevailing theme, perhaps reflecting Lindsay's personal experience, is the burden created by the father to be carried by the son. Lindsay was sixteen when he lost his father in 1745, and if his claim to have written the novel in his seventeenth year has some truth, he must have begun writing immediately after Henry's death, making their relationship a fertile field for contemplation. Most of the fathers in *Memoirs* struggle to do the right thing by their sons but persistently fail in their care and responsibility. As the Old Testament warns, the sins of the fathers are visited on the children unto the third and fourth generation (Exodus 20:5). There is a strong suggestion that the fathers would have done better if they had been less headstrong and more willing to permit their sons to follow their own stars and be allowed liberty to form their own beliefs and allegiances.[43]

In early eighteenth-century English drama, the stage rake fathered children in the manner of a barnyard cock, crowing about his numerous offspring but showing little interest in their upbringing. The virtuous father was domesticated and concerned, but it was the father who disowned or abandoned his children who generally had the strongest – though negative – role in the novels of the period.[44] In order to give weight and context to the odyssey of Telemachus, Lindsay narrates in much detail the relations between earlier generations of fathers and sons. Doing so also enables him to locate his story in the context of real events and to recite the turbulent political history of England (and Scotland) in the seventeenth century. Bible history and Creation history spill over into early modern English notions of kingship as fatherhood and patriarchal government – understood as a specific relationship, not mere metaphor.[45]

The founding Hughson, the first Sir John – grandfather of the Sir Thomas Hughson and Joseph Williams of the title of *Memoirs* – is given a plausible connection with real events and people (figure 3.1). Lindsay pushes his story back to Sir John's time in order to begin with the beheading of Charles I in 1649. Sir John is introduced as "a baronet of very ancient and honourable family: his education had been very liberal and much improved by travel, and judicious observations of different countries, customs and manners". He has taken the tour of Europe and lived some years in Italy, where he married "a lady of great fortune and distinction". On their return to England, Sir John sides with Parliament against the Royalists and "was extremely tenacious of the opinion he had imbibed with regard to Party, and had been very active and zealous, even to a degree of enthusiasm, in those civil wars and commotions which ended in the ruin of Charles I". Oliver Cromwell gives the regicide Sir John "a very lucrative employment", which stands him in good stead when the Restoration in 1660 makes him a "persecuted Protestant". Taking the title Chevalier Hughson della Cozzonico, Sir John, with his wife and son, retreats to Germany.[46]

Sir John's wife falls ill and dies in about 1662, and he turns his affections to his son, also named John. The elder Sir John does everything he can to "please and gratify his son; whom he made his friend and companion, without any of that formality or overbearing, which often make parents rather the objects of fear than affection". The son "never omitted anything in his power, to shew his filial duty and regard". The father, however, becomes increasingly aware "how much his rash and unhappy politics had injured his posterity, with regard to a paternal estate and the enjoyment of their native country". In 1672 he joins the Dutch army to fight the French, "hoping for an opportunity to revenge his quarrel with Charles II", who has made an alliance between England and France against the Dutch. Sir John fights bravely but suffers wounds in a series of battles and dies in 1675.[47]

Before his death, Sir John delivers an extended speech to his son that serves as a set piece for the expression of ideas about family, society and politics. Sir John regrets the actions that jeopardized the family's fortunes in Britain, but explains that he chose the side he did believing the country was "tending to the absolute monarchy of the prince and slavery of the people". With death in sight, Sir John expresses his "loyalty to a good prince" and his "most sincere patriotism". Regretting the "bloody catastrophe" represented by the beheading of Charles I, Sir John now declares, "The character of a king I allow to be sacred; but it is not a zeal for prerogative, it is the study of his people's welfare which makes a prince great and valuable." He fears the possibility of "a popish king" and recommends that his son keep open his ties in Germany, from whence – prophesying the Hanoverian succession – a prince might be given to Britain who will "restore the infringed liberties and properties of the people in general; and you, my son, on your posterity in particular, to your paternal inheritance and possessions".[48]

Following his father's death, the son – the second Sir John, Chevalier Hughson – is encouraged by friends to return to England and place himself at the mercy of the king. He prefers caution, his father having warned him about dangers surrounding the king's brother, the Duke of York. While the Chevalier bides his time, the duke – the popish Pretender – retires to Scotland; in fact he was sent out of anti-Catholic England, in the midst of the so-called Exclusion Crisis, to act as his brother Charles II's high commissioner (1679–82). Lindsay remarks that "when he came to *Scotland*, his usage of that people was so arbitrary, and shew'd such a spirit of persecution, as obliged many of the enemies of popery to leave their country, and transport themselves to Carolina". These events were both "extraordinary and hazardous to the protestant subjects of Britain, should the king's death open a way to his succession". Not only are they sufficient to prove that it would be dangerous for the Chevalier to return to England, they also "added the appearance of prophesy to his father's injunctions".[49]

While waiting for the right moment to return to England, Chevalier Hughson becomes acquainted with Marchioness von Guyshander, "a lady of great family and fortune". He marries her daughter Maria in 1683. Within a year they have a son, Thomas, and two years later another, Joseph-William, both of whom appear in the title of *Memoirs*. Soon after, on the abdication of James II in 1688 and succession of the Prince of Orange to the British crown, Maria travels to England to pave the way for the Chevalier's return. The Chevalier, however, believes that "The state of Britain appears in some distraction: there are various opinions of this surprising and glorious revolution", and remains cautious. His father's legacy weighs heavily on him. Eventually he decides to go to England, in 1692, but leaves his sons behind to be educated. Thomas is sent to Leyden, in Holland, and Joseph-William "to *Leipsick* in *Saxony*" to be placed under "two professors of the greatest ingenuity, probity and learning" (figure 2.5). To prevent suspicious enquiry into their family, Joseph-William loses the surname Hughson and becomes known as Joseph Williams.[50] In this way, readers of *Memoirs* are told early in the novel that these two men are brothers, though they themselves are forced to spend another thousand pages in ignorance of their relationship.

The Chevalier writes a long letter setting out how he wishes his sons to be taught. In the letter sent to the tutor of Thomas – aged eight – he begins by declaring that he personally "greatly suffered from the unfortunate principles of my father" and expresses a desire that "my son should be educated so as to have his own principles, and not his father's".[51] He is equally open on the question of religion, wishing that the boy not be brought up in the beliefs of any particular church. Here it is impossible not to suppose a direct parallel with Lindsay's own strict upbringing in the Church of Scotland and his father's strong views. The Chevalier hopes for a similar initial innocence of politics, declaring, "I would have him read no history of persons, times, or nations". The Chevalier returns to these topics once more towards the close of his letter, concluding: "as to matters of church and state, I should not be displeased if he comes out of your hands moral, virtuous, and polite, as to the one, and of no professed party with regard to the other. For when both shall be the effects of a good judgment, and mature consideration, I will answer to God for his religion, and to the king that is to govern him for his loyalty and fidelity."[52]

The care the Chevalier (Sir John) takes to separate the identities of his sons, by renaming the younger and keeping the two tutors unaware of one another, is vital to the plot of Lindsay's *Memoirs*. The possibility that the sons might live in mutual non-recognition is compounded by Sir John's failure to advise his wife or his mother-in-law of the arrangements. Within days of despatching the boys to their tutors, Sir John sails from Holland for England, but his ship is lost, and both his wife and the Marchioness assume not only that he is dead but also that the two boys have perished with him. The brothers, Thomas and Joseph, lose touch with one another; the father is in fact dead, and their mother is unknown to them.[53]

Sir Thomas Hughson grows to manhood, marries, and has two sons, Philip and Thomas (who is eventually revealed to be Telemachus). Philip, born 1711, is an evil character who conflicts with his father from an early age. Sir Thomas is not even certain of his paternity and suffers the indignity of hearing Philip called a bastard and his wife a whore. To remove his family from the temptations of the metropolis (London), Sir Thomas establishes his household in the Scottish countryside north of Glasgow. Philip grows up with his older cousin Francis Devereux, the son of Lady Hughson's sister (figure 3.1). In this rural setting the boys are first taught by Theodore Williams, who, unknown to the Hughson household, is the son of Joseph Williams, the separated brother of Sir Thomas. In 1723, when Theodore's pedagogy is found wanting and he offends the family, Sir Thomas places Philip and Francis with professors in Edinburgh.[54]

On their way to Edinburgh, Sir Thomas delivers a homily on the boys' duties:

> Want you to be the *fine gentlemen*, or the complete scholars? Read much: *ethicks*, will make you grave and considerate; *natural philosophy*, will stock your memory with a collection of useful ideas: *logic* will arrange your knowledge into proper assortments: *mathematics*, will accustom you to think justly, keep you to the point, and learn you to argue closely and subtilly. While *rhetoric*, and *elocution*, will make your discourse agreeable, and your style manly. Some time hence, after the more useful branches are attained, *history*, will make you wise; *poetic fancy*, witty. Above all, gentlemen, consider you are baptized; learn to be Christians.

Sir Thomas warns them particularly of the hazards of dancing. He declares that "it is without contradiction; that if dancing introduces a young man to the acquaintance of the ladies, they in return, will introduce him to idleness, sauntering after them, and a carelessness in every other more laudable pursuit and business".[55]

The following year, 1724, Sir Thomas leaves his family in order to free himself of Lady Hughson's debauchery. She is pregnant, but once again he is uncertain about his fatherhood. Although it is eventually revealed that on her deathbed she declares "she never had known man, but her Sir Thomas", Lady Hughson is portrayed as a promiscuous pleasure-seeker, "a disgrace to her sex".[56] She is just one of several "debauched young women" in *Memoirs*. Lindsay frequently disparages women, quoting Pope to the effect that "every woman is at heart a rake". Sir Thomas, now living in Glasgow, seeks guidance from a new-found friend, Joseph Williams; the two do not know that they are in fact brothers.[57]

PROSLAVERY PRIEST

Sir Thomas writes to Joseph, telling him that he plans to flee to Leyden and committing to Joseph's care his son, daughter, nephew and "an embryo as yet in the womb". Foreshadowing his own death, Sir Thomas tells Joseph, "My will you'll find at the hundred and seventh page of Cudworth's *Intellectual System*." Here he refers to the Cambridge philosopher Ralph Cudworth's *The True Intellectual System of the Universe: The First Part; wherein all the Reason and Philosophy of Atheism is Confuted; and Its Impossibility Demonstrated*, published in London in 1678, a work of 899 pages. Probably it was among the books in the library of Lindsay's father. At page 107 Cudworth specifically attacks what he calls "hylozoistic" atheism, in which God is abolished by making him one with his creation – an alternative version of pantheism.[58] Sir Thomas sails for Amsterdam, leaving behind Cudworth's weighty tome, without telling his wife or children of his plan. Lindsay debates Sir Thomas's choice at length but ultimately approves, saying: "To his children, his friends, his fortune, even his country, where-ever they are, he must some time or other bid adieu. It is the same for him whether by death or otherways. And if every one had the time of their *exit*, from those enjoyments, at their own choosing, it could never be more wisely made, than at a season, when any one of them makes the others intolerable."[59] Perhaps Lindsay felt something the same about his own journeys, past and future, and the wisdom of suiting his own best interests.

Nothing is heard of Sir Thomas, and after a time he is presumed dead. Lady Hughson dies soon after giving birth to another son, Thomas – the embryo in the womb. When Philip discovers that the newborn stands between him and his father's wealth, three years after his mother's death he "persuaded the child's nurse that it was an adulterous bastard, and with a pretty considerable sum bribed her to strangle the infant". Philip marries in about 1733 "but turned out so loose and wickedly cruel, that his lady, soon after marriage, died of a broken heart". His marriage increases his wealth but he falls in with "sycophants who spent his fortune for him through the day, and harlots through the night". Penniless and fearing gaol, Philip Hughson changes his name to Philip Tomson and plans to become a common sailor.[60]

Philip next appears as the teacher of Telemachus Lovet, freshly arrived in Scotland from America. Neither Philip nor Telemachus has any inkling that they are brothers, let alone that Philip had ordered the murder of Telemachus (who is Thomas, presumed dead). Both are lost to their father, Sir Thomas. The story is further complicated by Telemachus's mistaken search for his supposed American heritage. Volume 2 of *Memoirs* begins with this uncertainty, introducing "Telemachus Lovet, as some say the son, others the nephew, others a very distant relation, while not a few pretend to affirm him to be of no degree of relation at all of Brig—r *—, a wealthy and well known gentleman in *New England*; and not less now remarkable in *London*". The Brigadier has children by his wife, and some assume that Telemachus Lovet is his natural son, but the Brigadier claims that Telemachus is "the child of the Prince of the *M—k Indians*". According to the Brigadier, the prince sent his son Telemachus to be educated in "the best academies which *Boston*, or *Philadelphia* in *Pensilvania*, could boast of". However, the Brigadier advised sending Telemachus to England, where he arrived in 1732 on board a ship under one Captain G—, with "a very handsome annual allowance" and "attended with one servant only", the enslaved man Sicco.[61]

How Telemachus finds himself sitting at the feet of Philip requires a greater stretch of the imagination. It happens because Philip has turned to teaching when his desire to become a common sailor is cured by the hard labour of a single voyage. He sets up a school in Haddington, which Lindsay calls "a little village nigh the borders". The real Haddington was an important town east of Edinburgh, close to Prestonpans, and William Robertson's first parish (figure 2.2). The fatal coincidence comes about because the one voyage taken by Philip was under the same captain who brings Telemachus across the Atlantic. Captain G—, impressed by Philip's apparent knowledge of the classics, considers it of mutual benefit to bring Telemachus to the school of this "cunning, cruel, and ignorant wretch". For too many years Telemachus endures the brutal behaviour of Philip, but by about 1739 he comes to realize that he is "more obliged to his dictionary and grammar for his progress in learning, than to his insufferably inhumane preceptor". Telemachus escapes.[62]

After various adventures across Edinburgh, Telemachus is taken in by Lady Maria von Guyshander, his father's mother, but not recognized as such. She takes over his education and sends him to Leyden for a year to perfect his Latin and French and to be instructed in the history and geography of Europe. Telemachus goes next to Vienna, where for almost two years he "studied the polite accomplishments of fencing, riding, dancing, drawing, and music", as well as mathematics and "the art of war". Early in 1742 Lady Maria sends him on a tour of Italy, "the antient and parent nursery of arts and sciences", accompanied by the Reverend Dr Douglas, his Mentor.[63]

Philip and Telemachus do not meet again until 1745. Telemachus, on the run following the Battle of Prestonpans (in which Lindsay claimed to have fought) and having survived a storm off the Fife shore, is rescued and taken to an inn to recover, where he finds himself in the same room as Philip Tomson. They recognize one another as teacher and pupil but still do not know they are brothers or that Philip ordered the murder of Telemachus when he was a child. The prodigal Philip is now penniless, an invalid and much subdued. The too-forgiving Telemachus allows Philip to accompany him, which he does cunningly disguised as a valet in livery, using his dress to provide a "masque". They travel together, through the turmoil of the time, to Perth and Edinburgh.[64]

In 1747 Philip accompanies Telemachus when he sets out for America in search of his father. Castaway on Zophil Groam Ba, they eventually learn that the island's king is none other than Sir Thomas Hughson, father of Philip. Reunited with his son, the aged Sir Thomas shows preferment to Philip, and the latter becomes a monster of lust and cruelty, hoping to inherit the kingdom.[65] Bloody battles follow in which Telemachus is eventually victorious. In June Philip returns to Britain along with Sir Thomas.[66] Telemachus leaves later.

Back in Glasgow, Philip stirs up more trouble and Sir Thomas banishes him, though with a small allowance. They meet again in London, following the return of Telemachus. Not recognizing one another, Telemachus and the "despicable" Philip fight and the latter is wounded.[67] Finally it is revealed that the child who Philip ordered murdered was in fact Telemachus – saved by his nurse, Mrs Lovet, who took him to New England and then entrusted him to the Brigadier – and that Telemachus is the son of Sir Thomas. At this revelation, Sir Thomas, tears streaming down his face, declares, "Just heavens! . . . who shall henceforth dare to grieve at cross-grain'd fortune, when watchful providence from that very source does bring us joy so unexpected and so great. My child! My son of comfort. My Telemachus!" His sins revealed, Philip cuts his own throat.[68]

A Grateful Slave

Sicco, the enslaved African who travels with Telemachus as his servant, has an ambiguous role in *Memoirs*. Unlike the novel's other principal characters, whose kinship ties are as complex as tangled string, Sicco is never shown to be related to any other person with a role in the novel. He is frequently at the heart of the narrative but often explicitly distinguished from the others as a black African man, bereft of kin. Like his master, Telemachus, Sicco also dreams of being reunited with his father, but his dream is not fulfilled. Unlike Telemachus, however, Sicco does know the identity of his parents. He never doubts his African birth, yet his name is taken from the Greek, a variant of *sycophant*. In ancient Athens a sycophant was an informer, tale-bearer or slanderer. By the eighteenth century English usage had made the sycophant a servile, cringing type or a self-seeking flatterer, a fawning parasite. Lindsay had in mind this essential model of servility.

Lindsay portrays Sicco as a strong, though flawed, character. He is wise, faithful and self-sufficient and embodies elements of the "noble savage" as well as the "grateful slave". Appropriately thankful for his many blessings, he is not afraid to openly express his criticism of white society. The "grateful slave" is a dominant trope in eighteenth-century fiction concerned with slavery, though it has roots in the classical world and is found too in the image of the good and faithful slave of many Gospel proverbs. The trope is not a precursor of any antislavery argument; rather, as George Boulukos contends, it assumes the persistence of brutal regimes of bondage and – more important for Lindsay's theory and practice – "that Africans can be induced not just to accept slavery, but to embrace it, to be overwhelmed by ecstatic gratitude toward someone who continues to claim mastery over them". Boulukos traces the immediate origin of the figure to Daniel Defoe's picaresque novel *Colonel Jack* (1722) and argues that it "represents a moment when the still inchoate category of race is being actively theorized".[69] It was only in the early 1750s that fiction began to introduce the "grateful slave" as a standard character. Thus, although Lindsay was not the creator of the figure, he was certainly an early adopter.

Sicco makes his opening appearance in Lindsay's *Memoirs* when Telemachus is sent to England for his education, "attended with one servant only; a negro, exceedingly handsome, beautiful in his kind, and in reality a young captive prince, who, being taken amongst a number of prisoners in *Africa*, was, in the *English* trade, sold amongst the rest, to the common buyer". Telemachus's patron, the anonymous brigadier, bought Sicco, "not out of any intent to put him to work, as many unfortunate *African* prince and princess are to be seen on *American* soil; but to be the companion and attendant of the young Squire Lovet".[70] In this way, Sicco and Telemachus become parallel representatives of a type popular in mid-eighteenth-century drama: the fabled "native prince", in both its American (Indian) and African versions. Examples of ransomed African princes had some notoriety in Britain through the Atlantic slave trade; some of them were brought to Britain for education, where they were feted by court and gentry before being returned to their African homes. These men were exceptions within the slave system, favoured for their royal status in the midst of the great sea of Africans taken to the Americas with so little regard. Showing favour to Africans of such power and authority was essential to profitable running of the slave trade; it was not merely a matter of social grace.

Both Telemachus and Sicco fit this exemplary model. They recall both the theatre surrounding the Mohawk/Iroquois kings/princes brought to

England in 1710 and the African prince of Aphra Behn's novella *Oroonoko: or, the Royal Slave* (1688). Set in Coramantien, on the coast of Africa, and in (British) Surinam, the story of Oroonoko is founded on known biographical and historical facts.[71] Contemporary with Lindsay's composition of *Memoirs* was the staging of Thomas Southerne's dramatization of *Oroonoko* at Covent Garden Theatre in London. Notably, a performance in 1749 created its own public spectacle when the audience included an African man – William Ansah Sessarakoo – said to be a prince sold through treachery into slavery in Barbados and recently ransomed, his personal saga paralleling that of Oroonoko (though Oroonoko was ultimately killed and dismembered rather than being ransomed). Ansah was the son of a Fante chief and slave trader, John Corrente, from the region of the Gold Coast, whose plan had been to send his son to England with a companion to be educated. Deeply moved by the performance, Ansah himself became the subject of *The Royal African: or, Memoirs of the Young Prince of Annamaboe*, published while he was still in England.[72]

Without challenging the moral basis of slavery, the writer of *The Royal African* advocates the "humane and generous" treatment of all peoples because "human nature is the same in all countries, and under all complexions; and to fancy that superior power or superior knowledge gives one race of people a title to use another race who are weaker or more ignorant with haughtiness or contempt, is to abuse power and science". In spite of his experience, Ansah proved truly princely, as shown by "the gracefulness of his person, the nobleness of his sentiments, the modesty of his deportment, and the grateful acknowledgments he continually expresses for the justice that has been done him, and the favours he has received".[73]

In Lindsay's *Memoirs*, Telemachus resolves to "dedicate his life to the most servile employment" when he can no longer suffer the brutal tutorship of Philip Tomson. In spite of this dire decision, he has his "faithful slave" Sicco still with him when they are rescued from the streets of Edinburgh and taken into the household of Joseph Williams (the unknown uncle of Telemachus).[74] Joseph shelters them but at the same time places an advertisement seeking the parents of this "young gentleman, . . . whose habit and behaviour point him out to be of more than ordinary birth; and who himself says, has fled from the severe treatment of a tutor, attended with a Negro slave of his own age, or a little more". By chance, Telemachus sees the advertisement and decides to escape, leaving Sicco behind in order to make himself less visible. In the real world of contemporary Scotland, "run away" advertisements stood out prominently in the newspapers, partly because they were so few. There were then less than a hundred black slaves in the whole of Scotland, making individuals highly visible there, compared to the more than ten thousand in

England. This is what makes Telemachus nervous. Most of the slaves were, like Sicco, personal servants. In Lindsay's fictional world, Telemachus writes a note to Joseph saying, "if you have any use for him [Sicco], tell him 'tis my pleasure he should serve you, and he will do it even on his knees. Be not too hard upon him; he is a prince by birth."[75]

The strategy fails and Telemachus is quickly brought back to Joseph and locked in a room with Sicco. Desperate, Telemachus decides to jump from a high window, but Sicco thinks it hazardous and says, "Suffer your faithful Sicco, at least, to jump before you, and learn you of the danger." Telemachus rejects his offer and tells Sicco: "It grieves me much, believe me, though 'tis said I myself am born a prince, to think a captive heir to royalty should be my slave; so be it no more. There are frequent voyaging to the gold coast from *Britain*; and sometime hence, by the means of some ingenious and tender heart, you may be returned to the arms of a sorrowing father." Sicco responds by saying that a life of service to his friends in Britain would be better than "any thoughts of returning to mere titular happiness or gaudy slavery". He tells Telemachus, "I was bought by your father for your use – to attend you, as your slave – even to die, if to die can do you service". But Telemachus interrupts: "I know not that I have a father – if I have: whatever he may think of the matter; or whatever the barbarous *Americans* may do with their *African* dependents; nature ne'er designed one to play the tyrant over another. In *England* – bless thyself for the tale – there be no such thing as slavery." Telemachus is mistaken. Mansfield's judgement, which applied to England, did not come until 1772, and it was not until 1778 that Scotland's highest court declared that slavery had no place there. However, a case had been brought by an Ayrshire merchant in 1756, seeking to detain his Virginian runaway slave Jamie Montgomery, which was not tested because Montgomery died in gaol before the case came to court. Perhaps Lindsay was aware of the case as he completed his novel, and perhaps he predicted a verdict in favour of Montgomery.[76]

Sicco cannot endure the thought of parting. After Telemachus safely descends, using a bed sheet to reach the ground, Sicco throws himself out the window. He hits the ground hard and dislocates an arm, but he rises to his knees to declare:

> In *America* I was your parent's purchased slave; *here* you say, I am free: am not I then obliged to your father's generosity, who put that freedom in my power? And shall I abuse it? May heaven and earth pour forth their heaviest plagues upon thy slave, the moment he is ungrateful. Look not so wildly on me; kind sir, your frowns are death but believe me, I had rather, in a country of Christian knowledge of arts and liberty, pine, starve by piece-meal, as a slave to thy good pleasure, than range an *Afric* prince on the wide plains of my father's barbarous dominions.

Telemachus has no counter. "Let us go hence, you have overcome me with this extravagant generosity; and has obliged me to take to my arms a friend; perhaps a monitor; a hidden blessing sent me from above."[77]

PROSLAVERY PRIEST

Generally Sicco appears as Telemachus's "faithful" appendage but is given the occasional chance to display moral qualities or even become a rival. Sicco accompanies Telemachus on his Grand Tour, but on their return to Edinburgh he lives in the household of Joseph Williams while Telemachus wanders independently during the troubled months of 1745. While Telemachus is away, Sicco grows closer to Luisa, Joseph's "daughter" and Telemachus's true love. Here Lindsay observes that "we" are "apt to o'er look the misery of the slave! He was a man: had passions, open to beauty, and strong: he was a Prince; had the spirit of a monarch; and while he disdained a life of obedience, was a slave to gratitude and duty!" Luisa, however, wants only to hear Sicco recite the virtues of Telemachus; Sicco "found himself the most miserable of beings; obliged in pain to recount his master's virtues, to conceal an unhappy passion!" He thinks of ending his life, "as faithful as noble". Lindsay's straightforward account of Sicco's passion for Luisa is not painted as an impossible love; indeed, contemporary precedents existed in reality and fiction.[78] It was simply unable to prosper in the shadow of Luisa's devotion to Telemachus.

When Telemachus returns from his wanderings, he is (wrongly) accused by Joseph of ingratitude to Lady Maria and also of murder. With Telemachus in disgrace, Sicco declares his love for Luisa and says he hopes to die if his suit is denied. He tells Telemachus, "Sicco no longer lives thy slave, but thy rival! Pardon me the presumption; though of *Indian* [*sic*] dye, I have that blood which runs in royalty: from that, proceeds ambition". Telemachus, with his mind on his own troubles, responds, "Be this some comfort to your pains, your Lovet suffers wi' thee!" Telemachus fears he will be banished the next day. "Could I then with thee exchange complexion! with thee dwell under this roof a slave to so much goodness, 'twere a joy inexpressible!" In the end, the faithful Sicco determines not to stand in the way of Telemachus but rather to save him from anguish.[79]

Sicco becomes an intermediary between Telemachus and Luisa, carrying letters between them. Luisa writes to Telemachus, telling him that he has disobeyed her commands and saying she is happy she did not take up the encouragement to wed and wishes now only to forget. She reads this letter to Sicco, who then carries it to Telemachus. When Telemachus scans it too hurriedly and assumes that the trouble lies in Sicco's passion, "in a rage, twisting the letter in his hand", he "threw it at the faithful Sicco's face", saying, "Hence perfidious slave: nor let me see the blackness of thy face, till your heart is cleaner from presumption." Sicco, "sweating with revenge at the affront", cries: "Great heaven! . . . is the blood of *African* royalty, because by the fate of war a captive, to bear insults like these? No, by the gods! This heart but a moment ago the faithful slave, recoiling at its folly, breaks all bonds of servitude; and I shall see thee, unpitied shall I see thee fall below my notice!" Sicco leaves the house in indignation. Telemachus calls him back from a window, but Sicco responds, "No. *This* heart hitherto faithful as your wishes, shall now drink deep in ill design; shall grow as black as *this* face, to be revenged of the insult."[80]

Here the author ponders the passions that led Telemachus to act this way. He did wrong to throw the letter in the face of "the faithful Negro", but, says Lindsay, "who of us all, even the most philosophick, receiving so passionate and braving an insult from a servant, . . . is able to bend low to his dependant, and beseech his pardon?" Telemachus seeks to make atonement by sending Sicco a letter, "which tho' in the stile of a superior, was moderated with the contrition of one sensible of his faults". Sicco recognizes the handwriting and returns it unopened, revealing his character. Although he "had not so great a command on his passions as his Lord", he possessed "[m]any excellent qualifications, and was indeed a person of great understanding: and having in his education, under the direction of Telemachus, lost the natural savageness of his climate, was not given to its irreconcileable revenge". Sicco has regrets but "his roused pride was not tractable enough to confess his fault, or make any acknowledgement of his haughty behaviour".[81]

Sicco finds himself "[a] st[r]anger in a land of white savages". He seeks to "endeavour quietly to bury my wrongs" but declares he will never "as a spaniel, fawn upon his insulter, kneel at his feet, or thank him for the blow". While he understands that some may think it strange "that I, a servant, a negroe slave, should be so arrogant", he says that so long as he was "repaid with gentle acknowledgement, I was ever the faithful, submissive dependent; but being treated with disrespect, and repaid with contempt; I know myself too well to yield to indignities, till I have received that acknowledgement of wrongs, one prince expects of another". Eventually Telemachus confesses his fault and asks pardon of Sicco, who is happy about the reconciliation. Telemachus asks, "Are we friends?" And Sicco replies, "If my good lord . . . will accept my faithful service; I am your slave." Telemachus claims, "As my slave, Sicco, . . . I have never used you: I receive your services, as those of a friend."[82]

When Sicco, along with Telemachus and Philip, reaches Zophil Groam Ba in 1747, the simple islanders view Telemachus as "no less than a God" because he can order the thunder (he fires the ship's cannon), but they think Sicco "no other than a devil; whom the God had under his command to punish and destroy his enemies". In the battle that ensues with Philip and his island army, Sicco is captured, bound to a tree and tortured.[83] Telemachus comes upon Sicco, who expects to be burnt to death, the faggots already piled around the tree. Sicco beseeches Telemachus to despatch him with his sword to save him further suffering (why he cannot simply be cut free is not made clear). In extremity, Telemachus does what Sicco asks, saying, "No, butchers! – they shall not broil thee! Tortures and confusion rack me – but it must be so – heaven receive thy spirit; thus – and – thus I free thee from a world of woe! Just heavens be merciful! farewel, dear, mangled Sicco! I shall not meet thy equal." Lindsay concludes: "Thus fell, tho' a slave, a prince! tho' the most faithful, the most endearing, most valuable, and most loved dependant, fell, thro' a fate most cruel, in circumstances unparalleled, by the tender hand of a most humane and indulgent master!"[84]

PROSLAVERY PRIEST

Real and Living Personages

Although Lindsay located his narrative firmly in a fictional world in which characters performed as exemplary types – the grateful slave, the son searching for his father, the debauched woman – he also sprinkled this world with the occasional real person with a speaking part. Lindsay claimed that "many real and living personages" appear in *Memoirs*, but their numbers are in fact few.[85] Further, although these real people interact with the fictional characters, they are never attributed kinship – the quality that is the essence of the story – and most appear in places other than Britain.

The closest Lindsay comes to establishing a kin relationship occurs in the case of Sir John Hughson, the founding father of the story, whose fictional life closely parallels the life of the real but not living Colonel John Hewson (he died in 1662). Lindsay realized that readers might see the likeness, and opines: "It hath been conjectured that Colonel Hewson, one of King Charles's judges, was Sir John's near relation: but waving any consideration of this kind, certain it is, there was a great political alliance, and both had a large share in the transactions which brought about that fatal catastrophe." The John Hewson of history (figure 3.2) was lieutenant colonel of a foot regiment in the New Model Army and a signatory of the warrant for the execution of Charles I. A shoemaker by trade, he was a zealot who opposed the Levellers and defied the ordinance against lay preaching. He believed that a vengeful God approved of the parliamentary conquests of Scotland and Ireland, in which he played an active and sometimes brutal role.[86] Lindsay's Sir John is a softer version but still a man led to extremes by an overzealous enthusiasm, a trait Lindsay distrusted.

Most prominent among the real and living characters was Madame de

Figure 3.2 Colonel John Hewson. Engraved by Michael van der Gucht after an unknown artist, 1713. Author's collection.

Pompadour (1721–64), mistress of Louis XV (1715–74). She serves as a counterpoint to the pious Luisa, who in 1746, disturbed by the ambiguity of her relationship with Telemachus, travels to Rheims, where she enters a convent. In her journey she is accompanied by a nobleman whose son, Count Bellair, falls in love with her. She calls him "a young fop" – another male failure, known for pretentious artificiality, especially in dress, and lacking the corporeal masculinity of a rake. While in the convent, Luisa somehow remains a determined Protestant and, in confession, debates issues of theology with the priest Père Lohier.[87] Although Lindsay gives no clues, the name at least seems to be borrowed from a real person: the "French Counsellor at Law (P.A.M. Lohier)" who was on board the *Newcastle* in 1755 as a prisoner when Lindsay was chaplain of that ship.

Rebuffed by Luisa, Bellair visits Père Lohier, whom he thinks is an advocate for his ambitions. Bellair accuses Lohier of not pressing his suit: "But why did I expect – fool that I was – 'tis ever so where Jesuit can thrust his hand – Thou false, insinuating treacherous priest." Bellair continues to abuse Lohier:

PROSLAVERY PRIEST

> As for thy callous knees and hollow stare, as they become thy gaustly office, in them you ought to boast. But all will soon be well again. Courage! Having me bereft of e'ery pleasing hope, to continue in the schemes – the lovely *Scot* may now be yours. But when she sits to hear thy love tales at the [confessional] grate; while eyes with sharp-set looks do pierce through op'ning lawn; thy luscious fingers press upon the yielding bosom, or use her necklace as a rosary, thy scraggy gums, keen, watering in the scene, think of eternity and this much injur'd Bellair! Thou bawdy, lascivious – thou very priest![88]

Here Lindsay introduces Madame de Pompadour, taking the opportunity to mock her style. This occurs when Bellair fights a duel over Luisa, is wounded and has an arm cut off to save his life. Other military men are given advancement by "the French king" and Bellair feels slighted. Lindsay interjects the following:

> *Madam de* Pompadour soon after, by one of her pieces of wit, gave the public to understand the king's thoughts of the matter. She was sorry (she said) that the poor *Count* [Bellair] should have rendered, himself an invalid at the very time when his foot had got into the stirrup of preferment, and the kings pleasure only wanting, that his lordship might ride the saddle of command. Tho' at the same time she could not help thinking, he had acquainted the public with his qualifications in a very proper season: His majesty had but little need for commanders who knew their business so poorly as to allow an enemy catch them in their own stratagems; and then said something by way of *double entendre*, about a lady's dying under his tongue, – which as we think too gross for any of our readers to hear, we shall leave to those who like that besotted monarch love to sit with their doxies, at the expence of sobriety and modest conversation. Thus however she concluded, he seemed a heroe equally cut out for the service of Mars as of Venus. Madam de Pompadour as a sort of royal echo, intimated what the count might expect from his majesty: and his lordship taking the hint was prudent enough not to put his honour to a trial. Under pretence of the loss of his arm, he gave up all thoughts of rising in the field, and buried himself with as little noise as possible in the country at Bellair.[89]

The second appearance of Madame de Pompadour has her conceiving of Luisa as a rival for the attentions of Louis XV when she visits Versailles after leaving the Rheims convent in early 1747. The young Luisa, "gay, noble, blooming, beautiful as ever", is introduced to the king and he is captivated.

Madame de Pompadour maintains a close watch but Luisa gets the better of her when, in the presence of the king, they debate matters of modesty, virtue and honour. Madame de Pompadour contrives a story that has Luisa believing she will be ravished by the King if she joins a pleasure party to Fontainebleau. Luisa bids a polite adieu and returns to Edinburgh.[90]

Although lusted after by French nobles, monarchs and priests, Luisa does not forget her "Telemaque". She hears from Edinburgh on 5 April 1747 that Telemachus is "[g]one! Transported to Virginia! But, thank heaven, 'tis voluntary; and in search of his parents." Anxious to see "*old* Britain once more", Luisa travels to Amsterdam in August 1747 and arranges passage to Leith, the port of Edinburgh. The only other passenger on the ship happens to be Colonel Francis Devereux, cousin of Philip and, unknown to them both, Luisa's father. Wounded at the Battle of la Veldt (Lauffeld, near Maastricht, Holland, where Cumberland was defeated on 2 July 1747), he has been advised to return to his "native air" to recover. They meet with "mutual happiness", but when Luisa speaks of her hope to be reunited with Telemachus, Devereux declares that, for himself, he wishes Telemachus "may ever remain the happy son and husband of some American prince and princess!"[91]

Theatre

The year before, in May 1746, Telemachus has an unexpected encounter with Luisa and Devereux in a London theatre, when by chance they sit, along with mutual friends and family, in opposite boxes. Thinking that his love Luisa has married Devereux, Telemachus leaves the theatre, unable to stand the pain. Luisa is equally confused, and soon after this unhappy meeting leaves for the convent in France. The play they had all gone to see, identified in *Memoirs* as a "pantomime", was *The Orphan*, a tragedy written by Thomas Otway (1652–85) and published in 1680. It proved one of the more enduring stage plays of the period, and all the great English actors played parts in it up to the early nineteenth century. It was also popular in the American colonies and was performed in Jamaica from the 1750s to the 1780s.[92] Probably Lindsay chose *The Orphan* above the many alternatives because of the play's popularity and familiarity, or perhaps because he found in its themes a resonance with his own story, taking the opportunity to deploy a fiction within a fiction.

In Otway's play, twin brothers vie for the love of Monimia, an orphan, their father's ward. One of them, Castalio, conceals his marriage to Monimia, while the other, Polydore, deceives her into allowing him to share the wedding-night bed. The only solution to this concoction of incest, rape and deception is suicide. Critics found fault with the play's "morbid moral tone" and the improbability of its plot. In Richardson's *Sir Charles Grandison*, for example, Lady G uses *The Orphan* to make a general point about the perversity and unreasonableness of men when denied what they have set their hearts on. She opines: "Whenever I saw this play, I pitied the impetuous Polydore, more than I did the blubbering great boy Castalio; tho' I thought both brothers deserved to be hanged."[93] Lindsay has one of his characters say: "I have seen to-night, . . . a tender infant set in a goodly soil; grown to maturity; encircled and fenced about with the most liberal endowments: pluck'd in the bud; and her patient hopes of glory filled at length with disappointments, misery, and death. A play, from whence many salutary lessons may be drawn!" But he is countered by another who says she found it too much of a "sermon" and wished for something more "modern" that put aside the "glories, and miseries" and was "sweet and short in the matter".[94]

The second dramatic performance described in *Memoirs* occurs when Telemachus returns from Zophil Groam Ba towards the end of 1747. He lodges temporarily on Pall Mall in London, where he makes friends with a young clergyman, his wife and her sister and they go together to Drury Lane Theatre to see *Romeo and Juliet*. Telemachus fears the clergyman will feel obliged to discreetly "retire into the gallery", but "[t]he Doctor soon set him right in this; he said it was a play so much run after, and Mr Garrick's attitudes so much admir'd, that there was hardly such a thing as getting into the house, unless seats were previously procured". He has obtained seats for them in one of the front boxes. Telemachus is "not a little admiring the good sense of the people of England, who deny not their clergy those decent liberties they themselves enjoy; and are not displeas'd to see them partake of those recreating amusements, which tho' the laws permit, the narrow minded would be apt to condemn". However, when Telemachus asks his friends whether the clergy go "also as publicly to see comedies", being told that they do, he expresses regret: "he was afraid they would not always make a becoming choice: and as many of our comedies were notoriously unworthy the ear of our mob; they certainly did not deserve to be encouraged by the countenance of our clergy".[95]

The question was a matter of contemporary debate that reached a crescendo as Lindsay was completing *Memoirs*, but it was cast more broadly as "Whether it is lawful for the professors of the Christian religion to go to plays?" One answer, published in London in 1757, declared it sinful because "tragedies, comedies, and such diversions" encouraged "a fondness for sensual pleasures" – the "lust of the flesh, the lust of the eyes, and the pride of life" abhorred by Saint John. Attendance at plays also took people to places of temptation, away from domestic devotion, increasing "the number of the devil's slaves". The "divine dramatist" Whitefield, in a twist of irony, took on the theatre seeking to destroy it, but players learned from his emotional style and caricatured religious enthusiasts on stage. Adam Ferguson, a Scottish philosopher who left the church in 1754 and was soon to be professor of natural philosophy at Edinburgh University, also wrote on the subject, in 1757 defending the essential morality of stage plays and finding nothing in Scripture to prohibit attendance. Since 1737 the Stage Licensing Act had established the theatres royal – Drury Lane and Covent Garden – as the only legal providers of drama in London; as a duopoly they competed directly for audiences, a situation that continued until to the middle of the 1760s. The texts of new plays had to pass the censor, who was particularly concerned about undesirable political attitudes but also sought to maintain decency and morality.[96]

Telemachus takes a liberal stance on the issue but favours licensing by archbishops. He believes that "Churchmen then might not only enjoy the diversion, but be eas'd of a burthen: Moral duties might be inculcate from a stage; and the pulpet be no longer debauch'd with the dull insipid harangues of a moral philosopher, but be fill'd as it ought with ministers of the Gospel of Christ". His lady friends assert that people might learn as much from "the behaviour of a Bevil or Lord Townly" as from the Prodigal Son in a sermon. In this way Lindsay offers an unusual image of the playhouse – particularly the box – as a site for serious, respectable society rather than merely offering opportunities for seduction.[97]

Returned home to drink tea, Telemachus offers his thoughts on the performances. Of Garrick, who played Romeo, Telemachus says he was "sorry to see the public . . . give him such immoderate applause in what is not only turning tragedy into harlequin machinery, but what is most unnatural". He finds Garrick's attitudes and gestures exaggerated and accuses the "scene shifters" of playing to the gallery. Telemachus concludes, however, "Mr Garrick has pleas'd me in his alterations on the play: and he is the only gentleman ever charm'd me as an actor." When the clergyman-doctor asks, "[W]hat have players to do with philosophy?", Telemachus responds, "Pardon me sir, . . . no people have more; is it not their art to copy nature? Nature is always best studied with the assistance of philosophy."[98]

In addition to these scenes set in the real world of London's theatre, Lindsay locates his story firmly within the scope of dramatic performance: the living of life on a stage. In the very first chapter of *Memoirs* he declares his prime objective to be the true "representation of the fine gentleman", a type "very rarely seen in its full dress and proper requisites". Too often, claims Lindsay, contemporaries "either made him the faultless monster, or have mistaken the genteel rake, and pretty fellow, for the fine gentleman". Here he elides the contemporary type and the theatrical character, blurring the line between fact and fiction – within his own fiction. Thus he observes that "Our English comedies have made some progress in the character . . . but there are vicious qualities and too strong propensities to fashion in some, and a formal stiffness of civility and affected amiableness in others." He summarizes his own expectations: "great perception and great resolution, grafted upon great goodness of heart, are the necessary ingredients, and produce that true politeness and delicacy of manners, which form the character and render it complete".[99]

Lindsay goes on to observe that the Prince of Wales (soon to be George III), when asked "what he thought of Dorimant in *Sir Fopling Flutter*", replied that he could not "allow a fine gentleman so many vices". This is a reference to George Etherege's popular play *The Man of Mode; or, Sir Fopling Flutter: A Comedy*, first performed in London in 1676, in which Dorimant, not Flutter, is the hero. Etherege (1636–92) had written two earlier successful comedies: *The Comical Revenge; or, Love in a Tub* (1664) and *She Would If She Could: A Comedy* (1668); the first performance of the latter was attended by Charles II. Ambivalence was a common reaction to the character Dorimant, who is not only exuberant, masculine, charming, attractive and witty – deserving his place as the hero of the play – but also a rakish libertine who keeps three mistresses and treats all of them shamefully, yet finds time to dupe even them. At the same time the boundless, ungovernable passion of the jealous Mrs Loveit – a parodic character much enjoyed by Restoration audiences – is a source of Dorimant's disgust: he sees her as reduced to a slut.[100]

Although several characters in Etherege's *The Man of Mode* share names with characters in *Memoirs* – Mrs Loveit, Old Bellair, Young Bellair, Emilia (the daughter of a Glasgow merchant who hopes to make her Telemachus's bride) – Lindsay does not, however, insert a Dorimant or a Flutter into his epic. Neither of these two fitted his picture of "the fine gentleman". Richard Steele (1672–1729) had made the point much earlier, in *The Spectator* in 1711, saying that "a fine gentleman should be honest in his actions, and refined in his language", whereas Dorimant was "a direct knave in his designs, and a clown in his language".[101] In *Memoirs* Lindsay declares: "Sir Richard Steele's Bevel [*sic*], in my opinion, comes much nearer to the character: and yet many defects are visible, both in his sentiments and behaviour."[102] Bevil is the sentimental hero of Steele's *The Conscious Lovers* (1722), described by Doody as a play in which "family duty is presented with exaggerated seriousness". Steele is concerned particularly about the duties of sons and the proper behaviour of young gentlemen, as well as the inhumanity of arranged marriages, within an understanding of benevolence in which doing good for others brings joy to the heart. Although this makes *The Conscious Lovers* unusual as stage comedy – in which the rules of conduct and social duty were ignored with impunity – the sentiments are similar to those found in Lindsay's *Memoirs*.[103]

The scene in *The Conscious Lovers* most enjoyed by audiences was that in which Indiana learns the identity of her father, the Bristol merchant Mr Sealand. It was this scene that unsettled Lindsay's positive assessment of Bevil; he found that Bevil lacked the resolution and goodness of heart required of the fine gentleman. "For tho' he is sensible of Indiana's virtue, and nobly touch'd with her distress", writes Lindsay, "yet, out of views which seem low and narrow, he leaves her too open to the world's censure and his father's suspicions; and in his conduct to the lady herself is too reserv'd for a great goodness of heart". Bevil "takes great pains to gain her affections" but "the knowledge of the suspence, private uneasiness and torture, which he is convinced she suffers on his account, border rather upon cruelty; it speaks a mean fear, mixed with his filial piety; when the man of great resolution would have at first been open and honest without any arts, shifts or disguises". Further, comments Lindsay, "Equivocation and double-dealing deviate from that delicacy which is inseparable from the character: I cannot admit it complete where there is a deliberate fraud; nor agree with Bevel, that dissimulation can be honest."[104]

Lindsay also made use of the social space of the theatre to locate the qualities of his characters. It is in this way that Clarissa, Lady Hughson, is judged when her debauchery drives Sir Thomas into exile. She lacks culture as well as morals. Clarissa, says Lindsay,

> was very handsome; had a number of lovers; and, like the harlot with her customers, received them one after another; as well pleased to hear a tender sentence from the last, as from the first. This habit, a happy marriage could not wash off: she was still admired, still loved going to places of diversion; not that she enjoyed the design of these amusements, for if an old aquaintance would be amorous and gallant in his speeches to her, she would sit down in a box or by-corner, and hear him for hours together: . . . and thus would she waste her time, insensible all the while, that [Isabella] Burchell sung or Garrick played.[105]

Such failure Lindsay reverses in the case of Telemachus and Luisa. Although earlier they informally consented to be partners, joining hands in a domestic betrothal ceremony known in the Scottish border country and remoter parts of Britain as the "handfast", Telemachus and Luisa are not married in church until January 1749.[106] They have six children. *Memoirs* concludes with Telemachus and Luisa, allowing him to perform the role of the "fine gentleman" in the context of the theatre: "As he lov'd his wife, he lov'd to be near her he saw no indecency in sitting by her; he would beg the companies pardon, but always chose it when possible: he dar'd to sit with her, – to sit next her even in the play-house, and never thought himself obliged to a man to give her his hand when he was present himself. He would walk with her: walk with her alone."[107]

Thus, even when Lindsay introduces literary fictions into his own fictional narrative, the central themes remain the same: the nature of kinship, the association of individuals, and, above all, the relationship of father and son. Biblical in its tradition, this last was a persistent problem that directed Lindsay's own choices and spilled over into an understanding of identity and nation. It also inhabited the small world of the naval sailing ship, unnatural in its male exclusivity and mobile insularity. This small world did not limit Lindsay's imagination; rather, particularly in his role as chaplain, it allowed him to assume the perspective of an onlooker, an observer, taking in the drama being played out before him.

CHAPTER FOUR

An Imaginary Island

IN CONSTRUCTING *Memoirs* and presenting his moral lessons, Lindsay borrowed from classical and contemporary models but firmly established his narrative in a modern Atlantic world. He did not invoke wonders or supernatural interventions, nor did he supply his tale with a fundamentally imaginary history or geography. Whereas Fénelon's Telemachus journeys through the ancient world of the eastern Mediterranean and Swift's Gulliver travels among peoples extraordinarily short and tall, the central action of Lindsay's *Memoirs* takes place in a relatively familiar contemporary environment. The troubles of his Telemachus are classical but they are played out on a modern stage.

Lindsay's writing was firmly located in a style identified in 1750 by Dr Samuel Johnson as the new variety of "modern romances, or novels". With *Tom Jones* and *Roderick Random* in mind, Johnson opined: "The works of fiction, with which the present generation seems more particularly delighted, are such as exhibit life in its true state, diversified only by accidents that daily happen in the world, and influenced by passions and qualities which are really to be found in conversing with mankind." He termed this style "the comedy of romance" and declared: "Its province is to bring about natural events by easy means, and to keep up curiosity without the help of wonder: it is therefore precluded from the machines and expedients of the heroic romance, and can neither employ giants to snatch away a lady from the nuptial rites, nor knights to bring her back from captivity; it can neither bewilder its personages in deserts, nor lodge them in imaginary castles."[1] Lindsay followed these rules.

Many strange things happen in *Memoirs*, certainly, but they happen within the framework of a real natural and historical world. Coincidence, accident and mistaken identity are all part of this and therefore open to study and understanding, whereas giants, monsters and knights on white horses can only be marvelled at and are not potential subjects of science. Surprise is natural; the incredible is not. Lindsay guided his readers through his fictional world by means of Johnson's "curiosity without the help of wonder". On one occasion Lindsay lapses into a temporary credulous vision of ghosts, but he quickly provides its natural, rational explanation. His characters, whether fictional or real, possess no superhuman powers. They act out their stories on a natural world-stage, living real lives and fighting in real battles, much as in Homer's *Odyssey*.[2] This is why Lindsay felt comfortable in claiming that in *Memoirs* "the story is founded on facts, with the characters of many real and living personages" and asking his readers to accept its "historical faith" without expecting them to take literally the truth of its histories.[3] Similarly, Lindsay rarely distorted the shape of the political or military history of the period or the topography of geographical space.

The one great divergence from the real world allowed in *Memoirs* is the fictitious geography of Zophil Groam Ba, an imaginary island that is given a precise geographical location. Lindsay was drawn there by literary sirens. He could not resist the delights of constructing a place and a community – a microcosm – with its own topography and social organization and its own political model. Islands had long been favoured sites for imaginary places, having the advantage of isolation and the potential for creation of microcosms. Homer's *Odyssey* mentions more than ten imaginary places, most of them islands, from breezy Aeolia to Ogygia, the home of Calypso. Imaginary islands also served as testing grounds for ideal societies, the most influential of these being Thomas More's 1516 *Utopia*; the word means "no place" but More's example is set on an island off the coast of South America. Again, it is on a nameless island near the mouth of the Orinoco – sometimes claimed to be Tobago – that Daniel Defoe's *Robinson Crusoe* (1719) places the first modern individual of fiction, a man confronted by slavery, on the fringes of the Caribbean colonial world.

When Lindsay published *Memoirs* less than fifty years later, real islands – prime sites of imperial exploration and experimental exploitation – had come to outweigh the islands of the imagination. At the same time, the idea that an unknown island could be discovered in the North Atlantic, with a secluded, isolated population, was not far-fetched. In the middle of the eighteenth century, Europeans still often thought of the Atlantic as an ocean full of islands.[4] For Lindsay to find Zophil Groam Ba in the North Atlantic was an obvious act of fiction, but making this imaginary place an island, rather than a lost continent, and populating it with modern migratory peoples gave it a readily acknowledged verisimilitude.

Lindsay constructs Zophil Groam Ba as a real place, neither an island paradise nor a utopia. It has a precise location and is subject to the normal forces of nature. There are no monsters and things are no more likely to be governed by supernatural forces than anywhere else. It is this normality that enables Lindsay to use Zophil Groam Ba as the place to set out some of his more abstract ideas about good government and social organization. Perhaps because Zophil Groam Ba is the only substantial imaginary geographical site in *Memoirs*, Lindsay feels obliged to give a detailed idea of its topography, something he does not do for real places. Indeed, he created his own map of the island – at much the same time as he was producing his hydrographical map of Cork Harbour – to assist the reader's navigation of the narrative and draw attention to its details in his text (figure 4.1).[5]

An Imaginary Island

Figure 4.1 Lindsay's map of Zophil Groam Ba. [John Lindsay], *Memoirs of Sir Thomas Hughson and Mr Joseph Williams* (London, 1757), 3:173. Beinecke Rare Book and Manuscript Library, Yale University Library.

Fictitious Geography

PROSLAVERY PRIEST

There was nothing imprecise about Lindsay's geography or chronology of Zophil Groam Ba. At 11 p.m. on 6 April 1747 Telemachus and his companions aboard the *Union*, which sailed from Glasgow for America eleven days before, are at latitude 50 degrees 18 minutes north and longitude from London 24 degrees 48 minutes west (figure 2.3). The next morning they discover an island with bays and headlands and a "very spacious river", and on its banks "a very pleasantly situated town" but no forts or defences. The bay on which the town sits is "one of the finest in the world".[6]

Lindsay's certainty about the location of Zophil Groam Ba is set in the context of a display of nautical knowledge (gained during his several Atlantic voyages and in the Bay of Biscay) and an awareness of the latest technologies. Soon after the *Union* leaves Glasgow, "the horizon being extremely clear", the captain "had an opportunity of trying the new invented *azimuth* compass". A few days later they take a French privateer, called the *Adventure*, and Telemachus is given command of it. When changes in the wind force the ships to undertake some complicated tacking, they are separated and the ship under Telemachus suddenly finds itself in shallow waters. "[U]pon perusing their charts, finding no known land so near them as *Cape Clear*, they began to have hopes that this must be the island, so often spoke of by seamen, under the name of New Brazil."[7] Here Lindsay makes the claim that the island may have been discovered, but not visited, by Christopher Columbus in 1492–93 and "laid down in Mr. John Spad's map, printed by Mr. Dawson at *London*, in the year 1627, by the name of *New Brazil*". In fact John Speed (1551–1629) had shown in his *Prospect of the Most Famous Parts of the World* of 1627 an island called Brazil on two of his maps, located approximately at the coordinates recorded by Telemachus and west of Ireland.[8]

The hopes that Telemachus and his men have stumbled on New Brazil are quickly dashed, however; "they found themselves by their *reckoning* too far to the northward, as well as to the westward, for the *bearings* of that supposed tract". There is no chance that Telemachus has made a mistake. Since leaving port just a week before, they "had fine observations every day, with Hadley's quadrant" – the English octant, patented just twenty-five years earlier – so that "[e]rror in the *latitude* was impossible; and the *longitude* must have been very correct; as every day's *dead reckoning* agreed with their observation". The "first discoverers" of New Brazil lacked these technical advantages, says Lindsay, and "not only had come from the *West-Indies*, by which long run they must have had an incorrect *longitude*; but also by their own accounts, having had a long passage, from the time they discover'd the island, before they *made land*; and that, attended with very tempestuous weather, their *longitude* could not by any means be depended upon".[9]

Once the ship is anchored off the island and remains unmolested, Telemachus goes towards the shore with other crew members in a pinnace and they take as prisoners some island men found in a canoe. One of these men speaks "an intelligible sort of broken *English*", and from him Telemachus discovers that the island is "called by its inhabitants, *Zophil-Groam-ba*; a name, which, when interpreted, signifies, the *Land of the two kings*".[10] He then extracts from the speaker of broken English a concise history:

> the island was formerly governed by two potentates, one of whom was called Zophil; the other Groam. That about twenty years ago and upwards, some differences with the borders of each nation, was the cause of a very grievous war, and which, in all probability, would have in a short time been the destruction of both nations; had not Heaven, in pity for their distress, sent them in a miraculous manner, a deliverer; who, by the consent of both contending parties, was made ruler over the whole island; when the two kings by the public voice, were compelled to retire into their several kingdoms, and live in the character of private gentlemen. . . . [And] that as the present king lived in *Zophil-ba* and at a great distance from the populous and warlike inhabitants of *Groam-ba*, Groam their late king, had with great industry gain'd over the dispositions of that people to a war, with the present king of the united nations. And that they were now with a great army within a few days march of *Yettaa*, the principal city of *Zophil-ba*, and that which was discover'd lying on the bank of the river, already taken notice of.[11]

On hearing this convenient summary, Telemachus writes a letter, dated 10 April 1747, addressed to the island's king, saying that

> Being cast upon this island by contrary winds, in my voyage to New-England, and not knowing by whom it was inhabited, I have taken possession of these coasts and seas surrounding, in the name of George *the Second, King of* England, Scotland, France and Ireland, &c. &c. &c. But finding the *English* language corruptly spoken by your subjects, I have hopes this ceremony has been already done; and in the same name. Learning also your majesty's unhappy circumstances, threatened with an army of rebellious subjects; if it is to assist the friend of his *majesty* of Britain, this ship and its stores of war shall be dedicated to your service.

The same day Telemachus receives a response from "Zophil y Groam *Rex*" saying that "tho' I am here the *King* of Zophil Groam-Ba, I am still as yourself, a loyal subject of his *Majesty King* George of Britain". He proposes a meeting the following day, on the plain between the river and the city of Yettaa.[12]

Telemachus forms a guard from his sailors, dressed in their best and carrying the British ensign as their colours, and some of the French prisoners. They land, and "Multitudes of the ignorant islanders were assembled on this occasion; who like a concourse of devout Roman Catholicks at the passing of the host, shew'd their veneration and dread of so unusual an appearance, by falling down on their knees, and using a number of very romantic gestures, with acclamations hideous and mournful: but having the dread of the papist, without the love, they kept at too far a distance to intimidate Mr. Lovet's guards by their numbers." Telemachus then observes the king approaching with a troop armed with bows and quivers. Speaking English, Telemachus encourages his men to behave like "resolute Britons", but if outnumbered to be ready to retreat to the ship. In French he tells the prisoners to forget the war in Europe and combine with the "redoubtable *Brittons*".[13]

Zophil y Groam seeks the assistance of Telemachus in overcoming the island's rebellious subjects, offering his crown if victorious. He tells Telemachus: "You are welcome to these lands. I can see the kind providence of the God of nations in this timely assistance; and accept your generous offer in behalf of the king of Britain, and of me, with a heart as full of gratitude to you, as thankful acknowledgment to that almighty disposer of events." Telemachus offers his service, but says: "I do it without hopes of recompence. I am now in my voyage to New-England, in search of my parents, whose high station in Indian boundaries, I am told, gave me the honour of royalty by birth. Sent early from them, for a British education, I am now ignorant where or how to find them: but till filial curiosity is satisfied, no thoughts of grandeur can possess my mind."[14]

The narrative of *Memoirs* is interrupted at this point to fill in the "history of Sir Thomas Hughson" from the time he left Britain in 1724 to 1747, the novel's present. He has gone to Leyden as planned but, attempting to return to London, is blown off course and castaway on a sandbank. Eventually he gets to the small island of Ba-heizer (figure 4.1), a "dominion" of Zophil Groam Ba used for banishment of unfit persons. However, Sir Thomas finds the people of Ba-heizer more honest and humane than those on their parent island: "Our barbarous cut-throats of *Cornwall*, would have here gazed at humanity, and our unpladded gentry in the north of *Scotland*, as well as our broad-brims in *England*, would have confessed they never saw honesty in a light so beauteous before." These people were originally from Holland and their language Dutch, but corrupted perhaps by peoples from America who had adopted various Indian customs, "at length allowing the pagan to get the better of the lukewarm Christian, [which] may have been the cause of the few heathenish superstitions, which was then found in their form of worship". It is here that Lindsay introduces his description of the Virginia custom of "huskanawin", discussed in chapter 2, saying it had been followed in the island but was now abolished. He also says that the dress of the people is "almost Indian" and "their alertness in the use of the bow and arrow, point them out to be rather from this quarter, than from the northern parts of Europe".[15]

Lindsay reflects that

> It may seem strange to some that a few *Dutch* families going abroad to make a little money, should on their return be covered and armed like *Indians*. But this I think will be no objection of force. Their *pagan* customs grew from ignorance; which would be the same case with *England*, herself, were she for some time deprived of her *churchmen*. And the families, in their return, being here shipwrecked, tho' they had perhaps small arms on board, might not save one from the wreck: and tho' then cloathed like *Europeans*, having no communication with other nations, a short time might oblige them, for food, to use the bow; and for raiment, the skins of beasts, &c.
>
> . . .
>
> A question may here arise amongst *naturalists*, What sort of birds? What sort of beasts? Or how came they hither? But as that scene does not lie in my way, as a *memoirialist*, I leave it to the curious, who may perhaps favour the *Royal Society* or that of *Antiquarians*, on this point, with something new and useful.[16]

Here Lindsay reminds his reader that Sir Thomas was born in Germany and educated in Holland, and that Dutch is as much his native language as English. The summer following his being castaway on Ba-heizer, he goes over to Zophil Groam Ba, where he discovers conflict between the two principalities. Sir Thomas addresses the nobles, including Latin quotations from Cicero's orations, but the two princes fight and die, leaving behind the infants Groam and Zobaesti. To save the situation, Sir Thomas is offered "supreme authority" by "universal consent". He accepts, but on the condition that he be given "the liberty to prescribe for them a new form of government, and to make them laws agreeable to that constitution" (described in an appendix in the next volume of *Memoirs*). However, young prince Groam comes to see Sir Thomas as a usurper and stirs up the "civil broils" that Telemachus finds in process.[17]

The power relations are further disturbed by the presence among the shipwrecked travellers on the *Union* of the cunning Philip, Telemachus's former teacher and, unknown to both of them, brother. When Zophil y Groam (Sir Thomas) discovers that Philip is his son, he is overjoyed, and immediately gives Philip command of the "Royal army" against the "rebels". In the first battle between these forces, Telemachus is tricked into bringing only the French prisoners ashore, and Philip turns them against the British and "the *Virginian desperado*" Telemachus.[18] Philip leads the "King's army" to a rout of the rebels, who are unused to firearms. Telemachus, in the thickets after the death of Sicco, observes this unequal battle and breaks into a soliloquy: "Just heavens! what a state? into what a plunge of misery is my hopes and fortune fallen! banished! banished by that mouth which but yesterday eat of my bread, and thanked his master's kindness!" The rebels are led by Prince Groam, cousin of Zobaesti. Groam believes he should succeed as king and wishes his sister Princess Adonisa to be married to Zobaesti, but Philip hopes that he will himself both become king and win the hand of Adonisa. Telemachus enters the rebel camp after dark, arriving by chance at the tent of Adonisa, who is pondering her choices. He agrees to lead the rebels with the support of his sailors, but traitors enable another rout. Groam is killed and Adonisa taken prisoner. Telemachus escapes.[19]

At the same time Philip is being hailed as the new regent – with the title "Gi hom rattaiah" – at Yettaa Palace. Soon after, by the light of the moon, Telemachus and a small band of sailors storm the palace and take as prisoners Sir Thomas, Zobaesti and Adonisa, but they find that Philip is not there. Acting as a servant of "my royal sovereign George *of Britain*", Telemachus declares that Philip must be punished as a traitor, "who having been born a subject son of England, durst in rebellion, raise in these lands, a *Gallic standard*". Sir Thomas rejects Philip, but Telemachus puts aside his personal grievances and declares that his one goal for the island is "to reduce it to the subjection of the *British* flag".[20]

Telemachus goes with his men to establish a military presence on the far side of the island, using their ship's cannon, and there follows a bloody battle with Philip's forces. Eventually Telemachus is victorious and the people from all parts of the island seek the protection of Zobaesti. Telemachus, responding to calls for vengeance, pleads that Philip, as the deposed regent, be treated with dignity. This, Telemanchus tells Zobaesti, was essential "politically" for his own future security. Telemachus explains: "If you should begin at court to use with indignity that person who was formerly sacred; those subjects, who, as venerate your commands, will be taught that princes are only men; and that men may be abused. England, tho' the fav'rite isle of heaven; seat of the muses; the magazine of arts and science, has nevertheless made herself infamous, in a direful event of a like nature." Philip is taken as a prisoner to Yettaa but later allowed to leave the island with Sir Thomas. Telemachus seeks no reward from the House of Seniors but declares the islanders subjects of the British monarch, with their prince being only "regent hereditary". Zobaesti receives this title and, following a triumphal march into Yettaa, is married to Adonisa.[21]

"The Idea of a Patriot King"

Chapter 9 of volume 4 of Lindsay's *Memoirs* forms an "Appendix to the History of the Island of Zophil Groam Ba", centred on "the idea of a patriot king". Its aim is to provide "a description of that most extraordinary form of government" found in the island by setting out the character of the king, foreseen by Sir Thomas in the young Zobaesti. Lindsay adds the tantalizing comment that "as he [Sir Thomas] in his dictates, followed the maxims given by Charlemaign to his son; I shall not think I do the Baronet an injury, if in transcribing his idea of a patriot king, I follow that of a celebrated French orator".[22] Although Lindsay later admits to forgetting the orator's name, he acknowledges that this section of *Memoirs* was composed while he was on board the *Newcastle* in 1755 and had access to the library of the French prisoner Lohier.[23]

In referring to Charlemagne, Lindsay wished both to apply an ancient aura to his imaginary polity and to make obvious the parallels between its problems of government and the recent rocky progress of the monarchs and parliaments of Britain. The era of Charlemagne – the eighth and ninth centuries – saw consolidation of ideas about rulership that had been forming in the Christian West since late antiquity, in which an emperor might rule several settled realms and peoples, sharing power with Church and aristocracy, rather than imposing hegemony through barbarian plunder and tribute.[24] Charlemagne played a central role in ensuring the continuity of these developments. From his numerous offspring he singled out three of his sons for preferment in order to establish on a firm foundation the succession to his vast kingdom. To ensure peace between them, Charlemagne's *Divisio regnorum* of 806 allocated each of the brothers a realm for which he was to be responsible – to rule and defend – in the event that they outlived their father, and he went out of his way to prevent bickering between sons and grandchildren. They were jointly responsible for the care and preservation of Saint Peter's Church. It turned out, however, that only one of the sons – Louis the Pious – survived Charlemagne (who died in 814), which may explain Lindsay's reference to a son rather than sons. In making his sons both his partners in rulership and his heirs, Charlemagne provided a vital model for the future of government in Europe. Such precise arrangements were unprecedented, and in order to establish their authority Charlemagne sought the Pope's blessing.[25]

In *Memoirs*, Lindsay begins his outline of the "idea of a patriot king" by rejecting divine right, a notion rooted in Biblical genealogies that had persisted into the 1740s. Strangely, Lindsay makes no mention of Bolingbroke's widely influential *The Idea of a Patriot King* (1738), a notorious work that parallels Fénelon's *Telemachus* in its objective of preparing a young prince for kingship. As in Bolingbroke, Lindsay's emphasis is on the importance of instruction and preparation in order to give the king/prince the best chance of withstanding the many demands and pressures that come with the role. Once installed, a prince is immediately seduced by the splendour of his office and the adoration received, while those around him simultaneously seek special favours and preferment.[26] Pride has to be put to one side, says Lindsay, and the prince must constantly keep in mind the tribute he owes "the majesty supreme". The Bible has to be followed: "In that sacred volume, the faithful guide of kings, are contain'd those treasures of knowledge; that wisdom which became the object of the desire, and eager pursuits of Solomon the wise." In the Scriptures can be found "the maxims and the laws of a perfect government", as well as the "means whereby the deity is attach'd to kings of justice" and the "chastisements he prepares for princes, proud and disobedient". The prince, declares Lindsay, has to recognize the power of the Almighty in his "dreadful instruments of vengeance", He who in an instant could destroy armies and overturn empires and put "the conqueror in the place of him who is vanquish'd".[27]

The king who through hubris thinks himself divinely appointed is headed for a fall, says Lindsay. On the other hand, the "perfect prince" understands his greatness to be derived only from "a resign'd performance of Heaven's laws", and knows that "to God alone belong majesty, honour and power". The ruler is "obliged, by duty indispensible, to render a perpetual homage to him who is alone great, powerful, alone formidable, the principal, the only master of all".[28] Thus the prince is required to exhibit "modesty in the midst of stations the most illustrious" and "to establish, to enlarge, and maintain, the true worship, of an almighty superior". It is not enough for the prince to be privately pious and follow "religion's principles" and laws:

> He makes 'em to flourish in the whole extent of his estates. Scandal is punished; impiety reduc'd to silence, or forc'd to render homage to the truth; while virtue protected, receives her proper recompence. What sensibility for the true interest of the Church? What attention to make her councils observ'd! To establish the glory of her priesthood; and sees episcopal! What care that pastoral charges be fill'd with subjects distinguished for their knowledge; for their piety; for their modesty; for their zeal; and by all those virtues which become a servant to the altar![29]

With a proper attitude to God in place, the prince needs next to think about his responsibilities to mankind. The most important of these duties, Lindsay declares, is justice, meaning the capacity of rulers to "govern with equity their subjects; defend the weak against the oppression of the strong; fix properties; and render every one, that which properly pertains to 'em".

However, kings should not themselves dispense justice, as they did in the past, because "the spirit of fraud, interest, and divisions, have so disfigured the face of the world, that kings are obliged to make partners in their functions, the sages of their realms". The responsibility of the prince is simply to appoint "magistrates knowing, judicious, and incorruptable". Beyond the prince's love of justice, he is required to be vigilant in the protection of rights and to extend "gentleness-paternal" towards his subjects. The people he rules are in turn required to show respect, fidelity and obedience.[30]

In the light of statements about the supposed absence of slavery in Britain, discussed in the previous chapter, it is interesting that there is an "abundance of servants" but apparently no enslaved people on Zophil Groam Ba.[31] Perhaps the many servants mean there was no need for slavery in Lindsay's model, but even if he had constructed the society as a utopia he might have seen a place for the institution, just as slavery was often essential to island-utopian dreams of the ancient and modern worlds.[32] In Lindsay's *Memoirs* more broadly, social hierarchy plays a strong role, expressed most clearly in the descriptions of servants, women and enslaved people, all of whom are regularly disparaged and put in their place.

The prince in Lindsay's realm has the challenging task of selecting office-holders. It is his responsibility to be "[a]ttentive to examine the genius; to discern talents; to be acquainted with characters, and with manners" so that he can place "every one according to their merit, and that degree of usefulness, the public may receive from their labours". He has also to ensure that the office-holders carry out their commissions. This daunting task was less onerous than it might sound, since in the ideal prince's world injustice cannot flourish, fraud and violence are banished, usury and extortion suppressed. By gaining respect through justice, he can lay by "the sword of power".[33]

With the prince triumphant over his enemies and peace restored to the land, a prosperous agriculture and trade flourish once more and the youth are brought up in "obedience, fatigue, sobriety, and the love of letters".[34] It is here that Lindsay mentions the unidentified French source he copied from Lohier's library and again refers to the "patriot king", the idea announced as the subject of the chapter but strangely missing from the body of the essay. Even here Lindsay makes no explicit reference to Bolingbroke's *Idea of a Patriot King*, which approves of hereditary right in spite of its lack of philosophical foundations. Lindsay, like the Prince of Wales – the soon-to-be-crowned George III – may not in fact have read Bolingbroke's tract and probably had no need to do so, since its ideas were popular knowledge and rooted in classical models. On the other hand, there is no doubt that Lindsay was aware of the grooming that was in process and of the political jockeying that surrounded the ascension and high expectations of the new king.[35]

Lindsay concludes boldly, with a nod towards Sir Thomas, ruler of Zophil Groam Ba, and towards his own monarch, George II, and his son: "Such the idea of a patriot sovereign! Such the happiness these islanders enjoy'd under our Baronet's administration! Such too, thrice happy subjects, the blessings we ourselves have in view under that amiable young prince who discovers all the good qualities of an unparallel'd father. But which God long avert, by the continuance of that royal life, so much the blessing and glory of Britain!"[36]

Island Polity

Chapter 10 of volume 4 of *Memoirs* sets out the ways in which Sir Thomas introduces changes to the ideal model of government. When first made ruler of Zophil Groam Ba, he finds a government "entirely *monarchical*; and the crown hereditary", but he "altered it very much into that of a *republic*". The king retains a good deal of power but "by new regulations, became much limited by his Parliament and College of Seniors". The House, or College, of Seniors is "a body of men to whom, the whole nation, even king, ministers, and chiefs, (or Parliamenters) are subjected".[37] Sir Thomas makes these changes rather than reigning as "an arbitrary monarch" because he himself has "tasted of Britain's liberty", and "like a true father of his people, he parted with much of his grandeur, that it might not henceforth be in the power of any prince to rule with tyranny". The crown ceases to be hereditary. Although it is agreed that normally "the nearest in blood should succeed the deceased prince", the parliament, with the agreement of the House of Seniors, is given power to "not only divest a reigning *prince* of his authority, and choose a regent" but also to "set aside the next heir, if suspected, and retain the regent in his stead; or by want of proper succession can give the right of sovereignty into a distant family".[38]

No doubt Lindsay expected his readers to recognize parallels between the imaginary polity of Zophil Groam Ba and the real political history of Britain. Although the question of succession remained alive in Scotland at least until Culloden (1746), Lindsay could see in the Glorious Revolution of 1688 a growth in English liberty that seemed to have resolved the contest between Crown and government in favour of parliamentary sovereignty. Lindsay's account looks back to the roots of this contest, particularly the struggle over the doctrine of divine right and the sacramental character of hereditary monarchy, which precipitated the Exclusion Crisis of 1679–81. This crisis had its origins in the *Test Act* of 1673, which was designed to exclude Dissenters from political influence but more specifically to prevent the Catholic

James, Duke of York, from succeeding his brother, the Anglican Charles II. It established as a precondition of civil office a sacramental test and rejection of the doctrine of transubstantiation. It was during this crisis that James was sent north to Scotland. Succession to the crown, from William and Mary to the house of Hanover in 1714, followed shifting principles manipulated by Parliament that clearly deviated from a theory of divine hereditary right. It came to look very much like an elective monarchy along the lines of the changes introduced to Zophil Groam Ba by Sir Thomas.

Here Lindsay also displays a more radical streak, liberated by his fictional polity but mixing his ideas with models derived from ancient Greece – where kingship began with Homer's Odysseus – as well as Rome.[39] In the event of dethroning of a sovereign or disagreement between the parliament and House of Seniors, the matter is to be put to "the *public voice*". This means not "the majority of the Parliament, altho' the representatives of the people", but rather a public vote, or "The voices of the whole nation, that is, such as are married, be they of what age soever, . . . abstracting those only who are in servitude for public misdemeanours, and women; provided always that the College of Seniors, and not the Trustees of Orphans, have a power to represent the deceased father."[40]

The Seniors number twenty-five, elected to represent the sixteen counties of Zophil Groam Ba. They are drawn from the nobility, but this is an earned rather than hereditary rank. In order to be admitted, it is required that a man "behave himself in his country's service for a considerable space of years, with signalized assiduity and courage". Those who demonstrate such fine qualities might "attain the first mark of distinction, which is Knight of the order of the *Sword*". Behaving with honour in this rank, together with "accumulated heroism in arms", leads to the next rank, "Knight of the Holy-Cross", and an almost certain call to court and public office. To be eligible for election to the House of Seniors – says the twenty-seven-year-old Lindsay – a man has to be at least sixty years of age and to have advanced to the rank of Knight of the Order of the Sword. Such status demonstrates not only that he has been "raised by that means, above the common tribe" but shows also that "his sphere of life may have been led amongst such people, as may have given him a perfect acquaintance with the island in general; as well as his own county in particular".[41]

Although Lindsay saw the House of Seniors as serving much the same function as the (British) House of Lords, its composition is different. In footnotes citing, *inter alia*, Cicero, Juvenal and Ovid, his debt to Roman political practice is made explicit.[42] Lindsay's House of Seniors does not exactly match the Roman Senate, or even the council of elders portrayed in Homer's *Iliad*, but the relationships of senators and magistrates, nobles and office-holders, are loosely similar. In practice, the Senate under the Republic made policy following debates in which its senior members were allowed to have the first word, showing respect for their experience and authority. And often the first word was also the last.[43]

PROSLAVERY PRIEST

What of religion and the church in Zophil Groam Ba? Lindsay uses the island as a stage on which to act out the way in which a decline in religious observance might lead to social chaos and the necessity for a revival of faith to enable good government. In the absence of godly leadership, there has been no form of "regular worship or devotion" amongst the inhabitants, "from the time of their landing on this island, to the reign of their third king Groam Vanderskan, grand father to Groam Jataskan". By this time, after perhaps several generations, "superstition, ignorance, and heathenism, had very much defac'd all marks of a Protestant profession". In this situation, "finding the state of the isle growing into anarchy, and that no laws, distinctions, nor properties could be maintain'd, as they ought, unless founded on religion", Groam Vanderskan took up the challenge and sought to give to his people "a *form of worship* and *Summary of Faith*, or *Creed*". A "sort of liturgy" was composed and some of the island's elders, known for "virtue and prudence", were appointed "to teach, instruct, and after the method propos'd, to do reverence to the deity in the presence of the people".[44] The content of this faith is not detailed.

It is this primitive form of religious life that Sir Thomas Hughson finds when cast onto the island's shores. Under his direction "religion and virtue took a higher turn". The liturgy of the Church of England is introduced and "*Books of Prayer* were wrote on parchment in the language of the isle", while the island's "lay priests" master "the doctrines of sound Christianity". These refinements enable Sir Thomas to "reform and polish" the islanders "in mind and manners". He sets up "houses of religious retirement" under the direction of the College of Seniors, some for men and some for women, as temporary refuges or asylums, but under no particular orders or vows. There are also Houses of Penitence for debauched women. Telemachus establishes the "Holy Order of St. Peter", reflecting "that apostle's great apostacy, and his being again by repentance admitted into favour". This is a means of granting "respect" but not "honours", designed to rehabilitate penitent criminals and save them from the gibbet.[45]

When Zobaesti becomes ruler of Zophil Groam Ba, he "made very considerable amendments in the government of their church (if we may so call a body of men without *episcopal order*)". In order to govern the church, Zobaesti establishes a special court, "called the Reverend, but under the inspection and censure of the Seniors". The task of this court is to "oversee the churchmen, in their deportment to their people; to hinder oppression amongst themselves; to take cognizance of all innovators of doctrine; and many other irregularities".[46]

"Citizen of the World"

The people of Zophil Groam Ba face questions of allegiance and identity that parallel those raised across the Atlantic world in the midst of the Seven Years' War. The inhabitants are from Holland but creolized, with infusions of American (Indian) social mores. They are subjects of Britain (probably) but required to wonder about becoming French. They are perhaps Christians but on the edge of returning to heathenism and social chaos. Degeneration is not far away. In these ways, the islanders parallel the situation of Telemachus, who himself has every reason to question his identity, his race and his nation, as well as his parentage.

Lindsay used *Memoirs* to ponder fundamental questions of allegiance, and not only in the context of Zophil Groam Ba. Early in the novel, when Sir Thomas makes his fatal decision to leave his wife and family in Glasgow and travel to Amsterdam in exile in 1724, Lindsay intrudes his opinions in support of Sir Thomas's line of action in making himself a vagabond in a strange land, and takes the opportunity to advance a broad-ranging homily. He asks:

> But what, if we consider it rightly, are nation and property to a wise man: or what are those loans, family and friends, which nature indulgeth us in for a season, to a man, who learns to restore them thankfully, when the giver and owner shall be pleased to ask them. Since almighty pleasure gives us a being, what matters it, whether nature drops her burden in *Britain*, in *Turky*, or *Peru*. Nature all the world over is the same: religion and virtue, the most valued treasure a rational mind enjoys; no change of place or fortune can rob him of: his mind is free and uncontroled: his soul far above any human disaster, freely roams from corner to corner; and while he enjoys, what in spite of fortune he calls his own; while he with pleasure admires the peaceful cares of the lowly cottager, or grieves for those who bear the tawdry trappings of cumbersome state, it is alike to him whether it is the *Arabian* poppy or *Virginia's* intoxicating weed he treads on. A citizen of the world, and a sovereign in himself; in his nobler faculties, owns subjection to none but the King of Kings. True it is, one's friends, the nation of one's kindred, and country of one's birth, lies near the heart; a bleeding country sometimes needs one's help; a tender offspring a paternal care! When *Britain* is touched, a *Briton* warms! And sympathy in kindred-wrongs, is nature's beauteous law! But what are all these boasted virtues, but nature's best deformities? Infirmities, which degenerate mortals have stamped with esteem; and view them how you will, at best are marks of fallen partiality.[47]

Lindsay then refers to classical examples, including the story of Anaxagoras, praising him for regarding his country as his "lodgings" and being willing to leave behind friends and property when they became burdensome. Anaxagoras (c. 500–428 BCE) was the first philosopher of classical Greece to live in Athens, where he was the teacher and friend of Pericles. Accused of impiety for his astronomical theories, Anaxagoras was helped by Pericles to escape to Lampsacus, where he founded his own school and lived an honourable life. When Anaxagoras was asked if he could leave his country as easily as he left behind friends and possessions, he pointed to the heavens, writes Lindsay, saying:

> *There is my country*. . . . Go where I will, a citizen of the world, I shall still have the same sun to guide and comfort me; the same moon to give me light by night; the same bespangled vault, will every where surround, and roof my habitation. These are blessings I shall for ever enjoy in spite of kings or fortune. And when death shall close the scene; whether in my country or amidst my friends, I shall find a short cut into the other world every where.

It is the same for all of us, says Lindsay, "whether by death or otherways" we must "sometime or other bid adieu". Faced with his choices, Sir Thomas made a wise decision in forsaking a desperate household for exile and a wider world of citizenship.[48]

CHAPTER FIVE

A Voyage to Africa

EVERYTHING CONTAINED IN LINDSAY'S *Memoirs* depended on his experiences before he joined the *Fougueux* as chaplain on 26 April 1757. His earlier service as chaplain on the *Newcastle* certainly contributed elements to the novel, and no doubt he spent some of his time on board that ship, and ashore, completing his writing. Lindsay did not, however, leave evidence of having kept a journal while on the *Newcastle*, and the same applies to his first voyage on the *Fougueux*. Only his final venture as chaplain resulted in a literary record: his *Voyage to the Coast of Africa*, published in 1759, the year he turned thirty. This was Lindsay's second and last printed book. Although he produced weighty manuscripts in later years, none of them found a publisher.

Cork

The *Fougueux*, built by the French and launched in 1747, was captured the same year at the Battle of Finisterre. A third-rate ship of sixty-four guns and 1,400 tonnes, it was used first to escort convoys of merchantmen to the West Indies. By 1755 the *Fougueux* was based at Halifax, where it was one of six ships commanded by Francis Holburne which joined a squadron from Britain led by Vice-Admiral Edward Boscawen (1711–61). It is interesting that Boscawen was one of the few commanders known to have held a religious service at sea and that this occurred in 1755, but it was aboard his flagship, the *Torbay*, and confined to the ship's officers. In early June the squadron captured ships from a French fleet carrying reinforcements to Canada; the *Fougueux* (under Captain Richard Spry), together with the *Defiance*, took the *Lys*.[1] These captures marked the effective beginning of undeclared war between France and Britain and drew further attention to the British ambition to blockade ports on both sides of the Atlantic in order to prevent a build-up of French forces in North America. Lindsay's voyages on the *Newcastle* were one side of this enterprise, in the Bay of Biscay under Hawke. On the American side of the Atlantic, the focus was on the fortress settlement of Louisbourg.

Located on Cape Breton Island, Louisbourg was central to Anglo-French conflict in North America because it guarded the only navigable approach to Quebec. As the most strongly fortified French settlement in North America, Louisbourg was intended to protect Acadia, effectively the modern province of Nova Scotia. Acadia had been colonized as a region of peasant-style French settlement beginning in the 1630s, but the fragmented island coastline drew it into maritime conflict between France and Britain and connected it with New England to the south. The British came to dominate in Nova Scotia and the French in Cape Breton (called by the French Île Royale); the latter had strong trade links with the French West Indian sugar colonies and commanded the fishery that was so important in trade with the islands (figure 2.3). As a counterbalance, the British had established Halifax in 1749 as their principal base for naval operations in the region.[2]

At the end of 1755, Holburne's small squadron was left to blockade Louisbourg while Captain Spry of the *Fougueux* wintered at Halifax. Boscawen returned to Britain and joined Hawke's fleet off Ushant in May 1756, where Lindsay was on his second voyage as chaplain aboard the *Newcastle*, as discussed in chapter 2. In 1756 the *Fougueux* served in a squadron that sought to harass French shipping and blockade Louisbourg and the St Lawrence, taking six vessels and aiding in the destruction of the fishing village of Little Gaspé. The *Fougueux* then accompanied Holburne's fleet back to England.[3]

When Lindsay joined the *Fougueux* in 1757, it was being prepared to sail with a squadron assembling for Louisbourg, with the objective of attacking the French fleet harboured there and destroying the fort. Its new master was Sam Shepheard.[4] The squadron was commanded by Vice-Admiral Francis Holburne, though apparently the original hope had been that the fleet would be led by Hawke, Lindsay's former commander and Holburne's long-time associate (some critics came to associate Hawke's absence with the venture's ultimate failure).[5] Holburne (1704–71) had served in the West Indies in the 1740s, and in Barbados he married the widow of Edward Lascelles, of the planter-merchant dynasty. Edward was one of the less successful members of the Lascelles family, and indeed was suspended in 1744 as collector of customs for Barbados by Dinwiddie in the course of his investigations. Probably Holburne was chosen to command the fleet in 1757 because of his earlier experience off Louisbourg with Boscawen, and in recognition of his service under Boscawen and Hawke in the Bay of Biscay in 1756, where Lindsay also sailed. Holburne was not particularly liked by his naval contemporaries, partly because of his Scottish origins and his failure to adopt English manners, and perhaps also because of his wealth.[6] Lindsay was more comfortably British – even English – in his attitudes.

Holburne's squadron left Cork on 7 May and arrived off Cape Breton on 9 July 1757. The *Fougueux*, however, was not among the fleet. It had suffered damage at sea even before reaching Cork and had sought shelter in Plymouth Sound, where, in and out of dock, its rigging and masts were repaired and its bottom caulked. On 8 July the *Fougueux* joined a convoy of three ships, anchoring at Cork four days later. It remained there until the end of August, returning to Plymouth in the middle of September and finally mooring in the Downs, off the south-eastern corner of England, on 5 October.[7] Thus Lindsay saw no action and spent his time, frustrated, in port.

The fleet that reached North America had a similar experience, so Lindsay did not miss much. By the time Holburne's squadron had joined the forces assembled at Halifax in July, the French had strengthened their defences and both sides regarded caution as the best strategy. Holburne waited off the coast for his chance until 25 September, when a violent storm damaged many of his ships; one was lost. Leaving some of the ships to be refitted at Halifax, the fleet limped back to England, arriving in December without ever engaging the enemy. A definitive British victory at Louisbourg did not come until the following year, 1758, and only with the peace of 1763 did Cape Breton become British territory.[8]

Like many of his contemporaries, Lindsay was critical of the "inglorious campaign" of 1757. His complaints are directed particularly at the use of Cork as a port of embarkation. Exhibiting his nautical knowledge, he observes that the expedition was "detain'd in this harbour, for some months, by winds which almost constantly sit in one quarter, during the winter, from the time of the equinoctial gales". The delays made the entire enterprise a waste of resources, he complains.[9] No doubt Lindsay was frustrated during this period, kept from the centre of action and equally distant from London, where his novel was at the booksellers and being reviewed, but once again he was fortunate not to have been on board a doomed vessel.

Cherbourg

The early months of 1758, following Lindsay's abortive first voyage on the *Fougueux*, were marked by the successful taking of Louisbourg by the British and by attacks on the European continent. Lindsay did not participate in these events, but his elder brother William, the soldier, was killed in battle in France, at Cherbourg. The port of Cherbourg sits on the northern tip of the Cotentin Peninsula, at the midpoint of the English Channel and immediately south of Portsmouth (figure 2.5). As a naval port its value was limited by its exposed situation, and in the 1750s its fortifications remained incomplete. It was wide open to a British skirmish.

Rev. John Entick, in his contemporary history of the Seven Years' War, describes how, following the English landing at Cherbourg in early August 1758 under the command of General Thomas Bligh (1685–1775), the town was taken and "the light horse were detached to scour the country, and to lay it under contribution" by bringing in hostages for ransom. Some of these units ventured too close to the enemy, and "the brave Captain Lindsey, one of the most intelligent, active and industrious officers in the service of the light horse, was wounded by a musket-shot; of which he died universally regretted". The dragoons – mounted infantrymen – with whom William Lindsay fought at Cherbourg were commanded by Ancrum (William Henry Kerr, c. 1712–75), the fourth Marquess of Lothian. Ancrum had previously (in 1745) joined the Duke of Cumberland's forces in England in pursuit of the Jacobite army and had commanded the cavalry on the left wing in the slaughter at Culloden.[10]

Although the assault on Cherbourg was considered a success, Bligh's leadership was found wanting. Contemporary British critics questioned the significance of capturing a town that could not be held, but others declared: "By taking and quitting, at pleasure, the towns of France, we convince all Europe of our naval superiority; we shew to other nations that the French have no fleets that can oppose us on the sea, and to the French themselves, that they have no troops that can guard the coast."[11] Entick argues similarly that, although the attack did little damage, "it gave life and spirit to our people: it made them feel their own legs again, and to look a Frenchman in the face, without any of those apprehensions that had grown out of past miscarriages". In the middle of September 1758, trophies taken from Cherbourg were "carried in triumph through the metropolis of the British empire: a spectacle to which this generation had been a stranger; and the first enterprise upon the coast of France, for several ages past, which had done honour to our country, and brought disgrace upon the French".[12]

Gorée

In November 1758, three months after the death of his brother at Cherbourg, Lindsay was once again chaplain aboard the *Fougueux*, bound for

Africa to fight the French. In the account he published of this voyage, Lindsay mentions William in the first chapter, saying, "our author's brother, captain William Lindsay, brigade-major, and captain of a troop in Lord Ancram's dragoons . . . fell a sacrifice to bravery in a desperate attempt; to prove the usefulness of those light troops, he himself had the honour to introduce to the British service".[13] Lindsay was well aware that he had a personal investment in his nation's conflict with France, declaring at the outset:

> altho' I have of late been averse to going any more abroad, I now follow fortune with cheerfulness wherever she leads – and, however unbecoming a Christian to confess it, am so warm'd since the death of our poor friend at Cherburg, that I rejoice in going upon immediate action; and could be happy, if I were a soldier, with his skill, to revenge his death! But alas, my peaceful robes, entangle my arms; having nothing left to me but Cato's comfort – *Thanks to the Gods, my boy has done his duty!*

As a "British Christian", Lindsay pities the families of the French but prays that his nation's government "may never sheath the sword, until an enemy so treacherous are on their bended knees". Embarked on his voyage, however, he soon confesses his fault in expressing these feelings and, in the midst of stormy seas, began, he says, "to learn a Christian's prayers, should be for peace".[14]

Lindsay's *Voyage to the Coast of Africa in 1758* was published the following year. As the subtitle explains, it contains "a succinct account of the expedition to, and taking of the island of Goree, by a squadron commanded by the Honourable Augustus Keppel". Keppel (1725–86) was only a few years older than Lindsay but had already enjoyed a distinguished naval career, including sailing with Anson on his voyage of circumnavigation. He was the son of William Anne Keppel, second Earl of Albermarle, commander of the right wing at Culloden and, as mentioned in chapter 2, governor of Virginia in Dinwiddie's time.[15] In contrast with the cautious anonymity attached to *Memoirs*, the title page of *Voyage* boldly declares it to be "by the Reverend Mr. John Lindsay, Chaplain of his Majesty's Ship Fougueux".[16] The work is written in the present tense as a letter addressed to an unidentified London friend.

Gorée Island nestles under Cap-Vert Peninsula, the most westerly point of Africa and site of the modern city of Dakar, with the River Senegal to the north and the Gambia to the south (figure 5.1). Although small and barren and needing even water to be brought from the mainland, the island proved important particularly because there was good anchorage in its shelter, whereas the bars at the mouths of the rivers Senegal and Gambia made them useless as harbours.[17] Gorée was settled first by the Portuguese, who were displaced by the Dutch in 1621; they were ousted in turn by the French

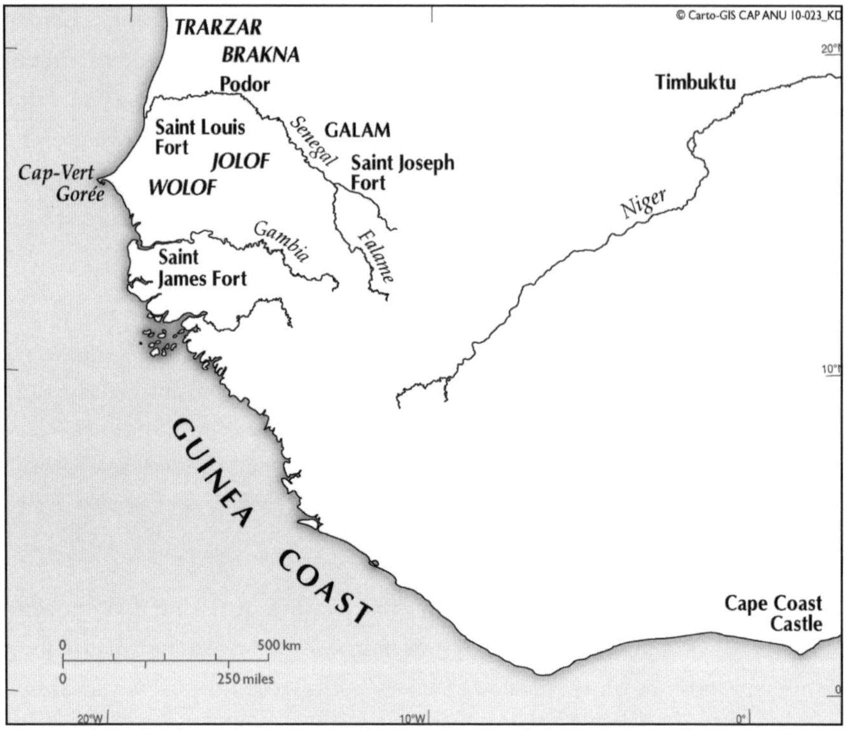

Figure 5.1 West Africa, circa 1758

in 1677. The coast had emerged as an important area of Atlantic commerce following the arrival of Portuguese traders in the fifteenth century, giving the rivers a new role in the downstream trade in gold, ivory, hides, spices and, increasingly, enslaved people. The seventeenth century saw the coast divided into spheres of European influence in conjunction with development of the Atlantic slave trades of the Dutch, French, British and Portuguese. The French established Saint-Louis in 1659, on an island opposite the mouth of the Senegal, and the British had Fort St James at the mouth of the Gambia from 1651. Before the entry of the Europeans, the region had looked inland towards the Sudan, the Sahara and the forest and it remained a dependency of states to the north, but political disintegration had followed the break-up of the Jolof confederation, accompanied by persistent violence between warlord regimes and Muslim theocracies.[18] The presence of the Europeans created an Atlantic Africa.

Matching their control of coastal zones through the establishment of forts or castles, the European states set up chartered trading companies with the objective of monopolizing Atlantic trade, namely the French West India Company and the (British) Royal African Company. The French attempted to use Gorée to capture trade from more distant points, including the Gambia, and together with Saint-Louis it became an important place for the shipment of commodities. The most important of these trade goods was gum arabic, derived from the bark of *Acacia senegal* (first described by Linnaeus as *Mimosa senegal* in 1753 using specimens collected in the region). Known also as gum senegal or gum senega, it is used as an emulsifier or an adhesive for various products, particularly in the sizing and dyeing of silk and cotton cloth. With the French in control of the southern Saharan coast, British customers had no choice but to purchase gum arabic from Dutch merchants who had trade with the French. Gorée was also a centre of the French slave trade across the Atlantic. By the middle of the eighteenth century, hundreds of enslaved African people lived at the forts and castles, serving the companies and the individual traders stationed there, performing domestic and manual labour, and developing skills needed by the European factors. The total population of Gorée, including the European troops and traders, was about one thousand.[19]

The 1750s saw famine across the region, a product of drought and locust plagues, as well as pressure on grain supplies resulting from the demands of the slave traders and war between the ruling families of emirs – the Trarza and Brakna – who were in competition for control of the gum trade. The shortage of food hit particularly hard at Saint-Louis, and this crisis contributed to development of trade to the Americas and drew activity away from the ancient trade across the Sahara to the north. With the spread of the Seven Years' War into the imperial theatre and the accelerating demand for enslaved workers in the plantation economies of the tropical Americas, control of the forts became vital to the European traders.[20]

It was the British desire to displace the French both on the coast of Africa and in the Americas that led to the expedition against Gorée in 1758. The venture combined commercial and military objectives, the British seeking to cut off the supply of slaves to the French West Indian sugar plantations as well as the export of gold dust, ivory, silver and gum arabic for use in the French silk industry. In May 1758 the British succeeded in taking the French settlement of Saint-Louis on the Senegal River but failed to secure Gorée. Realizing it was impossible to hold Senegal without control of Gorée, they organized the expedition commanded by Keppel.[21]

Lindsay begins his *Voyage* with Keppel's squadron at Portsmouth, waiting for a fair wind "to waft us to those sultry regions, where the pride of France is once more destin'd to endure the additional warmth of British thunder". A fleet of thirteen ships had been assembled, seven of them transports carrying seven hundred soldiers under Lieutenant-Colonel Worge.[22] Keppel's squadron sailed first to Cork, where Lindsay had been delayed the year before. In *Voyage* Lindsay recalls that he took advantage of his lengthy time in port "to make a few loose observations upon the harbour" and discovered that the existing charts were inadequate.[23] While at Cork in 1758, on his way to Gorée, he completed an improved hydrographic chart by taking "the principal angles, with Hadley's quadrant as well as the theodolite".[24] His map appears as the first plate in *Voyage*.

Soon after leaving Cork, on 11 November 1758, the squadron ran into an immense "tempest". Lindsay's vivid account of the storm was copied by later writers.[25] An error in calculation of the fleet's course, caused by failure to take proper account of variation in the compass, placed the ships perilously close to the African coast. One of them, the *Litchfield*, a man-of-war with fifty guns that had been part of the squadron based at Halifax in 1757, along with the *Fougueux*, was wrecked on the Barbary Shore. The survivors were "employed as slaves" in Morocco but released in June 1760 when a ransom was paid. The *Fougueux* survived under its new master, Joseph Knight, and continued its voyage with the fleet.[26]

In all of this, Lindsay makes no mention of his spiritual duties. He shows more interest in the natural world, making brave comments on navigation and the reading of winds and currents, and drawing the land as seen from his ship. When the squadron eventually finds its way to Tenerife in the Canary Islands, he describes the landscape in some detail but finds little "curious" except some plants and animals that he drew and had made into plates for his book. The fleet, now comprising eighteen vessels, left Tenerife on 20 December 1758, and on arriving at Gorée it laid siege to the island.[27]

The French surrendered on 29 December 1758. Considering the ease of the British victory over the French, Lindsay comments that the fortifications of Gorée were inadequate for defence against attack by sea and useful "for the purpose alone of keeping the negroes in subjection". In spite of this strategic imbalance, there was contention over the effectiveness of the tactics applied by the naval officers in taking Gorée, which implicitly questioned their courage and honour. Lindsay, having lived through the heat of battle, is forthright in his interpretation of events and confident of his own assessment and intervention. He defends himself by saying he did not go beyond his rank, though he was well aware that there were "sea officers who, from their little knowledge of mankind, think it lessens their dignity that any one but themselves should know things of this nature, and will immediately ask, *What the d—l has the Parson to do with fighting of ships?*"[28]

As he had done at Cork, Lindsay busied himself with his theodolite, making a plan of Gorée Island (figure 5.2). The result was, he thought, vastly superior to the existing chart by P. Labat, which Lindsay calls "wild, ridiculous, and incorrect". The beauty of the mainland seen from Gorée, with its

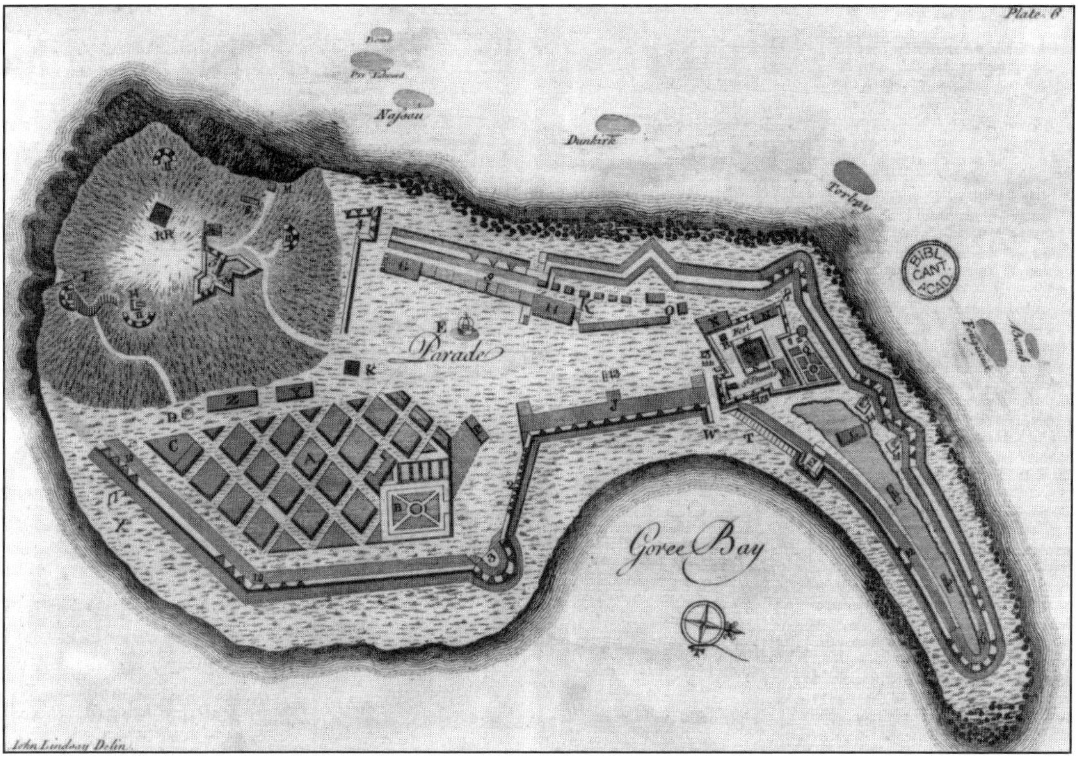

Figure 5.2 Lindsay's plan of Gorée Island, 1758. John Lindsay, *A Voyage to the Coast of Africa in 1758* (London, 1759), plate 6. Reproduced by kind permission of the Syndics of Cambridge University Library. Explanation:

> A, the negroe village; B, the company's gardens, &c.; C, the slavery; D, the negroe's fountain; E, the company's fountain; F, the governor's fountain; G, the hospital; H, the chapel; I, the officers houses unfinish'd; K, huts for labourers; L, the barracks for carpenters; M, the apartment for bombadiers; N, offices, storehouses, and barracks for soldiers; O, the pharmacy and engineers laboratory; P, the armourer's apartment and forge; Q, the governor's apartment and garden, &c.; R, a cistern; R.R., a cistern unfinish'd; S, a powder magazine; T, shades for water-casks; W, the landing beech, and entry into the parade; V, the court of the fort of St Francis; X, the shambles; Y, the burying-place; Z, ditto for the negroes; &, a rain water cistern.; 1–15, batteries.

long, white beach, soon beckoned across the water and, says Lindsay, "made me long to set my foot on Afric shore". Drawn to the mainland by "curiosity", he plunged into the forest, keeping an eye out for snakes and alligators but discovering no food crops to be enthusiastic about. He was more impressed by the delicacy and beauty of the fish taken from the bay. Although Lindsay's ventures to the mainland did not reveal "any thing that afforded me great satisfaction", he made drawings of the more "remarkable" plants and provided descriptions to match the images.[29] The published *Voyage* includes plates illustrating the fish, plants and land animals that caught his eye (figures 5.3 and 5.4).

Following his visit to the mainland, Lindsay observed that such wonders could easily be multiplied,

> if not from knowledge, at least from books; but that is the source from whence most of our histories are rendered ridiculous and obscure. I have, for instance, read of trees a gun shot in height, and the like: I believe there are no such trees – I saw none at least – and shall not say any thing but what I had from the best information or personal knowledge. . . . A lover of natural history might be here very agreeably entertained with numberless trees, shrubs, plants, and roots; but it will be highly necessary for the naturalist, to become first well acquainted with the country in general, and to cultivate in particular a good understanding with some of the more

Figure 5.3 Lindsay's drawing of plants and animals, Senegal, 1758. John Lindsay, *A Voyage to the Coast of Africa in 1758* (London, 1759), plate 4. Reproduced by kind permission of the Syndics of Cambridge University Library. Numbered elements named in Lindsay's text: "1, monkeys-bread tree; 2, fruit of monkeys-bread; 3, another remarkable tree; 4, palm tree; 5, arbor drago or dragon's blood; 6, palm tree; 7, pappau-apple; 8, houseleek; 9, aloes or dildo-bush; 10, calabash".

> sensible and best skill'd of the natives; and not in that loose way, that voyagers generally pick up their information.[30]

The acknowledgement that understanding the natural history of the region depends on extended observation suggests that Lindsay was aware of the work of Michel Adanson, whose *Histoire naturelle du Sénégal* was published in 1757 and had been translated into English before the middle of 1758.[31] Even though he rejected the Linnaean system, Adanson (1727–1806) has a significant place in the history of botanical taxonomy – for example, he introduced the term *mutation* – and it was his African years that proved formative. A "love of natural history" took him to "the burning sands of Senegal; where he spent five years [1748–54], in making a diligent inquiry into the various curiosities, natural and artificial, of Negroland". He was "the first philosopher, who adventured to visit the torrid zone, for the propagation of knowledge; and who in search of this valuable treasure, may be truly said, to have encountered more monsters, than those ancient heroes, represented in fabulous story, to have gone in pursuit of the golden fleece". Adanson explains at the beginning of his account that from an early age he had "felt a particular liking to the study of philosophy and natural history", but that his parents had destined him for the Church. He "resigned a benefice, with which I had been already provided, that I might be intirely at liberty to pursue the study of natural philosophy".[32]

A Voyage to Africa

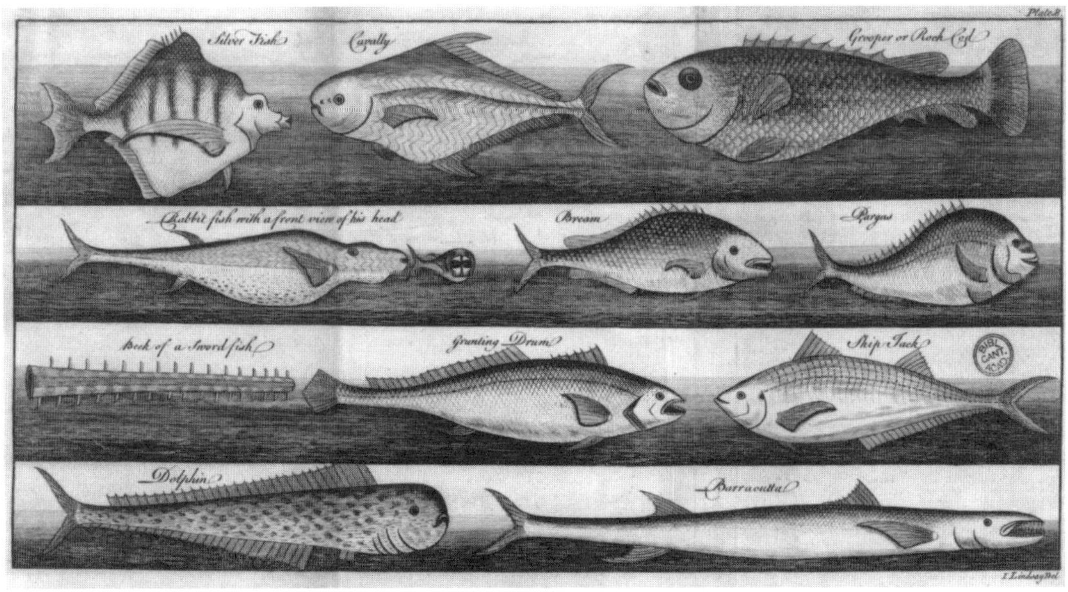

Figure 5.4 Lindsay's drawing of fish, 1758. John Lindsay, *A Voyage to the Coast of Africa in 1758* (London, 1759), plate 8. Reproduced by kind permission of the Syndics of Cambridge University Library.

Lindsay visited some of the places described by Adanson and often shared his opinions, though Lindsay was less preoccupied with the "monstrous".[33] Lindsay also shared Adanson's positive assessment of the people of the region, saying that those he met on his adventure to the mainland behaved "wonderfully civil". He did his best to communicate by signs but was happy to be able to speak French with a "marabout or [Muslim] priest". He soon became aware of the need to respect local customs. When the squadron needed water and fresh meat, Lindsay observes, "The cadi wou'd by no means permit of our coming ashore either for water or refreshments, unless a dashy or present, was made to their prince; one of the jalof [Jolof] kings, and, who is call'd (I think) Buiram." He notes further that when hauling in the seine, "Care must be also us'd, to oblige the negroes, nor refuse them a part of the draught, which they expect as their due, and will wait upon him for that purpose."[34]

Senegal

The squadron stayed only two weeks at Gorée. One ship was sent back to Britain with news of the action, and three vessels and a contingent of soldiers were left behind to hold the fort. The others reached the mouth of the Senegal River on 16 January 1759 and remained there for a week. Lindsay ventured upstream with a group of flat-bottomed boats, sailors at the oars, crossing in the process the dangerous sandbars at the mouth of the river. The passage across the bars was indeed frightening, with waves breaking in a heavy surf. The intrepid Lindsay claimed: "few chose to go over those places for pleasure, yet I could not think of leaving the coast of Africa, without seeing some old friends, left there from its first surrender, and who had doubtless, undergone many of those hardships, of which we had dismal accounts".[35]

European visitors to the Senegal Valley in the early eighteenth century typically described it as a highly productive agricultural zone, cultivating African rice along with New World crops such as maize and tobacco. On the coast, fishing was important and salt was traded into the interior. Much of the land was in forest. Islam had long been the dominant religion in Lower Senegal – since the eleventh century – and the people followed the laws of Mohammed, fasting at Ramadan and drinking no liquor. Other Mande-speaking peoples of the region followed their own systems of belief, and conflict between groups created the potential for enslavement.[36]

Saint-Louis was on the small, narrow island of N'Dar in the Senegal

River. The British found there in 1758 a population of two or three thousand, dominated by thirty or forty families descended from *signares*, local mulatto women who were wives of the numerous transitory Frenchmen posted to Senegal. The *signares* and their children had a prominent role in these slave societies, both as substantial owners of property and as influential entrepreneurs in their own right. The Europeans depended on African merchants for trade with the interior. Lindsay found the "negroe town . . . wonderfully regular". Many of the inhabitants were "of high rank and family" and had "adorn'd the island with several lofty and gay buildings". As he had done at Gorée, Lindsay made "a plan and perspective" of the island, the site of the fort Saint-Louis.[37]

While at the island, Lindsay witnessed "a scene of a very extraordinary nature; the arrival of Tresor Mughtard, king of Leghiboli, – a considerable prince in those parts, who came to congratulate the new governor on his arrival at Senegal". The Trarzar kingdom, north of the Senegal River and towards the coast, was the country – an emirate – of the Trarzar Moors. The "king" (emir) was attended by his "nobles and retinue, mounted on horses and camels, to a very considerable number". Major Mason, who was to be replaced by Worge as governor, waited on the island while a barge was sent to bring the king across with two military officers, captains Allen and Hamilton.[38] The king, according to Lindsay, thought this insufficient honour, since under the French the governors had gone in person to conduct kings to the island, but "captain Hamilton represented to his majesty, that he was not to expect those submissions formerly paid by the French". Whereas the French were merely "a company of merchants, trading men, and their governor a private person only", said Hamilton, "the English were the immediate servants of the king of Great Britain" and their governor his representative. The king eventually agreed, but when the boat reached the island, another dialogue ensued when he expected to be carried ashore by the British marines, who had done this for their own officers. Lindsay records that "major Mason, with captains Allen and Hamilton, being of opinion that it would be improper to begin them with any sort of treatment they would think too servile to continue", told the king "it was not the custom of the kings of England to be supported by any but Englishmen, and for the same reason Englishmen must not suffer themselves to become the servants of any other potentate whatever". Following "consultation with his nobles", the king came ashore on the shoulders of his own attendants.[39]

Once on the island, the king was greeted by a salute of seven guns. Walking across the parade to the fort, "he was met by a company of negroes attach'd to the Leghiboli moors, who danc'd before him in a manner the most uncommon imaginable". The leading dancers were women, in rows of

PROSLAVERY PRIEST

three. The woman in the middle, "while she danc'd stooping she spread out her garments like wings as a token of submission; and the two outermost women, dancing, sung also a song, in the chorus of which they were join'd by the other six dancers, with certain notes, or rather screams, some treble, some tenor, some counter, some base; and all of them at the same time clapping their hands, and throwing their bodies into many extraordinary, extravagant, and some into indecent postures". The king was then "led up to the governor's apartment, where was placed a great chair, with a shewey covering or carpet thrown over it, in some degree to imitate a throne, in which governor Worge, with much civility, seated the king; and during the audience, sat himself uncover'd in his presence".[40]

The king, says Lindsay, was "a man of six feet, well made, of a grave aspect, his beard decent, abating his colour, comely; dress'd in a loose robe of coarse worsted gawz, broad striped in blue and white, his robe sleeves of fine white linnen, loose and flowing in the manner of a surplice; his crown made of scarlet cloth . . . or rather a sort of ancient diadem than crown, encircling his temples". His legs were bare and he wore sandals on his feet. Lindsay asks his readers to picture the king so dressed,

> lolling on the arm of the chair set for a throne; one leg laid on the other knee, and all of the time the audience (as a farther mark of indifference and superiority), diverting himself by picking or rather cleaning his teeth, with a short twig from a tree which he had pick'd up in his way hither; now and then diverting the scene a little, by whiffing from a short tobacco-pipe which one of his nobles presented him with, and which his majesty, afterwards wiping the end he had in his mouth, was graciously pleas'd to honour his principal counsellor with a whiff of the same tobacco.

The "counsellor" sat or stood at the king's left-hand, "while his guiriot [*griot*] or chief musician, upon a seat at his right-hand, during the audience, thrumm'd most wretchedly upon a lute or instrument of the guitar kind, made of a calabash, and strung with horse-hair; besides these, the interpreter sat betwixt his majesty and the governor, and the rest of the nobles took their seats; some of whom were armed with swords, some with musquets, and others with lances, or bows and arrows, made up this strange court!"[41]

Questions about the health of the king and queen of Leghiboli and of King George were understood and answered easily, says Lindsay, "but when they came to talk of business, they hobbled terribly". The "Arabs or Moors" quickly raised "an old and favourite scheme of theirs, *viz.* the destroying of Poydore [the fort at Podor] and erecting a fort at *Port en Derrique*, or *Portendique*; and the English as soon got to their favourite and substantial topick – *roast-beef to their plumb-pudding*". The fort at Podor had originally been built in 1743 and was used by the French trading company. The negotiations made little progress, and "alas, each gave the other so little satisfaction, that I began very heartily to pity the poor colonel in his government!" Lindsay believed that little was understood by either side, "so that after a long conference, they spoil'd their dinners to very little purpose, and 'twill be well for them if this proves the only one: it seems this was to be their constant amusement for several days to come". He understood that the king and his retinue might stay for a week or two, maintained by the governor of the fort, and given presents when they left.[42]

Lindsay closes his account of this "mock court" with a description of a woman present at the meeting, whom he took to be "the favourite mistress of one of these great men". She was, he says,

> small in stature, differing nothing from the colour of the males, had her forehead concealed with one part of her head-dress, while another cover'd the lower part of her face, even to her eyes, and was sustain'd in that position by her nose only; for at times she would let it fall under her chin, to regale herself with a pipe of tobacco, the smoak of which she took in at her mouth, but threw it out in a surprising manner from her nostrils. Her dress was loose; but what was extreamly singular, her ancles were encircled with two large clumsey rings, and as I imagined of pewter, about an inch and a half in breadth (as in fig. 8, plate VII [figure 5.5]) and rounding off on both edges, like the rim of a pewter jordan, design'd doubtless to preserve them from galling her ancles but, nevertheless seem'd vastly inconvenient, and made her straddle in her gait most shockingly, putting me in mind of a horse fet-lock, and seemingly design't for a like purpose.[43]

Of the people, Lindsay declares the men to be "tall, strait, and well made" and lacking "that thickness of the lip and flatness of the nose, that common slaves and negroes farther to the south are always found to have". Lindsay had not himself travelled south, so this was an opinion no doubt gained from his time in Virginia or from reading accounts written by others. His high praise of the local (Wolof) women has been cited by modern historians as an example of the assessment typical of European travellers. Lindsay declares: "As to their women, and in particular the ladies (for so I must call many of those in Senegal) they are in a surprising degree handsome, have very fine features, are wonderfully tractable, remarkably polite both in conversation and manners; and in the point of keeping themselves neat and clean . . . far surpass the Europeans in every respect." Moderating a common European prejudice, Lindsay adds: "Their hair, for it differs a little from wool, very neat and curiously plaited; and their persons otherwise adorn'd, by earings, necklaces, and bracelets, of the purest gold."[44]

Probably with Virginia in mind, Lindsay tells his readers:

> Negroes to me are no novelty; but the accounts I receiv'd of them, and in particular the appearance of the females on this occasion, was to me a novelty most pleasing. They were not only pretty, but in the address in which they appear'd, were even desireable. Nor can I give you any drapery more nearly resembling theirs, than the loose, light, easy robe, and sandal, in which we see the female Grecian statues attir'd; most of which were of exceeding white cotton, spun, wove into narrow slips of six or seven inches, and sow'd together by themselves.

Similarly, Lindsay's contemporary Adanson says of the "Negro" women of Senegal (as distinguished from the "Moors"): "Their skin is surprisingly delicate and soft; their mouth and lips are small; and their features regular. There are some of them perfect beauties. They have a great share of vivacity, and a vast deal of freedom and ease, which renders them extremely agreeable." Their costume was "a modest dress enough for so hot a country".[45]

Not only does Lindsay say almost nothing of his own religious practice and chaplaincy in the course of his *Voyage*, he also finds little to say about the religious ideas of Africans.[46] Other travellers were less reticent. In 1744, William Smith, for example, states boldly: "All the natives of this coast believe there is one true God, the author of them and all things", and claims that the people believed that

> in the beginning God created black as well as white men; that he having created these two sorts of men, offer'd two kinds of gifts, viz. gold, and the knowledge of art, reading, and writing, giving the blacks the first election, who chose gold, and the whites was oblig'd to take the knowledge of letters; and that God granted their request, but being incens'd at their avarice, resolv'd, that the whites should be for ever be their masters, and they their slaves.

Lindsay does not venture into such arguments in his *Voyage*, though these were matters that would later exercise his mind; the myth was later recounted by Long in his *History of Jamaica*.[47]

As to "the progress of Christianity" in Senegal, Lindsay does give credit to the "Romish clergy" who had "been at vast pains to make converts to Christianity" and achieved "good success in snatching many from the ignorance of Paganism, and many from the delusions of Mahomet". However, he observes, these converts had developed "such a veneration for the religion taught them and things sacred, that they held the English for some time in very great contempt; and seeing neither priests nor ceremonies amongst them, would hardly be persuaded they were Christians, and would by no means permit them to bury their dead in their hallow'd ground". Lindsay says he heard that "a lady of distinction there, the princess Pennetica was heard to say, *That while she was ignorant, and a Pagan, she was happy; but now she began to find, that being a Christian would make her miserable!*"[48]

In spite of his apparent lack of interest in keeping any records of his spiritual practice, Lindsay does express concern at the neglect of Christian rituals. He worried that the British who were to be left behind in Senegal would be condemned to live "in a strange land, in a land of infidels, in a land of sickness and death; unattended by the chaplain of any of the regiments, either to administer the sacraments of Baptism and the Eucharist, either to instruct them in their duty while in health, to give them ease or comfort on a death-bed, or to attend their ashes, like Christians, to a grave, must strike every reasonable and sober-minded person with an awful concern!"[49] Without offering his own services in Africa, Lindsay ponders how this neglect could be excused before God, asking how it is possible "for a priest to stay by the flesh-pots at home, when some hundreds of those for whom he must answer, are gone to so desolate a country as this". All is not lost, however, because although "the English, to their dishonour", carried no pastor with them, "God in his good providence, has not left those infant Christians without a guide". Here Lindsay remarks that there was on Senegal Island "a gentleman (although a negroe) of extraordinary good sense, a good education, and withal polite; and not from authority, so much as the knowledge of his honesty and other amiable qualities, has obtain'd such ascendancy over the minds of the inhabitants, that his voice is with them a law in every thing". His house served as a chapel on Sundays, and there "a very decent and considerable community meet together, the gentleman himself officiating to them as pastor; so that Mr. Charles, for so he is call'd, may be truly stil'd their king, priest, and lawgiver".[50]

"Of Things Curious"

Lindsay commenced the eleventh chapter of his *Voyage* with a section titled "Of things curious". He had found few "natural curiosities" worthy of notice, attributing this to the shortness of his time in Senegal and his experiences being confined to the winter season. He did, however, search for shells and collected "some uncommon herbs". He made himself sick by eating beans from a vine but brought some seeds back to Britain; he claims in *Voyage* that some of these "are now growing at Sion-House, the seat of the right honourable the earl of Northumberland; and at Mr. Lee's nursery at Hammersmith". He lists elephants, lions, tigers and other animals, "most of which I saw at that place", but says that "the numberless descriptions we have had of those most common and remarkable, makes the bare naming them at this time sufficient".[51]

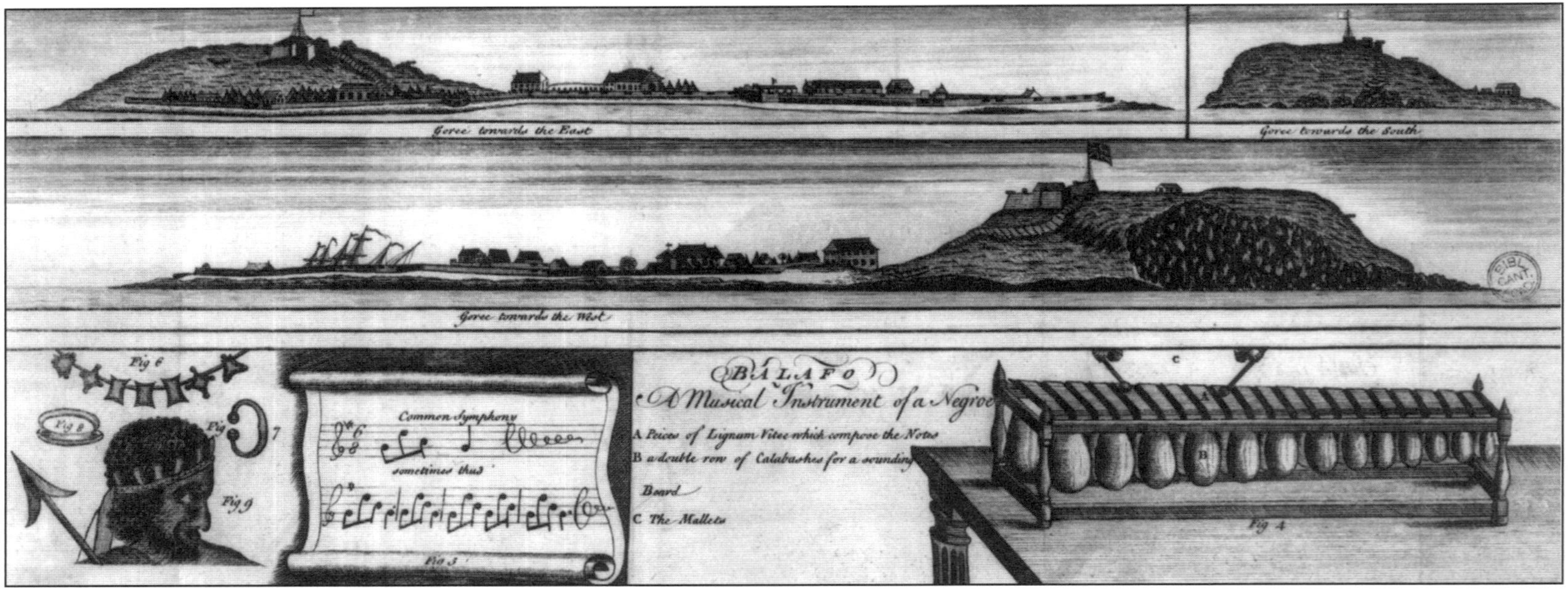

Figure 5.5 Lindsay's drawing of rings, balafon and grisgris, Senegal, 1758. John Lindsay, *A Voyage to the Coast of Africa in 1758* (London, 1759), plate 7. Reproduced by kind permission of the Syndics of Cambridge University Library. Numbered figures named in Lindsay's text: "4, balafo; 5 and 6, gris-griss; 7, bracelet".

Finding little of interest in nature, Lindsay moved on to "a curiosity of a mechanical nature", a musical instrument (figure 5.5). This was "the ballard, balafo, or balafeu" that had been "purchased by the late French governor of fort St. Joseph, at Galam, at a considerable price, design'd as a present to the duke de Richlieu". Lindsay provides his own drawing and a detailed description:

> The frame of the instrument is of wood, of about four feet in length, one foot in height, and on the left hand, or base, its breadth is about eighteen inches, falling off to nine or ten on the right or treble hand: on the top of this frame, lengthways, are stretch'd large gut strings, clear of the frame, upon which are placed nineteen pieces of lignum-vitæ, of different lengths, the longest eighteen inches, placed on the left, diminishing to ten on the right, about an inch and a half in breadth, and a quarter less in thickness, which serve for notes, and are still farther diminish'd in these dimensions, as the artist shall find requisite in tuning the instrument. Under these timbers are stretch'd a convenient number of smaller gut-strings a-cross the frame; and thereupon, to lengthen the tones, are hang'd calabashes, a sort of dry'd gourde, two and two a-breast, and of different sizes, from eight or nine inches in diameter, under the base notes, to two or three under the treble (fig. 4, plate VII). This instrument is play'd upon by two small hammers or mallets; the heads of which, to sweeten the sound, are made of gut-strings wound up, and sew'd firmly together; and altho' its music cannot be but incompleat, it has a certain soft and melancholy sweetness, extreamly pleasing, resembling the tone of no other instrument I have ever heard, and is a music fitter for a lady's chamber, than a ball-room, altho' Jobson says he heard it above an English mile.[52]

Although aware of it, Lindsay did not borrow from the more detailed description of the balafon offered by Richard Jobson in *The Golden Trade; or, A Discovery of the River Gambra, and the Golden Trade of the Aethiopians*, based on travels in 1621. Nor did Lindsay borrow from William Smith, whose *New Voyage* of 1744 includes a plate of "A Negro playing on the Ballafoe", said to have been seen at a reception given by the "King of Barra" for the English of Gambia Castle.[53] Smith's drawing, and his description, is simpler than that offered by Lindsay.

Generally known today as a balafon, the instrument belongs to the percussion family and is most closely allied with the xylophone. Examples existed in parts of Central and West Africa by the twelfth century, but the instrument is typically associated with Senegal, where Lindsay encountered it. Although the balafon may be indigenous to Africa, it has been argued that it diffused from Indonesia in an ancient process of coast-wise colonization. The Atlantic slave trade carried balafon players to the Americas. Examples of the instrument constructed from local materials were observed in seventeenth-century Barbados, eighteenth-century Virginia and St Vincent, and early nineteenth-century Surinam and Jamaica.[54] Whether Lindsay saw it again after Senegal is unknown.

Lindsay wrote also of "another part of the ingenuity of those natives – their proficiency in musick itself, as well vocal as instrumental". The king's visit was accompanied by "people of various abilities"; Lindsay "had the pleasure of being entertain'd by one of his guiriots, and who was it seems a principal performer". He guessed that the song described "some battle or great man's history". It was "sung in a sort of recitative; and at the end of every sentence (upon a lute, or instrument of the same kind that the mughtard's chief musician entertain'd his majesty withall) he play'd a sort of symphony, most commonly of four notes, especially in the passionate parts, and at others, he lengthened them out to four bars (fig. 5, plate VII [figure 5.5])".[55] Lindsay was most impressed by the vocals, in which the singer

> put himself into violent passions, 'till he would sweat and foam like a madman; and in accompanying the words with an action suited to the story, would sometimes stamp with his feet, and threaten with his hand, would kneel, and even lie down; would sooth, and threaten again, so that it appear'd to me, the performer was enthusiastically possest with some ideas of inspiration, or at least seem'd desirous his audience should think so; which last is most probably the case. The negroes believe those impostures are all of them inspir'd, or at least are familiar with the devil, and altho' they humour and enrich the sycophants, to have their praise while alive, they deny them even the common burial rites when dead, and are stuck up in hollow trunks of trees, least the earth or water should be poison'd with their carcasses.[56]

Believing that the people were "greatly given to superstition", Lindsay observes: "those who go to war are plentiously loaded with grissgriss or gregories, small cloth or leather bags containing little slips of written paper, which they purchase from the marbuts or priests, . . . : in these they put great trust, and are charms they imagine will prevent them from almost every kind of danger, and which they hang about their necks and arms (fig. 6, plate VII [figure 5.5])". Lindsay thought the crown of the king of the Leghiboli Moors, described earlier, was stuffed with "griss-griss". *Gris-gris*, meaning fetish, charm or amulet, comes from the Mande word *gerregerys*. The term was known in Louisiana from the early eighteenth century and survived in Jamaica as *gri-gri*. Lindsay goes on to contend that "all these fooleries those who have embrac'd Christianity, and were much amongst the French, have entirely cast off". On the islands formerly settled by the French, he says, most of the people were "very decently apparel'd, and in the French taste".[57]

Kingdoms and Empires

With the squadron preparing to sail for home, Lindsay offers "some account of our situation with the neighbouring powers" and some thoughts on the potential for British trade and settlement within the region. In terms of basic geography, he was aware that to the north of the Senegal River "the desart of Sahra" spreads over "a vast tract of ground". He describes the course of the Senegal River and what he thought its tributaries as far as Timbuktu. Some of his knowledge derived from the account of M. Compagnon, who had travelled there in 1716, and some of it from Mandingo traders. He also mentions gold mines recently established along the river.[58]

Politically, Lindsay believed the "neighbouring princes" were "very formidable" and capable of fielding "thirty thousand men, five thousand of which mounted on the finest Arabian horses, arm'd with various instruments of war".[59] He distinguishes between the Trarza ("those arabs subject to Tresor Mughtard, king of Leghiboli") and the Brakna ("the moors of Brackna") realms (figure 5.1). The problem was that the highly valued gum forests lay between these two "kingdoms", so that their rulers were constantly in conflict. Lindsay thought that the British had established an alliance with the Trarza while the French sided with the Brakna, and claims that the Trarza promised to fight alongside the British in taking Saint-Louis from the French, in return for destroying the fort at Podor. They did not in fact participate, and modern historians, notably Philip D. Curtin, regard Lindsay's account with scepticism.[60]

In general principle "it is our business to be well with every nation, to offend none", Lindsay asserts. Specifically, the best policy for the British in Senegal was to act as an "umpire" between the Trarza and Brakna, helping them achieve "an honourable peace, and . . . live together like brethren". From the traders' point of view, competition between the forts was the best way to keep the price of gum at a moderate level. Lindsay is enthusiastic about the gains Britain made in Senegal, arguing for "the great value of this easy purchase, and of the great necessity there is of keeping it in our possession". His principal objective was gold, and in opening the market to the British he expected the most "obstruction" to come from the Mandingo traders. The Africans had no fear of losing their gold, says Lindsay, because "they very well know, that it is not in our power to take away their gold, without giving them an equivalent". He argues that the local rulers need not fear lessening of their authority, because they could easily starve the Europeans by denying them provisions, and the forts were "no more than places of rendezvous, and strong warehouses, to guard our wealth against the lawless, a people from whom no nation is free, and our lives against the wild creatures of the woods".[61] He appreciated the fragility of the European presence.

The French were insignificant as rivals in Lindsay's view. They had not persevered in trying to reach Timbuktu and had done little to cultivate trade. He declares that "the knowledge of Tombuto may be attain'd, because by all accounts the natives have never shewn any aversion to Europeans settling amongst them, but rather have encouraged them". He believed the English could establish trading posts in the interior, which would save "the traders from Tombuto, coming down yearly with slaves, &c" and having to travel on to the English settlements on the Gambia. Lindsay thought the English had an advantage over the French; they offered better prices, so "the traders from Tombuto are our friends, and we need no mandingo, nor distant negroe guides, since themselves may be brought to protect us". Lindsay then advances a plan for a gradual spread of forts into the interior, with Timbuktu the ultimate goal, smoothing the way by giving presents to the rulers.[62] He also raises the possibility of cutting a channel directly to the ocean where the Senegal River first comes close to the shore and then turns south. And he proposes building a "moveable factory", or "a flat floating vessel, fitted to contain a director, with miners and soldiers to row upon occasion, as well as to support the company; which I would also have made arrow proof, and strengthened, over and above the soldiers firelocks, with musketoons, blunderbusses, and a couple of short light brass cannon or swivels".[63]

Lindsay warns against the joint stock company as a tool of trade and settlement. Companies, he argues, start strongly but quickly become torpid and unenterprising. He writes:

> The management of a company would never have peopled a tract of ground like America; and if ever trade is carried on as it ought on this river [the Senegal], it will be when we become numerous. For which purpose, all capital criminals (murderers excepted) might by the king's clemency be sent to work in the mines for life; male convicts, instead of America, might be sent as servants to Africa; and by introducing our religion with our language, and doing every thing possible to encourage a regular marriage betwixt our servants and the natives, a few generations would spread along the rivers very populous settlements of European descendents. A free and open trade, for these reasons, is to be preferred: but, altho' under this trade improvements flourish in time, yet as it meets with vast oppositions and discouragements in its infancy, the government must lend a strong hand in establishing and encouraging it.[64]

In laying out this model of colonization, Lindsay favoured the French example and looked to the development of a mulatto society on the coast. This model of settlement and social development was strikingly opposed to the typical British Atlantic style of imperialism. Thus Lindsay argues that the British should send no white women to Senegal, because a small number amongst many men would find it impossible to remain chaste and would suffer from carrying out heavy labour – washing, ironing, cooking – in the hot climate. Better, he thought, to have the white men find partners among the handsome women of the country, who were both acclimatized and chaste. Further, he says, "our mixing with the natives settles their affections on the most lasting foundations".[65]

Lindsay also proposes a model of economic development on the African coast which differs strongly from that followed in most of the British Atlantic colonial world. Although he bemoans the "natural inactivity and laziness of the people", he believed that increased trade with Africa needed only the stimulation of demand. This leads him to write in praise of consumption and the seduction of earthly goods: "Every one in trade must be sensible how far a curious shew-glass at a window, induces a passenger to step into the shop; how far varieties gain upon our fancy, to purchase what we have little occasion for." Applying his model to Africa, Lindsay confesses to feeling that

> there may be an unfairness in endeavouring to debauch a hardy people with effeminacy, yet, as a member of a trading nation, I cannot help representing that whereas the Mandingo traders never carry into their countries but one and the same sort of commodities, the greater number of forts or settlements we have in the country, will introduce a new and greater variety of conveniencies: by sometimes giving their princes and great men presents of various sorts of raiment, we should introduce amongst the whole an extravagance in this article, and so of others. Great quantities, and shewy choices of European fineries, be they ever so tawdry, would learn them gaiety; and to support which, we would not force them upon any unlawful methods, since digging and washing [gold] the oftner would do the business.[66]

As well as the naturally seductive power of consumer goods, Lindsay expected that the spread of civilization would contribute directly to the growth of commerce. As the "English" extended their forts and settlements, through gifts and friendships, the "natives . . . must of course grow more polish'd, and of course need more traffick, and in greater varieties". The people would discover needs unknown, "learning at the same time conveniencies they knew not of before, their ideas must expand, their wants must grow upon them; and which must still the more increase, when they find that by copying the English (and they have the ingenuity to do any thing) they can also find gold in greater quantities". All of this argument was directed at trade in gold. Lindsay sought to increase output, particularly by developing mines rather than depending on the washing of river sands. He also expected that other minerals, such as silver, tin, lead, copper and iron, would become important, and he saw prospects for marble and dyewoods.[67]

Trade in enslaved people was not prominent in Lindsay's scheme. He simply took it for granted, saying that, along with the gold and ivory brought from the interior, came each year "no less than two thousand of the best slaves (strong, gentle, faithful, and tractable)". Later, in 1788, he does however claim that "the inhabitants of Africa, have the custom of selling their own children, at this very day, without any consideration of their being subjects to their several princes". He recounts: "I could myself, in 1758, have bought an exceeding good looking boy, about eight years old, from his mother, for a very trifling price indeed – a pair of very common ships pistols, not worth ten shillings – a price so inadiquate that suspecting the morals and mischievous disposition of the youth, I avoided the purchass." According to *Voyage*, Lindsay believed that, after the defeat of the French, prices could gradually be brought down since it would be less necessary to compete, and the English had much to gain from the trades; "it will prove a heavy article, if, in accommodating a peace, we should be oblig'd to give up our acquisitions upon the coast of Africa".[68] This was, however, what happened at the end of the Seven Years' War.

PROSLAVERY PRIEST

Contemporary British accounts saw the capture of Gorée as an essential element in the larger scheme of empire and the development of Atlantic slave economies. British forces at Guadeloupe received news of the capture of Gorée in less than two months, in February 1759, and took the opportunity to enjoy "much hearty celebration". In 1762 the London *Gentleman's Magazine* declared: "Much importance was attached to this conquest. Amongst other indications of this, was a fine bronze bust, put up at the Senegal and Goree Coffee House, of the Earl of Halifax, 'under whose auspicious patronage the plan for conquering the French settlements of Senegal and Goree, on the coast of Africa, was happily carried into execution, in the year MDCCLVIII'."[69]

Entick, in his history of the war first published in 1764, declares the reduction of Gorée necessary "in order to complete the ruin of the French trade on the coast of Africa, and therewith to put the last and finishing hand to the destruction of those colonies, which our enemies could not cultivate without black slaves". For Entick, Gorée had an importance for the plantation colonies of the West Indies, not simply for trade with Africa but equally as "an effectual check to the perfidy and ambition of a nation, whose repeated insults and usurpations obliged your Majesty to enter into this just and necessary war".[70] Later historians came to see the British expedition against the French in West Africa as the beginning of widening the scope of the conflict from a limited to a more broadly imperial and international war. Keppel "finally established" the British in West Africa with the capture of Gorée. It has also been declared "the first successful combined operation of the Seven Years' War", in bringing together the army and navy.[71]

"So Old and So Crazy a Ship"

The final chapter of Lindsay's *Voyage* recounts the return from Senegal to England. Sailing on 23 January 1759, the *Fougueux* ran quickly ahead of the wind but had to reduce sail "for the safety of so old and so crazy a ship, as well as for the consideration of five hundred souls on board of her". Men were lost overboard. One of these, "on the lee arm of the yard, was wash'd entirely from us; and altho' we saw him swim strong in the water, until the towering seas separated him from our views, and might struggle with death for a considerable time longer, yet it was not in our powers to yield him the least assistance!" They made the Lizard on 29 February 1759, Ash Wednesday. The "old complaining vessel" was "so bruis'd with her misfortunes at Corke, and so weaken'd with our distresses at sea, that she was render'd unfit any more for that service", and was "raz'd to the keel for the value of her old iron only". Closing his account, Lindsay tells his imagined correspondent: "These are the dangers your friend has past – which now are turned to praise."[72] He does not refer to the significance of Ash Wednesday, and he does not give thanks to God for his safe return.

The manuscript of Lindsay's *Voyage* moved quickly towards publication. In October 1759 the London *Gentleman's Magazine* devoted its first five pages to a review of the work but said that it contained "no event that is not common to almost every other voyage". Some years later, in 1772, Rev. Thomas Percy identified the anonymous reviewer as Dr Samuel Johnson. This was denied by Johnson, who told James Boswell "he never heard of Lindsey nor that Gorree was conquered, so that to the best of his knowledge this cannot be". Whether it was Johnson or some other, the reviewer is dismissive of the account of the taking of Gorée, saying that it was no different from any other battle between unequal sides, pitching ships against land forces.[73] Much of the review consists of a summary of the book.

The reviewer does, however, take "the Rev. Mr Lindsay" to task on one point in his recounting of "an adventure of his own". Writes the reviewer, "This adventure was crossing some shallows of the river Senegal, where the water is very rapid, and consequently the navigation dangerous. It consists principally of altercations between him and a Dutchman, who directed the boat he was on board of, the Dutchman expressing his fears, and the chaplain his courage." The reviewer complains that

> To display his courage seems indeed to be his sole view, and so very solicitous is he to represent its vehement ardor and impetuosity, that he tells us he could not contain himself at a behaviour so dastardly, and that he is afraid he forgot himself a little in his expressions on the occasion. If Mr Lindsay had really been betrayed by the indignation of his valour into any expressions unbecoming his function,

> the consciousness of that valour would have prevented him from taking any method so indecent as this declaration to display it; and I know not what apology he can make for the shameless publication of such a fault. That a clergyman, merely to make a parade of his courage, should with an air of levity insinuate, that he broke out into oaths or execrations, is a disgrace to his function, and an insult upon the religion which he ought to inculcate at once by his precept and his example.

On the other hand, the reviewer finds that Lindsay expressed "a very becoming zeal in behalf of the negroes that have been converted to christianity by the popish priests".[74] Praise is also given for the quality of Lindsay's copperplates, with the exception of the fourth, which shows "several African trees and plants, composed in picture, but with so little skill in perspective, that the ear of an elephant on the farther side of a river is as long as a two mast vessel that is sailing down the river much nearer to the spectator; and the whole width of the river, in which this vessel is sailing, is not more than the height of a bulrush at the same distance".[75]

Modern historians have made little use of Lindsay's *Voyage*. Curtin describes the account as a "dubious report", at least in respect to his knowledge of military intelligence and local negotiations at Saint-Louis. Military historians have been more generous.[76] Anthony J. Barker offered a broader assessment in 1978, comparing Lindsay with his contemporaries. Barker includes Lindsay among those writers "most hostile to slavery" yet relatively unaware of the cultural diversity of West Africa. This lack in Lindsay may be explained by the short time he spent there and the narrowness of the territory he observed personally, but his hostility was muted, and soon to evaporate.[77]

1759

At the beginning of 1759 none could have foretold how momentous the year would prove for the expansion of the British Empire. Guadeloupe was taken from the French in May and Quebec in September. The British succeeded in thwarting French invasion plans through the bombardment of Le Havre. They defeated the French fleet at Lagos (Cape St Vincent) in September and at Quiberon Bay in November (figure 2.5). Hawke's victory at Quiberon Bay decisively destroyed the naval power of France and made Britain master of the Atlantic, the "global superpower" of the eighteenth century.[78]

It was this last great victory that Lindsay was fortunate to avoid. He was assigned to the brand-new HMS *Resolution*, a seventy-four-gun third-rate ship of the line, about 1,600 tonnes, with a crew of six hundred – a larger vessel than the *Fougueux*. However, he seems never to have joined the ship. Launched in December 1758, the *Resolution* formed part of Hawke's fleet at Quiberon Bay, but was lost when it ran onto a shoal during a terrifying storm the night following the battle. Many perished.[79] By this time Lindsay was already on his way to Jamaica – a life-saving decision.

CHAPTER SIX

God and Mammon

IN THE PREFACE TO HIS *Voyage*, Lindsay declares that he has "of late been averse to going any more abroad", suggesting the attractions of a settled parochial life. He chose instead to go to Jamaica. It was a brave risk. The island's ecclesiastical institutions had no high reputation and Lindsay was no missionary. The wealth of Jamaica was greater than that of any other colony in the British Empire until the American Revolution, with Virginia being its closest rival, but alongside the chance of great profit stood the risk of an early death. Lindsay was well aware of Jamaica's reputation as a place of frightening mortality.[1]

In Lindsay's *Memoirs* of 1757, Jamaica appears only once. The merchant Mr *****, first encountered in Virginia, where he had "made a very handsome fortune in his younger years", returns to his native Glasgow and there "carried on an extensive trade, not only with *Britain*, but with the *West Indian* islands, and the slave-trade".[2] When his son Periander, under promise of marriage, debauches his betrothed, Polly Young, and she becomes pregnant, he chooses not to marry but rather "determined as privately as possible to leave his country, and go over for a few years to *America*, in whose colonies, his father had great trade". Finding that a "ship for Jamaica was ready to sail", Periander "took the shortest time possible to acquaint his father of the design, being to embark in two days time".[3]

Mr ***** asks Telemachus to intervene, saying, "I argue, but argue in vain, to make my son, even mindful of his own wellfare – *Jamaica!* the burial place of our country-men, a climate abhorr'd by even its inhabitants. What is it can create so unaccountable a desire?" Periander appeals to Telemachus: "Why surely, . . . *you* cannot think so little of me; as my father's too great love, makes *him*. Why, while my fellow-traders, the sons of those much inferior to my father in substance, visit these colonies from whence our riches spring; must I, alone, of all this flourishing city [Glasgow] be the loitering house-keeper? and that while wealth and honour, in foreign climes, are sharing with bountiful hand, their choicest blessings." Mr ***** responds with passion: "Has not your father, traversed the globe – the mighty globe, for wealth to give to you: and when I have with the sweat of my brow earn'd a competency – if five hundred a year is such – you must, forsooth, and when my hairs grow thin and grey, leave me to myself. Undutiful boy!"[4]

Telemachus encourages Periander to reconsider: "Moderate your ambition: those who go abroad, go to obtain a fortune; bless your father's industry, you have not that to do." Periander, not wanting to offend his father, tells him: "I would not indeed forfeit your favour for *Jamaica* itself." However, returning to a theme noticed earlier in Lindsay's own life and in *Memoirs*, Periander is so "fright'ned at the consequences of his father's rigid notions of virtue: and particularly of the public penance enjoin'd by the Scotish clergy, under pain of excommunication, to such as are found guilty of fornication – the consequence of which is, either to be publickly pointed at, in submission to the decrees of the church" that he "resolved (against all entreaties) to take the first opportunity of going abroad". Periander goes to Polly Young to say farewell but finds she has already "been told of Periander's preparation for *Jamaica*", and in consequence has admitted her indiscretion to her parents. When Periander calls Polly a whore, Telemachus lectures him on truth and honour and gentlemanly behaviour. The couple marry and Telemachus settles them on an estate near Glasgow, asking, "Ah, Periander, what is this, to being broil'd at *Jamaica*?"[5]

"Broil'd at Jamaica"

In the face of this negative assessment, the reasons for Lindsay's decision to become a priest in Jamaica are less than obvious. His father had been dead more than ten years and there was no need to defy his wishes. A rural parish in England would have been enticing, but Lindsay was a Scot, with a confirmed enthusiasm for imperial adventure and an interest in the exotic. He was not afraid to risk his health and faced death with stoic fatalism. He was simply one of many who travelled west across the Atlantic, though most of his countrymen saw their professional opportunities in planting, trade, medicine or law, and many thought of themselves as temporary sojourners, hoping to make a quick fortune, with every intention of returning home.[6]

Probably Lindsay was a beneficiary of patronage, the system his father abhorred. The colonists of Jamaica rarely sought to call a particular priest to a parish, and happily left appointments in the hands of the governors. In

1759 Jamaica was governed briefly by Sir George Haldane, who replaced Henry Moore, lieutenant-governor since 1756. Lindsay later mentions his close relationship with Moore, but this seems to have developed later and had nothing to do with his initial appointment.

Henry Moore (1713–69) was a creole, born in the parish of Vere, the son of a planter descended from an English family that had first settled in Barbados in the time of Charles II. Moore went to Eton, then studied at Leyden University and travelled through France, Italy and Germany before returning to Jamaica in about 1735, along with a band of musicians. There, being heavily in debt, he sold most of the family's plantations. His wife, whom he married in 1751, was Catherine Maria Long (1727–1812), sister of Edward Long and daughter of the planter and member of Council Samuel Long. Moore rose through the Assembly and the Council and became island secretary in 1753, then lieutenant-governor in 1756. He was replaced in April 1759, when Haldane was appointed governor, but reinstated as lieutenant-governor following Haldane's death in August of the same year.[7]

The more immediate source of patronage for Lindsay in 1759 was Haldane, who himself owed his appointment as governor to the patronage of the Duke of Newcastle, First Lord of the Treasury, who had a hand in much Crown and ecclesiastical appointment. The connection with Lindsay was most likely a local, Scottish one. For more than a century the Haldane family had dominated the parliamentary seats of Stirling and Perth. George represented Stirling Burghs from 1747 to 1753 and again in 1758. His chosen career was a military one, and he rose to become colonel of the Third Regiment of Foot. However, Haldane incurred the wrath of George II and had therefore to work through Newcastle. The duke was eventually able to secure for him both the governorship of Jamaica and the rank of brigadier general in an expedition to the West Indies that saw him present at the taking of Guadeloupe in April 1759. Haldane embarked soon after Lindsay's return to Britain on the *Fougueux*. His term as governor lasted only from his arrival in Jamaica in April to his death on 26 July, but it was long enough for him to make appointments.[8]

As well as these potential connections between the Haldanes and the Lindsays, the new governor demonstrated a particular interest in the church. According to George Metcalf, "Haldane was the only governor of the period who took seriously the Royal Instructions that the duties of the Church of England be strictly observed." He wrote from Spanish Town to the Board of Trade soon after his arrival, complaining that "the neglect of publick worship is in the clergy themselves, and the vices and immoralities of this island, derive from the many shocking examples of those gentlemen". If Haldane was looking for priests of superior quality, Lindsay, with his Scottish background and ordination in the Church of England, together with his naval experience, would have seemed a good prospect. However, Haldane did not live to see the day. He died of "putrid fever", perhaps a consequence of eating contaminated, mouldy food. Epidemic in the first half of the eighteenth century, putrid malignant fever in the early stages was marked by dizziness and nausea, followed by skin lesions and cold sweats and finally intestinal ulcers, haemorrhages and bloody diarrhoea. It was the sort of end Lindsay feared for himself.[9]

Lindsay arrived in Jamaica towards the end of 1759. The island was not an element in the new empire that was then forming in the forge of the Seven Years' War but rather one of the longer-established and more profitable of the British colonies. Cromwell's Western Design of 1654 had among its primary goals a mission to remove Catholicism from the New World, and the taking of Jamaica from the Spanish in 1655 – more by default than by design – was part of that grand goal. On the other hand, Cromwell's words of encouragement to the godly colonists of New England to create a pious community in the island had fallen on barren ground.[10]

During Lindsay's time in Jamaica, the Roman Catholic church was proscribed in order to prevent "the growth of popery". Its priests were not allowed to set foot on the island and Catholics were prohibited from holding any public office that required swearing oaths of "abjuration and supremacy". The relatively prosperous Jewish community was similarly excluded from public office and military service, but it supported synagogues in Kingston and Spanish Town.[11] However, although these groups were denied full civil rights because of their religious beliefs, they were not prevented from settling in Jamaica so long as they were willing to swear the oath of allegiance. Many of them made large fortunes from enterprise and trade, including the buying and selling of enslaved people.

The Church of England was the church of the state and Jamaica's governors were required to profess this variety of Protestant Christianity. The governors played a direct role in the life of the church. Like the other British colonies, Jamaica had no bishops and was regarded as part of the diocese of the Bishop of London. His jurisdiction was, however, limited by Jamaican law and confined to the "ecclesiastical regimen of the clergy". Although the Bishop of London had a representative in Jamaica who reported complaints, even the power to dismiss clergy lay with the island's governor, "as supreme head of the provincial church". Clergy had to be licensed first by the Bishop of London, but the induction of rectors was made under the great seal of the island and put in the hands of the governor, who inspected testimonials to ensure that candidates were qualified – that is, that they had taken priest's orders according to the canons of the Church of England.

The salaries of Jamaica's clergy were set by law rather than depending on tithes and were raised by the parish vestries, which also set fees for registration of births, burials and marriages. Residence in the parish was a condition of priests' pay, and plurality was prohibited. These conditions were more restrictive than those applied in England, but they were compensated for by the fact that the salaries of Jamaica's parish priests were relatively good and came with superior material comforts.[12] Further, the clergy in Jamaica were independent, perhaps even isolated, with no local head of the church, no synod or ecclesiastical conference to attend. Clerks were appointed to keep records of the marriages, funerals and christenings performed by the ministers. The clergy had a good deal of leisure time.

Parochial responsibilities did, however, spill over into secular matters. The parishes, governed by their vestries, formed the basic building blocks of local administration in Jamaica. Although the parishes were amalgamated into three counties – Cornwall, Middlesex and Surrey – in 1758, these new administrative units played no significant role. From the late seventeenth century each parish had a vestry made up of twelve elected representatives, all of them men and two of them churchwardens, together with a number of magistrates, all of them required to be "conformists" of the Church of England. Elections were annual and the voters the same men who were qualified to elect members to the Assembly; vestrymen were sometimes also assemblymen. The rector was a member *ex officio* of the vestry, but its chairman was the custos rotulorum, and was often also a member of the Assembly or Council and appointed by the governor. The vestries were answerable to the Assembly. In Lindsay's time the vestry of St Catherine probably met around twenty times each year – rarely enough not to be a burden but sufficiently frequently to ensure that the rector came to know well his fellow vestrymen, even if they were never part of his congregation.

Churchwardens had responsibility for the collection of parish taxes, rents and fees, and in turn they were expected to ensure maintenance and care of the parish's common lands, water supplies, bridges and roads, through the supervision of way-wardens and surveyors. The vestries built markets and looked after the poor but generally took a direct approach to social control, by building and repairing barracks, magazines and arsenals, running the gaols, pursuing runaway enslaved people and the like. They made no investment in social change. Typically they were even more conservative than the Assembly. The objective of the vestries was to ensure smooth running of the economy and peace in the community at the local level, with the support of the militia and the army when necessary.

Although the vestries dealt largely with secular matters and were not seen as ecclesiastical agencies, their origin in church government and the continuing role of the rector in their deliberations were sufficient to cement the intimate association of church and state. The rector was required to join with doubters and unbelievers in governing the parish. It was one of the ways in which he came to be aligned with the interests of slave-owners, planters and merchants, and one of the routes by which the rector might be recruited to their cause.

Throughout the eighteenth century, the Church of England was concerned almost exclusively with the white Anglican population of the island. The Church Missionary Society was not founded until 1799, and earlier glimmerings of Anglican missionary endeavour – seen in the Society for Promoting Christian Knowledge (1698) and the Society for the Propagation of the Gospel in Foreign Parts (1701) – had little impact in Jamaica. Indeed, everywhere they played an ambiguous role in the slave societies of the British Caribbean. The Church of Scotland showed no interest in Jamaica before the end of the eighteenth century, building a kirk only in 1819. It was not until the 1820s that the Scottish Missionary Society sent missionaries (members of the United Secession Church) to Jamaica, and even they were accused of teaching subservience.[13]

Moravian missionaries were brought to Jamaica in 1754 but had a small following. Methodist missionaries appeared only after Lindsay's death. None of these missionary churches had the kind of impact on Jamaica that they had in North America before the Revolution, where many colonies were "awash in a sea of faith" long before they were touched by the Great Awakening of the 1740s. Black Baptists came to Jamaica following the American Revolution but did not begin preaching until about 1784 and only slowly built up a congregation, centred in Kingston and made up largely of enslaved people. The British Toleration Acts were overruled by local statutes. Licences to preach were placed in the hands of magistrates, most of them planters. The Christian religion struggled to prosper in the midst of an ungodly British settler community bent on the pursuit of wealth through sugar and slavery rather than caring for the life of the soul. Jamaica's Britons were called "the most irreligious" people on earth.[14] Unable to serve two masters, they chose Mammon.

Curate, Spanish Town

It was to this godless community of planters and merchants that Lindsay came to minister. He did not come to preach to the enslaved people, who formed the great majority of the island's population, though he thought them at least as benighted. When Lindsay arrived in Jamaica at the end of

1759, the population was roughly 165,000, of whom enslaved black (African) people made up more than ninety per cent and white (British) people nine per cent (15,000), with sprinklings of Jews (of Portuguese and Spanish origin) and free coloured and free black people (including maroon communities). In this period the great prosperity of the plantation economy, based on sugar and slavery, contributed to rapid growth in the number of wealthy planters, and these white families increasingly became absentees, living in Britain rather than Jamaica. Only this diminished community of whites – and some free coloured families – might be expected to worship in Lindsay's churches.[15]

Lindsay served first as curate at the parish church of St Catherine, in Spanish Town (figure 6.1). The rector was J. Venn, who had been there since 1748 and had previously (from 1742) been rector of the interior sugar parish of St John.[16] With no bishops and no cathedral, the parish church of St Catherine, situated in the colony's capital, was by default the "metropolitan" centre of the Church of England in Jamaica. It had been built on the site of the former Spanish (Catholic) Red Church, in which the English had commenced services after the conquest of 1655. Ironically, the original building withstood the great earthquake of 1692 but not the great hurricane of 1712. The English replaced it with a brick building but retained the cross-shaped plan; in 1760, the year of Lindsay's first known sermon, they added a bell-tower to call the faithful to worship. Although the "large and commodious" parish church of Kingston was a strong competitor, echoing the port's rivalry

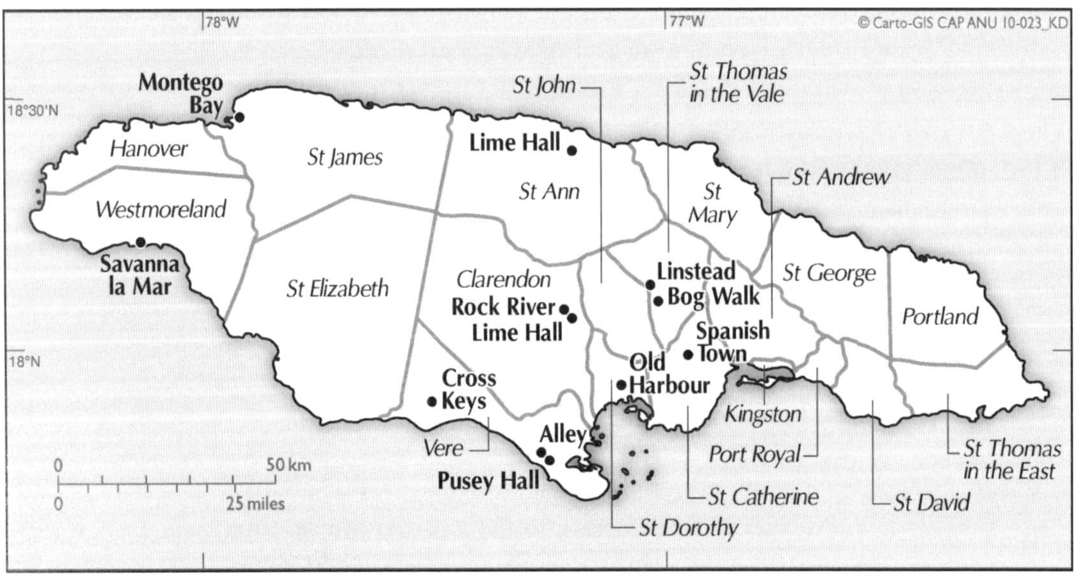

Figure 6.1 Jamaica: Parishes and places, 1760

for Jamaica's seat of government, the parish church of St Catherine was called "the finest and largest church in the English colonies in America".[17]

Spanish Town was enjoying its glory days at the beginning of a Georgian building boom. The institutions of government had long occupied the core of the town, represented in a series of buildings surrounding a parade ground. Construction of grand new versions of the governor's residence and the House of Assembly, facing one another across the parade, had begun. As well as the parish church two blocks away, there was a chapel with a cupola and a clock built in the "religious panic" that followed the earthquake of 1692, but by Lindsay's time it was used as an armoury. The parish church had its own Church Parade, on White Church Street. A little farther away was the Jewish synagogue, on Monk Street.[18]

In 1759 the population of Spanish Town was about fifteen hundred, distributed among five hundred houses. Of these people, two-thirds were free and white; they included two or three hundred Jews together with a few Dissenters, but most of them were British and Anglican. The other third was made up of enslaved people – black and coloured – and a few free coloured and free black.[19] It was a mix strongly contrasted with that on the plantations and in the population at large. Spanish Town's houses and compounds were often extensive, even occupying an entire block. Many had piazzas extending out onto the pavement, enclosed by shutters or jalousies, that impeded the progress of pedestrians and the carriages that filled the streets. Enslaved people occupied rooms in the houses and yards of slave-owners or lived in separate yards on the outskirts of town. Spanish Town's population was, however, partially seasonal; influxes were associated with the meeting of the Assembly – generally from October to Christmas – and sessions of the law courts. Planter assemblymen came to town for these sittings and the associated social whirl. Some planters had town houses of their own intended specifically to accommodate them during the season. Led by the Mistress of the Revels, processions, balls and horse races gave the white people of the town opportunities to display their finery. Theatre flourished, with performances, *inter alia*, of *Romeo and Juliet* and Otway's *The Orphan* – plays that had important roles in Lindsay's *Memoirs*.[20]

Lindsay reached Jamaica and Spanish Town in the midst of this social and political season and in time for Christmas festivities, which saw the town enjoy an exceptional period of holiday and street theatre. Jonkunu dancers, most of them enslaved people, joined other masqueraders in performances which combined cultural elements from diverse sources – from Akan costume to Scottish airs. On the streets, slave children known as "actor boys" recited scenes from Shakespeare's plays. The whites looked on from their piazzas or balconies, tossing coins to the performers but worried (correctly) that these performances were a mask for the plotting of rebellion. Raucous parties continued into the night.[21] It was closer to Carnival than a deeply religious celebration of the birth of the Christ Child. Lindsay must have found it difficult to read.

Jamaica was a significant market for British books between 1700 and 1780, importing more than Pennsylvania, for example. Some of these books went directly to the libraries of men like Lindsay, others to local booksellers and circulating libraries. A weekly newspaper was published in Spanish Town, but it had to compete with the more frequent Kingston newssheets and papers brought by ship. Spanish Town had its own printers, stationers and booksellers who competed with the larger establishments in Kingston. There were several schools, though the wealthy sent their sons to Britain for their education. A free school, established by the will of a former lieutenant-governor, Peter Beckford, had about fifty students.[22]

Another Spanish Town school was run by Francis Williams (c. 1690–1762), a free black man who taught reading, writing, Latin and mathematics. The son of John Williams, who had been freed and had established extraordinary rights for his family, Francis inherited the wealth his father had built up in land, slaves and trade. Taught the doctrines of the Church of England and educated in Britain (probably at Cambridge), Williams could have been Lindsay's intellectual saviour. However, Lindsay later observed that he knew "Black Williams" only in his "latter days, when reduced to keeping of a Negroe school – nor did I ever hear much of the success of his labours in this line". Williams was the first black writer to come to prominence in the British Empire, but little of his work survives apart from his Latin poems, including one written to celebrate the arrival of Governor Haldane in 1759. Williams was known for attending governors' levees in wig and sword, and it was in this style, surrounded by books and globes, that his image was painted in about 1740 by an unknown artist (plate 1). Williams died in 1762 and was buried in the churchyard of St Catherine. By then Lindsay had already moved to Vere.[23]

"God's Judgements"

Although he held the subaltern post of curate upon his arrival in Jamaica, Lindsay was soon in demand as a writer and deliverer of sermons. The preaching of sermons, however heavily plagiarized and however little listened to or read, was a central element in the colonial (and English and Scottish) clergyman's practice.[24] How often Lindsay preached and how many sermons he produced during his years in Jamaica are likely to remain a mystery. Only two of his sermons are known, the first delivered in 1760, when he had been in Jamaica less than a year, and the second at a funeral in 1777. It is in his sermons that Lindsay not only shows a public religion but also reveals his changing assessment of island life and of his congregation.

Lindsay's first known sermon is formally titled "A Sermon Occasioned by the Commemoration of the Annual Fast in 1760: for the Dreadful Earthquake on June 7, in Jamaica", under the banner "God's Judgements a Call to Repentance". It was delivered from the pulpit of the parish church of St Catherine, or, as Lindsay liked to put it, the "metropolis" St Jago de la Vega. The earthquake commemorated was that of 1692, which destroyed Port Royal and gave birth to Kingston. The only other day observed the same way was 28 August, in commemoration of the hurricane of 1722 (on the same day of the year as that of 1712), which did great damage to the island. As Charles Leslie observed in 1740, these two days of "solemn fasting and humiliation", authorized by the Assembly, were "observ'd sacred" and "most devoutly kept". He commented further: "The people have at least on these days the exterior shew of religion, and they may be called the only two holy-days in the year".[25]

How Lindsay, the newly arrived curate and thirty-one years old, came to be chosen to deliver the sermon at this great church on this great occasion is not certain. He had been in the island little more than six months, was most familiar with the exceptional small world of Spanish Town and was not yet kin with the planter class. He acknowledged that his "age and experience may seem to some unripe" and declared that he did not "presume to be too free with my elders: or to teach them what they must do". At the same time, he was not unwilling to accept the responsibility of his office, to direct his parishioners on a more godly way. He had arrived in the island with years of experience as a naval chaplain, his education at Edinburgh, his theological heritage and his recent reputation as a writer (though he still had not publicly admitted to authorship of *Memoirs*). He had few competitors and, according to Lindsay, Rector Venn was more concerned with secular matters and happy to pass along his preaching responsibilities.[26]

Lindsay takes his text from the Old Testament book of Joel, running together several appropriate verses from the second chapter: "Turn ye unto me saith the Lord, with weeping and with mourning: Rend your hearts and not your garments, for the Lord is gracious and merciful. Call a fast, a solemn assembly; and let the Priests, the Ministers of the Lord, weep between the porch and the altar: and let them say, Spare thy People O Lord and give not thine Heritage to reproach. Then will the Lord be jealous of the Land and pity his People." Lindsay turns immediately to wonder at the smallness of his congregation – "the many empty spaces that are every where to be seen in these pews" – considering that he preaches in "the metropolis of so great an island". He is struck by "the strange indifference and lukewarmness" shown by his parishioners to the memory of the "Divine Vengeance" that fell so heavily on Jamaica that day in 1692, when the city of Port Royal slipped beneath the sea and the sides of mountains tumbled down to leave raw wounds in the landscape.[27] The great Lisbon earthquake of 1755 was of even more recent memory, if reminders of divine retribution needed to be repeated to jolt sinners from complacency.

Doubters might question the exercise of God's will, Lindsay declares, by thinking that "judgements are the mere effect of *Blind Chance,* and to fix annual commemorations thereof, is the political & crafty insinuation of Church and Statesmen over the minds of the people when the weak heart is frightened, and as it were fitted to subjection, through the magical remembrance of natural calamities". Putting aside the "infidelity" of those who have gone to the extreme of disputing "sacred authority", and ignoring the fact that he has been in the island for less than a year, Lindsay declares it his obligation to "cry out against the rottenness of our worship and our lazy indifference about attending the house of God" and to show that "there is a God, whose Providence can spare, and can destroy his people". Citing a series of texts, he seeks to show that "to meet in assemblies, and to preach repentance, and a rending of the heart before the Lord, is not the political insinuating scheme of crafty Church and statesmen, but the way wherein God is to be found".[28]

Lindsay seeks not only to confirm the necessity of faith but also to justify the existence of priests whose role is to expound the laws of God. He challenges his congregation boldly, asking, "Are there not several, who like Satan assembled with the sons of God, now within these walls, look upon the ministers of God as a class of men the most useless – the most numerously burdensome of all society." Decrying the motives of some of those who seek to put on the cloth, Lindsay confesses that "numbers, like the sons of Eli, seeking to get into the priesthood, like a trade for a livelihood, do at this day thro' mere want, in all the English territories, fall upon such methods of thriving (unfortunate men!); when, forgetting themselves, they become a reproach to not only God's portion in particular, but in the general to religion herself". It would be better for the priestly class, he says, if "more of us consulted our abilities in preaching and expounding the sacred mysteries, before we undertake so holy a function, so tremendous a charge as that of souls! It were to be wished indeed, that all of us considered the taking of holy orders, as a dedicating our whole lives by example and precept to the service of the Gospel altar: and not as a channel whereby to earn a morsel of bread". Further, he confesses, "with shame and confusion for myself and many of my brethren, that there are great reasons to fear, that our dissolute lives and unepiscopal conversations, is no small addition to those provocations which draw down such judgements as of this day upon a nation".[29]

In a footnote to the sermon that was not part of what Lindsay declaimed from the pulpit, he admits that it is "hardly possible to give a just idea . . . of the almost general neglect of the worship of a supreme being, in the island of Jamaica". The island's priests are "not the choice of God's servants", he concurs, but thinks it equally true that "their flocks are very far from being the pick of the fold". However, Lindsay considers that the lack of respect shown the clergy derives more directly "from their being supposed to be the *teachers and instructors of their flocks*". They are confronted by "an unconquerable aversion to all kinds of instruction", their potential congregations seeing in the clergy "a constant remembrancer, and like a faithful mirror, putting them in mind of their ignorance and shewing them their wants, which of all lashings, is to them the most grievous". Lindsay then disparages the creole population, cut off from its British demographic heritage and made wealthy by pursuits unconnected with learning of any kind. "Philosophy they meddle not with", and wisely so, thinks Lindsay, considering it beyond their grasp. Rather, he says, "Religion is the butt their arrow's pointed at", since all and sundry have an opinion – and an eye out for failings of the priesthood which they might set against their own depravities.[30]

From the pulpit, Lindsay appealed to his congregation as a superior body of people, declaring the impolicy of reviling the clergy of the island as a class, since doing so would pander to the "common herd of mankind . . . the low bred, and the ignorant", who need to be provided with examples of reverence. Whatever "the nature of the priestly office", there are "blessings, obtained of the Lord, thro' the intercession of his ministers, for the interest of his people", and for this purpose it is vital for his listeners to have faith. "When you are directed by faith, to obey the Gospel", he says, "fly with the wings of impatience, for the Lord is waiting to receive you: humbly on your knees join with your watchmen in intreaties for your families and for your country; for his promises are unto us and to our seed, as many as the Lord our God shall call". Too many of his listeners were "apt to run into a fashionable course of irreligion; and look upon repentance, fastings and prayers, as mere technical terms". To those who lack faith in God's answering of prayer, Lindsay declares that "his promises . . . are sure and certain; since God is not a man, that he should lie, but faithful having promised".[31] Only patience and belief are needed.

Having established that "there is nothing more certain than Religion and the Laws of God", Lindsay says: "it must follow of course, that there are and must be Religious Duties necessarily to be performed, agreeable to those

Laws", and that "a religious life ought to be our principal aim and study". Repentance is necessary and urgent. Indeed, Lindsay tells his congregation in 1760, it is a matter of "dire importance, in every quarter, in every corner of the world; but in none so much as in this island, and at this time!" He does not treat his listeners gently but tells them they are a people "amongst whom, in the very face of the most justly deserved punishments, never did barefaced vice, luxury, and bold infidelity, reign so triumphantly!"[32]

This was no condemnation of his listeners for their ownership of enslaved people or the cruel treatment they meted out. Even less did Lindsay mean his sweeping accusation to be applied to those oppressed people. Rather it was a condemnation of behaviours he found lacking within a limited definition of sociability, but still deserving of God's wrath. Warning signs were evident enough. He points to drought and the threat of plague. Sitting in their pews, their feet resting on the tombstones that line the floor of the church – respecting an ancient tradition to be prohibited in Jamaica only in 1789, after Lindsay's death – he reminds his listeners of the inevitability of earthquake: "Hark! hark! the hollow rumbling of that coach as it passes by the Church-yard, strikes us with alarm! Nor is it unlikely, the dreadful havoc – nor distant from us, is already begun – and in a twinkling, those peaceful graves, o'er which we sit, may yawn wide and deep their horrid cheeks, and in their putrid maws, crush us to our eternal fates, whether of well or wo!"[33] Lindsay asks his listeners to contemplate "the employment of the greatest part of our metropolis, nay of our whole island, at this very instant . . . while God from Heaven's high throne looks down on the workings of our hearts, to see if in the midst of our threatened punishments, our sincerity deserves to be curs'd or bless'd at all?" In a remarkable passage in which the audacious newcomer Lindsay seeks to suggest an intimate knowledge of the way his contemporaries live their lives, he asks:

> Where are those Christians, my brethren, who should have filled these empty spaces? Perhaps they are under God's afflicting arm already; sickness prevents them; and they have with pious humility in their closets joined us in our intercessions: and God for their sakes peradventure may bless us all! *Christians*! is this the case? Charity could wish it were; but alas! how much the contrary? Is not the *Tradesman* even now (as is his practice every Sunday too) enslaved to his mercenary gains, peeping thro' his half shut gates, in greedy expectation each passing foot will bring a customer? The *Magistrate*, who should be virtuous, who should be here to enforce our prayers; is he employed as well? is he endeavouring thro' his office, while absent here, to put the wholesome laws in force against the profaners of this *National Solemnity*? Alack a day! are there not those, who, even now, are close immured: and in some house of vanity and riot, are deep engaged in *dice*, in *blasphemy* and *oaths*! Our *Great Ones* of the land; those who frame our laws; whose prudence and wis-

dom support our constitution; whose grave experience has brought them to guide the helm of society; whose encouraging example God demands; whose resolution, like Joshua, ought to be *as for me and my House we will serve the Lord*, – their belly, is their God – their heaven, debauchery! Where are they? do ye ask me? At their Farms. Perhaps reviewing their hard-work'd Slaves around their sultry fields: Their Wives (if they are decent and honest enough to have such), like Martha, little regarding the one thing needful, are busied directing the luxuries of the day: And should we enquire for their offspring – or seek the retirements of a Great Man's heir, to view his humble deportment, on this day of *direful memory*; O how much akin to their wretched Parent; heir to his wrath, as well as wealth! As yet untaught the All-seeing eye of God, he but now, at this late hour, wakes from his horrid slumbers – the *dark-hue'd* partner of his bed steals thro' some private passage: and in his rank abomination dares not to think of, far less to thank his Maker that he has yet another day to live! My brethren! I appeal to your honest hearts; is this picture *true or false?* O dreadful! Dreadful.[34]

God and Mammon

Returning to his central theme, the vengeance of God through earthquake, hurricane and drought, Lindsay adds another sign: the threat of rebellion by the enslaved. Tacky's Revolt, an ambitious rebellion concentrated in the parish of St Mary that saw the deaths of several whites as well as enslaved people, was going on when Lindsay delivered his sermon. Although his reference is allusive, it was readily understood by his congregation. Lindsay observes that "we ourselves" (meaning the white slave-owning community) have denied the "common support of nature [food and drink] in a very exemplary manner, . . . but a few weeks ago, [to] two of our fellow creatures in a neighbouring town". Here Lindsay introduces a footnote stating that in May 1760 two enslaved men were executed as rebels, "hung up on one gibbet together in chains alive, at Kingston; who lived in the scorching sun, one of them for seven days, the other eight".[35] He does not mean to condemn such barbarous treatment but rather to use it as an allegory. He tells his listeners:

Mistake me not, my brethren, I speak not this in the face of justice, forc'd with regret to a measure which the preservation of our own lives rendered indispensable: but to put you in remembrance, that if for one offence (and that too, the favourite British virtue, the struggling after liberty) . . . we are blameless in taking away the lives of our fellow creatures in so rigorous a manner, what do we ourselves deserve, grovelling, despicable maggots, for thousands of rebellions against the Majesty of Heaven?[36]

Whatever his justification of barbarity, Lindsay recognizes the "slavish rebellion" as "a new scene, a new judgment, to call us to repentance!" The perversity of his listeners and their class, "obstinately blind to Divine pleasure" sent upon them in plague, pestilence, earthquake, hurricane and famine, finds "Pharoah's last plague is now let loose, to rage amongst us! God having put the sword of his vengeance in the barbarous grips of our own Slaves, we know not whether the throats of ourselves, or First-born, or Friends, shall be the next to pay the public debt of delinquency." He implores his congregation not to spend the remaining hours of this special day "in idleness, in sleep, in chambering, or wantonness: but with repenting hearts, let every man for himself, implore the favour and acceptance of Heaven". Rather, Lindsay concludes,

> It is highly becoming us to frequent and meet together in the public courts of God, to interceed for public blessings: Here indeed we may appear in sackcloth, and rent our garments, but the renting of the heart, most pleasing unto God, will be best performed when we go home, and retire to ourselves. This is the proper employment of this day. And O that we had more secret prayers amongst us! The supplications of this Fast might then perhaps be more successful for *Jamaica*, than Lot in his for the prayerless sons of *Sodom*. Go then, my brethren, from the altar to your Closets! – Go! and may the God of Grace and Supplication go with you! Amen.[37]

How Lindsay's listeners received his admonitions is hard to tell. Merchants and planters were no strangers to the concept of risk, and in their material world they were rarely able to insure against hazards. They often enough thought of their investments as a kind of lottery and did their best not to fear death at the hands of the people they oppressed or from disease. Planning for an earthquake was impossible. For the godless, fearing the consequences of their behaviour and beliefs would be unlikely to fix their minds on the need to set one's worldly house in order in preparation for the next. Many of Lindsay's listeners were thinking about leaving Jamaica for a better world elsewhere on earth, but they hoped first to exploit the opportunities given them by slave society to build a fortune on the backs of others.[38] Lindsay himself hoped for advancement and found his best prospects within the island.

Rector, Vere and St Thomas in the Vale

Lindsay left Spanish Town for Vere in 1761, moving up from curate to rector and taking charge of his own parish. Vere was one of the longest-settled sugar parishes of Jamaica, forming the island's most southern point and stretching to the west into the territory of the modern parish of Manchester (figure 6.1). Its population was relatively small, dominated by six thousand enslaved people, most of whom laboured on the parish's twenty sugar plantations.

The parish church, St Peter's, was in the hamlet of Alley (plate 2). One of the oldest churches in the island, St Peter's was surrounded by large cotton trees, with a rectory nearby, some acres of glebe and a more distant piece of land that added to the stipend's £200.[39]

It was in Vere that Lindsay made his entry into Jamaican society and began to discover the island's natural world. He married in May 1762, taking as his wife Grace, daughter of the planter John Pusey, Esquire, and identified in the marriage register as "Grace Booth widow". They were wed in the Vere parish church and were described as "both of Vere". Probably Grace was a creole, born in the parish. Lindsay later identified her as a former schoolmate of Mary Ballard Beckford, who married Edward Long at the parish church of St Catherine in 1758, before Lindsay arrived as curate. Mary Ballard Beckford was also a creole, born in 1736 and baptized at St Catherine.[40]

As well as her immediate past husband, Norwood Booth, Grace was the widow of earlier unions: with Jonathan Gale, who died in 1756 and was memorialized on the Vere church wall, and before him Thomas Gardner the younger, owner of Lime Hall Estate, a sugar plantation with a watermill on Rock River in Clarendon, in the territory of the Beckfords and the Longs. Gardner's will of 1749 left Grace unprovided for and bequeathed his property to his sisters and other relatives. In 1769 a dispute came to court at the death of John Gardner, brother of Thomas, and it was agreed that Grace should receive an annuity. The agreement was, however, abrogated when the property was sold to pay off its encumbrances.[41]

By marrying into a local planter family Lindsay firmly established his alignment with the creole elite. Berating a congregation from the pulpit became less likely, even had the pews been filled. Lindsay turned his energies to the curious and the natural world around him. While at Vere he used his location to investigate the life of sea and land, beginning the drawing and writing that would become his preoccupation for several years. His father-in-law, John Pusey, taught him the names of the fish of the island. He was also introduced to the virtues of herbal medicines. He does not say by whom, but it could equally have been an enslaved person as a creole planter. Specifically Lindsay notes that, although the seeds of the red bead or wild liquorice vine can be fatal, the leaves and branches of the vine make a salutary infusion. Before coming to Jamaica he was troubled by a persistent cough, "But on my settling myself in a regular family manner, and taking a cup of this liquorice tea every evening going to bed, and every morning getting up, I found myself by degrees relieved; till I became perfectly freed of every complaint." He had been taking it for six years without ill effect, and observes further that he had not been "in the least costive, in bodily habit, since I took this medicine but every way regular and easy".[42]

When John Pusey died in 1767 at the age of seventy-five, he was buried under a slab in the floor of St Peter's. A mural declared him: "Disinterestedly sincere, and uniformly steady in the interest of his native country; he lived truly and justly venerated. Unsolicitous of public honours, he knew no ambition but that of doing good; and possessing a soul rich in humanity and benevolence which poured forth its bounty with a generous and unbounded hand." His executor was William Pusey (presumably his son), who represented the parish of Vere in the House of Assembly and died in 1783 at forty-two; his wife, Elizabeth, had died in 1780, at forty years old.[43]

In 1768 Lindsay left his position as rector of Vere and moved to St Thomas in the Vale, north of Spanish Town and now part of the parish of St Catherine. St Thomas in the Vale had for a century been settled in sugar plantations that spread across the interior valley where most of the parish's eight thousand enslaved people lived. Flowing through the valley was the Rio Cobre, which entered narrow Bog Walk Gorge to the south to run on to Spanish Town and the sea. Little is known of Lindsay's time in St Thomas in the Vale, and by 1773 he was securely installed as rector of St Catherine.[44] His time in Vere was the most formative, but while there, seemingly secluded in a distant parish, he had not been forgotten in Spanish Town.

"Images of Gods Sovereignty"

In 1763 Lindsay was called from Vere to deliver an "oration" before the governor of Jamaica, William Henry Lyttleton, "on the day appointed for *Thanksgiving & Public Rejoicings* for the late *General Peace*". Like his sermon of 1760, the oration was not published until after his death, and although delivered in church it was not regarded by Lindsay as one of his sermons.[45] Indeed, as noted in chapter 4, sections of the oration concerning the idea of a patriot king were drawn from his *Memoirs* of 1757.

The precise day of Lindsay's delivery is unknown. The Peace of Paris, which marked the end of the Seven Years' War, was formally proclaimed in March 1763 but the news took several weeks to reach Jamaica. The treaty involved a number of the sites where Lindsay had been over the years. From France Britain secured, *inter alia*, Canada, Nova Scotia, Cape Breton, Senegal, Tobago, Grenada, St Vincent and Dominica. France regained Gorée, Martinique, Guadeloupe and St Lucia and was guaranteed fishing grounds off Newfoundland.[46] Lindsay greeted the peace with enthusiasm, particularly in view of the hegemony awarded the British over the French.

In his preface to the oration, written in 1766 or 1767, Lindsay observes that some thought that his description of "a good governor" was directed unfavourably at Lyttleton, and more particularly "that the paragraph concerning church preferments, was a sarcastical reprimand, for being myself overlooked, in the disposal of vacant livings". Lindsay defends himself, saying that he regards "making use of the *chair of verity* for so mean a purpose as private revenge, to be a species of *sacrilege*". He explains that during the administration of Governor Henry Moore "there happened vacancies in the church". However, even though he was "on good terms with Sir Henry" and "particularly intimate with Lady Moore's nearest relations", he recalls that "a living was given to a person, then in a distant part of the world, and from as distant an application, while I troubled not his Honour either by own, or application of my many friends". Lindsay declares himself, "thro' Gods goodness, blest with sufficiency, and content" and, having cleared away any charges of self-interest, observes that he has always "endeavoured to avoid offending my conscience, by not being burdensome to the altar".[47]

When he delivered the oration in 1763, Lindsay remembers, "there were no less than six vacant benefices in the island". Lyttleton (governor from 1762 to 1766) had tried hard to fill these posts, "even to sending to his brother the then Lord Bishop of Carlisle, for gentlemen unprovided for in England". Lindsay reflects:

> The rectory of the parish in which my own estate is situate [perhaps St Thomas in the Vale], was then also vacant; when agreeable to my function, I shrunk back from no toils: but to oblige my fellow parishioners [of Vere] in their distress, even through the most mountainous recesses, and from my own family by day and by night, have I been instant in season and out of season, in the several offices of the Church; yet still had I not by any method whatever made application to his Excellency for preferment.

Even as he was writing the preface, says Lindsay, although three livings were vacant and he received "kind proffers of service" from Roger Hope Elletson (lieutenant-governor from 1766 to 1767), he chose to "remain as before, retired to myself & my friends".[48]

The final proof that his oration was not intended to offend Lyttleton, declares Lindsay, is simply that "the discourse with very little alteration was wrote a considerable time before his Excellency's arrival in the island". George III, whose reign began on 25 October 1760, was not crowned until 22 September 1761, and the date of the coronation was known well before the event. Its celebration in Jamaica occurred at the same time as in London and included elements from the metropolitan ceremonies, such as the coronation anthems. Composed by German-born George Frederick Handel (1685–1759), these four anthems were first used in 1727, for the coronation of George II and Queen Caroline. They formed part of the coronation liturgy, beginning with "Let Thy Hand Be Strengthened" (for the recognition), followed by the most famous of the four, "Zadok the Priest" (for the anointing), then "The King Shall Rejoice" (for the crowning of the king) and "My Heart Is Inditing" (for the queen's coronation). The coronation ceremony of 1761, at Westminster Abbey, turned out to be rather a shambles.[49]

In Jamaica, Lindsay says, "On the evening preceding the day of his *Majesty's* coronation, the rehearsal of Mr. Handels four coronation anthems (which were to be sung upon the occasion) was performed before Sir Henry Moore, then Lieutenant Governor, in the Kings House." It was at this late hour that "his Honour begged me to join to the service a short discourse suited to the ceremonies of the day. I could not help excusing myself from the task, from the shortness of the time; but pressing me further, with a compliment, (*he knew I would not be at a loss*, he was pleased to say) I obeyed his will, and soon after supper retired to my study." This was when Lindsay recalled his chapter on the idea of a patriot king and revealed his authorship of *Memoirs*. He soon had a discourse ready for delivery, but on the day of the coronation ceremonies Moore "was pleased to alter his mind with respect to the Sermon", believing the anthems, proclamations and gun salutes would fill up the available time. "Thus was the Oration (for Sermon I cannot call it) being unfit for a common occasion, thrown by as useless."[50]

Having made these excuses, Lindsay needs only to account for the delivery of the oration "in nearly the same dress in which it was to appear on a widely different solemnity", namely celebration of the general peace in 1763. Lindsay explains the circumstances simply, saying:

> The Rector of Spanish Town, Mr. Venn, having for some years past given himself intirely to secular concerns: and now not very fond of moral or sacred compositions, had put off all thoughts, of preparing for the service of this day, till he found it too late; and then applied to the Governor's Chaplain for his assistance in the Sermon: but he excusing himself from that trouble, by going down to read prayers to half a dozen people in his parish, joined Mr. Venn, in an application to me.

Lindsay got their letter "on the Sunday Evening – the day appointed for the Thanksgiving was the Friday following", but he was "unluckily seized on the Monday with a fever". Having agreed to assist, Lindsay says,

> I set my thoughts to work; but not being in a condition for service study, I had recourse to this very discourse, and found that by a few alterations, it would suit the nature of this solemnity, full as well as the former. Finding myself on the Wednesday a little clear of the fever, I drove up to town [from Vere] in the afternoon: but by the fatigue of the journey, I was again cast upon the hands of my apothecary: And instead of having a day to polish and add a little to the design, I

took the eighteenth dose of bark the instant before I stept into my chariot, to be drove to the Church.

All of this Lindsay tells to convince his readers that "whatever be the nature of this composition, no degree of satire was in the least intended by me".[51]

Lindsay claims to have mined *Memoirs* for his idea of a patriot king and suggests that he had little opportunity to add to what he said there, but the oration was in fact a substantially expanded discourse. On the other hand, it certainly did contain many paragraphs taken almost word for word from *Memoirs* and did use much of the material originally found in the novel. Here it is necessary only to consider the ways in which the oration developed the argument beyond that advanced in *Memoirs*.

Although Lindsay was determined not to call his oration a sermon, he was comfortable beginning with a text – Isaiah 32: 1, 16–18 – establishing the righteousness of peace. Aligning himself with Saint Paul, Lindsay declares that "a contentedness in our present state and condition, is the surest road to bliss". He then tells his audience that man's restless desire for "places of *honour, trust* and *preferment*" is simply destabilizing, indicating no more than "so many steps of ascent leading to anxiety, disquiet, disgust, and often to the precipice of ruin itself". Claiming that "a state of subjection yields the purest comfort", he argues further that "he who can with the best grace submit his conduct to the direction of his superior will in all cases find himself the happiest man". Even a king is ultimately subject to the "Almighty disposer of all events". So, says Lindsay, "Miserable the wretch, who restless and discontented, is constantly climbing one condition to another! And happy he, who in whatever state providence shall cast him, can therewith be content."[52]

By making this argument in the context of Jamaica's slave society, it might seem that Lindsay wished to instil a satisfaction with one's lot in life, whatever it might be, the acceptance of a compact in which a stable social order is more to be desired than individual fortune. His oration was not addressed to enslaved people but intended rather as an argument for obedience to church and state. It was a message to himself – to be content with his ecclesiastical station and not to hanker after preferment – and a lesson the (white) colonists needed to learn. Speaking in 1763, on the eve of the great debates that were soon to tear apart the British Empire, Lindsay warns his listeners of the risks they face in challenging the negotiated constitutional status they have achieved, one which respects their right to rule Jamaica in the way they wish – preserving their "liberty" – while at the same time ensuring the security and protection of their lives and their trade. What is to be feared, he says, is "rank rebellion . . . born of libertinism, arrogant pride and partiality, . . . flourishing in the soil of British liberty, under the sheltering branches of

British freedom". Although Britons live under "the mildest government", he says, there remains "a most rebellious appetite, struggling hard with the governance both of reason and religion". Some were calling for ever greater conquests, perhaps even taking France itself or cutting every French throat, but Lindsay says it is the "genius of Britain" to be gracious in victory.[53]

Rather than upsetting the order of things or craving for advancement, Lindsay tells his listeners in 1763, the loyal subject should hope only to be "governed by a superior who reigns in righteousness, and who consulting the quiet of the dependants, will appoint them princes & governors who will rule with justice". Only thus can the subject's "native *rights* and *privileges*" be secured. What Lindsay sought to achieve in the oration, something he did not attempt in *Memoirs*, was to consider the role of the king's representatives rather than the "glorious *aristo-democratical monarchy* which Britons providentially enjoy". He did this because of his colonial location and because "a King of Great Britain, in the great extent of his dominions, cannot in person attend to every part of his government", and therefore depended on the authority of his governors and civil magistrates. Godly government was essential: "truly, were our *rulers* and *judges* often to consider themselves as *images of Gods sovereignty*, his viceregents in this lower world, to distribute to his people, the blessings of his *All gracious attributes*, we should oftener than we do, find them rule as God rules".[54]

With ideas about the right relationship between father and son not far from his mind, Lindsay argues that the ruler should love truth and justice:

> Equally equitable in the distribution of punishments as of rewards, he punishes, not but with regret; and flies not to the resources of awe and dread, till he has patiently tried every other remedy. But firm and inflexible against blasphemy, impiety, and libertinism, he will employ all his authority, with the severities of law, to purge his estates. For fully convinced that in Heaven there is a sovereign master who will judge the rulers of the earth, he will give constant attention to the commandments of God, and to the observation of his laws.[55]

Under the "happy constitution" of Great Britain, "which preserves with the royal prerogative, the liberty and property of the subject", its subjects could want nothing more than to "sit under those sheltering branches of our vine and fig-tree, and bless the God or Armies, that calm peace". With much reiteration, Lindsay draws his oration to an end by praying for "the preservation of his Majesty's sacred person and government".[56]

Doctor of Divinity

Although occupied by his parochial duties, Lindsay found time to travel around the island. Many of his references to localities are to the lowlands of southern Clarendon and Vere, but he also went farther afield. His travels and observations contributed to the accumulation of writing and drawing that came to form the volumes known as the "Elegancies of Jamaica", to be discussed in chapter 7. In 1770 he sought the help of the House of Assembly to bring this work to publication, but was rebuffed.

Lindsay gained more respect in Scotland. In April 1772 he boarded the *Lady Juliana* and sailed to Britain, taking with him the manuscript volumes of his natural history. On 12 January 1773, Edinburgh University bestowed on him the degree of doctor of divinity.[57] The grounds on which Lindsay was awarded this degree are unknown. He may already have received an MA from Edinburgh, earned for attending classes and passing examinations. As to the doctor of divinity degree, it was left to the faculty to decide on the merits of each case, and degrees could be awarded so long as there was proof of learning and perhaps publications to demonstrate achievement. Honorary doctorates in divinity and law were awarded in the later eighteenth century, as approved by the faculties and without strict rules of qualification. Probably Lindsay got one of those, on the basis of good report, his published works and, possibly, his unpublished manuscripts.[58]

Lindsay received his DD while William Robertson was principal of Edinburgh University. Regarded as the leading historian of his generation, Robertson was equally interested in natural history, creating the chair at Edinburgh in 1770 and later playing a role in the founding of the Royal Society of Edinburgh. He dominated the town council that had charge of the university and dominated the General Assembly of the Church of Scotland, in which he was leader of the Moderates. Robertson's views on Presbyterian belief and its accommodation with Anglicanism were shared by Lindsay. The religious tests that had been applied to professors were removed in Robertson's time, but he took for granted their orthodoxy. He put scholarship ahead of preaching but regularly occupied the pulpits of Edinburgh churches.[59] It is possible that Lindsay was corresponding with Robertson when the DD was granted, though the earliest known letters between them are from 1776. Perhaps Robertson already knew of Lindsay's work in natural history and perhaps Lindsay showed him the "Elegancies" sometime in 1772. Without doubt, if Robertson had opposed the award, it would have been denied.

Rector, St Catherine

On his return from Edinburgh with the DD proudly appended to his name, Lindsay was installed as rector of St Catherine in 1773 and held its tenure until his death in 1788. His qualifications easily outshone those of any other clergyman in Jamaica. His stipend was £300 per annum, making him the best paid of the island's rectors.[60] Lindsay, however, may have hoped for even greater preferment. In the *Lives of the Lindsays*, compiled by Lord Lindsay in 1849 – shortly after the parish church of St Catherine was formally declared a cathedral – the claim is made that when installed as rector at Spanish Town, John Lindsay was "promised that see, if erected", suggesting a status not otherwise recognized (plate 3). He was long dead by the time Jamaica got its first bishop.[61]

Spanish Town was more elegant in 1773 than it had been when Lindsay first saw it. The grand new King's House – the governor's residence – had been completed; it faced the even more recent House of Assembly across the parade. Close to the parish church, a theatre was built at private expense and opened in 1776. In his *History of Jamaica*, published in 1774, Long identifies "Doctor Lindsay" as the current rector of the Spanish Town church, "an elegant building of brick". Pulpit and pews were made of mahogany and cedar, the aisles paved with marble. The governor's pew was raised above the others and "crowned with a canopy", the communion rail running around it as well as the altar. Chandeliers hung from the ceiling. A gallery held "an exceeding fine organ" installed in 1755; the organist was paid £120 per annum and "generally required at the funeral obsequies even of the free Negroes and Mulattoes buried in this parish". As rector, Lindsay was provided with "a very convenient dwelling-house in the town" together with "sixty acres of rich pasture-land, within a small distance of it, the donation of Mr. Edward Morgan in 1674". Long also mentions "upwards of five hundred acres in the neighbourhood, patented in the same year 'for the use of the parish of St. Catherine, towards the maintenance of the minister' ". Beyond any benefits from these resources, Long believed Lindsay could double his stipend simply from the substantial "occasional fees".[62]

From the time he was made a doctor of divinity to his death in 1788, Lindsay continued his interest in the natural world, but increasingly he became absorbed in the philosophical and theological discourse that came to centre on the problem of explaining human diversity and the emerging notion of "race". Probably he spent more time in his closet reading and writing, and less time wandering and wondering at the plants and animals of Jamaica. How much time he devoted to the management of his "estate", where it was and what it produced are unknown. No doubt he officiated at many funerals and did his best to maintain his congregation. The one sermon he delivered in Spanish Town known to have been published in his lifetime was delivered at the funeral of the governor Sir Basil Keith in 1777.

During this period Lindsay corresponded with William Robertson in Edinburgh, writing to him first in May 1776. That letter was sent by the hand of a young man going to the university to complete his studies in "Phisick"; he was the son of a judge and member of the House of Assembly, and Lindsay introduced him as unusual in not sharing the common "dissipated turn" of the Jamaican community. The main point of Lindsay's letter was, however, to provide abstracts of the baptisms and burials recorded in the St Catherine parish registers for 1750 to 1756 – years before his arrival in the island – and more recent numbers for the period of his incumbency, with details of causes of death. Lindsay believed Robertson would have an interest in these data: "as you have turn'd your thoughts of late a good dele to the history of Jamaica". It was Lindsay's reading that the island was becoming more healthy. He had found in his parish five thousand Christians, four hundred Jews and ten thousand slaves, and he offered his services in supplying any other information Robertson might desire.[63]

Lindsay wrote again to Robertson in August 1776, responding to a letter recently received from him, dated 1 January but slow to find its way to Spanish Town. It came by the hand of Robertson's nephew Nesbet, who had found work in the counting house of a cousin, William Harvey. Robertson asked for help in finding further employment for Nesbet, and Lindsay and Harvey agreed to recommend him to the governor, Sir Basil Keith, for an appointment as master in chancery. Lindsay goes on at length to give Robertson his thoughts on the "bold disaffection" of the North Americans and the instability this was creating in Jamaica, with fears of military attack from the French or Spanish, along with the fears of the island's whites stirred up by a recently exposed slave "conspiracy".[64]

Although slave risings are common, says Lindsay, the current conspiracy is new and frightening because it involves for the first time the creole island-born people and "those brought up about our houses". This cut home to Lindsay because it introduced into his domestic context what might have seemed located in the harsh environment of the plantation. Lindsay explains to Robertson a scenario that has become a commonplace: the image of a dining room, white diners seated and a black waiter behind each chair, equally attentive to the needs of the diner and to the table talk. The diners make bold declarations of "virtuous heroism" and a preference for death, however terrible the mode, rather than submission to "slavery" in political life, oblivious to the message this might send to the waiting blacks. Lindsay saw the sedition and ingratitude of the North American rebels and the vocal support given them by sympathizers in Jamaica – Lindsay calls them "Wise-Acre Patriots" – as sources for models of disobedience to law and authority that the enslaved could not but take notice of in their own situation. The American war had brought rebellion into the Jamaican household, increasing dramatically white fears of poisoning and massacre. Lindsay paints a vivid and detailed picture of Jamaica under martial law, the burning alive of suspected conspirators – house slaves – and the "troubled waters" of island life.[65]

"The Prosperity of the Soul"

The one sermon by Lindsay known to be published during his lifetime was *Preached at the Funeral of His Excellency Sir Basil Keith, Knt. Governour of Jamaica.* The funeral took place in Spanish Town on 16 June 1777, the day following the governor's death. A Scot, Keith had served in the navy before his appointment as governor of Jamaica in 1774. Although only forty years old when he arrived, he was in poor health for most of his time in the island. In spite of his incapacity, his government was hailed by the colonists, helped along as it was by the prosperity of the planter class in the years before the American Revolution. In his honour, the Assembly spent almost £1,000 to erect a marble monument placed in the chancel of Lindsay's church in 1780. It was so imposing that Lindsay was voted £30 to compensate for fees lost from the crowding out of other potential memorialists.[66]

The title page of the sermon declares that it was preached "in the Parish Church of St. Catherine, and Town of St. Jago de la Vega" by "John Lindsay, D.D. Rector of that metropolis". Shortly before leaving Jamaica in January 1780, the classically trained closet Methodist William Jones – who does not mention Lindsay in his diary over his previous two years in the island – records that "Dr. Lindsay, Minister of Span-Town, did me the honor of requesting my perusal and judgment of a sermon, (for so he calls it), which he is about to publish relative to Sir Basil Keith, late Govr. of this island".[67] The published version is dedicated to Sir Alexander Dick (1703–85), an Edinburgh physician who boasted various scientific and cultural achievements and who with Robertson played a role in establishment of the Royal Society of Edinburgh. Keith was Dick's nephew, the son of his sister Margaret and the Scots diplomatist Robert Keith (c. 1697–1774). Lindsay addresses Dick, saying that "our assembly, having voted a very noble monument to perpetuate his memory, I suppose thought that sufficient". Once again, Lindsay's appeal for a publication subsidy had been rebuffed by the Assembly. Dick covered the cost.[68]

As well as the dedication to Dick, Lindsay includes an "apology" designed to explain the content of his sermon. He says: "Religion and the public ordinances being here at the lowest ebb, I have customarily, on occasions, when common decency has drawn our better people to church, strove in my compilations, to throw as many doctrines, which can yield reflection, together; as the compass of a sermon can well allow". This is what he had done for Keith's funeral, to which he might assume to have drawn a superior but infrequent community of listeners. He explains, however, that while he had been "fully explicit, for the learned – opulently educated – and liberal congregation, for whom I composed it", he realized that it might not satisfy those "slow and scrupulous readers" who would prefer to see a single issue "critically and minutely handled". In order to suit the circumstances, he had "given to some passages a turn of freedom and boldness, which may not be altogether pleasing to those whose manner of thinking is more close and cautious". Bearing in mind his Edinburgh Enlightenment contemporaries, Lindsay tells Dick that he fears this might be the view of "many of my late reverend and eloquent fathers, friends amongst you". However, with his Jamaican audience in mind, Lindsay concludes his dedication by reflecting "[t]hat the natural genius of a people breathing this airy elevating region, is so lively – so quick and penetrating, that the grave, polemick reasonings of deep divinity would only have led to inattention and disgust". Rather than berating his listeners, as he did before in the same place, Lindsay tells his congregation: "Few eulogists as I, have so respectable an audience to address. Few, such a friend to praise!" He comes not, however, "to offer the incense of adulation" or "sublunary panegyrick", but rather to offer divine instruction.[69]

Lindsay's text was the Old Testament injunction "Set thine house in order for thou shalt die" (2 Kings 20:1). These were the words of the prophet Isaiah to Hezekiah, who was "sick unto death". His remorse and supplication led the Lord to grant Hezekiah another fifteen years of life. Lindsay does not detail the story but assumes that his listeners knew it well enough. Rather, he leads them to "thoughts on eternity".[70] But he is no puritan or ascetic. He considers "the good things of life" to be "God's blessings", and the passions "given to us by heaven's own gracious will – to sweeten the many nausious draghts of human slavery". Although he describes passions "of the pleasurable kind" to be no more than "lightsome inns through our pilgrimage; which Nature's God intends shall allure us on to more intense and intellectual enjoyments", he equally condemns "that zealot, who would doggedly refuse or neglect, the prudent and proper bounded use of our pleasurable passions, [who] is as absurd as the dissatisfied enthusiast, who would refuse on his death-bed the apothecary's cordial; lest reviving his burdened spirits, and catching another glance of God's good world, he should have obtruded on his pious mind, one other wish for length of days".[71]

This "doctrinal observation", says Lindsay, leads naturally to "a most serious warning to all those, who too rigidly adhere to ill digested opinions in the salutary doctrine of predestination". He relates this specifically to Keith, who, thought Lindsay, denied his physician the chance to prescribe, believing "our end being in every circumstance and purpose of life predestinated". Equally unacceptable to Lindsay's mind is the idea of "the *free* grace – the *unmerited* grace of God" obtained by lucky conversions, through "weeping contritions" or "pious, saintly looking upon a cross, even at the point of death, whatever has been their life". He accepts that the only way to heaven is by the blood of Christ, the Redeemer. However, Lindsay continues, "St. Paul as well as James the *brother of our Lord*, argue well to this purpose – both allow that the efficacy of faith rests firm on the merits of Christ: but both carefully introduce our own examplary conversations and good *works* as the threshold at least to any door of hope through that quarter. Let the righteous, therefore, go to reason, before he talks so boldly of his *faith*."[72] Christ's acceptance of the last-minute penitence of the thief on the cross was a singular case that should not be made general, and the "ungracious" lepers healed by Jesus, who failed even to give thanks and glorify God, were made fit for human society by their "*simple faith* in his preternatural power", but not by this alone made "*faithful children of paradise*". Rather than clinging to such hopes, says Lindsay,

> If we have occupied *well* our day and generation – if we have lived *well* under the influence of faith – and left our house in order, we deserve well – we shall at best, indeed, make but unprofitable servants; but if we shall have done our best – *properly speaking done it* – we may look up with courage: for God never will withhold that grace or favour we shall in the *general* have deserved, to punish in *particular* some small failings . . . .[73]

Setting his argument more precisely in the Jamaican context of the desire for great wealth, the objective common to his congregation, Lindsay tells his listeners that it is more important to care for "the prosperity of the soul". Developing the accounting model, he says: "To neglect the setting our house in order, my dear friends, and in that work the business of our souls; while we are in health and ease, is a neglect of the most alarming nature." Lindsay points to the fragility of life in a land where death comes so often and speaks of the hazards of fortune. He continues:

> God seems to have left this business much to ourselves – we may make what use of life we will – 'tis in our hands. But *reason* declares, that if we make not of it, a state of probation – when death shall call – it will most assuredly be, to a court of

> retribution! ... O happy! happy then, the soul who shall have so settled his worldly affairs, that when his fatal knell is heard – and when death's glare hath struck across his gliss'ning sight – he may have nothing left to do – but fix them, with his thoughts, on God – and die![74]

In the face of death, Lindsay asks, "What avails thee, here, my gay friend, the splendor of thy luscious couch – the softness of its pleasures – the pamp'ring delicacies on thy table – or all those fields and villas, which called by thy name administer to thy rank and ostentation?" The "charms of beauty", of wealth and power, "rank and dignity", are nothing when "drenched in the cold, wintered sweats of death". Equally useless in the face of death is the ingenious reasoning of the falsely wise who have no faith. Lindsay challenges his congregation, asking, "And what advantageth it thee, my philosopher, the thousand questions of the curious – the various modes of subtile nature, eloquently turn'd to interweave our vices with our virtues; and make a right of wrong – ingrafting sin, upon the choice stocks of pleasure".[75] In contrast to his oration of 1763 and in spite of his warnings to the foolish, Lindsay does not conclude his funeral sermon in honour of Keith with hopes of meeting together in heaven, let alone any mention of hell.

Clergy and Congregation

Writing near the end of his life, Lindsay developed a theory that church attendance was an element of fashion and depended on the example set by the governor. It was unfortunately the case that "religion in Jamaica, to our eternal and shameful disgrace, is a meer *wether cock of fashion,* pointing and veering about, as a Governour shall be pleased to be at leisure".[76] Although Lindsay was applying his theory strictly to the case of Jamaica, it fitted well with later assessments of the eighteenth-century clergy of the Church of England, in Britain as well as its colonies, which often found their quality wanting and charted a general decline over the century. The church was seen as becoming spiritually moribund and filled with priests more interested in feathering their own beds – their luscious couches – than in bringing sinners to salvation. Even when they did attend church, in Jamaica the ritual of the Eucharist – the sacrament of the Lord's Supper – was rarely practised. In some rural parishes it was never celebrated, and even in Spanish Town communion was offered only once a month and at the great festivals.[77]

Lindsay recognized that he lived in a land where belief struggled to prosper and church attendance was notoriously unpopular. In a note to his oration of 1763 he observes the "almost general neglect of the worship of a supreme being, in the island of Jamaica" but argues elsewhere that attendance declined rather than grew during his time.[78] In the 1720s the rector at Spanish Town reported that "a considerable number of the parishioners constantly and religiously attend" and that the Kingston parish church was "generally pretty full" on Sunday mornings. Priests then mostly bemoaned the poor attendance at liturgies during the week, typically the reading of prayers on Wednesdays and Fridays. Because the wealthy subscribed to pews, ensuring their regular place within the ranks of society, their absence was easily identified.[79]

Only funerals brought the plantocracy regularly to church, and Lindsay was well aware of the need to catch his congregation whenever he got the chance. Sunday was, however, best known as the great day of commerce, when the grand "Negro markets" took over town squares and crossroads throughout the island. It was the sole opportunity enslaved people had during the week to buy and sell, to exchange the produce of their provision grounds for consumer goods and to interact on relatively equal terms with the free people, their one day not devoted to unremitting labour in field and factory. The markets, attended by all and sundry, commenced at dawn and continued, according to law, until an hour before the time of divine service. This "profanation of the Sabbath" struck British visitors.[80]

Most of Jamaica's Anglican clergy came from Britain. The church was an unusual calling for the island-born, but Lindsay did encourage a relative in this direction. In 1781 he wrote in favour of his "nephew" Richard Pusey, who was travelling to England "as a candidate for holy orders". Lindsay stated that Pusey, baptized at St Catherine in 1756, had been "known to me since his infancy; being entitled to a considerable landed inheritance" and had received a legacy from his grandfather (presumably John Pusey, Lindsay's father-in-law). When about fifteen years old, Richard Pusey expressed a "desire of going to Cambridge to prosecute his studies in the line of the church" but had no encouragement from his "guardian uncle" (presumably William Pusey, son of John). On his return to Jamaica five years later, in about 1776, "virtuously disdaining the libertine practices of this island", he "soon married, made a considerable purchass of land and Negroes . . . and meant to continue in the planting line". By 1781 he had rented out his property and sought once more to become a priest.[81] He was unusual.

In Jamaica, some clergy spent time managing the estates of absentees, and indeed this was something Lindsay himself later advocated. William Jones in 1778 claimed to have seen a parson who neglected his parochial duty though collecting his stipend, but "so void of shame, before God and men, that he travels in the face of open day, accompanied by his *sable* favorite, as a necessary appendage of a West-Indian life".[82] Long's well-known 1774 assessment of the "character" of the clergy in Jamaica was relatively generous. Although some were "detestable for their addiction to lewdness, drinking, gambling, and iniquity", there were always others "respectable for their learning, piety, and exemplary good behaviour". Some were "better qualified to be retailers of salt-fish, or boatswains to privateers, than ministers of the Gospel", but on balance he thought "the major part, worthy the public esteem and encouragement".[83] Lindsay, with his university education, was one of the latter.

In advancing his theory that church attendance followed fashion, with parishioners taking their cue from the governor of the day, no doubt Lindsay had Spanish Town particularly in mind. He attempted to put his own tenure in a good light and took the opportunity to make an assessment of the island's governors during his time in Jamaica, though he seemed anxious to cloak them in obscurity. Lindsay begins with his first years in the island, saying:

> In 1759 and 1760, his honour H—y M—r [Henry Moore] was a regular attendant at church – I say nothing of his religious principles – but as the first representative of royalty amongst us, he considered public religion, and under the forms of England, to be an important part of the constitution of England, to which he was, as Governour publicly instructed to be attentive – and whatever it was, right or wrong, 'twas his part *ex officio,* to support and enforce its observance.[84]

These were the years when Lindsay was serving as curate at the St Catherine parish church, and when he preached on the earthquake.

Lindsay claims that in Moore's time, "The public worship, was then attended to by all ranks of citizens – it matter'd not that the rector of the parish [Venn] had left the metropolis to a curate [Lindsay], the church was crouded." Further, he says, "The public officers – every man in public life, seem'd to vie with each other who should make the most constant appearance – even families of colour, were in the fashionable rage." Without identifying himself, Lindsay says that in 1760 or 1761 he made a special effort to instruct the free coloured in Spanish Town, but that by the 1780s they only "attend the public worship when conveniency serves them" and remain "as ignorant as pagans can well be, in every spiritual and mystical doctrine". This assessment is contrary to the view that by the middle of the eighteenth century the free coloured and black people of Jamaica were "all Christian". Reflecting arguments he advanced in relation to trade with Senegal and the encouragement of consumption, Lindsay asserts that this fashion was such that "silk-mercers, drapers, and every dependant on commerse and taste, profited from the growth of religion and orderly behaviour". There was also a good effect on the stability of the community, to the advantage of the whites, Lindsay argues: "Even the safety of our persons, and strength of our islands security, was supported from this very quarter – for while the Governour went to church . . . our militia was kept up and in readiness to be called upon, on the sudden."[85]

Moore was followed by William Henry Lyttleton, who was governor from 1762 to 1766. Lyttleton travelled to Jamaica on HMS *Deptford*, the ship that carried one of John Harrison's famous chronometers designed to ascertain longitude, and indeed Lyttleton was a witness to the daily winding of the watch. The watch was tested in Jamaica at the end of January 1762. No doubt Lindsay heard of this great event but he was then mostly in Vere, about to be married in May, and how much he knew of Lyttleton is uncertain. Regardless, in 1788 he declares boldly: "His Excelly Wm Hy Lit—ton . . . a strict attendant on the church; and most examplarily decent, in all the devoirs of a ruler: and during his administration, the house of prayer, was throng'd both weekdays and Sundays."

Although Lindsay offers high praise of Moore, the creole of Vere, he quickly dismisses Roger Hope Elletson, lieutenant-governor in 1766 and 1767, saying: "I speak not of his Honr. Rog. H—pe Ell—n: for being a native here and a planter, he seldom spent a Sunday here, in Spainish Town – and indeed his short administration, leaves me little to say of him, in the matter of example." Elletson was a third-generation Jamaican, born in 1727 and educated at Eton and Cambridge. Whatever his attitude to religion, he had support from an Assembly that had wrecked the administration of the righteous Lyttleton. Next came Sir William Trelawny, governor from 1768 to 1772, whom Lindsay calls "a most punctual man in every species or point of duty: and rigidly supported every means which tended to the advancement of every thing honourable and becoming in a community of English Protestants. If he was not a *pious* Governour, he wore the semblance of a *religious* one: and religion was honoured and throve under his auspicious administration."[86]

The real decline came after the death of Trelawny, with the tenure of Lieutenant-Colonel John Dalling, lieutenant-governor from 1772 to 1774. At this point in Lindsay's manuscript the identifier "His Honour Coll. D—g" is crossed out and no alternative offered. Lindsay's text would have said only that following the "much lamented death" of Trelawny "came the first curse this community met with, both in faith and morals. . . . a gentleman who, not only had not religion, but was deficient in a political disguise, to hide the unseemly want of it". According to Lindsay, Dalling "never went to church unless invited to a funeral". Even worse,

> the great festivals of the church, which governors, as such, had never before neglected, but always attended in the highest magnificence of state – even the national fast days for storms and earthquakes – were all by him equally neglected – while

he gave himself up with extream readiness, to every species of dissipation and bad example before, and accompanied by, a people, whose dissolute manners, ought rather to have been judiciously led, by the winning insinuations, and attractive charm of a gay and lively superior, into the ways of industry – not the extravagances of apeing too genteel and fashionable a life.[87]

Following the deplorable Dalling, relief came in the form of Sir Basil Keith, governor from 1774 to 1777. At first Lindsay had some doubts about Keith's orthodoxy, because "born in Scotland, and brought up in the bosom of Presbeterianism, he might perhaps have been naturally such (or partly such) by inclination". However, says Lindsay, "being the representative of a king, whose etiquete as such, is constantly to pay court to the King of Kings before he expects a subject to pay court to him, he affectionately followed royal example; and when in health constantly led the way to church. And religion which had droop'd with Coll. D—g, came again into fashion." Keith saw the island through the first months of the American Revolution, steering the colonists away from any rash thoughts of rebellion.[88]

The early death of Keith saw the return of Dalling, "the former scourge to religion, . . . when the worshipers of God, turn'd immediately to their former fashionable neglects". This time Dalling was promoted to governor, a position he held from 1777 to 1781. Lindsay introduces himself here in the third person, reflecting that "it is very remarkable, that altho the same person ministered now as rector, who in 1760 gave satisfaction as curate: yet was there now, no more any church attenders on *weekdays* – and soon after the *prayers even on Sunday evenings*, was also obliged to be given up". A soldier, Dalling's main interest during this period was the prosecution of the war with the northern colonies and its effects on Jamaica, most immediately the threat posed by American privateers, and later famine. The Assembly believed he was jeopardizing the island's security, exposing it to capture by the Spanish. Dalling was also haunted by personal enemies – political rather than spiritual – and eventually the imperial government came to see him as incompetent and he was dismissed.[89]

Next came Major-General Archibald Campbell, lieutenant-governor from 1781 to 1783 and then governor until 1784. Lindsay observes that Campbell was "another Scotchman – and perhaps a Presbiterean too – but oh! sad reverse": rather than following the example set by Keith, he "followed closely the heels of . . . his predecessor and intirely forgot, that his *duty was constitutionally to support the established religion of his country* – whatever *his own* might be – and his country was Jamaica while Governor there". Campbell, another career soldier, had been badly wounded at Quebec in 1758 but went on to fight in India; he returned to Scotland in 1774 to represent Stirling Burghs, Lindsay's stamping ground and the parliamentary seat held earlier by

Haldane. Compared to Dalling, Campbell proved a strong leader, with military as well as administrative skills.[90]

Finally, and outliving Lindsay, Lieutenant-Governor Brigadier-General Alured Clarke occupied King's House from 1784 to 1790. Lindsay declares him to be "a gentleman extreamly ready to fulfill every part of his duty, and I am told that a desire of shewing respect to God and his worship, is not by any means wanting in him – but perhaps he is affraid, religion has left us so long and is now so far gone, that any endeavours or good example of his, will avail but little". Lindsay thinks Clarke should make an effort, believing that "he might yet, give a fashionable turn, towards religion and virtue amongst us".[91]

Concluding his review of religious observance, Lindsay finds that "*religion in Jamaica is in and out of fashion as its Governors shall be pleased to lead the way*". He believed the pattern was not confined to Spanish Town but repeated across the parishes. From his point of view, writing in 1788, Lindsay found both the security of the island and interest in religion "*in a horrid decline*" and called on public officers to set a better example: "Those judges, barristers and magistrates – those Privy Councelors and Assembly men, who *would not* be *unfashionable*, while under the view of the court, must needs also carry back the fashionable modes into their several families in the country."[92] This argument was directed at ensuring the security and continuity of slave society rather than instilling fear of punishment at the hands of a vengeful God. By 1788 Lindsay had spent almost thirty years in Jamaica and his concerns had shifted over time. By then he had been definitively recruited to the side of the plantocracy and the cause of proslavery ideology. The result was a growing gap between what he thought and what he preached, and between what he could say from the pulpit and what he was willing to argue on paper under the veil of anonymity.

Deists, Dissenters and Freethinkers

In his *Memoirs* of 1757 Lindsay found an opportunity to put into the mouths of others ideas that perhaps reflected his inner ruminations. These occur in the letter sent by Chevalier (John) Hughson in 1692 to the proposed teacher of his son Thomas in Leyden. It is in this letter that the Chevalier recalls the suffering he experienced in consequence of his own father's "unfortunate principles" and desires that Thomas be "educated so as to have his own principles, and not his father's". He has accepted Calvinism from his father but believes equally that "had he been a member of the church of Rome, of the Jewish synagogue, or a follower of Mahomet, I should have thought theirs the purest worship, and their tenets most rational and proper". Thomas is not to be brought up in the beliefs of any particular church but simply exposed to "those general maxims in divinity, which are the uncontroverted foundation of all religions, and ecclesiastical bodies", so as to ensure "knowledge of a Supreme Being, and a veneration for religion in general, . . .; being sensible that the good of individuals and society itself depends upon it, and that no clear stream of virtue can possibly flow (in a Christian country) which proceeds not from the pure fountain of true religion".[93] Here Lindsay rehearses relativist, theistic views that he could not announce from the pulpit, even in so marginally a "Christian country" as Jamaica.

By the 1760s, when Lindsay began preaching in Spanish Town, the Church of England had emerged from a long period of intense religious conflict. Denominations labelled Old Dissent were now on the wane, the Deists had been neutralized, Evangelicalism domesticated and Roman Catholicism diminished as a threat to church and state. Extreme forms of scepticism were less common. A broad compromise had been reached in which true religion – directed at ensuring moral order and sociability – was easily tolerated by freethinkers so long as belief was placed on a "rational" basis and observance distanced from the supernatural. Even David Hume, whose objective in *A Treatise of Human Nature* (1739–40) was to build a godless "science of man", had to work out ways to live with orthodoxy.[94] Although realist philosophies were essential to concepts of scientific measurement and proof, as well as the inner logic of nature's laws and perhaps even nature's God, the Enlightenment notion that humankind is itself responsible for its social organization and values (including religious beliefs), rather than their being the creation of a vengeful God, proved sufficient challenge.[95] The Anglicanism of Lindsay's days sailed a middle course, tolerating a good deal of honest doubt and alternately giving blows to both popery and enthusiastic dissent.

If these were liberal, modern values, it was the new brands of dissent associated with enthusiasm that became the common enemy, not only for Anglican orthodoxy but equally for deism and sceptical rationalism. When the Methodists burst on the English religious scene at the end of the 1730s, they were condemned both for their belief in instantaneous conversion and for their "enthusiasm", described by critical contemporaries as "a kind of a religious phrensy, that mistakes the dictates of an inflamed imagination, the vapours of a troubled brain, for the operation of a divine possession, the effects of an immediate inspiration". In its Methodist incarnation, enthusiasm replaced both the Calvinist notion of election and the sociability of Anglican theology with belief in justification by faith. Even Wesley struggled to distinguish appropriate forms of enthusiasm from those that were not. He regularly protested his loyalty to the Church of England, but Methodists were accused of destabilizing church and state.[96]

Believers were faced by a variety of forms of doubt. Free-thinking depended on reason and evidence, particularly in deciding matters of religious belief, but the label was commonly used by the more orthodox of the clergy to castigate opponents of every stripe. Most often free-thinking was equated with deism – belief in a single supreme being and a system of natural religion which valued reason over faith – that had its clearest expression in John Toland's *Christianity Not Mysterious* of 1696, which attacked both the doctrine of revelation and ideas of the supernatural. Deism challenged the historicity of characters and events in the scriptural narrative, including miracles (such as the Resurrection) which had long been deployed as fundamental proof that Jesus was the Messiah.[97] Most sceptics of Lindsay's time came to be associated with deism or a rationalistic variety of theism, often with the hope of establishing a universal religion stripped of all forms of particularism, mystery and supernaturalism. Some adhered to a belief in one true religion, tracing a continuous prophetic lineage through Adam, Noah, Moses, Christ and Mohammed.[98] Those who remained closer to Christianity aligned themselves with Arminians (who rejected predestination and believed all might be saved), Unitarians (who rejected the Trinity and believed in the unity of God) or Socinians (who asserted that Jesus was man, not God, and that nothing in faith can be beyond reason, yet wished to be regarded as Christians and took the Bible seriously).[99]

Christian thought provided the fundamental framework for Enlightenment philosophy, and most Enlightenment philosophers were brought up in the faith. Not a few of them – Hume, Turgot, Diderot and Franklin, for example – had been directed at one time towards a career in the church. The consequence was that religious belief, and particularly Christianity, proved a preoccupation. Religion in its particularist, intolerant, prejudiced, fanatical, enthusiastic and superstitious forms was subjected to intense critique and irreverent parody. Deists and their allies mocked the absurd claims of the Scriptures and the parochialism of Christianity. The ideas of inspiration and revelation were prime targets. Notions of a "chosen people" and providential predestination were laughed at. Miracles were seen as violations of the universal laws of nature. Letting go completely was too difficult for most, however. Thus Franklin clung to a Christian theism while Hume stopped just short of denying the possibility that an amorphous intelligent power had formed the universe.[100]

Some critics see deism as simply one element in a long tradition of Anglican compromise between the claims of revelation and reason, but this was a compromise that might be associated with a commitment to grace and priestcraft or alternatively lead easily to full-blown unbelief. Powerful arguments against God and revelation were well-known by the seventeenth century. The heat of the debate died down during the Enlightenment and extreme versions of doubt and free-thinking gradually became less popular. However, if deism had faded from view by the time of Lindsay's death, so too had Anglican orthodoxy. As Martin Fitzpatrick puts it, "Enlightenment religion can be characterised as rational, tolerant and non-mysterious and the Enlightenment God as a beneficent Newtonian hero who had designed the world as a system of benevolence."[101]

The Church of England in Jamaica, as the established church and an arm of imperial government, had no great difficulty in accommodating doubters so long as they served their public purpose. Thus, although John Wolcot (1738–1819) admitted to deist doubts when encouraged by Governor Sir William Trelawny to take orders, the governor was unperturbed. He simply told Wolcot "not to return with the hypocritical solemnity of a priest" and observed that he had recently "bestowed a good living on a parson who believes not all he preaches and what he really believes he is afraid to preach". A reluctant priest, Wolcot occupied the living of Vere from 1770 to 1772, preaching to a small, occasional congregation. He soon "relaxed into apathy and indolence" and joined the Vere plantocracy shooting ring-tailed pigeons on the bay, much like Lindsay before him. Following the death of Trelawny in 1773, Wolcot returned to England, where he enjoyed success as a poet under the pseudonym Peter Pindar.[102] Lindsay might have hoped for such literary acclaim, but he situated himself firmly in Jamaican society through marriage and orientation and maintained the struggle to relate his theology and philosophy to everyday experience.

Living through the age of Hume and Wesley – an age of reason and enthusiasm – Lindsay grappled with these ideas and attitudes, as a follower rather than a leader. While he remained firm in his ecclesiastical position, there were limits to the public expression of any scepticism that might have grown in his mind. From the pulpit in his early days in Jamaica, Lindsay had hard words for freethinkers. He addressed them directly in his straight-talking Spanish Town sermon of 1760: "Hear me, thou vain, blasphemous pretender to *Free-thinking;* thou saucy, grumbling mortal who ridiculously appliest thy poor insignificant line of Reason to fathom the infinite depths of God's council". Lindsay dared the freethinker to go home to his closet and there pray: "*Great and awful majesty, infinite, incomprehensible in all thy ways, judge of all things; I thank thee, for that thou hast given me grace above the ordinary measure, with a knowledge so celestial, that I detest as contrary to thine honour and dangerous to the welfare of my soul, those blasphemous writings called the Bible* – I say, go to your knees and pronounce these words if thou darest!"[103]

PROSLAVERY PRIEST

In 1760 Lindsay was aghast at the way in which the island's "little *great men*" proclaimed their "learning and knowledge". They might not be able to tell where it was they got their education, he says, "yet with a wag of their finger, they can knock down all Gospel evidence: and having heard of it, if not read Lord Bolingbroke's *Philosophy*, with a cunning sarcastic sneer, they make no bones to level the writings of Moses and the prophets with imposture and romance". In Jamaica there were many who, "poor and untutored at their beginnings, when waxen fat in affluence, vilify all holy men, and jest with every holy purpose: seeking thereby to make a shew of knowledge; and get the ignorant to admire their shining parts – choosing rather to have it believed, that their great wealth and wide extended possessions were amassed by their own skill and penetration, than to pay their bounden thanks to God, by whose especial gift alone they either live or prosper".[104]

Exploiting a rich vein of imagery, Lindsay tells his congregation: "We must not only be Christians by profession, because called to, and washed by water, in the mystical laver of Christianity; but we must be also Christians in practise, washed in the laver of real regeneration: and led as by the spirit of God thro' the streams of the Gospel, let its windings and intricate meanders be ever so mysterious."[105] Situated to the side of the healing stream were those troublesome souls who, says Lindsay, "to suit their inclination, put what they call the *Religion of Nature* (tho' more fitly called the *Religion of Convenience*) in the room of every Gospel method that leads to happiness". On the other side of the stream Lindsay found those "whom in charity I would place in the light of the young man in the Gospel, who was not far from the kingdom of heaven". Such people struggled towards righteousness but found "moral rectitude or justice" too hard, "everything centering in their niggardly hoards" and lacking any "spark of charity". These too might claim to believe "every article of our Christian faith" and "have no objection to obedience, provided the act may but suit their conveniency".[106]

In this way Lindsay sought to dismiss the idea of "natural religion" by associating it with opportunism and preoccupation with the things of the world, which were allowed to get in the way of true faith. The idea went deeper, however, and connected comfortably with more fundamental brands of doubt. Pope, for example, sought to promote an "ethical naturalism" in which happiness naturally inhered in God's creation. It was a cosmic scheme in which human beings had no reason to question their place in the order of things, because they had been so placed by God, whose purposes were beyond comprehension. Hume, on the other hand, declared the scheme reductionist, dominated by "the idea of a blind nature, impregnated by a great vivifying principle, and pouring forth from her lap, without discernment or parental care, her maimed and abortive children". Lindsay opposed the "modern moralists" who, he said, encouraged the view that good works and moral virtues might in themselves be enough to achieve salvation.[107]

What Did John Lindsay Believe?

Publicly, Lindsay declared his belief in the existence of God and Jesus Christ; in the authority of the sacred Scriptures; the need for man to worship God; the need for religion, together with church and clergy; the reality of sin and the need for a Saviour; the living of a good and godly life, in addition to simple belief, as necessary to salvation; and the hope of eternal life for those who love God. He rejected strict interpretations of the doctrine of predestination (though he did accept that God might be vengeful); dismissed the belief that salvation could be gained either by simple faith alone or through mere good works and moral virtues; had no time for religious enthusiasm; and denounced freethinkers. He makes no mention of the Trinity or the Holy Spirit, or of Christ as the son of God, though he does speak once of "God in Christ". He refers twice to Satan and once to the Devil but he seems less certain about the reality and character of hell, and his picture of heaven is vague at best.[108] He does not speak of the Resurrection of Christ and seems little interested in miracles. He might almost have been a Unitarian. Although he saw the presence of the Almighty in nature, he rejected natural religion and believed that reason can go only so far. Ultimately it was necessary to accept that God's ways are unknowable, a mystery to mortal man.

These were Lindsay's central beliefs as expressed in pronouncements from the Spanish Town pulpit between 1760 and 1777. They represent views common within the Church of England, which thought itself supreme in religion, the established church. It was the mission of the church to support the British state and the social order expressed in the British imperial project. Yet in spite of its authority and spiritual power, the beliefs of its priests and congregations faced threats from within and without. Questioning the inspiration and authority of Scripture undermined a view of the natural and spiritual world formerly founded on wonder and credulity, while the moral basis of varieties of social oppression was to place the church in opposition to radical dissent and political progress. Lindsay found himself caught up in this whirlwind of ideas and movements, both in relation to his curiosity about the natural world in which he lived, in Jamaica, and in his reactionary response to the emergence of attacks on slavery, all of which carried him to a new position in relation to the authority of Scripture and the secular history of humanity.

John Lindsay's religious ideas contrasted with those of his Evangelical father, Henry, whose essential theology can be similarly gleaned from sermons he preached between 1733 and 1737. Henry Lindsay's system of belief was not far from that adhered to by some of the more enthusiastic branches of evangelicalism, the ideas of George Whitefield and John Wesley.[109] In a sermon preached before the Church of Scotland synod of Perth and Stirling, Henry Lindsay sets out clearly the foundations of his faith, inveighing against "*atheism, infidelity* and *prophanity*" and deploring the "*youth of better fashion*" who had lost respect for the sacred. Many of these, he feared, had been led astray by books "wherein *Christianity* itself hath been openly attacked, our *dear Redeemer* . . . robbed of his *divine nature*, and degraded into the rank of a creature". He feared that the preaching of the Gospel had been replaced by "*abstracted schemes of morality*". Teaching Christ crucified, salvation through God's grace and the Holy Spirit might be "by some despised, by others laughed at, as enthusiasm, or *unintelligible jargon*", said Henry Lindsay, but they remained "the chief subjects of Christianity".[110]

In another sermon, preached in Edinburgh in 1734, Henry Lindsay discourses on "Christ's advocateship", emphasizing the relationship of child to father and of humanity to God the Father – "born of God" and "begotten again to a lively hope through the resurrection of Christ Jesus from the dead".[111] In 1736 he preached "*against the infidelity of the age*". Referring directly to "the Deists", he takes to task the "multitude among us who pretend to polite learning" and who direct their "sarcasms" against divine revelation and "the preaching of the Cross of Christ". All would be lost, he declared, if the church drifted towards teaching morality and lost sight of "the great end of the Gospel, the salvation of sinners" through "Christ crucified".[112] These sermons, preached when John was still a young child, foreshadowed the separation that was to come between Evangelical father and Moderate son.

CHAPTER SEVEN

Natural History

LINDSAY'S ECCLESIASTICAL DUTIES, his sermon writing and his reading left him a good deal of time to explore the land in which he lived. Although he began his Jamaican journey in the urban setting of Spanish Town, he spent most of the 1760s in the rural parishes of Vere and St Thomas in the Vale (figure 6.1). Vere included the barren limestone promontory of Portland Point as well as sugar and cotton plantations on the fertile plain around Alley. It was also famous for its extensive fields of Guinea corn (sorghum) and, in former times, indigo. The southern boundary of Vere stretched along an extended and varied seacoast, spreading to the west into parts of what was to become the parish of Manchester, largely uninhabited in Lindsay's time. St Thomas in the Vale was one of the island's rare interior parishes, lacking a coastal boundary. Large sugar plantations occupied the broad valley floor known as Sixteen-Mile-Walk, while forest clothed the encircling mountains, including towering Mount Diablo. Regular rain on the mountains fed numerous springs, while heavy falls could create violent flooding. On many mornings the vale was covered by a dense atmospheric fog.[1]

These two contrasting parishes enabled Lindsay to investigate the plants and animals of the sea as well as those of plain, mountain and stream. His pastoral duties took him through all these environments in all seasons, and other travels enabled him to see even more of the countryside.[2] He was in his thirties, in apparent good health, curious about the world around him and in need of projects to occupy his mind and display his various talents.

Lindsay's choice to illustrate the natural world was not eccentric. Natural history had become established as the "universal British pastime, if not the national sport" and declared by the *Critical Review* of 1763 "the favourite study of the times". There was a craze for books on natural history, as Lindsay was well aware.[3] He had already prepared drawings of plants and animals for the engravings included in his *Voyage*, published in 1759. In Jamaica he followed in the footsteps of several illustrious natural historians. The best known of all was Hans Sloane, whose *Voyage to the Islands Madera, Barbados, Nieves, S. Christophers and Jamaica, with the Natural History of the Last of those Islands* had been published in two large volumes, the first in 1707 and the second in 1725. There was also Patrick Browne, whose *Civil and Natural History of Jamaica* was published in 1756, just three years before Lindsay arrived in the island. Unpublished until 1770 but well known in Jamaica were the collections and manuscripts of Henry Barham, Anthony Robinson and the brothers Robert and Edward Long. Within this substantial but limited field, Lindsay had reason to feel he might make a significant contribution.

"Elegancies of Jamaica"

In December 1770 "the reverend Mr. John Lindsay" petitioned the House of Assembly of Jamaica, stating that he had "been engaged, for eleven years last past, in the expensive and labourious exercise of collecting drawings of the most curious and beautiful plants, trees, fruits, birds, insects, fishes &c. of this island". He had undertaken this task largely because of "the deficiencies and incorrectness which to him appeared to be, in the descriptive drawings of former collectors of this kind". Appealing to the creole enthusiasm of Jamaica's lawmakers, Lindsay opines that "nothing can more tend to the satisfaction of the learned, or give the world more just and agreeable ideas of this island, and the West-Indies in general, than to see before them a complete proportioned representation of those beautiful articles in the animal and vegetable part of the creation, which most particularly adorn and characterise our southern climates". He argues further that "the mutilated sections of botanic writers, in their plates and figures, the petitioner, with great deference, apprehends can give no general satisfaction; and flatters himself he has struck out such a clear description in the forms, proportions, and colouring of his designs, which are represented entire, and actually drawn from nature, that if published, will yield a satisfaction to foreigners in general, and prove an honour to this island in particular".[4]

What Lindsay wanted from the Assembly was assistance to bring his work to publication. He does not say exactly how many of the drawings are complete but declares that "his collection will consist of upwards of two hundred copper-plates, of very peculiar workmanship, in two volumes of royal folio" (620 x 480 mm), the publication of which "will be attended with great expence". Lindsay concludes his petition by "praying that this house will cause such inquiry and inspection to be made of the premises, as may be necessary, that such report may be made thereof, as to them may seem meet". A committee was formed; it reported two days later, stating that it had "examined his drawings of the plants, animals, birds, fishes and insects, of this island; and are of the opinion, that it is a work of great labour and ingenuity; that the drawings in general are well adapted to convey a proper idea of what they are intended to represent, and will merit the attention of the curious in natural history". The House agreed to the report, implicitly declining to contribute to the cost of publishing.[5]

Rebuffed by the Assembly, Lindsay carried his volumes of natural history with him when he sailed to Britain on board the *Lady Juliana* in April 1772. He obtained an introduction to Sir Joseph Banks from the antiquary Robert Ramsay, "who suggested Banks would be interested to see the paintings". The letter is preserved in Banks's papers, but what transpired is unknown. Lindsay may have carried his "Elegancies" volumes back to Jamaica without Banks or Robertson ever seeing them.[6]

The status of the work in 1770 is uncertain. Four bound volumes are known but there seem once to have been at least five. The surviving volumes are located in the Natural History Section of the Bristol Museum and Art Gallery in the United Kingdom. On the spine of one is lettered "Elegancies of Jamaica/Lindsay", and on the others "Vol. V/Lindsay Drawings", "Vol VI/Lindsay Drawings", and "Vol VII/Lindsay Drawings". How these relate to a possible volumes one to four, or to any missing volume, is not clear.[7] The "Elegancies" volume has inside its front cover a bookplate that identifies it as a product of Spanish Town: "Lowry and Sherlock, Printers, Booksellers and Stationers, At their shop in Spanish Town, make and sell all sorts of books at the lowest prices. Books bound, gilt and lettered, as neat as in any part of Europe." In this volume the pages are not of uniform size, and it appears the various sheets were bound together after 1770 by Lowry and Sherlock. There are two drawings dated 1771 and another two dated 1775, as well as one from 1758, the year before Lindsay reached Jamaica. The last is of the club-like *Dracaena draco*, or dragon tree, of the Canary Islands – called by Lindsay "the Arbor Dracco of Teneriff" – and it matches closely the same plant included in a plate from his published *Voyage* (number 5 in figure 5.3). He had seen it growing in a garden on the edge of the town of Santa Cruz.[8]

How did Lindsay's works on Jamaican natural history come to be in Bristol rather than remaining in Jamaica or being sent perhaps to Edinburgh? Two of the volumes have bookplates stating that they came as the "Bequest of A. Broughton M.D. 1796" to the Bristol Library Society. The Society recorded its thanks to "Messrs Lowbridge and Richard Bright for their very liberal offer of taking upon themselves the settlement of the freight of four cases of books and fossils the gift of the late Dr Broughton". Lowbridge Bright (1741–1818) and his cousin Richard (1754–1840) were wealthy Bristol merchants who traded with the West Indies; Richard was a Unitarian and a founder of the Bristol Philosophical Society.[9] Later the volumes became part of the collections of the Bristol Museum; for a time it was believed they had been lost, destroyed by bombing during the Second World War.[10] It was only after 1978 that bibliographers became aware that the works had survived.[11]

The "Elegancies" volume contains 121 drawings, 105 of them dated. The largest number from one year (twenty-nine) are attributed to 1769, the year before Lindsay approached the Assembly for assistance to publish. He made forty-six in the three years 1766–68 but only two in 1770. After his rebuff he effectively stopped. A similar pattern applies to the other three volumes. Some of the drawings in the "Elegancies" volume are simple pencil sketches, others are inked and a good proportion have been completed as watercolours. They are not bound in chronological sequence, and it appears that Lindsay decided on their order when he was compiling his text. Often the text was written some time after the drawing was made, and many drawings lack text or even titles.[12]

Only one of Lindsay's volumes carries a descriptive title. This is volume six, which states that its subject is "Insects and Amphibia" and includes an incomplete list of the contents. The other volumes are untitled but carefully organized. Volume five is devoted to birds, volume seven to fish, crustaceans and other marine life, and the "Elegancies" volume to plants. A basic principle of selection was that the species should be endemic or indigenous to Jamaica, but Lindsay did illustrate a small number of exotics. For example, he included an (undated) drawing of the coffee tree (*Coffea arabica*), which was a recent introduction to the island and relatively unimportant in Lindsay's time.[13]

Lindsay's 1766 drawing of the cotton bush (*Gossypium purpurascens*) was accompanied by a diagram of the planting layout of a cotton field as well as an unusually detailed drawing, dated 1767, of a cotton gin, showing the mechanisms of the gin and three black workers engaged in different tasks (plate 4). These drawings were made towards the end of Lindsay's time in Vere, the principal cotton-growing parish of the island, and reflected his close observation of the agricultural world around him. On the other hand, he ignored the major field crop of his region, sugar cane, partly on the principle that it was an introduced plant and partly because as a grass it was not particularly curious. Sloane similarly chose to illustrate the "curious" cotton gin rather than the sugar works, the latter constructed somewhat in the manner of a cathedral but suffused with sticky heat and sickly steam – nearer hell

Plate 1 Francis Williams, circa 1740. Unknown artist, oil on canvas. ©V&A Images/Victoria and Albert Museum, London.

Plate 2 Vere parish church, 1984. Photo ©Ray Chen.

Plate 3 Spanish Town cathedral, 1967. Photo: B.W. Higman.

Plate 4 Cotton gin, 1767. Lindsay, "Elegancies", 77. Bristol Museum and Art Gallery.

Fig. 1 the cotton gin, with its foot frame, wheels and rollers; Fig. 2 [the gin] bed; Fig. 3 perspective of a gin compleat, with all its apparatus; Fig. 4 a view of the method of hanging up cotton bags to be stove: A gin frame; B foot frame; C bed [of gin]; D feeding-board on which the stone-cotton is laid to be put to the rollers; E side jarrs, to keep the two rollers exactly over each other and in a proper distance from each other, by the means of circular notches (ZZZ Fig. 2) so that the stone cotton Q being sucked in by the rollers, is spew'd out as at P, leaving the seeds to fall down by themselves at O; F middle-jarrs . . . to keep the rollers from opening or yealding too much in the middle; G square pieces, that coming through mortices, by the means of screws or wedges (gggg) keep the jars fix'd, as a pair of nippers or vice; H wheels; I rollers, made of hard wood, and faintly notch'd long ways, or flutted, as it were, with the point of a sharp nail, the better to suck in the cotton; K [wheel and roller]; L small contrivance fix'd with a pin about 10 or 12 inches from the center of the wheel, to which the cords MM (figs 1 and 3) are fix'd and support the foot-frame by the two holes bb. And by which, crank ways, the rollers are set into motion: and as may be observed by MM fig 3, one roller turning to the right the other to the left; N a little space left between the rollers and feeding board for the cotton seeds to fall throw when seperated by the rollers from the cotton; O seeds falling down; P [ginned cotton] falling down into the Bag S; Q cotton with the seeds as laid on the feeding board and kept to the rollers by the opperator R; W basket with cotton V, placed for the use of the genner X.

Plate 5 Flowering hedge plants, 1767. Lindsay, "Elegancies", 166. Bristol Museum and Art Gallery.

Plate 6 Orchid (*Oncidium luridum*), 1769. Lindsay, "Elegancies", 279. Bristol Museum and Art Gallery. Identification based on A. Gloudon and C. Tobisch, *Orchids of Jamaica* (Kingston: University of the West Indies Press, 1995), 157.

Plate 7 Prickly pear tree, 1767. Lindsay, "Elegancies", 262. Bristol Museum and Art Gallery.

Plate 8 Strainer, 1768. Lindsay, "Elegancies", 200. Bristol Museum and Art Gallery.

Plate 9 Indean silk shrub, pods, 1767. Lindsay, "Elegancies", 114. Bristol Museum and Art Gallery.

Plate 10 Flying insects, 1762 and 1765. Lindsay, Drawings, vol. 6, 89. Bristol Museum and Art Gallery. Common grasshopper: (a) flying, (b) springing or jumping and (c) at rest; (d) Macacca beetle; (f–h) large newsmonger; (i) bishop; (k) brown cuckold or capricorn; (l) spotted capricorn or cuckold; (o) light green money fly or capricorn; (p) black money fly, mottled with green; (q) brown money fly; (r) light brown money fly; (s) large light brown money fly; (t) golden lady-fly or herold; (u) orange lady-fly.

Plate 11 Catechism, half-eaten by insects, 1770. Lindsay, Drawings, vol. 6, 95. Bristol Museum and Art Gallery.

Plate 12 Portuguese man-of-war, 1769. Lindsay, Drawings, vol. 7, 30. Bristol Museum and Art Gallery.

Plate 13 Jamaican red macaw, 1765. Lindsay, Drawings, vol. 5. Bristol Museum and Art Gallery. Identification by Ivan Goodbody.

Plate 14 July-flower tree, 1765. Lindsay, "Elegancies", 83. Bristol Museum and Art Gallery.

Plate 15 Papilios of the day, 1766. Lindsay, Drawings, vol. 6, 32. Bristol Museum and Art Gallery. Showing underside: (5) "dark brown butterfly, with double peeked wing" (*Marpesia chiron* Fabricius); (6) "dark brown butterfly, with azure and orange clouded wings"; (7) "large black butterfly with yellow spots" (*Papilio thoas melonius* Rothschild and Jordan); (8) "Lappet wingd black butterfly, with green clouds and spots" *(Graphium marcellinus* Doubleday); (9) "dark sea green butterfly, with yellow clouds" (*Battus polydamas jamaicensis* Rothschild and Jordan). Identifications based on F. Martin Brown and Bernard Heineman, *Jamaica and Its Butterflies* (London: E.W. Classey, 1972).

Plate 16 Portrait of James Ramsay by Carl Frederik von Breda, 1789. ©National Portrait Gallery, London.

than heaven. Lindsay did include corn (*Zea mays*) and Guinea corn (*Sorghum bicolor*), which grew abundantly in Vere; the first of these was indigenous and the second from Africa.[14] He devoted much more space to beautiful flowering plants, from lilies to cacti, bromeliads, ferns and orchids. His objective was not economic botany but rather promotion of the wonders of Jamaica's natural life.

Some of Lindsay's watercolours were constructed decoratively rather than being designed to depict the details of individual specimens. In 1767, his final year in the parish of Vere, he painted a "collection" of "the most common hedge flowers" that bloomed between December and May. Because "they grow promiscuously together", says Lindsay, "I have also thrown them together in the delineation, as a sort of representation of this island in the winter season". In order to achieve this arrangement, he festoons the flowers around a scene showing riders and a carriage passing along a road beside a church (plate 5). Lindsay does describe each of the flowers but with relatively little botanical detail. In other cases he seemed to lack the detailed knowledge needed to say anything specific, as, for example, his several images of orchids and bromeliads. His drawings are sufficiently precise, however, to enable identification (plate 6). In referring to his 1767 painting of a cactus (plate 7) – *Opuntia spinosissima*, as determined by Fawcett and Rendle in 1923 – Lindsay wonders whether "this curious plant" is the same as specimens named differently by Linnaeus, Sloane and Browne. He does not attempt to resolve the question but emphasizes the plant's spiny character and calls it simply "the prickly pear tree". Lindsay found this specimen growing among rocks at Milk River Bath, in Vere, where he went occasionally to take the waters for his health. His image places the cactus in a desolate rocky landscape.

Examples of Lindsay's attempts to provide more detailed botanical description at the same time as offering attractive images occur in his accounts of the loofah (*Luffa cylindrica*, as determined by Fawcett and Rendle in 1924) and the Indian silk tree. Lindsay calls the loofah, painted in 1768, "the strainer" and notes simply that when dried the fruit can serve to strain lemon juice and the like, whereas he devotes several pages to his study of the plant, flower and fruit (plate 8). He commits even more pages and separate drawings to the "Indean silk shrub" (*Calotropis*), drawn in 1767, paying particular attention to the pods (plate 9). At the end of this lengthy description Lindsay reflects on "the wonderful mechanism of this plant" and the fact that it has been put to no use by man or beast. Believing that the "Almighty Architect" created nothing in vain, Lindsay predicts that its "higher purpose" will in due course become known.

Although the volumes of Lindsay's natural history are organized in a broadly systematic manner, he seems not to have attempted a general introduction. He marvelled at the beauty and curiosity of the plants and animals he selected for illustration and description, but his aim was to reproduce as exactly as he could what he saw, only occasionally providing an exotic or fantastic backdrop. He made few explicit statements about the hand of God in Creation and more often referred to the role of "nature". For example, he says of the "large newsmonger" (not to be confused, as by Patrick Browne, with the common tumble-turd) that it was "by Nature designd" to carry burdens (plate 10). For the "quicker and more easy management of its body, Nature has placed (by way of rudder) the first pair of legs under the thorax", says Lindsay, and the joints of its legs are unusually crafted for their particular purposes by "the allwise Architect of Nature". With the mystery of God's ways in mind, in referring to the joints of another insect, he can only say: "for what purpose, by Nature designd, I cannot guess". In a sermon seeking to prove the existence of God, Lindsay declares that the fact is not only proclaimed in Scripture but "all nature cries aloud there is". However, he made no attempt to advance a seventeenth-century model in which the prime purpose of observing the God-created natural world was to learn God's lessons and draw from it spiritual guidance.[15] Only in the middle of the nineteenth century did the notion become well established that the natural world could be understood without reference to the guiding hand of God. Lindsay lived in a transitional time when European thinkers were wrestling with the problem of how properly to see the role of God in nature, and how to express it.

A telling image is that in which Lindsay precisely replicates the typography of the title page of *The Scripture Catechist: or, The Whole Religion of a Christian: Being a Full Explanation of the Church Catechism; Containing, a Comprehensive Body of Practical Divinity*, a spiritual guide "for the use of families" prepared by Clement Ellis and published in London in 1738.[16] In a watercolour image dated 1770, Lindsay shows the bottom half of the page missing, eaten away by a variety of insects (plate 11). Perhaps the catechism was simply to hand and Lindsay used it to provide scale rather than his usual playing cards, but it seems equally likely that his copy had fallen victim to termites. The duck ant munches through paper and binding materials with enthusiasm, loudly enough to be heard by the horrified booklover. The cigarette beetle drills fine holes from one cover to the other. Cockroaches prefer glue.

Curiosity and beauty competed for attention, only sometimes combined in one individual. Thus Lindsay could say of the "turbutt of Jamaica" that it was "a beautiful and curious fish". The same applied to the Portuguese man-of-war and the Jamaican red macaw, a species now extinct in Jamaica (plates 12 and 13). Of the granadilla, Lindsay says it is "a favourite vine; and much cultivated by the curious: not only on account of its thick foliage, but also its aromatic scented blossom, and its agreeable fruit". The parrot or soap fish he thought "the most lovely little fish I have ever seen", saying "Nature seems here to wanton in brilliance of fancy."[17]

Generally Lindsay is content to let his drawings speak for themselves. He supplies extensive text only when he believes he is correctly describing a species for the first time or possesses significant contextual information. For example, he offers three different views of "the small black catterpillar with white and yellow ribs", saying it is "a very beautiful worm: but will more easily be expressed by the description of the pencil than the pen. To which therefore I refer the reader." In describing the "red mouth'd, or grass grunt" in his volume on fish, Lindsay notes that it is caught in quantity at Old Harbour and forms a basic food for the poor of that district, then goes on to say: "Its colouring is striped; and so various, that I shall depend more upon my pencil than my pen in the description of this, as well as of most others: and I have been so minutely exact in the description of forms, proportions, and colours that I flatter myself the figures will be sufficient enough."[18] Lindsay was justly proud of the quality of his drawings. Although some strike the modern viewer as false in respect of scale, shape or colour, many are superb and demonstrate an understanding of the internal workings of the organisms.

Only occasionally does Lindsay place his specimens in context. Most of his fish lie inert, drawn in profile. But in his 1760 drawing of "the four winged flying fish", which he saw while at sea, he places the fish within an environment of sea, shells and reeds. Similarly, his 1765 image of a turtle shows it on its back on a beach, a man poling a small boat in the background. Often there was no context to paint because the specimen was delivered to him or he collected it himself and took it home to draw. For example, "when bathing" at Millards Bay, "near Portland Pitch", he took up a tiny "sea lizzard" in a calabash of water and carried it home alive. The rare July-flower tree (*Cordia*) he first saw in the garden and fences of a Mrs ***** in Old Harbour. He "had one dug up with the best part of the root intire, about eight or nine feet high (being then but young) and had it carried to my own garden in Vere, full twenty five miles, where it soon took fresh root and is now in the perfection as describ'd by the figure annexed" drawn in 1765 (plate 14). The "small silver spider" he found in his own house and among the pineapples in his garden. He was, however, wary of the venomous "red-arsed spider".[19]

Some things were hard to find. For example, Lindsay saw the blue grouper only once but declares it "a good eating fish". Occasionally he notes that an example caught in a net was brought to him by a fisherman. He was cautious about the qualities of some of the fish he was given, as, for example, the stad-holder, which he was not sure was good eating, suggesting that he did not risk consuming what he had to draw; it might simply not have been fresh enough to eat. Clearly his enthusiasm for the curious had become known, and no doubt he offered rewards to those who plied him with what he was looking for and what seemed out of the ordinary. The extensive stretch of coastal waters that bounded Vere was well known for its fish, and Edward Long noticed that "some marine animals, extremely curious and remarkable, have been hauled ashore here by the Negroes in their seines".[20] Probably some of the people who brought specimens to Lindsay were among these observant – and curious – enslaved black people, though he never acknowledged their contributions.

Lindsay's drawings certainly seem original and drawn from nature, and indeed he claimed it was his dissatisfaction with existing works that impelled him to commence his own labours. He was not alone in criticizing or amending the work of his predecessors. Another large unpublished manuscript now found in the Bristol Museum, apparently deposited by Lowbridge Bright, is titled "A Supplement attempted or Appendix and Addendum to Sir Hans Sloane and Dr. Pat. Brown in Notes and Observations *Natural* and Moral on the Native Blacks, the Quadrupeds, Reptiles, Insects Plants Birds Fishes Air and Clime &c. of Jamaica by Rt. L'g, – Being occasional Remarks and observations from 1752 to 1762, inclusive." Its author was Robert Long (1729–75), older brother of Edward Long (1734–1813) and a friend of Dr Anthony Robinson.[21]

There is no doubt that Lindsay consulted the works of earlier writers; he referred to some of them frequently, notably "Dr Brown" – meaning Patrick Browne and his *Civil and Natural History of Jamaica* of 1756 – with whom he regularly disagreed. In describing "the cutlash or sword fish of Dr Brown", Lindsay not only disputes Browne's description but claims that "in Jamaica he is commonly called Blundering Brown".[22] He also criticizes engravings in Sloane's *Natural History*, and others in *The American Physitian* (1672) of William Hughes. On the "papaw tree", Lindsay declares that it has been "but indifferently described by any author hitherto", including in his list of failures the illustrious Swedish scientist Carl Linnaeus (1707–78) as well as Sir Hans Sloane, Patrick Browne and William Hughes. Lindsay fills several pages in covering the botany, culture and uses of this tree and its fruit.[23]

Generally Lindsay is respectful of Sloane. Thus, when he describes "the brown butterfly with a broad yellow stripe across the upper wings", Lindsay notes that "this undoubtedly is the Papilio No. XXII of Sir Hans Sloane: but hardly can guess how it comes to pass my figures should differ so widely from that great collector. Perhaps they are the variations of different islands: perhaps his may have been taken from old dried subjects whose colours might have sufferd from accident and perhaps some parts of the fly been hurt or lost in the catching." Lindsay painted in watercolour. Most of Sloane's drawings are full-scale and based on tracings of specimens, living or dried, but all of them came to the viewer engraved. Lindsay also refers to oral sources, including the marine expertise of his father-in-law, John Pusey.[24]

Did Lindsay have a collection of preserved plants and animals as well as his drawings and watercolours? There is no clear evidence, but it was common for amateur natural historians of his time to keep cabinets of curiosities. The layout of his drawings of insects does suggest a board or case of dried individuals pinned in a permanent arrangement (plate 10). On the other hand, his butterflies are laid out to show opposing images of the colours and patterns of both their upper and undersides, requiring the specimens to be turned over and aligned for the purposes of illustration (plate 15). The birds and fishes may also have been preserved and displayed, and thus available for painting at a later date. Sloane's collections created the base for the British Museum in London, earlier in the eighteenth century, but Jamaica does not seem to have had a public or private museum during Lindsay's time. Such institutions came later.[25]

It was the arrangement of specimens in groups that led directly to the formal taxonomy that underpinned the emergence of natural history as a systematic discipline. When Linnaeus visited Sloane's British Museum, he was appalled by its lack of organization, but his study of those materials, including the Jamaican species, contributed substantially to establishment of systematically classified and labelled collections of specimens for display and study. Linnaeus published two volumes on Jamaica (one of them together with a student, Gabriel Elmgren) in 1759, the year Lindsay arrived in the island.[26] Although Lindsay was well aware of the work of Sloane and Linnaeus – and ready to contradict them on points – he did little himself towards taxonomic study that progressed beyond natural curiosity. Occasionally he is not even able to offer labels for what he has drawn, as, for example, a group of locusts which he had no trouble drawing but says of three specimens that he is "at a loss to give names".[27]

"A Refin'd and Civiliz'd Country"

None of the authorities Lindsay refers to – Sloane, Linnaeus, Browne and Hughes – lived in Jamaica in his time, but he was not alone in his interest in natural history. Prominent among his resident contemporaries were doctors of medicine and physicians and the occasional planter. Few of them were island-born and most were short- or medium-term residents. Standing out from the ignorant majority berated by Lindsay from the pulpit, these few kept up with the literature and politics of their homelands and of Europe more broadly. They sought also to contribute in original and systematic ways to the knowledge of the natural world at large. They knew Jamaica not only as a source of great wealth through sugar and slavery but also as the home of an exotic tropical world which had contributed fundamentally to the study of nature and its classification. They felt neither marginal nor isolated.

Edward Long in 1774 observes that the study of Jamaica's natural environment and meteorology is "reserved for men who are at entire leisure from the avocations of business and office; and who, to the incentives of a laudable curiosity, can join all the abilities, both of genius and fortune, that are necessary to pursue its full gratification". He thinks the island has never lacked "gentlemen of distinguished taste for the fine, as well as the more useful and œconomical, arts", but argues that the Assembly should fund a person "thoroughly qualified in the branches of natural study". This was an uncommon view. Long says:

> The want of a liberal education, or an attention of the whole soul to get money, as if it were the only rational object of pursuit in this world, has occasioned men in general to treat the study of natural history, and its followers, with contempt and ridicule; all are indiscriminately confounded with the despicable tribe of insect-hunters, and collectors of gimcracks. We should, however, be cautious to separate from this dross all those, whose labours conduce to the most useful purposes of life; who not only disclose to us the wonderful mechanism of the creation, and the wisdom of the Deity; but exemplify his unbounded benevolence to man, while they instruct us in the means by which our health may be preserved, our life prolonged, our agriculture improved, manufactures enlarged and multiplied, commerce and trade extended, and the public enriched.

Long mentions Sloane, Barham, Browne and Robinson, noting that the unpublished work of Robinson corrected errors made by Sloane and Browne, "who, compared with him, were in various instances very superficial observers, or ill-informed". He does not mention Lindsay in this company or say where he might be ranked among the curious and the dross. Long particularly condemns the lack of botanical knowledge among Jamaica's medical practitioners, saying, "for what can be more reproachful than to have it said, and with truth, that many of the Negroes are well acquainted with the healing virtues of several herbs and plants, which a regular physician tramples under foot".[28]

Abstract statements of self-conscious purpose and policy – beyond notions of the curious and exotic – became more common towards the end of the eighteenth century, after Lindsay's death, but the spirit was already building. The transition was marked by the establishment of formal botanical gardens in Jamaica, financed and controlled by the colonial state, that served as outposts of the Royal Botanical Gardens at Kew. They were set up in 1759, the year Lindsay arrived in the island. Several months before Lindsay died, Thomas Dancer, MD, was appointed superintendent of a botanic garden at Bath. Dr Dancer was another correspondent of Edward Long's, sending him in 1788 a "Catalogue of some of the most rare and elegant and useful exotics in the Bot. Garden of Jamaica", as well as "a specimen of our cinnamon bark".[29] In early 1790, after Lindsay's death, Dancer was appointed Island Botanist, and he then delivered an "oration" to the "Board of Directors under the new Act (1789) respecting the Bath and the Botanic Garden in Jamaica". In this address he takes the opportunity to set out his ideas on the role of natural history and economic botany.[30]

> Utility is the grand object of every public institution and if a Bot. Garden is not subservient more or less to this end, it should meet with no encouragement: but it is not necessary, in such an enlighten'd age as this, so renown'd for the progress of science and when natural history in all its branches has made such rapid advancement, that I should in any part of the British Dominions undertake to demonstrate by formal and logical induction, the advantages of Botany, or of that part of natural history which relates to the vegetable kingdom, from whence we derive so large a portion of our subsistence; to which we are indebted for most of the comforts and elegancies of life and which furnishes us with the most simple and at the same time the most efficacious remedies for the various diseases incident to human nature.

Dancer means not to suggest any lack of good sense in Jamaica, he tells the Board, "for I am sure there is not a country upon the earth, that abounds more with intelligent men". At the same time, he warns that everywhere there are those who "estimate every thing by the standard of immediate self interest". He praises the efforts of Jamaica's gardeners, such as Matthew Wallen and Hinton East, but emphasizes the need for longer-term support through public institutions. Dancer declares that he has himself "hitherto considered a botanical establishment in the view of utility or as it relates to agriculture commerce and the arts; but should it when considered in this light appear an object of that magnitude I am willing to represent it; are there no other beneficial purposes to which it is subservient? Is not the institution an ornamental one? Would not the want of such an establishment be a disgrace to a refin'd and civiliz'd country like Jamaica?"[31]

If Lindsay engaged with no other of his contemporaries, in the years towards the end of his life and immediately before Dancer's encomiums, it seems certain he knew Arthur Broughton, whose collections came to include Lindsay's volumes, shipped to Bristol together with Broughton's papers in

1796. Born in Bristol circa 1758, son of the rector of St Peter's Church, Broughton worked first as apprentice to an apothecary in the city, and he developed an abiding interest in botany. On completion of his seven-year apprenticeship he left Bristol for Edinburgh in 1776 to train as a physician. In 1780 he was appointed as physician at the Bristol Royal Infirmary, maintaining there his interest in botany and publishing a small British flora. In 1783 he took leave to travel to Jamaica in hopes of recovering from an illness related to epidemic influenza, and that same year he published a pamphlet on the influenza then plaguing Bristol. He arrived in Jamaica in January 1784. His health did improve and he chose to remain in Jamaica rather than returning to Bristol. Broughton entered a partnership with a medical practitioner in Kingston, where he died in 1796.[32]

In Jamaica, Broughton used his "intervals of leisure" between 1786 and 1790 to collect a four-volume herbarium, the specimens in which remain in excellent condition. As with Lindsay, the organization is not systematic but the specimens are carefully named and attributed to their places of collection. Broughton also produced *Hortus Eastensis*, a catalogue of the plants in Hinton East's botanic garden at Spring Garden, near Gordon Town in the hills behind Kingston, which was first published in 1792. Broughton sent fossils to Sir Joseph Banks and living plants and seeds to the Royal Botanic Garden at Kew. He also prepared a Linnaean index to Barham's *Hortus Americanus*, which was eventually published in 1794.[33]

Henry Barham, FRS (1670–1726), began as an apprentice and then a surgeon's mate on warships before going to Jamaica in the 1690s and commencing medical practice there. Although he had not received a regular education, Barham developed through reading and observation a detailed knowledge of Jamaican flora and corresponded frequently with Sloane. Barham returned to England in 1716 and was made a Fellow of the Royal Society the following year, but he was soon back in Jamaica, where he died at Spanish Town in 1726, long before Lindsay arrived.[34] A manuscript copy of his *Hortus Americanus* was sent to Sloane in 1711 but remained unpublished until printed in Kingston by Alexander Aikman, with the full title *Hortus Americanus: Containing an Account of the Trees, Shrubs, and Other Vegetable Productions, of South-America and the West-India Islands, and Particularly of the Island of Jamaica*. Much of its information became known earlier, however, and Long borrowed freely from it in his *History of Jamaica* of 1774. For the revised edition of his *History* (never published), Long sought Dancer's aid in compiling a full catalogue of plants, but Dancer told him about Broughton's "Flora Jamaicaensis", which may have thwarted Long's plan.[35]

Disconnected from this genealogy of Jamaican natural scientists was

Patrick Browne (1720–90) who was born in Ireland but studied medicine in Paris and Leyden, where he received his doctor's degree in 1743. He practised medicine in Jamaica from 1746 to 1755. Returning to England, he published in 1756 *The Civil and Natural History of Jamaica*, just three years after the *Species Plantarum* of Linnaeus. Linnaeus was a subscriber, and Browne noted that the "vegetable productions" of the island had been "disposed chiefly according to the system of Linneus" and the animals "classed nearly according to the system of Linneus also; but where that seemed forced or unnatural, we have followed another method, in which we have endeavoured to be guided solely by natural appearances". According to Frans A. Stafleu, Browne was "the first true Linnaean follower in Great Britain to make a contribution in print". His Jamaican botany appeared before any North American or British-based publication used the Linnaean system, and his *Civil and Natural History* remained the most scientifically advanced account of the natural history of any British American colony until the Revolution. However, although Browne was an important pioneer in his application of the Linnaean system, he chose not to use binomials; instead he applied phrase names and "quoted as synonyms of his own diagnostic names the diagnoses of the 'Species Plantarum' ".[36]

Linnaeus and Browne corresponded, and in 1758 Linnaeus acquired Browne's herbarium. Linnaeus also acquired a copy of Browne's *Civil and Natural History*, in which he wrote the binomials and added further notes to identify the species for which there were equivalent specimens. Many of the new species supplied by Browne were included by Linnaeus in *Plantarum jamaicensis* and *Flora jamaicensis*, both of 1759, and in new editions of *Systema naturae*.[37] Browne was a significant figure in the history of botany; he was not merely a compiler but a systematic collector and classifier. In spite of his disparagement of Browne's work, Lindsay could lay claim neither to systematic collecting nor to taxonomic originality.

The physician Dr Anthony Robinson, who died in 1768, left a series of volumes of his drawings of plants and animals, some of which were copied the following year under the supervision of Robert Long. He thought Robinson's work served to "correct many errors in Sloane and Brown; who, compared with him, were in various instances very superficial observers, or ill-informed".[38] Not all of these volumes have survived but those that have are now in Jamaica, in the collections of the National Library and in the Science Library of the Natural History Museum. Robinson's "Birds of Jamaica" contains 163 large-scale drawings of birds and their eggs, from the "banana bird" to the "clucking hen of the Jamaicans", with minimal text.[39]

A second John Lindsay lived in Jamaica in the 1780s, working as a surgeon and also as assistant to Island Botanist Dr Thomas Clarke. The two John

Lindsays – the priest and the surgeon – have occasionally been confused. The second seems to have been also a Scot, and a student of medicine at Edinburgh University from 1776 to 1780. He went to Jamaica to practise, establishing himself in the parish of Westmoreland, far from the haunts of his namesake and apparently not in touch with him. The surgeon John Lindsay became respected for his investigations in botany and known particularly for his ingenious experimental approach to studying the sensitive plant, common in Jamaica as a groundcover called "shame-me-lady"; the leaves of the plant close themselves sequentially when touched. Lindsay wrote papers describing this work in 1788 and 1790. These were communicated to the Royal Society by Banks and presented at the Society's regular weekly meeting but not published.[40] The medical Lindsay also made detailed meteorological observations at his Westmoreland residence from 1785 to 1792, continuing the practice of Robert Long and followed by Thomas Thistlewood, a Westmoreland planter and diarist. Their records included temperature, winds, rain, thunder and lightning. The priest John Lindsay is not known to have attempted such systematic record-keeping and he showed little enthusiasm for experiment, or even measurement. He could do no better than speculation and mind games based on his observation of externals. But he did progress beyond the credulous concept of wonder, rooted in awe and fear, which was increasingly opposed to the more worthy notion of curiosity.[41]

Another medical doctor, William Wright (1735–1819), had a career more closely parallel to that of the Reverend John Lindsay. Wright was born at Crieff, Perthshire, in Scotland, and died in Edinburgh (figure 2.2). He was first apprenticed to a surgeon in Falkirk, then in 1756 commenced study of medicine at Edinburgh University. In the summer of 1757 he made a voyage to Greenland, and in 1758 he joined the navy as a surgeon's mate. He was present at some of the major battles of the Seven Years' War in European waters, in 1758 and 1759, though apparently not those witnessed by Lindsay. Wright sailed for the West Indies with Rodney in 1760 to protect the British colonies and take Martinique. He obtained his MD at the end of the Seven Years' War and in 1765 went to Jamaica, where he established a partnership based at Hampden Estate in Trelawny, with Thomas Steel, a former fellow student. Here his main occupation was the treatment of enslaved people, and Wright used the experience in his later publications on diseases, including yaws. The money he made was used to buy slaves and land.[42]

In the 1770s Wright began collecting specimens of birds and insects for Edinburgh University's new museum. His dried plants were arranged according to the Linnaean system, following a copy of the third edition of *Species Plantarum* (1764), in which he wrote the common names and references to the works of Sloane and Browne. Wright also sent living plants to Kew and many dried specimens to Sir Joseph Banks. In 1774 he was made Surgeon-General of Jamaica, "an office of honour and distinction", by Governor Sir Basil Keith. The following year a paper by Wright was read before the Philosophical Society of Philadelphia; it was an essay advocating the use of lime juice saturated in sea salt in the treatment of diabetes, and this became his first publication. He travelled to London in 1777, where he read papers before the Royal Society, met Banks, and was soon after made a Fellow. He was claimed to be "an original thinker, . . . who admitted no dictum upon mere authority, nor any theory without evidence".[43]

Wright returned to Jamaica in 1782 as surgeon to the Jamaica Regiment and was made physician-general of Jamaica. He renewed his collecting, maintaining his close correspondence with Banks, but left the island again in 1785 and settled in Edinburgh, where he published on the medicinal plants of Jamaica. By 1788 he was aligned with the Reverend John Lindsay in his indignation at the pamphlets published against the planters, telling the absentee Chaloner Arcedeckne, "In our happy Island the Negroe wallows in provisions every way calculated to make him healthy robust and opulent". In 1792 he gave evidence to a parliamentary committee on abolition of the slave trade, speaking in defence of the traders and his fellow slave-owners. He expressed a benign view of slavery that contrasted sharply with his observation in 1761, which was based on his first encounter with the enslaved of the West Indies: "no one, endowed with the common attributes of humanity, can witness their sufferings, and reflect on their hard fate, without pity for misfortunes which end but with their lives". In 1792 he declared the enslaved of Africa "cannibals" and wondered at the attention they were receiving, "while we lose sight of all the tender ties of relationship, colour, country, and christianity". In an age of democratic revolution, he feared "a levelling disposition".[44]

As Norris Saakwa-Mante comments, Wright "was never to give up the role of botanical collector and naturalist because it allowed him a vocation as a gentleman of science with social rewards that matched, and at times exceeded, those of his career as a surgeon". In a manuscript volume titled "Plants of Jamaica", Wright provides an introduction, dated 1786, in which he sets out his thoughts on the philosophy of botanical collecting. He emphasizes the "utility" of botanical study, which enables "commercial" transfer of plants within and from outside Britain's "colonies and settlements". He "spent the best of his days" in the West Indies, says Wright, and "appropriated every spare moment, from the duties of his profession to botany; his chief aim was to ascertain the properties of plants; whether usefull in medicine, in commerce, the arts or rural œconomy: how far he has succeeded is not for him to say". In his "Directions to Officers Going to the

West Indies", Wright observes: "An officer need never want amusement or exercise; in his quarters he may have books, musical instruments, or employ himself in drawing; and if he has a turn for natural history, so much the better, – he will find ample subjects for his purpose; in all the islands the scenery is new and beautiful, often magnificent and grand." Wright's career was particularly varied and commemorated in a memoir, but Saakwa-Mante concludes that "though an eminent physician, he was a minor player in late eighteenth-century natural history, a foot soldier of science". On the other hand, Wright certainly thought himself superior to Lindsay, telling Banks in 1783: "Dr Lindsay Rector of Spanish-town . . . is no less a blockhead in botany and drawing than in theology, and common sense."[45]

Lindsay has no claims to rank in science. He did his best to illustrate what he saw as accurately as he could, and he was as precise as possible in his botanical descriptions. But he did not pretend to be comprehensive or systematic in what he selected to illustrate, making his choices principally on the basis of what he understood as beauty, elegance and curiosity. He made no pretence at taxonomy, though he happily criticized the naming, description and images attempted by his contemporaries. He lacked the background in medicine that underpinned the advances made by Sloane, Browne, the other Lindsay and Wright. Elsewhere in the Scottish Enlightenment, examples are known of clergy who took natural history to mean the systematic organization of knowledge of "the works of creation" and who achieved advancement in the profession, but Lindsay had both less interest and fewer opportunities. He lacked the empirical imperatives that drove medical men and merchants. He lacked the fundamental desire to know the scale of things that drove the planter Thistlewood, for example. Lindsay was comfortable not measuring or weighing objects while at the same time declaring the superiority of his observations.[46] He also had no time for experiment but depended chiefly on the evidence of his eyes, his visual inspection of surfaces – sometimes apprehended merely in his mind's eye.

Lindsay was, however, unusual in the way in which he combined his duties in the church with his interest in natural history and, less surprisingly, theology. R.A. Minter has argued that in the whole period of slavery in Jamaica, among the clergy of the Church of England only "two, or at most four, seem to have engaged actively in the intellectual interests of their time" – namely Lindsay and John West, and perhaps H. Pasmore and R. Tabor. Pasmore and Tabor were Englishmen, both of whom arrived in Jamaica in 1698. Pasmore ministered in Spanish Town; he promised to send plants to Sir Hans Sloane but died before the end of the year. Tabor, a graduate of Oxford, was rector first at Vere, then at St Catherine, where his garden was described soon after his death in 1720 as containing a "good number of exotic plants besides the most curious vegetables that grow upon the island and fig trees and vines of the best sorts". He had two "small presses of books" worth £65.[47]

John West (1756–1817) was a Scot and a Presbyterian until he converted to the Church of England. He came to Jamaica in 1784 and first attempted a circulating library in Kingston. When this failed, he became a teacher at Manning's Free School in Westmoreland and was soon recommended as a candidate for the Anglican priesthood. He served as rector of St Mary and then of St Thomas in the East. A graduate of the University of St Andrews, West was a sophisticated expositor of the new field of mathematical analysis. While in Jamaica he kept up with the latest works of Lagrange and Laplace, and his understanding of Euler's contributions enabled him to produce work that placed him well ahead of his British contemporaries. West also developed a new method for finding longitude and laid it before the Admiralty in 1803. His isolation in Morant Bay might seem to make these achievements remarkable, but the situation suited him. West was by nature reclusive, and the lightness of his clerical duties gave him time to read, write and compute. Unlike Lindsay, he did not apply his intellectual energies to the mysteries of human diversity, the inspired status of Scripture or the natural world around him; he sought to comprehend a different plane.[48]

What Lindsay did achieve was recognition of the importance of observation, the application of reason and the rejection of credulous, opinionated theory. As a gentleman naturalist whose principal calling was the church, this was perhaps as far as he wished to go. He did not engage in public debate with his local rivals in the field of Jamaican natural history, though completion and publication of "Elegancies of Jamaica" might have changed this balance. His principal venture into public debate was rather with a distant philosophical competitor, Benjamin Franklin, about his interpretation of whirlwinds and waterspouts. These meteorological phenomena fell outside Lindsay's regular preoccupations but were commonly placed by British observers among the "exotic" phenomena of American colonial climates and continued to be associated with wonder.[49]

Waterspouts

Like Lindsay, Benjamin Franklin (1706–90) was brought up in traditional Presbyterianism and directed towards a career in the church. In adolescence, however, he "began to doubt of Revelation itself" and became "a thorough Deist". He believed divine power was remote and its manifestations open to human reason. At the same time he happily benefited from the arrival of George Whitefield in Philadelphia in 1740, printing and selling his works as well as conducting experiments to measure the distance over which the preacher's famous voice could be heard. Franklin's scientific mission was directed against superstition and his experiments were designed to show that physical phenomena such as lightning had natural explanations rather than signifying divine retribution. It was not such fundamental questions of belief that led Lindsay into debate with Franklin but rather his interpretation of a specific phenomena, the waterspout, first discussed in a paper written in 1753.[50]

In 1781, in the midst of the American War of Independence, the *Gentleman's Magazine* of London published "An Examination of the Hypothetical Doctrine of Water-spouts, in Opposition to the Ingenious Speculations of Dr. B. Franklin of Philadelphia, F.R.S. by the Rev. John Lindsay, D.D. Rector of the Parish of St. Catherine, and Town of St. Jago de la Vega, in Jamaica". Lindsay told the editor, Sylvanus Urban, that he had sent his contribution because of "the extensive circulation of your valuable miscellany, and the many useful discoveries in every species of literature that you have introduced to public notice".[51] The *Gentleman's Magazine*, begun in 1731, was indeed a prominent publication with its combination of articles on many areas of knowledge, literature and political affairs, including the notice it gave to Lindsay's *Memoirs* and *Voyage*. It encouraged dialogue and had already published accounts of waterspouts, even before Franklin's paper, in which writers pondered competing theories explaining their origin, from "various and contrary winds" to "an extraordinary rarefaction of the air by igneous meteors". The editor called Lindsay's contribution a "*curious letter*" on a "*curious subject*".[52]

Lindsay begins with "a voyage to America in July 1749, about the banks of Newfoundland", where he first observed the phenomenon. It is not known whether he made detailed notes at the time or whether his account of 1781 depends on his memory of occurrences more than thirty years before. Lindsay says of his experience in 1749: "In a clear air, the sea rendered smooth as glass by hot and calm weather, and heavy, gloomy looking clouds hanging all around us, . . . on a sudden we were surrounded with five spouts at once: one of which being within about half a mile of us, we felt severely." Lindsay directs his readers to figure 1 of a plate printed in the magazine (figure 7.1). This image, he says, resembles that made by Franklin

> in the bushy form at the base, and the joining of the column to the cloud, but many times higher in proportion: and instead of being particles of water, driven as from the vortex of a wheel, we had all that frothing, boiling, and fretting, which is occasioned by the fall of an overshot miln; or . . . the roaring tumble of cataracts from huge precipices, which naturally, also, throwing up a thin misty spray, obscured in a slight degree this boiling base.[53]

Figure 7.1 Lindsay's drawings of waterspouts at sea, 1781. *Gentleman's Magazine* 51 (1781): 558, figs 1 and 4.

Here Lindsay draws on his observation of noisy water mills on Jamaican sugar estates and on cascades that were well known and illustrated, for example, in Long's *History of Jamaica*.

Although Lindsay draws attention to the great height of the waterspouts he observed in 1749, this is not at issue. Rather, he says, "it is the rising of such a phænomenon I mean at present to dispute". Franklin believed that

> a water-spout is nothing but a whirlwind on the seas, which carrying more or less quantities of water with it into the air, gives it that denomination; and the waters at that time being by *pulsion* or *suction* forced up through a tube or void space in the middle of the whirl, is thereby carried up into the clouds to the height of thirty or thirty-two feet, provided the center of the whirl be really a vacuum; and less, if the void is less perfect. [54]

The foundation of Franklin's "philosophy", says Lindsay, is "that a fluid, moving horizontally from all points towards a center, must either mount or descend at that center". Lindsay accepts this contention but asks: "will a fluid do either the one or the other in extremes, to support a doctrine in extravagance?" He proceeds, not by "experimented truth" but rather by imagining in the mind's eye what might occur in an "artificial vortex" created in a tub of water spinning on a horizontal wheel. Visualizing the outcomes, Lindsay concludes that "water is too yielding and pliant to refuse the effects of any whirlwind; and has too many ways for a vortex to expand and escape by (near the surface) to have a whirlpool continued to any considerable depth, far less to be forced upwards for want of elbow-room (if I may be allowed the expression) into the very midst of the cause which gives the effect, into the whirlwind itself".[55]

Lindsay observes that small bays might perhaps suit "the Doctor's [Franklin's] tub with the hole in the bottom; but if we must have an *ascending whirl*, we must try another experiment". He proposes the rapid spinning of a cylindrical tube, as shown in his figures 2 and 3 (figure 7.2), and agrees that the water within the tube would mount up, even as much as thirty-two feet. However, says Lindsay, "I would not from thence conclude, that a huge body of solid water (which is the Franklinian doctrine) by any walls of embodied air whatever, could be held up, and kept in on every side, even to the height of twenty feet, nor the half of that."[56] In all of this Lindsay refers to Franklin's "experiments" and acknowledges the possibility of further practical trials, describing how these might be conducted but without ever claiming to have conducted any such himself, or wishing to do so. He was happy merely "apprehending" or "imagining" the results.

The fundamental point of disagreement between Lindsay and Franklin concerned the origins of waterspouts – whether they rose or fell. Whereas Franklin claimed that descending spouts were rare, Lindsay contended "the only certain-to-be-depended-upon accounts of water-spouts are falling ones". Modern weather science shows Lindsay to have been nearer the truth, though only for the most common variety of waterspout. At the same time, Franklin deserves credit as the true discoverer of convection (in 1749).[57]

Most often, waterspouts originate at the base of a rapidly forming convective cloud and extend down as a funnel to the water surface. These "fair-weather" waterspouts develop over high-humidity warm water bodies when the air is heated from below and becomes unstable. The warm air rises within this unstable atmosphere, is cooled to the dew point and condenses. The visible water in a waterspout has not been sucked up from the ocean; rather, it comes from condensation of vapour in the air and extends *down* in a rope-like manner from a cumulus congestus cloud. Waterspouts can be from

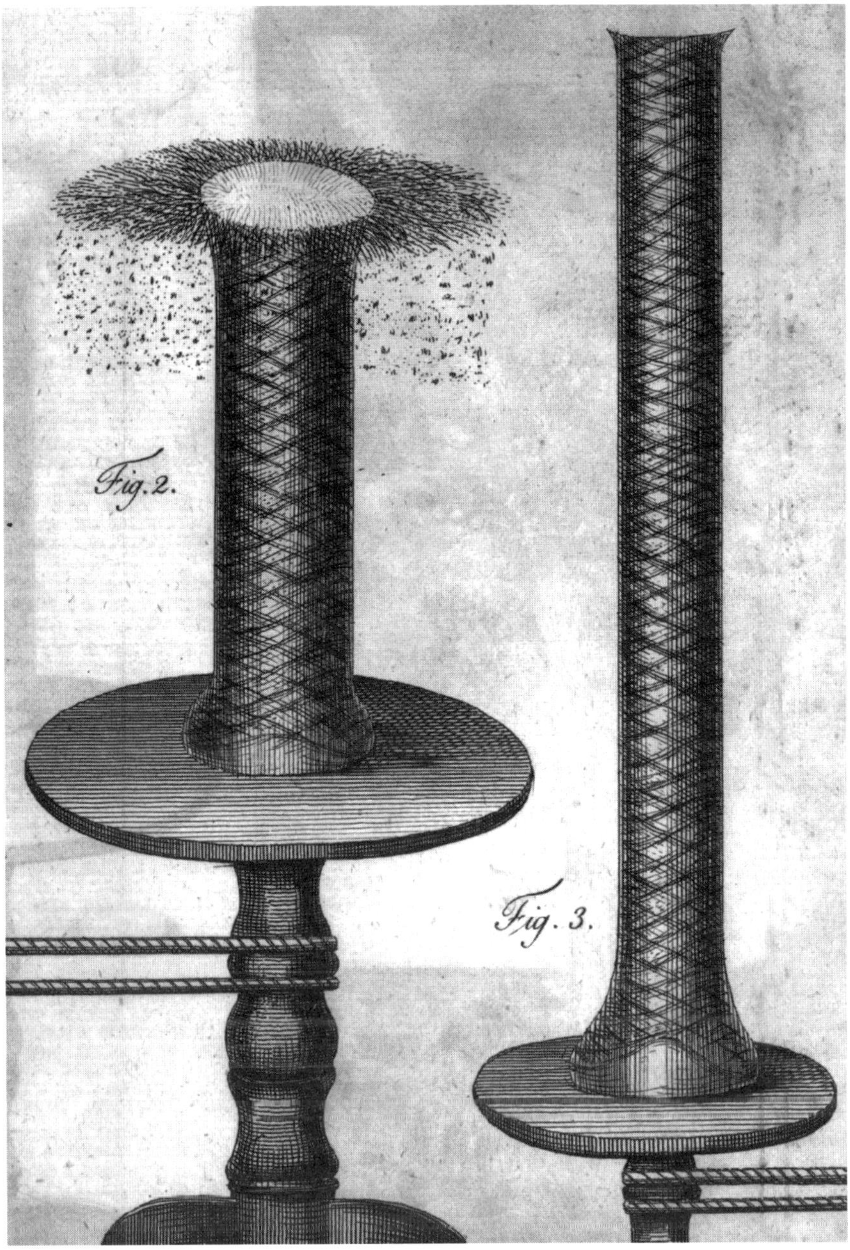

Figure 7.2 Lindsay's drawings of imagined experimental waterspouts, 1781. *Gentleman's Magazine* 51 (1781): 558, figures 2 and 3.

5 to 100 metres in diameter and have wind speeds up to 150 kilometres per hour, powerful enough to damage boats. Most survive only a few minutes, though the largest may persist for an hour or more. Occasionally a tornado can move off land to become a waterspout or become associated with tornadic thunderstorms over water.[58]

Lindsay argues that falling spouts are formed by "a local motion", probably "of a fanning nature, and gentle", but sufficient to initiate spiral motion. It is the spout's "foaming fall upon the ocean" that makes it appear as if the water is ascending, he says, and this false perception explains credulous "travelling stories". With this knowledge established, Lindsay argues, "I can make plain English of the worst-told tale amongst them; which, without it, are full of absurdities, contradictions, frighted confusions, half-understood, half-seen, and half-told systems." In this way Lindsay manages to associate Franklin's theory with the false observations of the credulous, and indeed there is no clear evidence that Franklin had actually seen a waterspout when he first wrote on the subject, depending heavily on the oral testimony of old salts and plausible whaling men. Franklin's trust may be interpreted positively as showing respect for testimony-based knowledge, but Lindsay expected a more sceptical attitude.[59]

In the course of this criticism Lindsay declares, at a location unspecified (perhaps in Philadelphia or Williamsburg in 1752), "I have spent some convivial hours with Dr. Franklin in a groupe of philosophic friends; and in numerous respects have, as an ingenious gentleman, the highest esteem for him." In view of the high regard in which he holds Franklin's contributions, Lindsay offers an excuse for his error in this field, saying: "Good men are often credulous – and it is too natural for us all to warp and coax a pliable story, when it will suit a fond hypothesis." However, he adds, "because I admire the Doctor's productions, I am not bound to put on his spectacles, and view objects only in his favourite mediums".[60]

Lindsay's letter of 1781 ends with a plea for close observation and the need to reject credulous accounts. Superstitions persisted among seamen in dealing with the menace of dangerous waterspouts. In the Caribbean this sometimes involved "cutting the waterspout" by pointing a knife in its direction and making slashing motions with the blade, or perhaps jabbing the knife into a mast. Alternatively, a cannon or rifle could be used to fire a ball into its centre, reflecting the idea that iron was effective against all varieties of evil and sorcery. Lindsay's near contemporary on the coast of Africa, land surveyor William Smith, who accepted the ascending hypothesis, observes that ships threatened by waterspouts "endeavour to break them by firing at them, for though the Ball should not hit them, yet the Concussion of the Air seldom fails to break them, and then they come down, . . . without any Damage to the Ship". Similarly, Charles Leslie in his *New and Exact Account of Jamaica,* published in Edinburgh in 1740, says: "seamen, when near, endeavour to disturb and break them by noises, and the firing of great guns, which puts the circumjacent air into a tremor and motion different to, and opposite in some sort to that whereby they are impelled".[61]

Lindsay mentions none of these, setting himself firmly on the side of reason.

In December 1783 the *Gentleman's Magazine* printed a second letter from Lindsay, noting, "Our philosophical readers will doubtless be pleased to see a continuation of Dr. Lindsey's ingenious and original hypothesis on water-spouts." Lindsay refers to two figures with the general title "Representation of Waterspouts at St. Jago de la Vega in Jamaica". The first of these (figure 5) shows a mountainous area overlooking a bay with no resemblance to the Spanish Town area, whereas the second (figure 6) seems a realistic representation of Lindsay's parish church and its surroundings (figures 7.3 and 7.4). It may be that figure 5 was incorrectly associated with the general title, but the style does match some of the more flamboyant landscapes in "Elegancies of Jamaica"; probably the original drawing was of his making. Referring to figure 5, Lindsay remarks that "in the Torrid-Zone, at some times of the year, the falling, or dropping of the clouds is exceedingly heavy", and that in Jamaica it is "very common, to see the rain streaming down in sheets and flakes; picturing an idea, somewhat resembling the ribbon-like webbing of the *Aurora-Borealis*". He also notes the truth that "we frequently see a heavy fall of rain, on one side of a fence or hedge, watering the thirsty fields of one gentleman, without blessing his neighbours with a single drop".[62]

Lindsay's figure 6 (figure 7.4), he says, draws on his experience on 5 May 1778 "at the burial of one of my parishioners, where there was at least a concourse of three hundred people". On this occasion he "beheld the sun-beams from the West shining thro' two clouds", making visible a shower of rain, and "we were presented with a most beautiful appearance of shining crystalline drops, as large as hasel nuts, which fell very thick and fast within the church-yard". Lindsay also refers to the rains that "fell from the leads of my rectory house at St. Jago de la Vega". As to the waterspout, Lindsay objects to those who make it a thing of wonder, saying, "it is charming, I confess, passing curious, but a chip in porridge withal".[63]

Running out of fresh things to say about the waterspout, Lindsay's third contribution to the *Gentleman's Magazine*, published in 1785, more broadly discusses whirlwinds – "phænomena, which under the torrid zone, are too frequent for any one who has made his residence there for twenty years, as I have done, not to be pretty well acquainted with them". Whirlwinds, he finds, are of "two essentially different kinds: the one always sportive and harmless, its progressive motion easy and gentle; and the other as constantly dreadful and destructive, swift, furious, and impetuous. Both have their degrees in motion; but so perfectly different and distinct from each other, that the sportive never wax turbulent, nor the destructive degenerate into pleasantry."[64] Whirlwinds of the "sportive" type, says Lindsay, often originate in flat, open

Figure 7.3 Lindsay's "Representation of Waterspouts at St Jago de la Vega in Jamaica". *Gentleman's Magazine* 53 (1783): 984, figure 5.

Figure 7.4 Lindsay's "Representation of Waterspouts at St Jago de la Vega in Jamaica". *Gentleman's Magazine* 53 (1783): 984, figure 6.

places, and are "sure prognostics with the experienced planter of a longer continuance of . . . dry and sultry weather". The other type of whirlwind is "caused by the rushing and contentions of contrary streams in a hard gale of wind; which is again always amazingly dreadful and destructive in its powers". Such winds include "all the several winds called by the names of *exhydria*, *ecnephia*, *prester*, *turbo*, *typho*, and *travado*, which are all hurricane storms, with some variations in climate and appearance. Thunder mixed in one, heavy rains in another, whirlwinds dashing down in one place, carrying up in another, hurling forward there, and havoc and destruction every where."[65]

Of greater interest is Lindsay's claim that the weather of Jamaica had moderated as a consequence of settlement. He argues that

> In former days, when our island was overgrown with woods, their thick foliage and spreading branches served as so many spreading grapnels, first to impede the flight of clouds in their course over the lofty mountains; and then by degrees, as it were, to arrest them there; these so highly embanked the whole length of the island, that the succeeding clouds, stopped also by their retention, did so deeply overspread the lower grounds, that heavy falls of rain used to settle over the whole island for several weeks together, in such constant and dark pours, that I remember for several days on a stretch to have sat down at noon to the light of a candle. Then were the former and the latter rains certain over the whole island. But now we are so cleared away below, and so much thinned by settlers aloft, that our seasons are become exceedingly precarious; and, when they come, are not only often of shorter continuance, but, at best, much more partial and inconsiderable. So, in former days, hurricanes were dreaded, and storms not uncommon: but now a short gust of wind is almost all that we know, unless, peradventure, the tail of a storm shall pass over us, after having visited some of our windward neighbours.

Lindsay was strangely mistaken about the frequency of hurricanes in Jamaica. They were in fact particularly common and destructive in the early 1780s. He did not keep systematic records of rainfall, temperature, clouds or thunder, as did the exceptional Thistlewood, or even attempt the more limited observations of Long and Wright.[66]

Finally, Lindsay laughs at those who think waterspouts miraculous, seeing God's hand intervening in the details of nature. He says:

> It seems then, that when this same whirlwind is to take its rise, or *sets itself to work* upon the waters, as they call it, to carry it up into the air, some 30 feet or so; the watchful Providence, which prepared the whale for Jonas, sends down at the instant, and in special readiness, a large cloud for its reception too, with some other unaccountably strange assistants, an apparatus of aerial chemistry; or, at least, some very supernatural exhalations, to disperse the ponderous and solid element; and with so amazing a degree of equality too, as to fall down soon afterwards in pleasant, gentle, dropping rains, to wash a few sailors jackets in the middle of the ocean.

Lindsay similarly dismisses the "ridiculous accounts" of the "strange story-telling mariner" and questions the powers of observation of "unlettered and barbarous" common sailors.[67] It was necessary to reject "the confident stories told and retold amongst them, of the wonderful, and hair-breadth scapes, from the dangers of these phænomena, which they have seen and felt, even at the distance of a *boat-hook's length*, or so near as to *chuck a biscuit* into the driving element – sensible landsmen may stare, but must not refuse to credit them". Such "positively told stories" seem to many listeners convincing observation, complains Lindsay, so much so that "sensible men have been drawn in to believe a cloud to be an ouzle [a thrush or blackbird], or a whale, without taking time to reflect whether 'tis a Hamlet or a Polonius that has said so". Among those deceived has been Franklin, who, on the basis of false reports, "has set his own ingenuity to work, to accommodate so preternatural a phænomenon to philosophic description, and to mathematical proof". These words, in his 1785 letter on whirlwinds, are Lindsay's last on water-spouts.[68]

CHAPTER EIGHT

The Creation of Race

A FEW MONTHS BEFORE his death, Lindsay completed a manuscript devoted to an investigation of the origins of human diversity and a justification of slavery. It was a work of study, a reading and interpretation of texts, a product of his Spanish Town closet. Rather than being an extension of his interest in the natural world or a work of theology, it combined a conjectural history with a pragmatic reaction to emerging threats to the stability of the slave society in which he lived. His purpose was proclaimed in the manuscript's title: "A few conjectural considerations upon the creation of the humane race; Occasioned by the present British Quixottical rage of setting the slaves from Africa at liberty". He believed his work to be substantial and timely. It was never published.

"Glimmerings of Directing Light"

Lindsay did not put his name to the manuscript. Its title page merely attributes the work to "an inhabitant of Jamaica".[1] As with his first work, the fictional *Memoirs* of 1757, he desired anonymity, though once again with little expectation that his identity would remain secret. The manuscript was sent to Edward Long in London, together with a letter signed only "Lindsay". He must also have confided in the powerful planter-attorney Simon Taylor, who found a ship captain ready to sail from Kingston and "trusted on his account would pay great attention to the delivery of the packet". The accompanying letter, sent on a separate vessel for safety, bears a note in a different hand, probably that of Long, ascribing it to "Revd. Docr. Lindsay, Rector of St. Jago de la Vega" and recording that it was "Received Oct. 1788". On the manuscript, beneath "an inhabitant of Jamaica", a similar note identifies the author as "The Revd. Doctor Lindsay, Rector of St. Katharine's in that Island". The work is dated "St Jago de la Vega, July 23, 1788".[2] Lindsay was dead by 3 November.

Within the manuscript, as he hoped it might reach the public, Lindsay gives few clues to his identity. Early in the text he declares himself "very peculiarly interested, not only as a voyager to America, a visitor on the slave coasts, but as a planter". It is interesting that he identifies himself as a planter in Jamaica as well as a voyager to America and visitor to Africa, hinting at different levels of knowledge and involvement without any mention of his being a clergyman. Although he makes no claim to more than a limited knowledge of Africa and Africans, Lindsay turns his extended Caribbean experience to advantage by arguing that "the most unerring line of getting at a general and consistant knowledge of that race of people, is likely to be had best in one of the largest and most populous of our West Indea islands (such, for instance as Jamaica) where the natives of every country meet together". Further, he declares that it has been "more than thirty years now, since a full knowledge of the African race led me to fancy them of a different class of beings to those of Europe".[3] In this way he dates the beginnings of his "full knowledge" to 1758, the year of his voyage to Senegal. He also makes a larger claim, saying, "I have known America, and have now become almost a native in it".[4]

Excusing the imposition of sending his manuscript to Long, Lindsay refers to their "old acquaintance" and praises Long for "standing forth as a warm friend for the West Indean planter against Mr. Ramseys idle charges of cruelty". This was the Reverend James Ramsay, the Anglican priest of St Kitts whose two publications of 1784 – *An Essay on the Treatment and Conversion of African Slaves in the British Sugar Colonies* and *An Inquiry into the Effects of Putting a Stop to the African Slave Trade, and of Granting Liberty to the Slaves in the British Sugar Colonies* – did much to arouse antislavery public opinion in Britain.[5] Lindsay's "Conjectural considerations" responds directly to these titles in advertising that his contribution has been "occasioned by the present British Quixottical rage of setting the slaves from Africa at liberty". In this way he connects his response to Ramsay with the foolishness of Cervantes' Don Quixote, who, coming upon a chain of galley-slaves, sees an opportunity to "redress grievances and give help to the poor and the afflicted". After hearing from the men their individual histories and crimes, and against the wisdom of Sancho Panza, the "not very sane" Don Quixote demands their freedom, declaring that he thinks it "a harsh thing to make slaves of those whom God and nature made free". In the commotion that follows, the galley-slaves escape, taking their guards' weapons and robbing Don Quixote and Sancho. The freed slaves become highwaymen, terrorizing the countryside, but Don Quixote takes no responsibility, saying that he did only what his religion and his chivalric duty demanded, and seeing evil in the plight of the people rather than their crimes.[6]

Ramsay's essays of 1784 were crucial in leading William Wilberforce and Thomas Clarkson to commit themselves to the cause of abolition. Clarkson's influential *An Essay on the Slavery and Commerce of the Human Species* appeared in 1786.[7] Although planters and merchants published their own pamphlets in rebuttal, Lindsay felt led "to throw in my own mite towards inlightening any of the dark strokes or perplexing passages which sometimes arise even in philosophic minds upon it", though without owning his status. It was his fear, Lindsay told Long, that "the ill inform'd people of England" might be led to impose "a total or at least some partial – and it may be improper restrictions – on the slave trade".[8] In January 1788 Wilberforce had been optimistic that a motion for the abolition of the slave trade could be brought to Parliament and approved quickly, but he soon accepted that more evidence of its evils needed first to be presented to a committee of the Privy Council. In early May a resolution put by William Pitt was agreed to. Although this merely committed the House to consider the slave-trade question at its next session, it was enough to trouble Lindsay. Further, also in May, Sir William Dolben, member of Parliament for Oxford, moved a bill to improve conditions in the slave trade by placing a limit on the number of people who could be carried in proportion to the tonnage of ships, and by paying bounties to captains and ship's surgeons for the enslaved people who survived the passage.[9] News of these developments reached Jamaica just weeks before Lindsay dated his manuscript at the end of July 1788.

Feeling the urgency of the issue rather than expecting his own imminent demise, Lindsay pulled his ideas together but found that they "accumulated too fast upon me to be entitled (in point of elegance or perspicuity of stile), to that severity of *review* which I could have wish'd to have bestowed on such a work". This was particularly true of the final chapters, he says, in which he proposes practical changes to the system of slavery in Jamaica, specifically "forewarding the situation of deserving Negroes". Lindsay considered these chapters "perhaps the most valuable in the design" and regretted being "obliged to hurry over, in *the dread* of being too late".[10]

Exactly why Lindsay came to these questions so late in life and why he felt impelled to write about them with such urgency in 1788 is not clear. Unlike his other literary endeavours, Lindsay's writing on race and slavery was reactive rather than driven by a desire to entertain or inform. When he first arrived in Jamaica, there was no antislavery movement or ideology to react to, no obvious necessity to justify what to slave-owners seemed natural and functional in a slave society. It was Anthony Benezet's *Observations on the Inslaving, Importing, and Purchasing of Negroes*, published that very year (1759), that laid the first foundations for an effective movement. Antislavery ideas and action developed rapidly though fitfully over the first twenty-five years of Lindsay's time in Jamaica – up to the publication of Ramsay's *Essay* in 1784 – but Lindsay was slow to join the ideological reaction. He was silent throughout the controversy over Lord Mansfield's judgement of 1772, which brought rapid responses from Edward Long and Samuel Estwick, agent for Barbados, among others, in essays which contributed to the foundations of a proslavery ideology rooted in legal history as well as material necessity, but without much reference to race theory or theology. Nor was Lindsay quick to respond to Ramsay's essays of 1784. A flood of books and pamphlets appeared rapidly, beginning the same year with *An Answer to the Reverend James Ramsay's Essay on the Treatment and Conversion of Slaves in the British Sugar Colonies by Some Gentlemen of St Christopher*, who questioned the truthfulness of Ramsay's personal history. Responses came also from planters in other British colonies, notably the *Cursory Remarks* of James Tobin, a leading Nevis planter, published in London in 1785. Ramsay responded with *A Letter to James Tobin* (1787), and critical reviews came also from Olaudah Equiano in the year before publication of his autobiography.[11] Lindsay was relatively slow to arms. Once convinced that the battle was necessary, however, he took up the pen with enthusiasm and commitment.

The text of the "Conjectural considerations" is about eighty thousand words in length, divided into twelve chapters. As Lindsay recognized, the work is marked by "numerous traverses from the straight line" and tempted into bypaths by the "newness and uncommonness" of the subject. The questions under consideration, he believed, were "so complicated that a trifling error in any one part, from want of strict attention to facts – or a deficiency of those facts; will marr and render doubtful the just proportions and fair effects of the whole superstructure – even where no bad or selfish design shall lead the fancy of the describer". It was his hope "to throw such glimmerings of directing light as may lead honest enquirers streight onward into the truth".[12]

Lindsay did, however, construct what he saw as a coherent argument and set out a summary of the contents of each of the chapters at the beginning of the manuscript. The first ten are concerned with "the creation of the humane race" and the final two (discussed in chapter 9 of this book) contain his proposals for the Jamaican slave system and his proslavery argument. In the first section of the work, he begins by setting out what he understood broadly of slavery and his reading of contemporary commentators and critics, together with his own qualifications to speak on the subject. Chapters three to six discuss the status of knowledge generally and more particularly the authority of Scripture. The next three chapters discuss the works of individual writers, notably Lindsay's fellow Scot Lord Kames (Henry Home, 1696–1782) and the Frenchmen the Count de Buffon (Georges Louis Leclerc, 1707–88) and Cornélius de Pauw (1739–99), while the tenth chapter discusses the place of slavery in Africa and the West Indies, creating a bridge to the proposals in the final two chapters.

Well aware of the unfinished state of his manuscript, Lindsay hoped "the editor" (presumably Long) would amend anything that was not "clear and intelligible". It was already much amended and corrected in Lindsay's hand.[13] He also included a series of "Observations for the printer", hoping for help in sorting out inconsistencies in his use of capital letters, for example, and deciding whether to include sections "which may be thought to bear too hard against religion and some church men" that he had bracketed. Although much editorial effort went into the sanitizing of late-eighteenth-century manuscripts – in order to temper animadversions and remove defamations of the living as well as creating more polite texts – it is easy enough to see why, particularly once Lindsay's death became known, neither editor nor printer had much enthusiasm for such responsibility.[14]

Explaining his desire that the work be published anonymously, Lindsay tells Long, "I need not remind my friend, that prudence will require my name should be kept a secret – at least till we shall know how the theologic critic shall receive it". He believed "much offence" might be taken at "the theologic parts". Without any sense of presumption, Lindsay opines that

> had either Luther or Calvin, when they struggled with the church on erronious points of faith, *protested* also against receiving *many*, if not all (the Books of the Law and the Prophets excepted) of the Jewish records – which however authenticated and held valuable by them, or however supported by the judgement of wrong headed Romish Councils, having no *proper claim* on the God of heaven as their author, there is not a protestant who would not have join'd in the matter, without the smallest hesitation.

The persistence of a contrary interpretation would, however, mean that his views would be likely to "raise a clamarous opposition from sectarists of every rigid denomination". Optimistically and with some apparent confusion, Lindsay hopes that such outrage might "give life to the subject – bring it into various and interesting points of view – make the tract, for various reasons besides the slave trade, be more generally read – may tend possibly to the discovery of truth and to emancipate the human mind from vulgar error, as well as human nature from the disgrace of slavery".[15]

Lindsay was ready for rejection, saying that "if after a thorough weighing of the matter, the bookseller shall think the sale will not be sufficient to support the publication", he wished the manuscript returned to him "for a further consideration – perhaps a little new modeling". Yet he had faith in the work, as well as in his own longevity: "I am strongly inclined to think, that, were the consideration of the African slave business, expunged from the work altogether, the tract as an improvement and criticism on the essays of Lord Kaims and Chevr. Buffon, Mr De Paw &c. with respect to the diversities of the human genus, would be received as a *standing book* and an acceptable present, amongst the liberal thinking and philosophic part of the world."[16]

In the letter Lindsay sent to Long together with the manuscript, he hints at a more extended correspondence. Lindsay promises to provide information "from the tombs", presumably inscriptions that might assist Long's genealogical researches. Two years before, in 1786, he had sent Long transcripts from the parish register for St Catherine. Lindsay also played on their relationship, concluding by saying, "Mrs Lindsay (an old schoolmate of Mrs Longs) joins me in warmest compts. to all your family", and he mentions "happy accounts of you" delivered by a mutual friend.[17] Lindsay seems to be clutching at straws in referring to such distant varieties of acquaintance, but no doubt he believed Long would share a fundamental interest in the particular philosophical contributions that might be found in his "Conjectural considerations". Long himself created a volume with the general title "On the different races of mankind", which consisted chiefly of notes made from contemporary writers of the 1770s and 1780s.[18] Lindsay's manuscript was just one of many volumes Long had among his collected papers. He did not destroy it or return it to Jamaica, suggesting that he thought there was value in it, but he added only the occasional comment or correction.

Four Hypotheses

The question at the core of Lindsay's "Conjectural considerations" is the origin of human diversity. He has been driven to this "very uncommon inquiry", he says, as a result of "being in some degree puzzled; and not at all myself fully satisfied of the *how*, in *what manner*, or by *what means* such strange diversities of the human race now appears – and in spite of all the arguments that learned men have produced in support of their several discordant theorys, there being still matter of much philosophical doubt remaining". Early in the work, in the third chapter, he identifies "four several hypotheses" bearing on the question, and it is these hypotheses he seeks to test.[19] He does not give them equal attention and much of his discussion is eclectic and diffuse, but the four hypotheses represent Lindsay's best effort at imposing order on his thoughts, and he does ultimately come down in favour of one of them as the best available explanation of human diversity.

PROSLAVERY PRIEST

The first of the hypotheses broached by Lindsay is that known as "the mark of Cain", a widely influential interpretation of Scripture attributed by Lindsay to Genesis, "Moses's first book". According to Lindsay, "It has been held by some that the contemptuous mark of distinction set upon Cain by almighty vengeance for the murder of righteous Abel, was the black skin and wooly hair of the Negroe". He argues that this is "an hypothesis not unworthy of notice; did not the subsequent flood of Noah, destroy such a position, in the opinion of all those who read this tremenduous judgement literally and without metaphor. The friends of this position however consider the universality of this flood as hyperbole, and at same time mixed with much allegory – that a great destruction happened, is unquestionable – but that all of the earth and the tops of the highest hills were covered are rhetorical figures." This "sort of writing was very common to Moses – as well as later writers".[20]

The second hypothesis refers to the scattering of peoples at the Tower of Babel. Lindsay associates it with "Lord Kaims, who supposes that the various appearances, colours, manners, and languages throughout the world, originated at the supernaturel confusion and dispersion of mankind, into a variety of latitudes at the building of the presumptuous Tower of Babel". This is an argument, observes Lindsay, "the truth of which he [Kames] himself suspects".[21] He gives it short shrift.

The third hypothesis is environmental, essentially climatic. Lindsay attributes it particularly to Buffon, who, "struggling hard against every hypothesis, which runs counter to the Mosaic account: endeavours to reconcile the contradictory appearances of nature, to one only pair formed in Paradice; attributing every subsequent difference to climate, food, and habits". Much the same view is held by de Pauw, says Lindsay, the difference being only that "his scene of proofs, are singular indeed – very strongly fought for – and laid in America – seeking to show that an impure air, and an imperfect and unfinished earth and atmosphere in the New World, is the sufficient and efficient cause, of all the varieties in mankind".[22]

The fourth hypothesis is in essence what came to be called polygenesis, according to which human beings had separate origins or creations in different parts of the world rather than being descended from an original single pair. The argument according to Lindsay is that "a diversity of races or species's in the human genus, had at the creation been provided by Providence sufficient for the diversity of all his climates". He attributes the idea to Kames and regrets that it is also the opinion of "a very sceptical gentleman, the celebrated David Hume Esqr." and equally "reprobated by the . . . much celebrated Principal, Dr Robertson". Lindsay finds himself on the wrong side. Despite its mixed pedigree and its general rejection by Scottish thinkers of the time, Lindsay considers that his fourth hypothesis would "perhaps be found the most concordant to the present systim of philosophy".[23]

All four hypotheses show the direct hand of God. The first three see God creating the human family from a single pair (monogenesis), whereas the fourth has God creating a diversity of peoples at the beginning (polygenesis). The first and second see God's intervention after the initial creation of a single "human race", in which the separation of races represents the response of the Almighty to social breakdown. Only the third hypothesis does not require God's active intervention beyond the creation of an original single race, with the emergence of separate races being a direct response to the God-created diversity of physical environments. Only the first and second of the hypotheses are seen to rest firmly on Scripture.

In order to demonstrate the truth of polygenesis, Lindsay had to traverse some difficult ground. He had to reject literal readings of Mosaic accounts of the Creation and the Flood, and of God's vengeance against Cain and against the builders of the Tower of Babel. To deny such readings Lindsay had also to reject pure versions of belief in the inspiration of Biblical texts. He had to advocate the plausibility of events not found in Scripture. Doing so placed him in conflict with the doctrines of the Church of England and on the side of heresy. Sceptical exegesis and free-thinking provided him with tools for the task, but these were attitudes he had himself publicly condemned. By 1788 they had been displaced by less extreme philosophies.

Conjectural Histories

Lindsay's approach to the problem of human diversity – the testing of his four hypotheses – is alternately philosophical, rational and theological. He disclaims the possibility of scientific observation and experiment but turns confidently to exegesis and reasoning. He says: "Hypothesis, speculation, conjecture and analogical conceptions, in their turns, go far we shall find, and must confess to form the foundation of this whole superstructure. For as neither mathematical reasoning nor positive evidence can be adduced in a business of *this kind* – we must be satisfied with the best arguments that present themselves."[24]

The closest Lindsay comes to mathematics occurs in his discussion of the depopulating effects of the Deluge, in which he promises to provide "a more fixed and even bordering upon mathematical demonstration, that *all mankind were not destroyed by this flood*".[25] This is not followed by any calculations or equations. In terms of collecting evidence, the best Lindsay can find to do is question washerwomen. To criticize Buffon's claim that "the sweat of Negroes" was "of a deeper shade or tinge than ours", Lindsay went out of his way "to interrogate in a very serious manner (and I conceive that was sufficient) a couple of laundress's on the point (one of whom my own; and by washing for a large and complicated family; of all colours and degrees – free and bond – white, black, and brown, makes her a competent evidence) but could not learn that a Negroe, *more than a white man*, left the smallest shade extraordinary discernable in depth or darkness of colour behind him".[26] He made no pretence of examining the sheets himself.

If science, mathematics and systematic observation seem of no great use to his task, Lindsay does take pains to establish his credentials and distinguish himself from the many uninformed commentators of the time. Occasionally he employs his botanical knowledge to undermine the authority of his rivals on philosophical and historical matters. Notably, he uses this method in his criticism of "Mr L'Abbe Renald" – meaning Abbé Guillaume-Thomas Raynal and his ten-volume *Histoire*, published in three successive editions (1770, 1774 and 1780) and appearing in English translation as *Philosophical and Political History of European Settlements and Commerce in the Two Indies* (1776). Lindsay devotes several paragraphs to exposing Raynal's ignorance of the difference between the cocoa tree and the coconut tree, taking the chance to relate his personal observations of palms during hurricanes. Raynal's descriptions, says Lindsay, are "express'd so very unlike a person who has been in any, tho a small, degree acquainted with the tree, that I know not what to say of it". Recalling his African experiences, Lindsay concludes that Raynal is equally mistaken about the oil palm, the nutmeg and the clove and "unfortunate in the manufacture of his arrack", making his book "an incoherent *translation* – an incorrect *copying*". Lindsay shows here an awareness of the multiple sources that made up Raynal's *Histoire*, though perhaps not that its radical discussion of imperialism came from the hand of the *philosophe* Denis Diderot. Lindsay's aim is to encourage suspicion not simply about Raynal's botanical credentials (as he will do for Moses) but also to show that so "cool and so fascinating a writer, is to be read with caution", to damp the "fire of zeal" that might be set alight by the politics of the work.[27]

Lindsay's title – "Conjectural considerations" – suggests an approximation to the method of "conjectural history", a concept shared with his Scottish Enlightenment contemporaries. Lindsay did not use the term; it was, in fact, coined only after his death, in 1793, but the essence of the approach is evident enough. The originator was Dugald Stewart (1753–1828), a Scots moral philosopher who used the phrase in an "account of the life and writings of

Adam Smith" presented to the Royal Society of Edinburgh. The remark occurs in the course of a discussion of Smith's "Dissertation on the Origin of Languages", first published in 1761.[28] In the absence of "direct evidence" to enable a reconstruction of the history of civilization, says Stewart, "we are under a necessity of supplying the place of fact by conjecture". He calls such investigation "*Theoretical* or *Conjectural History*" and says that it is "an expression which coincides pretty nearly in its meaning with that of *Natural History*, as employed by Mr Hume [in his *Natural History of Religion*], and with what some French writers have called *Histoire Raisonnée*".[29] Another important Scottish Enlightenment contributor to this theme, not mentioned by Lindsay, was Adam Ferguson (1723–1816), a professor of natural and moral philosophy at Edinburgh and teacher of Stewart. Ferguson's *Essay on the History of Civil Society* (1767) is devoted to tracing the progress of humankind, "the species itself[,] from rudeness to civilization". Working towards a "natural history of mankind", Ferguson advocates the use of descriptive and classificatory methods, as does John Millar in his *Observations Concerning the Distinction of Ranks in Society* (1771), a pioneering historical sociology.[30] It is not certain whether Lindsay was aware of this genealogy, but the ideas certainly appealed.

The generally positive attitude to conjectural history expressed by Ferguson, Millar and Stewart may be contrasted with the views of their German contemporary Immanuel Kant (1724–1804), the grandson of a Scot. His *Muthmasslicher Anfang der Menschengeschichte* was published in 1786 but not translated into English until 1798, as *The Conjectural Beginning of the History of Man*. Kant argues that whereas "[t]o intersperse conjectures in the progress of a history, in order to fill up chasms in the accounts, is by all means allowable", he believes that "to let a history arise out of conjectures entirely, seems little better, than to delineate the plan of a romance". With satirical intent, Kant uses Genesis to create a metaphorical "map" to underpin his hypothetical speculations, but he begins with man and woman (a single pair) fully formed and possessed of language and reason. Rather than original sin and divine providence, Kant makes humanity responsible for its progress towards liberty and equality. In this work, rather like Ferguson's, Kant's discussion of human diversity makes no use of the concept of race but looks rather to the developmental economic bases or "mode of life" of societies, with an emphasis on the conflict between pastoral and agricultural peoples located in a sequence of epochs. Kant came to race later.[31]

The Meaning of "Race"

It might seem reasonable to expect that Lindsay would have commenced his enquiry with a definition of race. The fact that he does not reflects both the fuzziness of the category in the middle of the eighteenth century and the lack of enthusiasm he showed for systematic classification in natural history. Lindsay's title refers to the creation of a singular human "race", not a plurality of races. Although the word *race* occurs often in "Conjectural considerations", Lindsay had no clear idea of what he meant by it. Typically, his use of the word offers only generalized references to physical, behavioural and moral characteristics. Lindsay does speak of "genus or race", "one race or species" and "a class or race of people", but the rules remain plastic throughout, sometimes connecting the individuals of a population, sometimes distinguishing subgroups within them. Lindsay's claim, noted above, that it was possible to identify black Africans as a "race of people" more easily in the context of slave society than in the great diversity of peoples within continental Africa, points to a process of generalization, though still imprecise. Here he plays on the advantage of his knowledge of Jamaica. There, he says, people from twenty or more African nations might be found in a single field, and "In such a situation, there can be no mistaking, no hiding, no paliating, no playing the hypocrite in their capacities nor in their dispositions."[32]

Modern dictionaries define *race* as meaning a subgroup of the human species that uniquely shares common physical traits. None of the dictionaries Lindsay might have consulted defined race in this way. For the British, the concept remained bound up with older alternative methods of classification, such as *nation* and *tribe* or specifics such as *Americans* or *Negroes*. Only gradually was *race* adopted to identify large units of population. For Lindsay it was a work in progress.[33]

The new emphasis on *race*, as against the finer distinctions recognized in *nation*, derived in part from the generalizing and homogenizing tendencies of slavery and imperialism. It was apparent in works such as Raynal's *Histoire* (1770) and Robertson's *History of America* (1777), as well as in the writings of Thomas Jefferson and Benjamin Franklin, though others such as Buffon persisted in emphasizing the internal diversity of Africa and the Americas. The mixing of African nations in American slave societies, as well as the emergence of a relatively homogeneous creole population, contributed to the European perception of uniformity. Black Africans – "Negroes" – came to be attributed "a general uniformity" or "race" that transcended region and nation. It was a way of reducing the plenitude of variation in human physical types to a (relatively) small number of possible classes or groups and placing them in a hierarchy of human worth.[34]

These European tendencies of thought, derived from imperialism and slavery, came to receive authority from science. It was only through science that *race* came to have a precise definition, taken to mean a set of physical characteristics, notably skin colour and morphology, or a biological classification that could describe or measure differences between human groups and between the individuals belonging to those groups. Only in the later seventeenth century did Europeans begin to include human beings within the scope of "natural history" and to think of people as varying in the same way as plants and animals, and equally open to systematic classification – an attitude of mind in which Lindsay showed little interest. Gradually humans came to be assimilated into the animal kingdom rather than distinguished because they were thought to possess souls.[35]

Linnaeus included humans only in the second edition of his *General System of Nature*, published in 1740, raising eyebrows by subjecting humankind to the same taxonomic principles he had applied to plants and animals. Linnaeus here divided people into four categories – *Europaeus albus*, *Americanus rubescens*, *Asiaticus fuscus* and *Africanus niger* – on the dual basis of continent and skin colour. This scientific system of classification not only departed from the biblical tripartite division derived from Noah's sons but also laid the foundations for a scientific racism that matched popular (European Christian) notions that distinguished red and yellow, black and white. Thus humans became a species, first termed *Homo sapiens* by Linnaeus in the canonical tenth edition of his work, published in 1758, rather than a special part of the natural kingdom distinguished by "reason". The orang-utan, lacking language, was not included. Linnaeus was a "special creationist", believing that each species was created specifically by God, and he came only reluctantly to accept that new species might be created by hybridization. He saw humanity as a continuum, divisible into "varieties", but the idea of "race" and its corollary, "degeneracy" – emerged ultimately as the dominant concept.[36]

The idea of race persisted in spite of the absence of any agreement on the number of races that existed or on how individuals should be allocated to them. Hundreds were named. Only in the later twentieth century, with the identification of the gene and DNA, did the concept of race come finally to be rejected as unfounded in biology. As a system of classifying people, race is now regarded as a concept both inaccurate and useless, lacking any foundation in human biology. This conclusion derives from the observation that, although popular markers such as skin colour are genetically transmitted, skin colour may be a poor indicator of shared genetic heritage. For humans (though not for all animals) the biological reality is one of continuous variation and genetic boundaries that do not define specific populations in isolation. All modern humans are now known to have originated in Africa about two hundred thousand years ago and to have spread around the globe over the past seventy thousand years. However, the rejection of race as a category is not the same thing as denying the fact of human diversity. Genetic diversity is in fact greatest in Africa, matching the continent's large number of languages and ethnolinguistic groups. Both in human genetics and in ethnography – as well as in everyday life – the recognition of difference remains important and intriguing. It is equally true that the historical roots of discrimination and exploitation based on human difference go very deep. But this ancient racism existed in the absence of a coherent theory of the concept of race.[37]

Lindsay was present at the birth of the idea of race. He struggled to make sense of it through the system of thought in which he placed his faith: Christian theology as interpreted through Scripture. His early encounters across the Atlantic did not equip him for the task. When he was in Virginia, in the early 1750s, British perceptions of difference were still in process. The "Indian" was seen to have a different skin colour, though the term *red* was not commonly used until the nineteenth century. In *Memoirs*, Lindsay's images of the African and the Native American are ambiguously romantic and derogatory but lack a theory of race. The blackness of the black African, or "Negro", was well established as a distinguishing feature in European perceptions, the colour being encapsulated in the name and its negativity. Lindsay learned this in Britain, but his perception of the Senegalese was broadly positive.[38]

Whereas he seemed comfortable enough with an anthropocentric teleology – the idea that God's creation was directed solely towards his plan for humankind – Lindsay struggled with the problem of what made "man" human and where he should be located within the cosmos. He defines his subject as "The human part of the creation – and I mean, the machine only – *Man*, as we see him". In doing so, he wishes not to suggest a lack of interest in the inner being ("soul"), and indeed he pursues alternative possibilities. Thus, for example, Lindsay recognizes that God might have chosen to create "a world of spirits" rather than men with a spiritual part (the soul), or beings "*immaterial* as well as *immortal*", or even immortal rational beings.[39] More important, he feels confident that the inner, spiritual being can be discerned in the outer shape, the body/machine. The implication is that the character of the soul – not the individual's state of grace – might vary, so that, for example, "a dull, heavy, lubberly clown, has in reality a soul perfectly concordant to his outward appearance". Although an argument for the inequality of souls might appear unorthodox, Lindsay uses it to ask "if God has not created from the beginning, different species's of the *human genus*, he has at least permitted (in the course of his Providence – and for reasons very obvious to society) the soul frequently, to degenerate with the body? . . . Or if on the other supposition, they are only the more refined part of the animal composition." However interpreted, says Lindsay, "the feelings of the *inward mind* is happily permitted to give way, and suit itself to the fate and circumstances of the *outward machine* – whither to command or to obay". Implicit in the argument is the notion that mental capacity is equally indicated by external form, with the best minds occupying the most perfect bodies.[40]

The notion that souls might vary in quality in tandem with the human body contributed directly to Lindsay's explanation of human diversity as well as his model of social order. He makes his case plainly, though recognizing that "such an opinion of different capacities of soul, may be obnoxious to some, who are now a days set agogg on *universal liberty* and who must plead doubtless for a *universal equality* too". Rejecting such egalitarian claims, Lindsay contends that "there certainly are people and races of men, intersperced by Gods providence, and design'd, or ordain'd by creation, to serve and to be in subjection, to those formed with superior gifts or superior enduements". Evidence can be found in Scripture (Genesis 27:40), in "the case of the elder brother Esau, who whither it was from the superior arts and contrivance of Isaac, or a deficiency in the brain or cloudiness in the intellects of Esau, that could not preserve his rank and birthright when he might; but certainly was by *divine permission ordeand to serve his brother*". Lindsay realizes such doctrine might startle "the squeamish religionist" but observes that it is a doctrine "as old as the creation; as it is also every day fulfilling". There is nothing strange in it theologically, he says, since in all nations there are "whole families nay whole districts, as well as single persons, who are so inferior – or so brutified . . . in their natural capacities, that all the instruction of the world, would be lost upon them – nothing could give them a capacity or fit them for any higher purpose than the lowest drudgeries of the community they live in". The law and the gospel, Lindsay is convinced, have shown that it is better that "poor, ignorant, and low-endued people, all the world over, . . . had fixed servitudes for life" rather than being "hired into service for some years or months – and turn'd out a begging, stealing, or starving for as many more".[41]

By these means, Lindsay is able to draw the conclusion that God's creation contains a natural and well-regulated hierarchy. Rather than man's being "a perfect individual – *independent* of every other", he was "created for a reciprocal intercourse with his fellows in society, each depending on his neighbour; the weakly constitutioned, to improve the genius, so as to direct to advantage – to guide and by improved skill to direct in peace, safety, and wisdom, the labours of the more robust – and those, on their part, conscious of an inferiority in the mental powers, thankfully to contribute their industry and labours, to the support of their venerable protectors". Not only do these distinct but interdependent human beings exist in nature, says Lindsay, but because "we find the whole species, in numbers properly proportioned, as well as in abilities properly fitted, both to serve, and to be in want of servants – we have only to admire the marvelous wisdom of kind Providence – and to be thankful".[42]

In these ways, Lindsay connects his discussion of racial difference with the concept of the great chain of being, in which the God-given ordering of things determined their relative statuses within a naturally interdependent and interlocking hierarchy. From the humblest to the greatest, from the most minute grain of sand or the smallest insect all the way to God himself, each link played a necessary and virtuous role. Although the essentials of the concept were ancient, the idea was by no means universal, and indeed it was anathema to animists and anarchists. The notion of cosmic harmony had its greatest currency in the seventeenth century, when it was broadly accepted by European philosophers, fiction writers, deists and orthodox clergy. Rather than existing solely as a model of the macrocosm, the principles of the chain were seen to work equally at smaller scales, as in the family or a kingdom. At every level, chaos threatened when any weak link was exposed. To maintain the natural and social order, sons had to respect their fathers, subjects their monarchs, and mortals their god. The chain was both incredibly strong and incredibly vulnerable. In the larger scheme, human beings came to be seen as the "middle link", located between the creatures of the earth and the much more numerous celestial species above, stretching at length to the infinite being, God.[43]

In "Conjectural considerations", Lindsay is quick to enter a disclaimer, saying:

> I wish to avoid giving the smallest offence upon the subject – there are those who are uneasy at the idea of making the African an *inferior link in the chain of nature*. I think them not so. The orang-outang or ape may be *inferior links* in the great chain – but the Negroe, as a rational animal, must be part of the *human link* itself – tho still of an *inferior nature* (mark me, not an *inferior link*) as steel and iron two distinct metals may be intermix'd in the formation of one and the same link.

Here Lindsay distinguished himself from the arguments of those who sought to assimilate the orang-utan as a "barbarous nation" of humanity. Reiterating the point, Lindsay says that "from the extreme brutification of Negroes in general, it being a vulgarly held received opinion amongst the unlearned of the Europeans in the West Indies that Negroes are not by any means of the human genus – this idea I willingly sunk with my own – cautiously timerous, lest in days of licentious infidelity, the smallest mite from me should be added to the train of opposition against the inspiration of God, thro Moses, the prophets and the evangelists".[44]

In taking this strong stand on the humanity of Africans, Lindsay places himself in opposition not only to "unlearned" Europeans but also to the "learned" Edward Long and his followers. Although Lindsay drew on ideas and information found in Long's celebrated *History of Jamaica* of 1774 and approved much of what Long had to say, he did not accept Long's interpretation of the chain of being that allocated the "Negro" a separate link, nearer to the apes than to human beings. Lindsay thought Long's model too close to vulgar opinion of the type reported by William Jones in Jamaica in 1778: "A creole gentle – I shou'd have said savage – man told me, 'that he believed the Negroes to be no more than overgrown apes, and that a man could not hurt them, except he killed them'."[45] Thus, whereas Lindsay became a strict polygenist, believing that God created separately unique varieties of human beings, distinct from the apes, Long included the "Negro" only by expanding his definition of *human* to encompass the orang-utan as well. Long's argument leads him to conclude that "we cannot but allow, that the Deity might, if it was his pleasure, diversify his works in this manner, and either withhold the *superior principle* entirely, or in part only, or infuse it into the different classes and races of human creatures, in such portions, as to form the same gradual climax towards perfection in this human system, which is so evidently designed in every other".[46] Long's view was less obviously polygenist than assimilated to a Linnaean version of the chain of being, in which humans sit comfortably in the amazing "series and progression from a lump of dirt to a perfect human being" but separated by a great gulf from "the most perfect angelic being" and, in turn, "the Deity himself".[47]

Although differences between races might be philosophically unpalatable, the contrasts are in practice observed "every day of our lives", says Lindsay, with the model of Jamaican slave society firmly in mind. He offers a simple proof:

> In a European stranger, his language is perhaps the only difference twixt him and us [in Jamaica] – but with his son, born and bred in the same country with ourselves, we make no allowances or considerations whatever – but it is not so with a Negroe. Let him be most carefully brought up among Europeans so that his language may be extreamly articulate; yet never will it be compleat: and here and there one out of thousands may be found wonderously correct but correct *considering he is a Negroe.*[48]

Lindsay continues:

PROSLAVERY PRIEST

> He is clever in some mechanical parts of operative business – But has never shown any *dexterity in inventing anything new*; however he does every thing that can be *expected from a Negroe*. Black Williams wrote Latin poems – tis true they were not equal in diction to the elegance of Virgil – Phillis Wheatly has the name of a volume of poems, tho not to compare even to the Ayrshire ploughman [Robert Burns, who was about to emigrate to Jamaica in 1786 when his successful *Poems, Chiefly in the Scottish Dialect* was published]. And Sanches may have wrote an account of his life and achievements; tho not in so flowrey a stile, as to be commended with rapture – yet all of them wonderously well, *considering they are Negroes*. Now, why this *consideration*? Tis true, 'tis what we constantly do – but 'tis as certainly a constant admission of an inferiority in the genus or race – and that the Negroe having fewer talents given him than the white, less is expected from him.

Here Lindsay follows critical contemporaries in not only questioning the authenticity of Phillis Wheatley's *Poems on Various Subjects, Religious and Moral* (1773) and of the *Letters of the Late Ignatius Sancho* (1782) but also disparaging the quality of their writing and associating them with Francis Williams of Spanish Town.[49]

Inspiration, Earth History and Sacred History

In spite of the importance of conjectural history and philosophy to Lindsay's task, and without a satisfactory definition of race to guide his study, it was the status of revealed religion and the authority of Scripture that exercised him most. Here he felt most vulnerable, most anxious to remain anonymous. He also had a practical fear, on behalf of the beneficiaries of West Indian slavery, that extreme scepticism might place "the *whole sacred volume* under the suspicion of error, or as one intire delusion", with the effect of "undermining and weakening the support of that religion which is, always was, and ever must be the very and *only* cement of society and of *every thing valuable in their country*, and which may suffer from this quarter".[50] Thus, in view of his own obvious scepticism, he ultimately rested his argument on a pragmatic social foundation rather than a philosophical or theological base.

On the question of inspiration, the belief that the Scriptures represent the word of God, Lindsay adheres to a qualified conception that enables him to pick and choose. Although he declares, "we are firm advocates for scriptural inspiration", he excepts interpretations which are "wild and enthusiastic" and concludes that "inspiration is by no means an *uniform idea*, but various in *kind*, and in *information*; in its *fullness* and its *precision*". He argues that not all of "the books received as canonical" are indeed "*in every part inspired*", and further that "even in the *inspired parts*, they are not *all, equally inspired*". The consequence is that some passages of Scripture are simply "traditional", or derived from "experience" and "learned observations". In spite of this, Lindsay manages somehow to argue that although he opposes "the general received opinion of thousands of ages; and more particularly in two very singular points", he holds to the belief that none of this will "shake or weaken, those parts of sacred truth which concern salvation".[51]

The problem of inspiration had several aspects. There was first of all the manner of transmission from God to the hand of the writer. Lindsay believed inspiration signified "a singular light, granted by God to peculiar men, on peculiar sacred occasions". These men were "like so many lamps with glasses of different perfections and clearness – the gifts and induements of some, will be (from their nature) more full and resplendant than others – there therefore must be, as many degrees of inspiration, as there are degrees of ingenuity in the persons inspired". Next came the problem of transcription. Here Lindsay adopts the brand of sarcasm for which freethinkers and deists were famous, saying, "Tis true God might have, *preventatively inspired* a *million of such copiers!* Tis to be rather wish'd however, that God had at this time gratiously inspired *one or two men of ingenuity* with the idea and invention of printing and making of paper."[52]

In a passage he thought might not be fit to print, Lindsay opines that ancient scriptural texts have to be "read with extream caution, and perhaps with some hesitation" and "held as doubtful, on particular points of record".[53] The central figure is Moses, purported writer of the book of Genesis. If Moses can be declared an "*inspired historian*", then there can be "an end put to all those difficulties, tropes, and figures which we have been supposing". However, Lindsay finds that Moses himself had no "ripe or ready ideas of *inspiration*" and lacked "any idea like to that idea of *inspiration* which the *influence of the Holy Spirit* thro' the *gospel* has given to Christians". For the purposes of his "investigations into the diversities of the human race", he begins with "figure and allegory", the use of which by ancient authors makes it difficult "to draw a satisfactory line" between their writings and "plain history". Lindsay opposes the "literal explaination" of Scripture and observes that even "our saviour himself . . . constantly taught in metaphor: and while privately expounding the plain meaning of his doctrines to his disciples, often declared, that if the world valued his instructions, it should cost them trouble to come at them". Moses too was often "hyperbolical", and his books contain "seemingly incorrect pieces of narration" together with "a mixture of interpolation, mistaken policy, and false copying".[54]

Consequently, Lindsay finds Moses "defective in his history of the creation", particularly because "his account is calculated to meet the old and erronius idea, of the earths being the principle object of the creators attention – the great – the fixed and central point of the whole creation". He declares that, in Genesis, "perhaps the very first verse – *In the beginning God created the heavens and the earth*, gives us as much instruction, as all the subsequent glimmering amplifications will ever do. Let us read the account figuratively – let it be *allegory* – and 'tis well." Lindsay concludes that Moses's first book "wants so much assistance, to support any other idea of it, than a collection of antient well authenticated *oral traditions*. And many a sensible Jew with whom I have conversed on their Books, think of Genesis, no otherways." In its modern, positive sense, "oral tradition" was a coinage of the eighteenth century and closely associated with James Macpherson's study of ancient Scottish Highland verse, as well as assessments of Homer. The concept was controversial, however, and Lindsay's attitude remained negative and dismissive, much like his challenge of the credulity of Benjamin Franklin.[55]

In Lindsay's argument, there is a close association of his interpretation of Scripture with his understanding of earth's history and human diversity. The question whether, and if so why, God separately created multiple varieties of humankind paralleled the creation of separate worlds. Lindsay confesses that he finds the "common received opinion" – placing the origins of humankind in the Garden of Eden – to be "a starved conception of the almighty creator". He considers it strange that, "having form'd so capacious a theatre as this *stary sphere*", the Almighty should immediately confine the action of the universe to one small spot. Lindsay argues that

> The continents even of a small part of which (this earth for instance) are yet so widely distant in connexion, by dividing seas – immense oceans – or barriered in from each other by impenitrable deserts or impassable rocks and mountains: that till the art of navigation led to communications with each other – the creator had kept or seem'd to keep all as it were under cover; designing them, it would appear, as *whets* to the *minds of posterity* – and to keep up a constant spur to the *curiosity* and *improvement of mankind*.

The outcome was that

> the vast inhabitable parts of that earth, by this account, must have remained for thousands of years uninhabited, uncultivated and wild (contrary to the very purpose of creation in human idea) except a small corner about Palastine; till by the very late invention of the loadstone adventurous men should cross the different oceans to find out or begin the population of new worlds. I say, such an opinion seeming fully as poor and confined as the miserable short-sighted idea, so long fondly hugg'd by the antients, both in philosophy and theology – that the solar systim with the innumerable host of heaven were all form'd for *earth-born-men alone*

– first to be enlighten'd by them then to divide their time: and after a vast round of centuries to divert a few pleasant fellows upon the top of observatories, by peeping through glasses at them, as they moved along![56]

Lindsay's God was more expansive, more philosophical.

As to the flood, Lindsay did not doubt its reality. He says: "The account handed down to us of the deluge, carries more the appearance of plain unadorn'd narration, than metaphor or allegory: and as such, is too incorrect and deficient, for modern experience and a more extencive knowledge of things, to be pleased with it." In the first place, Lindsay can find no wrong sufficient to justify God's drowning of the whole world. Second, he wonders at the absence of plant life in the account of Noah's flood, noting that it must have been wiped out if the Deluge was truly universal and prolonged. This was, says Lindsay, "a prodigious oversight", showing that "Moses was no critic – and but an indifferent botanist".[57]

Lindsay's conclusion is that the Deluge could not have been universal and therefore that the Mosaic account is at best misleading. However, he found in the Flood narrative grist for his polygenist mill. Lindsay wonders, "out of curiosity, . . . what became of that race of beings, mighty and gigantic: and who themselves it seems, had no small share, in provoking the almighty to that devastation we have been considering". In Genesis, these people "were positively (by Moses's account and the chronology of the antediluvian tradition) not the race of Adam" but called "*sons of God*", suggesting a distinction but also an ignorance of their origins and location. In Numbers, however, "we meet with a race of the same men: who inhabited Hebron in the hills towards the east of Palestine – where the spies of Israel found Abiman, Sheshai, and Talmai, three chiftians of the giants or children of Anak – whose bare appearance much alarmed the spies, and the accounts thereof broke the courage of the whole camp of Israel". In Deuteronomy they "were known to the *Moabites* by the name *Emims*, and called by the *Ammonites Zamzummims*". Lindsay found this interesting because "such a race could not have sprung by chance, from a few tall individuals keeping to each other: for it is observed of gigantic people amongst ourselves that they are seldom healthy or long lived – robust nor prolific". And "if such a nation had sprung up amongst the race of Adam they could not have subsisted, unknown to them, either by fixed genealogy, or some sort of tradition or other".[58]

The outcome, argues Lindsay, was that "if there were giants before the flood . . . they were *either drowned* or *not drowned*". So, "If the deluge was *universal, they were drown'd*. But we find they *were not drowned*. Therefore *their existance afterwards*, is as strong a proof as a matter of this nature can have, *that the deluge was not universal*." The supposed existence of such pre-Adamite beings – both giants and pygmies – not only contested monogenetic interpretations, in the same way that the European discovery of an inhabited New World challenged understanding of the descent of humankind – and the definition of what it was to be human and possess a soul – but also threatened the whole edifice of a universal salvation history, with its beginning in Creation and its end in the Final Judgement.[59] It was heresy, a siren beckoning Lindsay towards polygenesis.

The Mark of Cain and the Curse of Ham

Lindsay showed little interest in the "mark of Cain" – the notion that Cain, the first son of Adam and Eve and murderer of his brother Abel, was condemned for his crime to wander east of Eden. The story represents not only the severity of God's vengeance but also symbolizes the moral distinction between civilization and barbarism which supposedly left Cain marked by "the black skin and wooly hair of the Negroe". It is discussed by Lindsay only in relation to the Deluge, and promptly dismissed on the grounds that if the Flood wiped out all peoples except those in Noah's ark, then whatever happened before the Deluge mattered not at all. If other people survived the flood, then many other explanations offered themselves.[60]

Lindsay was more interested in the claim that black people were descended from the sons of Ham, who was cursed by Noah, but it is not one of his four hypotheses and he mentions Ham but once in "Conjectural considerations". The omission is significant because the curse was actively being developed as a central element of the proslavery argument being directed exclusively at black Africans at the time Lindsay was writing. The essence of the story is that all peoples descend from Noah's household, the sole survivors of the Deluge, and that one branch of the family was, through the curse, condemned to wear "the colour of hell" and subject to perpetual slavery.[61]

Versions of this meaning were argued by contemporary commentators, including those on whom Lindsay depended, notably Rev. Dr William Dodd (1729–77), whose three-volume *Commentary on the Books of the Old and New Testament* began to emerge in 1764. A graduate of Cambridge and a clergyman in the Church of England, Dodd had hoped for a literary career, publishing poetry and a novel before turning definitively to the production of compilations and digests, with which he had great success. Ironically, he was hanged for forgery in 1777 after being denied mercy by Lord Mansfield.[62] Dodd tackles the curse of Ham in his commentary on Genesis 9:22–25. There, when Noah's youngest son, Ham, "saw the nakedness of his father",

Noah said, "Cursed be Canaan [the fourth son of Ham]; a servant of servants shall he be unto his brethren." Dodd considers it wrong to think this curse specific to Canaan but argues rather that it must apply to "his whole race" or "whole nations", committing them to "the servitude and misery, which their more than common vices and iniquities would deserve". The Canaanites were, says Dodd, "abominably wicked", corrupt in morals and religion and regularly involved in "unlawful marriages, and unlawful lusts, witchcraft, adultery, incest, sodomy, beastiality, and the like monstrous crimes". The curse confirmed that "the natural consequence of vice in communities, as well as in single persons, is slavery". Dodd sees this servitude as spreading persistently, over many generations, through Carthage and Egypt ("the land of Ham") and continuing with the trade in people across the Atlantic. He concludes: "Nothing then, it appears, can be more complete than the execution of the sentence upon Ham, as well as upon Canaan".[63]

In spite of his general approval of Dodd, Lindsay shows no interest in this interpretation, not even questioning what might seem the wrongly directed nature of God's judgement and its unequal harshness. His only reference to the sons of Ham occurs in his extended discussion of the contested relationship of Moses with Zipporah, as well as that of Aaron and Miriam. Quoting the Hebrew, Lindsay disputes the supposed marriage between Moses and Zipporah, daughter of Jethro, and argues that, in any case, "the children of this lady, introduced as nephews into the family, were not a couple of wooly headed mulattos – but only a shade or two deeper in their own brownette – and that perhaps only from a little more southerly climate". Lindsay claims that "Jethro was actually sprung of the seed of Ham the father of Cush" and "settled to the southward of Arabea, built Babel and settled Nineveh". He therefore denies that Jethro was an "Ethiopean".[64]

The Tower of Babel

Another hypothesis given short shrift by Lindsay is that associated with the problem of explaining the diversity of human language. It is here that he parts company with Kames, who clung to the hypothesis for reasons of religion. Although a religious sceptic and a friend of David Hume as well as Adam Smith and Benjamin Franklin, Kames was neither a deist nor a dissenter. Threatened with excommunication by the Church of Scotland for his *Essays on the Principles of Morality and Natural Religion* (1751), Kames claimed to be a committed Presbyterian. A lawyer and judge, he had an eclectic interest in philosophical subjects and published on many subjects. It was his *Sketches of the History of Man*, first published in 1774, that particularly attracted Lindsay. Kames not only observed inequality between races or peoples, as many before had done, but also gave race a prominent role in his theory of society. In this he was a pioneer. Lindsay, in spite of his ecclesiastical status, pressed on where Kames drew back, daring to tread paths of exegesis that led into deep theological thickets.[65]

According to Lindsay, Kames concludes plausibly "that God at the creation created pairs of the human race, fitted for the different climates he had made on the globe; and placed each pair in their proper abodes – and left each, in time to form languages for themselves and their posterities". What Kames actually says is "that there are different races or kinds of men, and that these races or kinds are naturally fitted for different climates". However, says Lindsay, because this seems to Kames "so opposite to Moses's accounts of the creation and variety of languages, he tries to solve both by the confusion of tongues at Babel, and by that means scattered mankind all abroad upon the Earth: God, also miraculously changing the universal constitutions and colours of the emigrants to the different climates they should betake themselves unto". Lindsay considers this a tortured argument, requiring a "miracle . . . tantamount to a *second creation*". Kames contends that the confusion of Babel is "the only known fact that can reconcile sacred and profane history", but Lindsay thinks even Kames must have recognized that "there is more of allegory in that account, than plain history".[66]

Lindsay ponders further the problem of the development of language and its diversity and the various names given to things. He dismisses the notion that language and nomenclature were given by God at the beginning. Rather, he says, "we find every nation and language have since, given all of those particulars, names of their own; which if they had considered them as the language of God and heaven, they would never have been changed by any nation on earth, for any other words or terms of distinction whatever – but all the world over would have been the same".[67] And why should God have stopped at language? Adopting a sarcastic stance, Lindsay observes:

> There can be no doubt, but that the world might have been created . . . a more inlightened one. God, had he chose it, might have made Adam a present of a pair of globes, an orrary, a telescope, a mariners compass &c and while in Paradice he might have given him a few lessons on the sciences, and the uses of his instruments – and which would have been of more value towards the immediate cultivation of society and the civilization of mankind, than his making him a suit of cloaths, when from his disobedience he richly deserved to have gone naked – at least till his own ingenuity and necessity might have taught him to couple skins together, as he had already sow'd the fig leaves. But God, having given him an improveable mind, speech and every social attainment, was to be got in time and practice, without the aid of extraordinary miracles.[68]

In some general comments on the knowledge of the natural world available to the ancients, Lindsay argues that both in "the Old Testament accounts" and in passages of "gospel history", it is necessary to make "the amplest and most liberal allowances". He says: "Those early writers were perfectly in the dark respecting that philosophical knowledge which had then only began to dawn upon the learned world. The evangelists were inspired with gospel, not astronomical knowledge: at least not that part of it, which was yet in perfect infancy – the spherical formation of the earth, contrary to the old opinion of its being one spacious extended plane, was understood, but by few." Thus, for example, although the devil took Jesus to the top of "an exceeding high mountain" to tempt him, it was impossible for him to show him "all the kingdoms of the world" (Matthew 4:8). Even if the devil had taken Jesus to the moon, says Lindsay, he could not have shown "even the smallest village, on the opposite side of the globe – unless indeed his devilship had taken it into his head, to whisk the whole globe itself round, in that moment of time, for the Lords inspection". Lindsay concludes that "the evangelists" gave only a vivid picture of the temptation and that it is with "the same liberal degree of exposition, we must read many other passages, which is apt to assist the free thinker in his scepticism".[69]

Climate

Race theory rooted in environmental influences did not dispute the original Edenic Creation but sought rather to explain human diversity as adaptation to regional variations in nature, particularly climate. Lindsay first tackles this hypothesis in the seventh chapter of "Conjectural considerations" – titled "Observations on the diversity of men, from the Sketches of Lord Kaims" – and pursues it further in the following two chapters, which are devoted to the ideas of Buffon, de Pauw, Abbé de Brügel D. Pernety and Abbé Clavigero. No doubt Lindsay's strong focus on this hypothesis reflects his interest in the natural world and natural history, but the argument is mixed up with his advocacy of polygenesis. Writers enamoured of environmental determinism took centre stage in bridging the chasm between revelation and scientific observation. They also contributed to the construction of ideas about natural regions which overlapped ideas about human diversity and its geographical distribution. Both regionalization and racialization were essentially systems of classification, and it was in this context that Lindsay began to formulate a much more refined, modern definition of what he understood by race.

Once again Lindsay turned to the influential work of Kames, whose *Sketches of the History of Man* offered not only an appealing version of polygenesis but also contributed substantially to demolition of the environmental hypothesis. In *Sketches*, Kames distinguishes between his use of documents to elucidate recent history and his speculative, conjectural approach to deep time and the emergence of civilizations, claiming that he wishes to trace development towards civilization and maturity in all nations but being pessimistic about the chances.[70] Lindsay quotes extensively from *Sketches*, using the first edition of 1774. Kames also provided ready-made critiques of Buffon and Montesquieu, and his approach suited Lindsay's method. Strangely, Lindsay mentions Montesquieu only twice, but he was, after all, more concerned with political theory than with natural history and more important for his influence than for the originality of his environmental determinism. More broadly, Lindsay was unwilling to see good in almost any French writer. He completely ignored the aberrant polygenist Voltaire, whose ridicule of Buffon was at least as intense as the critique offered by Kames.[71]

In the environmental field, the basic argument of Kames, which Lindsay agrees with, was that "no animal nor vegetable is fitted for every climate; and from experience we also learn, that there is no animal or vegetable but what is fitted for some climate, where it grows to perfection". Lindsay applies his experience of the Jamaican environment to this general principle, noting variations by altitude as well as latitude. Taking the example of the camel, an animal "peculiarly fitted for the burning sands of Arabia", Lindsay observes that when "transplanted from thence to Jamaica, in hopes they would thrive as a useful beast of burden or of draught", they failed and were by the 1780s "extinct, and out of breed". From plants and animals, Lindsay follows Kames in moving on to argue that "all men are not fitted equally for every climate", noting the extremes of heat and cold but saying: "Even in Jamaica whose climate is moderated by a regular and constant sea and land breeze, by day and by night, the white people are obliged to recruit their numbers by fresh supplies from Britain – as well as to return thither at times to brace up and draw a little northern air."[72]

The next problem for Lindsay (and Kames) was whether people of a particular place or nation changed their physical characteristics when exposed to a different climatic regime, and whether over generations such change might be sufficient to make them seem natural to that new regime. These were important questions because proof that people change in response to climate would mean that a single original human pair could be responsible for all human diversity, the range of variation marking the range of climates around the world. Lindsay could find no support for this theory. Drawing on the American example, he declares: "Africans have had four complete generations in the northern climate of Pensilvania, and yet continue black as at first – and let a Europian expose for years his face, neck, and hands, to the meridian sun – and withering breezes – of the torrid zone, till he is as brown as an old rusty Spanish Jew, his children will yet be fair as a European."[73]

Lindsay's extended critique was directed particularly at Buffon, the prominent adversary of Linnaeus. Buffon's *Histoire naturelle, générale et particulière* began publication in 1749 but took eighteen years to complete; it was available in English translation by 1775, as *The Natural History of Animals, Vegetables, and Minerals; with the Theory of the Earth in General.* His discussion of "the varieties in the human species" is directed at defending the uniqueness and original unity of humanity. Differences in colour (including the colour of eyes and hair and the pigmentation of the albino, or *négre blanc*), as well as in "form and size" and "disposition", he explains principally as a response to variation in the physical environment. As Lindsay read him, Buffon was an advocate of the view "*that climate, custom and manner of feeding, cause all those varieties in the colour, size, make and appearance, we meet with in human kind*".[74] It was not a new view. Buffon was simply more obstinate in tracing all difference back to external factors. Opposing the binomial system of Linnaeus and rejecting measurement, Buffon preferred a holistic style of classification that made his attempts at taxonomy inexact and inconsistent, with slippage between concepts of race, species and nation. He believed that white was the "natural" or original colour of people and that deviations (notably Native Americans, Laplanders and "Negroes") were therefore degenerate "races".[75] This was an approach that matched (European) folk knowledge and consequently proved highly influential.

As an example of his errors, Lindsay attacks Buffon's account of cold-climate peoples:

> In examining the nations towards the north, the Esquimaux of America, the inhabitants of Greenland, Iceland, Nova Zembla, Norway, Swedland, Lapland, Finland, and all the northern parts of Russia, Muscovy, Samoides, Borandians, Siberians, the numerous extended Tartars, including even the northern Chinese, are to outward appearance the same people. Their visages are large, broad and flat, their noses like the Negroe, flated down; their cheeks very much raised; with very wide mouths; thick lips poking forewards; squicking voices; large heads; small feet and hands; course lank hair; and tawny skins – they are a diminutive race; from four feet to four feet and an half the highest: a deform'd, half-begotten race, even the very handsomest.

Lindsay concedes that these peoples, "unlike any other of the humane race", were perhaps "formed by nature for the inhospitable climate they posess". From his description of the miserable lives of these ugly beings, Lindsay leaps immediately to the problem of Creation, saying, "If the whole inhabitants of the earth are sprung from Adam and Eve – they must have been quick indeed in their migration; for there are very old standers, indeed beyond the knowledge of history, in these northern regions." More important, they were happy and at home in their bleak climates, "for even Paradice would seem so to them".[76]

The satisfaction of the world's peoples with their particular environmental niches, however forbidding, seemed to Lindsay proof that "the God of prolific nature" had created so vast and varied an earth with clear intention. It is foolish, he says, to imagine that, having "adornd and finished so compleatly from pole to pole (with trees, plants, nay grass for different soils – beast, fowls, and insects to suit each peculiar latitude – nay fish, for their peculiar and natural seas and rivers)", it could have been God's intention that all this "should lie so long unknown to mankind; and uncultivated continue in waste and neglected ruin, except to one infantine family in the environs of Palestine – when his own power and perfectitude could have set the whole prolific creation to work, with his first finishing fiat". It was an idea contrary to God's command to go out and multiply. Dismissing exasperatedly Buffon's climatic argument, Lindsay asks:

> Is it not more likely, to suppose, that God of his infinite power, goodness and mercy, would have done all this of himself and at once – at the creative instant, as he has unquestionably done in a numerous variety of his creation; rather than that handsome, beautious creature, form'd after Gods own image, when in obedience to heavens first and great decree he endeavoured to increase and to people, a distant quarter of Gods domains, he should first, be oblig'd to undergo a long and dangerous course of be-shriveling, be-stewing, frying, and boiling in his own grease, till he is burnt black as a fire coal, before he shall be in a proper and bearable tone to inhabit the several tracts in the torrid zone.[77]

In addition to his sustained attack on Buffon – a critique which often parallels that applied by Long – Lindsay devotes many pages to similar materials found in Cornélius de Pauw's *Recherches philosophiques sur les Américains, ou, Mémoires intéressants pour servir à l'histoire de l'espece humaine*, published in 1770 and 1771. Lindsay does not directly address de Pauw's physiologically based climate theory but complains that his description of the Americas left the continent an unfinished part of the Creation, unfit for habitation by man or beast, every living thing poisonous or a pest, dwarfed and degenerate. More specifically, de Pauw is taken apart for arguing "that the difference betwixt the Americans and other inhabitants of the globe, proceeds from an imperfection in the air and soil of that country". Not only does Lindsay find de Pauw "credulous" and "too much a slave to every travellers story", he reveals himself as "a disciple of Mr le Abbe Raynal, in regard to freedom and slavery". Worse still, everything in de Pauw was "selected as to chime closely with his own hypothesis".[78]

It is in his criticism of de Pauw that Lindsay expresses most clearly his personal experience and observations, saying, "I have known America, and have now become almost a native in it". Taking advantage first of his time in Virginia, Lindsay questions de Pauw's assessment of (Native) Americans as weak and incapable of heavy labour. While admitting they might have been unenthusiastic when required to labour for the Spanish, just as "labourers of whatever colour, and especially in the meridian sun of a hot climate, are inclinable to skulk and be lazy in a masters service", Lindsay is certain that "the Indeans when working for themselves shew no such marks of weakness". Perhaps recalling an expedition to Logstown, he observes: "In carrying their furrs from very distant lakes, and in their canoes, when coming to the falls of a river, they can whip up their packages of peltry on their heads, and mount their canoes on their shoulders and can (carrying all with but little to do, below the falls) launch their vessel, repack her cargo, and again pursue their voyage."[79]

As well as questioning de Pauw's qualifications to speak on the climate of the Americas, Lindsay joins colonials such as Jefferson and Franklin in objecting to allegations of New World inferiority, including a qualified defence of the aboriginal peoples. He does not look north to these figures, however, but happily sides with Abbé de Brügel D. Pernety, whose "dissertation" on America was included by de Pauw in *Recherches philosophiques* in order that his positive views might be disparaged. Known as Dom Pernety, the Abbé was Antoine-Joseph Pernety (1716–96), a sometime Benedictine whose knowledge of the Americas came from his participation in a voyage with Bougainville to the Falkland Islands and the Brazilian island of Santa Catarina in the early 1760s. His direct observation and his opposition to de Pauw's assessment of the climate of the Americas made him attractive to Lindsay, though "perhaps too far to the opposite extreme of exaggeration". Dom Pernety's Native Americans were almost heroic in their stature and, says Lindsay, "he puts sentiments in their minds, which disgraces the most philosophic of Christians". They despised riches and had only contempt for the energy expended by Europeans in the pursuit of gold, "the God of the Christians!" Thus, Dom Pernety argued, "the Caraïb" was not "the most miserable of beings" but in truth "much happyer than we".[80]

Lindsay was sceptical of the supposed "cultivation of both soul and genius" that Dom Pernety claimed to find in the Native Americans, saying that "when we wish to view them in a civilized light; and reflect that the vagabond, lazy, thieving, cowardly race of Jews, so early in their history, had a polished at least an established language reduced to letters and characters", it had to be asked why "a whole hemisphere – the half of the globe – has subsisted seemingly since the creation, . . . ignorant even in any tradition of their *own history* unless what is very vague indeed". Lindsay declares the Native Americans "in general, a mighty lazy, unwilling, and triffling people, in the cultivation of the earth, . . . more like savages still having little or no sort of improving contrivance". Here Lindsay accepts the judgement of Robertson, who in his *History of America* declares the indigenous people lacking in "curiosity" and "unacquainted with all the ideas which have been denominated *universal*, or *abstract*, or of *reflection*". In finding the Native Americans inferior, Lindsay identifies fundamental faults without attributing them to climate.[81]

Lindsay also found fellow cause with the creole Jesuit priest Francisco Clavigero (1731–87), who was expelled from Mexico in 1767 and was a forerunner of Mexican nationalism. It was perhaps an unexpected admiration in view of Lindsay's harsh treatment of the Jesuits in his *Memoirs* and his condemnation of the "Jesuitical arguments" of de Pauw.[82] He did it partly to show that he was up to date, thus giving a clue to the precise time of his composition of "Conjectural considerations". He says: "I have just now been favoured with a few transcripts from the Critical Review and Political Magazine for June 1787 (the work itself not having yet reached the West Indeas) of a late publication, by L'Abbé D. Francesco Saverio Clavigero, a gentleman who had lived it seems for 40 years in the Spanish settlements about Mexico, and which if I had seen sooner, might greatly have shortened this work." The work reviewed was translated from the first (Italian) edition, published in 1780 with the title *The History of Mexico*. The creole Clavigero traced his society's history back to the glories of ancient Mexico, establishing its classical antiquity and seeking particularly to answer the slanders of Buffon, de Pauw and Raynal.[83]

The general tenor of the assessment published in the *Critical Review* is positive but occasionally directed at defending Robertson's *History*; the reviewer thinks that if Robertson has "sunk the Mexican ingenuity too low, the abbé has undoubtedly raised it too high".[84] For his purposes, Lindsay was taken by Clavigero's belief that the animals of America "must have proceeded from the old continent by land". Clavigero observed that many Indian people in Mexico and Guatemala had flood myths and tales of their migration from the north. He found it plausible that North America had once been part of a land mass united with Europe and Asia, meaning that he had no difficulty picturing a migration to the Americas from Noah's ark and from Babel. However, the reviewer remains at a loss, saying that according to this account it has to be supposed "that the whole of the Atlantic was once land; and that of the races, from which many of the animals, and all the men of America proceeded, no one was left on that part of the land, to the east of the sea, which burst through the vast continent, and divided it into two worlds". Lindsay says that Clavigero fails to counter Buffon's opinion "that America has very lately emerged from the sea".[85] Lindsay was hampered by a catastrophist view of earth history, since he lacked a conception of geological time that made possible continental drift and geomorphological diversity.

"Distinct and Seperate Originals"

Lindsay did not know the term *polygenesis* – a nineteenth-century creation – but accepted the essence of the hypothesis that, contrary both to traditional scriptural interpretation and to arguments based on events after Eden, God intentionally created a diversity of humankind. Largely because polygenesis required abandonment of the biblical account of a common origin, belief in the model was relatively uncommon in the eighteenth century. Lindsay, as already noticed, attributed the theory directly to Kames and Hume, but Kames held back from full commitment because he was unwilling to abandon the biblical account of Creation. Lindsay was aware of the reluctance of "this learned judge" to go the distance in confirming the concept of multiple creations. He was more willing to surrender Scripture in order to build a practical theory of race and slavery.[86]

An advantage of shifting the emphasis from climate to race was that it rescued the problem of human diversity from the clutches of time. Lindsay had a precise notion of the length of time that had passed since the Creation, saying it was "now near 5500 years", thus indicating acceptance of Archbishop Ussher's 1650 biblical calculation that the earth had been created on 22 October 4004 BCE. The vastly greater time depth acknowledged today by science, in which account even modern humans have existed for about two hundred thousand years, was not available to Lindsay.[87]

Although Lindsay might have followed the path of contemporaries who realized that earth history extended over at least thousands of centuries and argued that the seven days of Creation and the forty days of the Flood had to be understood as epochs, this was too large a temporal leap for him. Buffon, whose advocacy of environmental factors as the determining causes of human diversity so provoked Lindsay and Kames, has a central place in modern attempts to estimate the history of the earth. He did not merely speculate but also conducted experiments, measuring the time taken by iron balls of different sizes to cool after being heated to near melting point. Buffon used his findings to calculate the time needed for a sphere the size of the earth to cool; in 1778 he published his answer: seventy-five thousand years. This was massively longer than the commonly accepted six thousand years, but in his unpublished papers Buffon pushed it to almost three million years. He must have known that his published number was already too large to satisfy those who depended on Scripture.[88]

To Lindsay it seemed that God's precious gift of time – designed to encompass the working out of earth history and salvation history – was simply too short to be taken up with waiting on the diversification of humanity through transformation by interaction with climate. Sacred history had an urgency that demanded a prompt resolution of such basic matters. However, whereas enabling the temporal foundations of sacred history by advocating polygenesis over climatic adaptation had obvious benefits for explaining human diversity, it did not resolve the theological problems. It was easy enough to follow Kames in saying that "God the great and provident architect created men for the several climates, rather than those climates now-form'd or moulded their inhabitants", but doing so required belief in multiple gardens of Eden and multiple Adams and Eves. As Kames says, "God in his creation, had most probably made races of men for every climate as we find he hath done with the animal creation". This was an argument not merely heretical but also opposed to the belief held by almost all the Scottish historical philosophers, including Hume, that human beings shared a similar character in the rudest stages of social development. Polygenesis complicated any notion of human progress. This made the theory unattractive to many thinkers, but not to Lindsay, who found in it a justification for slavery and for conservation of slave society.[89]

Fundamental to polygenesis was the fixity of race as a category, a visible indicator of human diversity independent of environment and nutrition. Before attempting to demonstrate the truth of this assertion, however, Lindsay first tackles Buffon's claim that "all men are one race or species, because they all procreate together". Lindsay questions the logic of this argument, saying that "if all men were of one original species (and we may add – fitted to all climates) there never could have existed, without a miracle, those different kinds we now meet with – the individuals of each so remarkably uniform: and yet differing not less remarkably from the individuals of every other kind". Here Lindsay agrees with Kames, declaring that "this uniformity and permenancy must be the offspring of design – never of chance". Lindsay also holds that "if a white man mixt with a black woman, in whatever climate", their offspring would be "a mongrel breed differing from both". On the other hand, suggesting perhaps a more personal observation of the community of Spanish Town, Lindsay disagrees with Kames's claim that this "mongrel breed" could be "no improvement of either kind", declaring that "the people of colour, descendants of the white and black immediately; but more so the mulatto, quadroon and mustee, are doubtless an improvement of one kind – and very often mend the breed of both". Lindsay was entirely empirical about miscegenation, in contrast to Long, who found it possible to believe that "mulatto" couples could not bear children, at the same time drawing "family trees" of colour mixing in order to demonstrate that "three removes are necessary to restore the primitive blackness".[90]

Although Lindsay did not attempt a systematic classification, he did identify a number of races. He sought also to show that features identified as racial were not so trivial as to be ascribed to "climate, food or other accidental causes" along the lines argued by Buffon. Thus Lindsay refers, for example, to "the black colour of Negroes, thick lips flat nose, crisped wooly hair, and rank goatish smell . . . [which] distinguish them from every other race of men – even from the Abyssinian, who nearly under the same climate, are tall – well made – their complexion a brown olive – with features well proportioned – large, black, sparkling eyes, thin lips, &c, a nose rather high then flat". None of these characteristics, says Lindsay, are localized or occasional but are "fully and generally" shared.[91] He does not lump together all "Africans" but thinks it obvious that "Negroes" belong to a distinct racial group – as distinct as white people – occupying a distinct geographical region: "Negroeland".

What exactly makes blacks and whites distinct races? Skin colour is there for all to see, but what caused its variation? Some, say Lindsay, believe that "blackness of complexion" can be ascribed to "the heat of the equator" or differences in "blood and bile". He finds, however, that the bile (a liquid secreted by the liver that aids digestion, known until the early eighteenth century as "choler", one of the four "humours") and the blood of blacks "differ not in any manner whatever from the fairest European". He did not accept that race was inherited through the blood itself.[92] He agreed, however, that there was a difference in the epidermis, and argues that this is "a most evident mark of a very seperate race: indued by the great creator, the more to fit him for his sultry abode". By denying the possibility of "metamorphosis of figure and colour from bad living, untoward manners, and heat of climate", whether for blacks or whites, Lindsay was able to both defeat his philosophical opponents and restore to God the power and responsibility for his creation. Nor was he blind to beauty, observing that some black African women possessed "bosoms as elegantly form'd as nature can bestow; and which they know full well the value of", and that "the delicate softness of their velvet skins (occasioned perhaps by the relaxed tone of their fibres) gives others no small degree of vanity amongst their own sex, and coquetish airs of triumph sometimes over ours".[93]

Within the Americas, Lindsay found Americans ("Indeans") "wonderfully singular" across many latitudes. He does, however, distinguish a "northern race" – the "miserable wretched Esquimaux" – who were not necessarily "the first settlers, or aborigines of the American Indeans". As to this "northern race", Lindsay was less than certain that they formed "a very distinct race and creation of people", uniform throughout the "polar and icey regions" and including all of "the clumsey, untoward figures we find around all the northern regions, of Russia, Lapland, Iceland, Greenland, Eskimaux, Labrador, &c. &c.". These peoples share "monstrous and hideous forms" but not language, says Lindsay, so perhaps Greenland was peopled from America rather than Europe.[94] He also sought to distinguish them from the Patagonians, "a permanent and old standing race" of "gigantic" people who had been "so long hid to the knowledge of faithful history, puts both the theologean and philosopher to their trumps". The discovery of this "race of giants" was such a blow to the "doctrine of one pair of progenitors only for all the humane race", says Lindsay,

> that like the Pope, who confounded with the idea and report of another half, to this world, being found out, or on the eve of it, declared in his plenitude of knowledge, that America *did* not exist – and *could* not exist (I think when his holiness was about it, he might also have added, *should* not exist) – however what was tantamount to it, he declared that he would excommunicate any one, who dared to believe, that this globe had an opposite hemisphere inhabited by rationable creatures.

The solution, he argues, requires thinkers only to agree "that the all-bountious and provident creator, has been pleased to suit various races of men, to various climates, and to various purposes. And according to each, their peculiar uses and purposes; they seem created with, or permitted by divine providence, to enjoy – superior, inferior, or middle degrees of capacity or inlargement of mind or soul."[95]

A separate, essentially theological, question concerned the existence of imperfect human beings. Since it was easy to identify grotesque and monstrous peoples, slothful and cowardly, with "vile habits and beastly ideas of propriety", it had to be asked whether such were "the corrupted races of a variety of people" or whether God had made them thus, so very much the "reverse of every thing noble and perfect". Lindsay believed that "originally they must have had a natural perfection" when dropped from the fingers of God, and therefore "much of their deformities have been augmented by their own vicious tastes, bad habits and beastly lives".[96] Representative of "the ugliest and most frightfully deform'd of the human kind", Lindsay identified "the course and robust *Calmucks*", distinguished by "a broad, flate, splatter face; the one eye five or six fingers breadth from the other – and pig eyed too; the little rising they have in the middle of the face, by way of apology for the want of a nose, has also two holes which serve instead of nostrils – their knees bending outwards, and wadling like parrots with their feet turned in".[97] He was not alone in awarding this prize to the Calmucks. He probably derived this idea from his contemporary Dr Peter Camper (1722–89), a Dutch professor of medicine whose lecture on natural variations in physiognomy, delivered to the Amsterdam Academy of Drawing in 1770, presumably reached Lindsay through Buffon or Goldsmith. Camper developed an influential method of measuring the "facial angle" and presented a hierarchy of skulls from monkey to Calmuck ("the ugliest thing in nature") and refined classical European statues. However, rather than identifying gradations in form, Camper, like Buffon, maintained a sharp dividing line between human and animal, divorced from an uninterrupted chain of being.[98]

Pondering the theology, Lindsay opines: "The habit of long thinking in one way concerning the creation doubtless renders it to our ideas a shorter finishing of Gods work to make one man and one woman only." However,

> surely God, who at the creative instant, must have seen the necessity of a variety in every thing animated and capable of growth, agreeably and suited with wisdom to have begun population thro the various zones in his creation even as he has done in the fishes of the sea, the birds and beasts, and the plants and trees of the various fields and forrests of every different climate: cannot be supposed to have wishd for a short way, for expeditions sake (as if to get through his labour and to gain a day of rest) to people his vast world with two rational subjects only, let the event afterwards be ever so slow. Nor can we see at least, any solid and substantial reason even in theology why the creation of man should have been confined to the solitary pair, in the regions of Arabia. Or why such extraordinary climates should have been created without suitable creatures to inhabit them from the first. Climates whose baneful air, were in process of time, to change the pleasing image and likeness of the creator himself, into the brutish stamp of those of Lapland, of Greenland &c. &c. Let therefore those who read their Bibles for sceptical purposes, only read them again, with a liberal disposition – and their Bibles, will be found to be their Bibles still.[99]

Closer to his conclusion, Lindsay declares that the more he pondered the latest geographical and other discoveries, the more he became conscious that human beings could never understand

> the designs of providence, in permitting so large a proportion of his rational creation, as downright dunces, to remain blind to all scientific knowledge – dark and stunted in the few natural talents that are theirs – while he has so liberally bestow'd on the remaining few every enduement that can grace and every ability than can adorn the humane nature. Whatever designs, I say, God may have for this seemingly

partial distribution of his benefits – or what purposes (out of our sights) he may have in design for them, thro the endless ages of another world – lies with him alone. But all put together, I am clearly perswaded that the all provident and unconfined creator, did form from the beginning more distinct and seperate originals – more races and species's of the human genius – than Moses in the time of his writing, could have had any information of – or we, as yet can well enumerate.[100]

Ultimately, Lindsay wished his God to remain incomprehensible. If only there were "a few sure postulata to build upon", it might be possible to construct a much more robust theory of race, thought Lindsay, but, as it was, his enquiry was necessarily "a matter more of curiosity, than satisfactory science". Ultimately, the ignorance of humankind on this and many more puzzling questions could only be seen as the wish of the Almighty. Here he stood steadfastly beside his patron Robertson. Says Lindsay: "God never could have meant that Man, altho indeed greatly favoured, should comprehend the depth of *his ways*, which *like his thoughts are so widely different from our thoughts*."[101]

"Many Mansions"

For Lindsay, polygenesis was immediately attractive because it was the one hypothesis that envisioned a fully conscious God looking far ahead in time, rather than a reactive or distant God, a mere clock-winder. Thus Lindsay considered that this concept should appeal to "those, who trust *in the constant watchings of a Providential care over man and all his affairs, even to the hairs of his head, and ever since the creative moment*". The faithful of this view should "have no vast difficulty of meeting this opinion half way at least", namely

> That the various colours, forms and constitutions of the varying nature of man, might have been the design, the pleasure, and permission of the first great creator; and act as seeds planted or sown in mans original formation, tho not to appear till nature in the distresses of unfriendly latitudes shall call those seeds into action – which opinion will resolve itself into that of the last [the third hypothesis], and the white race of Europe may become swarthy, to indure the sultry deserts of Africa.

However, contended Lindsay,

> every reader of a philosophical turn, and liberal way of thinking, are not pleased with this. Not desirous that man in his shallow knowledge should load nature with more than pertains to her – altho they admit of the indulgent creators condesending attention, even to the sparrow of his handywork: they shrink at the idea, that the *great first cause*, who had the *whole course* of the *solar systim* and its *consequences*

> before him at *one view*; should be found on peculiar occasions, mending, altering or superadding some necessary changes, different from his original design and model.[102]

A related question that worried Lindsay and his contemporaries concerned the fate of those peoples – in the Americas and elsewhere – unknown to the Scriptures and denied revelation. He had addressed the problem in his sermon of 1760: "All those who inhabit the vast unenlightened parts of the world, having nothing but pure nature for their guide – shall they in the end be doomed to misery?" The problem applied equally to those who had gone before in ignorance of Christ's message of salvation. Lindsay asks: "What shall be the fate of the justly admired philosophers of antiquity, who neither knew there was or ever would be a Gospel of Christianity?" He thinks the answer simple: "those who have no the law, are a law to themselves" and will therefore "receive virtue's rewards", whereas "those who live under the Gospel, God, from the Gospel will judge". The fate of the "untaught Ethiopian", "the wild Indian imboss'd with darkness dire and melancholy", the infant and the idiot was not for "finite mortals, saucily to determine" but rightly left to the "mysterious distributions of Grace and Providence".[103]

As in his attitude to religious doctrine, Lindsay sought above all to establish an applied theory of race. His objective was to provide a philosophical underpinning for the hierarchical social world he inhabited, a justification for the enslavement of some and the liberty of others. The consequence was that he had no need for a systematic list of races on a global scale. He was quite specific about what he needed to achieve in his attempt at a theory of race. He says: "as for my own part and for my present purpose, I only contend for an essential and necessary difference between the white and the black creation: the latter of whom appears to me, from their being little susceptible of care – vastly stupid and deeply degenerated in the powers of reason – to be destined, if not possitively from creation, at least subsequently by permission of providence, to be hewers of wood and drawers of water". They have, Lindsay says, been designed by God to serve "the more busy, more delicate colour and more inlightened inhabitants of the globe: whose frames tho form'd for active life, have not been created to labour in the latitudes of the torrid zone". Blacks, he adds, are fit for "no other purpose in Gods creation that I could ever devise or frame in their favour *amongst us* – and they are almost useless in their *own country*". Further, "while from the extreme unpleasant and unprofitable soil of Negroeland, though perfectly suited to the Negroe nature and disposition, no other nation under the sun, will wish to rob them of a single acre, except up the sea and river sides, for a few strong store houses for the purposes of trade".[104]

On folio 156 of his manuscript, Lindsay closes the first section of his work with this paragraph:

> Nor need the tender feelings of the sons of the church, be alarmed here. For the merits of Christ will reach the weakest and most ignorant sinner, as well as the most intelligent, or obstinate reasoner. The gospel is no ways affected here – it rather strengthens the idea of the apostle of the gentile nations; by showing us how far, those who without the knowledge of the law, will hereafter be judged from that law which nature has written in their own hearts. And as by Christs account there are *many mansions* in the heavenly domains, there will no doubt be a reception for the *most stupid rational being*, provided the honesty of his heart and good intentions of his soul, shall have conducted him to the grave.[105]

Christ sought to comfort his disciples immediately after foretelling his betrayal and death, by telling them, "In my Father's house are many mansions" (John 14:2). He was going to prepare a place for them. In pondering the will of God the Father, Lindsay understood this hope as symbolic of the ordering of diverse and multiple worlds, in which all earthly beings deemed worthy might find their proper destinations. Accepting the notion of a plurality of heavens ("many mansions") and hells, each perhaps with its own internal hierarchy, provided support for belief in a world made up of unequal beings created to work together as whole, each element of the Creation designed to play its own particular part. It also provided potential homes for the heathen of the New World, who had been kept so long in ignorance of Father and Son.[106] Doing so allowed Lindsay to glorify God, acknowledging His capacity to create multiple worlds and universes as well as the immense diversity of earthly plants and animals. Within this cosmic multiplicity, the notion that human beings had been created in multiple varieties and qualities at the very beginning seemed easy to admit.

CHAPTER NINE

Slavery and Salvation

The second part of Lindsay's "Conjectural considerations" is devoted to the theory and practice of slavery. Although it is much shorter than his discussion of the problem of human diversity, Lindsay considered this second section at least equal in significance. Aspects of his argument depended, he thought, on the conclusion reached in the first part. In particular, he found in his advocacy of polygenesis a justification of systems of social subordination, including slavery. He believed that the God-designed natural order entailed such hierarchical systems and that the separate creations of human beings represented the universal working out of this order, the ultimate purpose of which was known only to God. For Lindsay, these conclusions were not merely of philosophical and theological significance but had practical implications for management and government of the slave society in which he lived.

Lindsay was not concerned with simply justifying the existing order. He declared an interest in change, however cautious and hedged about, and he offered concrete recommendations. He firmly believed that his "proposals, as to raising the condition, and forewarding the situation of deserving Negroes", were practical and important, and hoped they would be implemented once the "political propriety of the slave trade" had been secured in the British Parliament. He thought himself well qualified to comment on these matters, declaring that he was "writing for the benefit of those, who cannot have had the experience I have had for forty years amongst this sort of people (thirty of which last in the West Indeas)". In the second as well as the first part of "Conjectural considerations", Lindsay never identifies himself as a clergyman, happily declaring himself a slave-owner, a planter, a long-term resident of Jamaica and a "visitor on the slave coasts" of Africa.[1]

"States of Subordination"

PROSLAVERY PRIEST

Lindsay did not look directly to the Bible for a justification of slavery. Rather, his defence emerged fully formed from his biblical criticism and his polygenesis. By putting aside literal and even allegorical readings of the weakly inspired books of Moses, Lindsay found it easy to understand why there should be "a variety, and perhaps an inferiority too, in the classes of men, for the necessary purposes of society". He felt compelled, therefore, to wonder "why *such a tumult* about the despicable services of African subjects in particular?" He thought it obvious that "God has been pleased to form originally, some men more coarse and robust, to bear the heavy and hard labour of northern climates, to give to others black skins, the better to endure the as necessary, but lighter fatigues of the torrid zone". Further, "if he hath in kind providence denied so manifestly to those destined to be *hewers of wood* and *drawers of water*, those *more delicate* feelings with which others are indued, what is the mighty difference, could we think without prejudice, between the service of seven, seventeen, or seven and twenty years?" This was not an order peculiar to the West Indies but the common experience of all societies in which "the greatest part of the lower class of people, *do* and *must* continue servants for life, in whatever part of the world they inhabit".[2]

Equality, Lindsay believed, was not part of God's providential plan. Across the globe could be found "individuals of every family or colour, the construction and conformation of whose intellects are so *inferiorly* design'd or permited, through Gods inscrutable but bountiful providence; that no education or experience whatever can raise them to any equality with their brethren". Even among "the most refin'd and best polish'd people of the world (Europe for instance)", fully one-third remained in ignorance and served another third, who themselves were no more than "docile assistants" and served in turn "a *remaining*, more ingeneous and useful, *third* part". The inferior naturally found themselves "contentedly drudging on through life in the *meanest offices of servitude* – and if not slaves, perhaps *much worse*". Therefore, says Lindsay, it is essentially a matter of indifference whether "these low class'd men, shall be fed or supported from their own starved wages or family charity as free or fed and taken care of, at the charge of an owner, *as slaves*". How individuals came to be allocated to a particular status was not a question that worried Lindsay – it was a product of the unknowable wisdom of God – but he does remark, in the context of his understanding that all human beings possess souls of varying values, "We cannot well affirm, that there is any thing in looks or appearance from the creators hands, has mark'd out one for *freedom* or another for *slavery* – all that happens in the life or history of man, is meerly according to the succeeding fasheons, customs, experiences or arts of the world."[3]

It is wrong, argues Lindsay, to contend that liberty is the natural state of man or that prelapsarian man was free. On the contrary,

> our first progenitor was not *created* free, nor are we *born* free. Free! yes, in some things – of every tree in Eden thou mayst *freely eat*. But of the tree that is in the midst of the garden though shall *not eat*. And every community of human kind since, for their mutual protection, have found it necessary, all the world over, to enter into certain restrictive and prohibitory law or engagements; giving up many, seemingly inherent, priviledges to enjoy others.

Thus Lindsay finds that "*liberty* judiciously ballanced by *authority*, is the law of God put into execution by a chosen appointment among men". At best, liberty seemed to him to indicate "man *in a state of savage nature*", whereas authority identified "man *brought into a state of social communication*". In God's world, "states of subordination" were essential.[4]

Lindsay was well aware that his concept of slavery as integral to an efficient social order had ancient philosophical and historical roots. Aristotle, for example, argues that civilized society can exist only where the labour of some is exploited for the benefit of others, and that it is natural and just that those who are incapable of full human development should be the slaves of those who can achieve the good life. In this understanding of "natural slavery", the slave is conceived of as intellectually and morally deficient, even subhuman, and thus incapable of living as an independent, autonomous being. The fundamental qualification for enslavement was simply that the person had been born outside the state, defined in some way as a foreigner or barbarian on the basis of language or geography. This system of slavery coexisted with ancient prejudices derived from the perception of physical difference, but it lacked the "racial" exclusivity that marked the Americas after Columbus. However, the practical and philosophical problem facing the ancient theory was that warfare netted both those who were natural slaves and those who were natural free men. Both categories came to form part of slave society, but whereas the first group "deserved" their status, the second did not.[5] This was an issue that concerned Lindsay.

Early Christian doctrine came to associate slavery with both sin and salvation. The judgement of God on the unrighteous was just; sin was not part of the order He had created but rather began with Adam, who misused the freedom he had been given in his natural state. Thus sin was the cause of all slavery, both physical and spiritual. However, in both pagan and Christian thought there was the idea that virtue existed independent of slavery and freedom. Judaism saw the relationship of slavery – the utter subjection of one person to another – as symbolic of the relationship between mankind and God. Jesus extended the metaphor so that the slave was ennobled by being made the symbol of mankind's place in the kingdom of God, and the faithful (grateful) slave was given a special calling.[6] It was this idea – rather than the idea that salvation and liberty were one – that Lindsay used to legitimize his system of Christian sociability, a community in which to do unto others as one would wish to be treated oneself formed the foundation of a moral community for all its members, regardless of their place within it. Even within a Calvinist context, both the elect and the reprobate were said to have reason to glorify God, and, therefore, whatever their earthly lot or their eternal destination, had reason to live virtuous lives.[7]

Whether they are considered in terms of ancient or modern histories, argues Lindsay, it is soon found "that *freedom and slavery, liberty and bondage* are meer *comperative* terms". In his own time, he asks, "What are the subjects of Persia? What are the subjects of the vast empire of Turkey? Slaves, every soul of them." The French, he felt, were little better off "in the scale of liberty". The Bastille offered "*freedom* to the *bow-string*" while the people were "under the slavish yoke of an absolute tyrant", himself in turn "the slave of his confessor", the "slave of the Pope". Writing just five years after the conclusion of the American War of Independence – the consequences of which he had foreshadowed long before – and on the eve of the French Revolution, Lindsay struggled with the idea that liberty was a natural human right. What was relatively new in Western discourse was the notion that this should be a matter for debate, in contrast to the long period from ancient times to the sixteenth century when Europeans had taken the justice of slavery to be self-evident, without need of theoretical underpinnings.[8]

In comparative view, Lindsay contended that there was little difference between slavery, bonded servitude (indentured labour) and even apprenticeships. In the north of America, he saw, "*slavery* is useless, because *servitude* is better and easier to be purchassed. *Purchassed!* Ay, I have said so – and to my mind, the difference is trifling: whither I bargain for ten pounds, for twelve months servitude – or pay seventy for seven years – and seven years is generally called a life." In apprenticeships, "seven or more years of youth are often bargained for, by their parents or owners, in no better form than a slave". The treatment of apprentices was often worse than that of slaves, thought Lindsay, because the loss of an apprenticed or indentured person was not felt so heavily by the master. More broadly, he argued that "*servitudes* are all *purchasses* – and tho the expression may displease an idle republican disposition, they are all of them slaves, tho in different degrees".[9]

On an even broader moral front, Lindsay wondered why those who attacked slavery did not similarly fight against warfare "and try to put an end to *man-killing* – for *man-stealing* is but a flea bite, a mere mote to the mountain". Perhaps recalling the impressment of men to serve on the *Newcastle* in 1755 and the ship-side lashings he witnessed, Lindsay remarks that "in *Christian verity* it is a shame that men should be kid-nap'd under the idea of hire, in short enslaved the greatest part of their lives – and trained up for the very unchristian purpose and business of slaughtering their fellow creatures; in ye cold blood of princely politicks". In practice, few princes could be convinced to disband their standing armies; those who did would simply hand the advantage to their more pragmatic rivals. The impracticality of a unilateral British abolition of the Atlantic slave trade or granting of liberty, argued Lindsay, was of the same degree of difficulty. The outcome could only be national disgrace: "when we shall have given up our African manufactures, lost our Guinea trade, and are obliged to go to some of those wiser nations to buy sugar, and rum, and coffee and cotton and all the rest of it, what a foolish figure would G. Britain cut amongst the nations of Europe".[10]

Slavery in Africa

It was Lindsay's view that slavery and the slave trade were natural to the West African coast and that the Atlantic slave trade was a blessing rather than a curse for the people involved. Rehearsing arguments first advanced in his *Voyage* of 1759, he claimed that the origin of the trade could be traced to the poor resource base of "Guinea", its soil and climate, which made the region "unworthy of the conquest of any civilized nation". Because it was unattractive to a civilized conqueror, the country would always be in the hands of "a set of restless, ignorant, and absolute chiefs, . . . constantly ingaged in paltry, jealous quarrels". The outcome was a ready supply of captives created by internal forces. He also observed that the sale of people taken prisoner in declared war was a practice not confined to Africa but found equally in many other places both ancient and modern.[11]

A further question was whether the trade in prisoners of war was fuelled by the Atlantic trade and therefore the direct creation of European traders. Some believe, says Lindsay, "that the English traders, blow the coal of war amongst them, to fill the slave market". He acknowledged that European traders on the coast sometimes "set the neighbouring kings at varience with each other, that prisoners may be bought", but this was no different to what "more polished kings, *do every day*". He also saw that "the profits thus received from Europe by the African chiftians, leads them the oftener to quarrel with one another . . . merely that they may have the more of their neighbouring prince's subjects to dispose of as their own captive prisoners

– by which it too frequently happens, that innocent victims are carried into bondage". The problem, thought Lindsay, was that "in Africa where can a poor subject travel to find a better prince – they are all in the same plan – and tho humane nature may feel for the wretched – they *may* be, and *are* most commonly much betterd in their slavery".[12]

Being sold and taken to the plantations of the Americas, thought Lindsay, brought redemption. It was indeed a gracious benefit that "[t]he trading nations of the north, secured in their wooden forts – their ships – have found the blessed means of softening the revenge of the proud conqurors on Afric shores – and by the exchanging Europian goods (valuable to them) for the redemption of the captive's life". In an improbably conjectural passage, he argues that enslaved Africans are also better off in the hands of European masters than if they should find themselves prisoners of "the Barbarian of the West", meaning the Native American. With the new (European) masters of the Americas, the enslaved African had merely to toil for his bread, the fate of every "subordinate subject", and was safe from "torture and vindictive scalping". It was a sign of civilization for Lindsay that "gain has supplanted the tomahac".[13] Africans could count themselves lucky that they had been enslaved by wealth-seeking Europeans rather than bloodthirsty Native Americans. God had created the people of "Negroe Land" as part of a grander design: to serve a worthy and superior race.[14]

Slavery in Jamaica

Although Lindsay's prime objective was defence of slavery and the slave trade, he does have critical things to say about the practice of slavery in Jamaica. These remarks are not necessarily directed at the mistreatment of enslaved people, however. With the Dolben Act of May 1788 in mind, Lindsay says: "I will not here say anything of the cruel, and avaricious custom of the African merchants from Great Britain, of overloading their ships from the slave coasts: because I find that has already been taken notice of in England – and will doubtless undergo an amendment."[15] He was more concerned that the sale of people from the ships that crossed the Atlantic was too often "done in an indecent manner". Taking up a long-standing complaint, he says:

> the first opening of a sale, on board a Guinea ship – the rushing in, of a numerous company of buyers, with eager looks, and rude keenness for the best choice amongst the apprehensive slaves is . . . shameful to the chaste feelings of many a purchassor, as well as full of dreadful apprehensions in the minds of the poor victims

(and which the several assemblies of the West Indeas might most easily remedy): – but this shock, is happily but for a moment – the wretched tremblers between hopes and fears, are quickly undeceived; and *the remainder of their lives, is more joyous* – and it is oftener more their own than the masters faults, if they are not the happiest labourers in the world.[16]

The real trouble, for Lindsay, was a lack of equity from the point of view of potential purchasers. In the course of his complaint he provides an unusually detailed account of a sale of enslaved people, suggesting personal observation. Indeed, he says elsewhere that he "found myself obliged, (altho my first beginning as a planter was with sixty choice, and almost all creole Negroes) from time to time since to go to market for new purchasses". As to the fairness of these transactions, Lindsay comments: "I know not whither the African merchant sold them fairly – but I am sure, that I fairly became a purchassor." Writing in 1788, he notes also: "I but lately bought a couple of Negroes (a girl and a boy) from a Jew trafficer, who had bought a large parcel of refuse Negroes, i.e. after the first sale on board of a Guinea ship – and many people who cannot stand the shock of so disagreeable scene . . . take such an opportunity to pick if possible such Negroes as may suit them."[17] Lindsay objected to such scrambles because "by meer effrontry and bullying, the strongest attended overseer or manager, is sure to run away with the best choice of the ship". To fix the problem,

> Proper, secure, and decent places on shore, should be provided for a Guinea ship cargo: persons under the police of majestracy, should see, that no unfair practices are used, either in oiling or shaving for a fortnight before the sale: and prohibit that unfair custom of encircling a larger number of Negroes, than any one means to be the purchasser of – and what else may be found in course necessary to be added, to the fairness of such a sale as well as the credit of the country.[18]

In this critique, Lindsay combined his faith in fairness and his idea that equitable treatment was at the core of Christianity and applied these notions to the harshness of the sale of enslaved people. He saw no paradox in making this connection but, rather, believed that the fundamental principles of right behaviour transcended social oppression and subordination as designed by God. Thus, although Lindsay noticed with concern the terror of the enslaved, his objective in seeking change was directed at improving the system of slavery by making its mechanisms more efficient and profitable. His ideas fitted neatly with those of the planter-directed "amelioration" that emerged in this period. However, whereas the planters typically understood amelioration in terms of the material conditions of life and the punishments inflicted on the bodies of the enslaved, as a means towards creating a stronger and longer-lived labour force, Lindsay's emphasis was on the mind and the soul. He wished to reward honest labour with limited freedom and to lead the people towards a limited education and limited spiritual salvation.[19]

Lindsay wrote in order to demonstrate the falsity of "those pretenders to humanity, who alledge that the cruel usage of the unfortunate slaves from Africa, not only brings on the unnecessary expenditure of his life; but also that the unnatural neglect of the female in her pregnancy, is the chief cause of the constant drain and yearly recruits by fresh cargos from Africa". Rather than legislating change, "if ever any reformation is made in further attention to the well being of our slaves, it must come from the care, right instruction and the scientific observations of the landed gentlemen on their several properties thro our islands – many of whom of late have shewn themselves, much inlightened in the paths of sound philosophy as well as the world". Lindsay did, however, approve regulations introduced by the Assembly that required the allotment of sufficient grounds for the enslaved to produce their own food. Thinking of Vere, he argued that these provisions should be in addition to the production of a store of Guinea corn (sorghum) managed by the planter. What was necessary was to ensure that this bounty actually reached the people, rather than being "left to the disposal of either a niggardly thoughtless master, or any unfeeling manager".[20]

In a more direct contribution to reducing infant mortality, Lindsay added his voice to the view that "a lying-in hospital near the mansion house should be provided" for nursing mothers. He was unusual in hoping that it would be "under the inspection if possible of a white woman". As to the plantation hospital – "commonly called hot house" – he (correctly) believed that many of the sick would be better off staying outside, but again he hoped somehow "to have our overseers or bookkeepers some of them married men, whose wives or daughters, for their additional wages, would oversee our hospital". He also advocated superior buildings and declared it "a strange idea, that some have imbib'd, that Negroes, because they sometimes sham sickness, a hot house should be contrived so disagreeable and inconvenient for *them*, that a *good Negroe* when really sick, will patiently work till he falls in the field, rather than go through the ordeal".[21]

"Easy and Comfortable"

When Lindsay comes to lay out his plan for the improvement of slavery, he begins with "a general axiom (though not without its exceptions), *that good and honest, lively and acceptable service, will always make a Negroes life easy and comfortable, let who will be his master*". He then adds a "corrollary or inference" to the effect that "*it has seldom happened, that where such a Negroe or slave has been found on an estate, he either has not long continued a slave – or his slavery has been made much sweeter to him, than had he been manumized, for his faithful behaviour*". What was just and desirable, he thought, was to make the "noble, princely property" represented by a gang of field slaves "*still more valuable than they are to their proprietors, by making that labour so necessarily imposed upon them appear in lights more easy and more delightful to the slaves themselves*". His aim was to have the enslaved "work from conscience and from principle" rather than because they were driven. Here Lindsay advocates a crude project of indoctrination derived from his notions of "fairness" and his recognition of death as the great leveller. He asks: "Is it not possible to make them thoroughly and practically convinced, that when *we* as well as *they* shall die, we should all go to *a world of spirits*, in which God will make us *eternally happy or without bounds measurable, according as we have behaved here, while alive*?"[22]

The desire for equity and fairness expressed by Lindsay did not derive from a belief that the subordinate state of the enslaved meant they were badly treated or unhappy. Rather, he argued that even a person enslaved for life had nothing to complain of other than "the *bare idea of bondage*" and that this was balanced by "the happiness of a slaves situation". He presents a romantic vision of slave life, with little relation to the everyday experience of those among whom he lived in Jamaica. He says:

> Free'd from a cloud of cares and perplexities through life, which the free are never without, and he will feel himself the happier man by far! No debts disturb his nightly rest – no dun's, nor dungeons harrass or frighten his security through the labours of the day – no table for wife or children to provide for, or haunt his wakeful hours. They are all cloathed too, as well as fed, at a masters expence: and even in sickness, his very life is his owners, more than his own concern!!! Weak nature, indeed, is often *fond of changes*, and there are pleasures in the *bare idea of freedom*: and which as I heartily myself wish, they could both *deserve* and *make a proper use of* . . . .

It is wrong, says Lindsay, "to speak of slavery as a state excluded from, and as it were the *negative of freedom*, and the reverse of liberty as every mans undoubted right".[23] He might have added that the definition or meaning of freedom is even more problematic than that of slavery, but the essence of his argument was that the natural order of society was one comfortable with hierarchy, a security undermined by the potential chaos entailed in unbridled liberty.

With these philosophical and theological assumptions in place, Lindsay reveals his equally pragmatic plan "to put up freedom and liberty (the greatest blessing, as is imagin'd, this life can give) to the Negroes views, *at the end* and as the same *reward of a certain number of years good trusty behaviour*". He thought this "*right and fair justice*" or "at least equitable", but quickly seeks to calm his readers by arguing that his scheme will not create "any great numbers of slaves as free men to overpower us: or that we shall be giving up the *labour of the best* Negroes to make *effectual examples to the worst*". If anything, Lindsay believed the general "ignorance and degeneracy of Negroes" meant that so few would be deserving of the "*reward of freedom*" that it might be appropriate initially to relax the requirements, in order to be able "to grant the premium of freedom now and then, tho not perfectly deserving".[24]

These exceptional individuals would provide examples of what was possible and open the way to "the clear understood *hopes of happiness with God* in another world imparted thro proper instructions, as the joint reward (with liberty) of an honest and faithful life, while under the service of a master". Even though the reward of freedom might be "distant and doubtful", many would think themselves as good as the person freed and therefore make the attempt. Lindsay expected an immediate improvement in labour, believing that the work which "the common run of drowsey soul'd Negroes, would now take six or seven days to accomplish, would not take the cheerful slave of principle (or at least spur'd on by incitement, in the appearance of principle) not more than three or four days". The outcome would not only be profit for the planter but also, ponders Lindsay, "how safely then might each of us repose in the most lonely retreat of our island, when we should sleep secure from all dangers of future attempts from rebellious disaffection".[25]

"The Line of Probation"

The core of Lindsay's plan was "the Line of Probation", which set out requirements for gaining freedom. He drew the idea from his broader theological understanding of human life as "a state of probation" preliminary to the "court of retribution" that all have to face at death. As he had preached at the funeral of Sir Basil Keith in 1773, God had put into man's hands the task of choosing between good and evil. It was up to the individual to take advantage of the probation offered by God, to qualify for blessings and redemption.[26] With this model in mind, Lindsay makes a list of qualifications.

First, a "candidate for freedom, must for the last ten years past, have an unblemish'd character, from *runing away* or absenting himself from his duty, excepting with his owner or overseers leave". Second, the candidate had to be "examplary in the plantation" and known for "*fair-dealing* with every one", as demonstrated by never stealing, maintaining a "*decent* and cleanly . . . house, tho it be but a hovel", well-kept provision grounds and whatever livestock might be allowed, all of which would prove that "he depends not upon fortuitous means for his subsistance". Third, the person should be "well known and respected by his drivers and overseers for a *quiet behaviour*, and an *active life* in his masters service in the field, as well, as when sent abroad and out of sight, intrusted with orders of any extraordinary nature". Fourth, "As the common run of Negroes are ever slothful and slow in moving about, or at work, a candidate for freedom (tho perhaps himself no driver) as he must be himself examplarily active, he will be constantly exhibiting a *faithfullness in spurring up the slothful slave*, who shall be near him and as it were under his eye; endeavouring to inspire into every Negroe, a like quickness with himself in their labour." Fifth, "it will be a principle and a very agreeable part of a candidates qualification, that *his* word for truth has been always to be depended upon" and that "he has been a constant monitor and punisher" of young liars. Finally, with Spanish Town and Kingston firmly in mind, Lindsay rules that candidates for freedom "should early be taught, that *strict sobriety – the most pointed honesty – keeping home* at night instead of becoming a *night-stroller* – hunting after Negroe revels – dancing, gambling, all which lead often to vicious consequences – cheating, stealing, and house-breaking – and are all of them vices too prevalent, amongst town house servants especially – and will *forever prohibit* such characters from passing examination for liberty".[27]

What could be given with one hand could be taken away by another. Lindsay did not mean freedom to be a natural condition of humankind; it had to be earned every day, forever. It was his idea that the freedom granted would be "conditional, binding the manumized to a continuance of good behaviour". The grant of freedom was not intended "for the purpose of filling the hive with drones or hornets" but rather "the manumized is still to labour in good example, for the public, by hireing himself out as a tradesman or labourer to some honest, faithful or trusty obedient service". Lindsay did not rule out the possibility that industrious individuals might cease to be hired labourers and eventually purchase "some little convenient spot of ground, whereupon he can himself, perhaps in time assisted by a wife and children – and to the full and satisfactory observation of an overlooking neighbourhood, he will very fairly and commendably support his freedom, to the benefit and support of the community". On the other hand, "he who settles himself in a suspected corner" could be "justly suspected of a design to prey (as a gambler and greedy huckster) on the needy or unsuspecting slave – unwarrantably and destructively selling liquor in the vicinity of his old fellow servants – keeping a rioting house for the conveniency and reception of any such customers – encouraging them to theft, to pay off their scores – and ever ready to receive as payment, what they know could not but be stole". Such bad – unfair and inequitable – behaviour would mean the immediate forfeit of freedom, and the offender "should be adjudged to serve the informant or prosecutor, as a slave for a second term of probation".[28]

Tightening the screws, Lindsay wished the revocation of freedom to be retrospective. Under his plan, withdrawal of freedom was to apply "not only to Negroes hereafter to be manumized, but to all Negroes already freed, or may have been born free". In order to justify such draconian principles, he claims European precedents; he saw "*transportation* for a term of years, from ones country family and friends", as no worse than "a *temporary loss of freedom*, from a life of vagabondism and malepractice". Jamaica's towns, he said, contained nests of "idle profligate varlets" ready to offer "villainous education" to the young, making them strong candidates for such legislation.[29]

On top of this, Lindsay wished to see his probationers constructed as informers. By keeping their candidacy secret, they "could mix pretty frequently in Negroe plays, gambling houses, burials, and such like – and by that means might privately give intelligence, how many a theft might be detected, runaways hants discovered, gaming parties watch'd" and so on. Lindsay was particularly concerned to bring reform to the urban scene, his home turf, where he thought the "industrious free people" outnumbered by the "profligate", many of whom "live under a pretence of selling to the best advantage the produce of their mountains, which they at the same time plant not by their own industry so much as by the labour of gentlemens servants, whom they inveigle and encourage to run from their lowland penns to help them in their provision grounds". Perhaps Lindsay believed he had suffered personally in this way. He thought it an evil of "vast extent" and argued, "No property in the mountains should of itself, unless some lucrative handicraft (and well employ'd in it too) be joined with it, excuse a man of colour for his living wholly in a town." Further, he believed "it should be held criminal in a high degree whether male or female for a white person to give any such idlers ye nominal protection of being servents to them – or employ'd by them in any particular branch of business – unless his employment is sufficient to maintain them: and that they can substantially and bona fide make that appear".[30] All who failed to satisfy these conditions were, for Lindsay, candidates for enslavement, forever on probation.

Although his proposed probation scheme seemed capable of taking away as much as it offered, Lindsay had no difficulty in thinking it just and equitable. Nor did he imagine that people released from slavery might deserve to be compensated for their past loss of liberty or that slave-owners should be made to pay for the gains they had gotten through theft. He thought the enslaved should be the ones to pay.

The Price of Liberty

Why should people who had been enslaved have to pay to obtain their own freedom? Lindsay worried little about this fundamental question but did debate the amount that they should pay, typically by equivalent labour rather than money. Like most of his British contemporaries – nascent abolitionists as well as slave-owners – he began with the constitutional position: "There is no denying our rights in a property which we have purchased with our money – a property too which is of itself continually increasing." On the other hand, "if with true honesty of heart we would for a few moments divest ourselves of the mean desires of usury, we would not expect, we would not indeed accept, for a saleable article of property, more than enough". More particularly, "in *a sale of liberty*" it was necessary to agree on a fair price.[31]

Without committing himself, Lindsay does throw around some numbers and makes calculations on the basis of initial purchase prices, interest, consumption of goods and the value of the person's output (estimated at £15 per annum). Typically, he thought that after twelve years of slavery a person could deserve freedom. A creole slave was to "have his time of probation to commence when he can be of use, I mean of *profitable use* to an owner and which with them cannot so easily be fixed to an year". He does not fix it to the age at which creoles normally commenced work, namely four years, or to adolescence or adulthood, which would see creoles qualifying for freedom in their early thirties. On the other hand, he thought "salt water" or "Guinea Negroes", whatever their age, should be "able to speak English, or at least sufficiently understand it, as to enable them to receive instruction, or information of the nature of the law" before they could be considered for probation. Here Lindsay advances a precise calculation, proposing: "for illustrations sake suppose that the labour of such a Negroe, as will be found to deserve freedom, is worthy of £15 per annum (supposing him to be a common field Negroe bought at £65 from a ship) in this, which will be a general, case – to fix probation of ten years, will give £150, as the purchass of his freedom".[32]

Although he thought direct bargaining between master and slave would be best, Lindsay acknowledges that, because "there are such hearts in our community so unfeeling, so blind to fair honesty", it would be necessary to appoint "umpires for such business appointed by the wisdom of the legislature, in every parish, to moderate and soften the strict line of power and right". Occasionally there might be cases "in which umpires may see reason to award some price to the master: but if the service of the slave secured by a certain number of months or years indentures, and at a certain awarded yearly value for his labour can be brought about, the manumission of the slave, being a public example, it should not be for a moment postponed".[33]

Lindsay then considers the social cost of his proposal, arguing strongly that "the advantages which will accrue from such manumissions, is a proposition the clearest in the world". The gains to the slave-owning class would be both direct and guaranteed by the system of regulations that was to underpin Lindsay's scheme. Thus Lindsay could argue: "there can be no great cause of fear, that an owner shall lose the service of a slave he has been perhaps so long used to in a certain line, that we cannot well be without him. For tho made a *free* man, he is not to be an *idle* one." In the first place, it was very likely "that such a servant is too much attach'd to family connexions – perhaps a wife or children – his own old and well improved feeding ground – an old and perhaps indulgent master or mistress". The slave-owner, in turn, would have pride in the "free servant" and therefore "be more and more assisting in his little property, and make him too happy ever to wish for another residence – even tho his faithfulness should be put to a cruel trial, by a secret offer of a rise in wages". Lindsay believed that many freed people would choose to continue with their former masters, but he did not propose a legal requirement that the manumitted person should remain bound to the household for some period of time as, for example, was the fashion in imperial Rome, where manumission was relatively common.[34]

A further hope was that his scheme would reduce the frequency and violence of slave rebellions. Lindsay believed this was a rational expectation, because those who sought to gain favour and ultimately manumission would have an investment in serving not only as exemplars but also as informers on the side of the slave-owning class. He thought "every honest fellow in the row [of field labourers], now begins to act as a second driver, to his neighbours; and the worthless next or near him, can no longer find room to sham – to idle away his time – or skulk from the duty required". Marronage would be made difficult. Because the "suspected harbourers or the places of concealment" were all "pretty well known to many of the gang", once "the busy anxious candidates for freedom, are amongst them, such desertions will be too liable to discovery to be frequent". The presence of so many "*private superintendands* scattered about the island" would be the "deathstroke to all Negroe rebellions in future".[35]

Another benefit of his proposal, thought Lindsay, was that rather than encouraging manumission at large, the granting of gratuitous manumissions would be limited and controlled. In particular, he believed this could be achieved by changing the rules that governed the granting of freedom to enslaved people who had white fathers, the so-called people of colour. Every claim for freedom was to be scrutinized. Thus, "young people of colour, and favourites brought up about white people, ought not after the passing of this Act to be freed at the whim or pleasure of an owner, till they shall first by the judges of freedom, have past an examination, and been found worthy, it will be highly necessary that an extraordinary care should be taken of their education in particular". This would result in a superior division of labour, because "when their moral qualifications shall be stamp'd with the seal of religion", the slave-owners of Jamaica could expect to be "served with honest, attentive, sober and obliging house servants", whereas "the saltwater, stupid, selfish, thieving, vexatious pack we are in common served with will be driven where they ought to be – to the hoe and bill".[36]

To ensure "so happy an issue", Lindsay contends that "the education of our female slaves of good desert, and promising expectations, should be peculiarly attended to – they should be taught that honesty, truth, virtue, and œconomy, will be their only – at least their best dowry, if marriage should be their lot". He saw a fundamental difference between the behaviour of females and of males which worked to the advantage of his scheme. The island's young females were "not in general so prone to many of those vices, which on examination for freedom will be constant bars to many of the males", such as "drinking, gaming, night rambling (and, its constant attendant, robbery)" as well as "sleeping of bad hours, and hunting improperly after the other sex". Because "many of our females will obtain liberty", said Lindsay, it was essential that they be taught "virtue and honesty". They would not be like "the present swarm of free women" who had been "let loose upon the public without the smallest tincture of virtue or good behaviour: and from whom is sprung that race of idle vagabonds, who at this day lurk so disgracefully and mischievously about our town". Lindsay considered it appropriate that legislation be passed "to deprive for the future any owner of slaves to free or grant manumission to any slave, either by will or deed, unless [they] shall have first pass'd an *examination of desert*, before they be let loose on the public".[37]

A more generous idea was Lindsay's proposal that "besides the bare manumission", the legislature should "find out some further reward or encouragement in money or lands to apportion or settle out some of the most notedly well deserving of such young citizens into the world – that it may prove an encouragement to honest matrimony". This way, the men, "instead of squandering their labours, upon an idle swarm of wicked and licentious street walkers, . . . might rather be supporting an honest, deserving and promising legal offspring". Such virtuous couples, "by their joint endeavours, . . . may see their little freeholds enlarging into respectable properties, to bless a deserving progeny – cloathing, at the same time, our barren and uncultivated lands and provision mountains, with every necessary article for our town markets; both in plenty, cheapness, and with the best of every kind".[38]

"The Vital Flame"

Lindsay leaves until late a discussion of the role of religion in his proposal. When he finally gets there, he claims it as "the *great desideratum* – the vital flame, which in my humble opinion, (as the blood in the heart) must actuate the whole design". But once again he immediately qualifies his argument and seeks to pacify his proslavery audience by declaring that what he means is "a religion, like to themselves, of a confined and narrowed cast".[39] It was to be a form of religion specifically designed for the "Negroe" and directed at shoring up the social order.

The teaching of religion was closely tied up with notions of secular learning. Just as Lindsay argued that the religion to be taught slaves should be narrowly conceived, so he thought secular education should be limited, even though it might be "the first step to make them the most useful and worthy of notice in a civilized society". He thought "Old Negroes can be made *to hear* at least – but young minds are *to be instructed*". Even for the brightest of the youth, reading, writing and arithmetic would be quite enough, and the reading confined largely to catechisms and fables that would encourage "the principles of *obedience, honesty* and *faithful servitude*". It was essential to limit the growth of knowledge "for fear of perplexity and confusion, which would ruin all".[40]

Hedging his bets, Lindsay thought it impossible to predict what "some few Negroes *may be* after a careful cultivation" though "at present I do not think that Negroes will ever make any remarkable figure in the school of divinity". Perhaps to ensure that he would never know the outcome, Lindsay contended that just as the education of Jamaica's slaves should not be "scholastic", so too their religious teaching should not be allowed to delve into "disputable knowledge in points of divinity".[41] They were to be kept ignorant of complexity and scepticism. What Lindsay wanted taught was "the *religion of Christ* – such as *he himself taught and enforced* – I mean not the *Christian religion*; for that at present, is, we know not what". The religion of Christ was simple, consisting mainly of "the adoration of the one great and generous benefactor of the universe, who will graciously accept of every creature, nation and kindred whatsoever, and will reward them in heaven with himself, according to the degree of their love and obedience – or punish them by his perpetual displeasure for their irreverance or disobedience, in some region where love, harmony, and happiness never will be felt". Lindsay did not want to produce Anglicans or Presbyterians or Moravians, let alone adherents of enthusiasm. "To bring up a Negroe to any particular sect or form of religion, in preference to others, were madness in extreme," he exclaims.[42]

Thinking more theoretically, Lindsay insisted that "it would be a bold ascertion in any person to say, which *form* of religion is the most agreeable (to the eternal council of God, in the plan of creation) for black or for white". There were so many candidates, so many different religions around the world, that not even their number could be known. For those "passionately fond of simplicity, our choice may fall on some one which to our taste has the least quantity of frippery about its furbelows or paraphernalia", opines Lindsay, but "this is by no means determining the most pleasing to the Almighty". All that was certain was that "the humble adoration of the heart, in whatever manner, form or words, it is conveyed, will be ever, and only ever a pleasing service to heaven". Rather than "the *manner* or *form* of the Phareces prayer", it was the "reverent and *humble address* of the self abased publican" that most pleased Christ. Similarly, contends Lindsay, "surely a Negroe may be allowed sincerity, in an adoration of the deity".[43]

In this broadly relativist declaration, Lindsay invokes passages first encountered in *Memoirs*, written more than thirty years earlier, indicating that he had little changed his position on the truth or authority of a particular religion in its fundamental tenets or the utility of preaching hell and hellfire. Choosing a religion to teach the enslaved of Jamaica was therefore fundamentally a pragmatic decision. All he could commit to was that in "the public worship of God (when they shall meet together under the superintendency of a minister) I would by no means in an English colony degrade the English constitution by preferring a different mode of worship". He preferred to "avoid the reading of any creed (the Apostles excepted) before such a congregation". In teaching the enslaved, "lessons might be chosen too, peculiarly adapted to them", whereas "all doctrines of mystic nature should be assiduously avoided . . . and the gospel in its utmost simplicity only, propounded". Further, says Lindsay, "I would not have an English or Scotch catechism taught them by any means – they are all of them too dark and perplexed – too full of clerical politicks, and difficult points of ecclesiastic faith." He believed a catechism should be "form'd on purpose, as milk for such infant proselytes".[44]

Lindsay accepted that the Africans already possessed "certain ideas concerning the true and heavenly God", most particularly found in the common expression "*God a-top, dont love ugly* – meaning that the all-seeing God in heaven hates evil doings: and will not make them prosper". He also observed that "their ideas of another life and a futurity" were "confused and incorrect", though without noticing that his own views on the subject were far from clear. Building on what he understood as the basic ideas of African belief, he declares:

> The foundation of Christianity itself, is but these simple ideas, more enlarged and improved – viz That there is a God – and that he will reward every one of those, who die deserving of his favour, by taking them to his own home – their spiritual country. And if a select few of such of our clergy who have been long and well acquainted with the dispositions of this people, would apply themselves to a purpose of this kind – a short and easy catechism of the fundamentals of religion, accorded to their ideas, would lead on step by step, improving those ideas which they now almost confess.[45]

Fundamentally, Lindsay put his faith in the golden rule, which he believed even the least enlightened of humankind, including the enslaved, could be led to understand. He declares: "The general rule of the gospel cannot be beyond their comprehension – *Do to others, as you would wish them do by you*." How he squared this principle with the practice of slavery Lindsay never says.[46] As Dean Tucker declared in 1785 in his condemnation of slavery and the slave trade, "The plainest dictates of morality, viz. *Do as you would be done by*, loses its influence in many cases when opposed by self-interest."[47] Certainly Lindsay does not advance a true principle of reciprocity. He does not argue that if people wish not to be enslaved then they should not enslave other people. Rather, Lindsay's basic notion was that wherever human beings might find themselves placed (by God) in the great hierarchy of being, and whatever their race or class, they had an obligation to treat other human beings with honesty and fairness, even when they were being exploited or oppressed themselves. This was his notion of fairness and equity.

It was a conception of social order attractive to those who found themselves at the top of the hierarchical heap, but equally an argument rooted in Christian notions of forbearance. In the New Testament the idea is attributed to Jesus on at least three occasions, once in the gospel of Matthew and twice in Luke. The fullest expression occurs in Luke, where Jesus tells his disciples, "Love your enemies, do good to them which hate you" (6:27), to turn the other cheek (6:29), and "as ye would that men should do to you, do ye also to them likewise" (6:31). In Matthew 7:12, Jesus says, "whatsoever ye would that men should do to you, do ye even so to them: for this is the law and the prophets". These were the principles that underpinned Lindsay's moral philosophy, outlined thirty years before in *Memoirs* – in his image of Sicco, the "grateful slave" – and essential to his construction of racial difference.[48]

Missionary Bookkeepers

Lindsay expanded his argument regarding religion by connecting it with the long-standing desire of the Jamaican Assembly to increase or at least maintain the white population of the island. The principal mechanism used by the Assembly was the *Deficiency Act*, which imposed fines on landowners who failed to maintain a sufficient ratio of whites to blacks on their properties.[49] Lindsay argued that the law "was not design'd as a money law, to inrich the treasury: but if possible to recruit our island with good and useful families or white people, as servants upon our several estates, emported from Europe from time to time". He admitted, however, that it was a failure and that "most of our white servants, whom we call clerks, book-keepers, distillers &c, in the general are but a sorry sort of make-shifts – an idle, be-sore'd, be-sotted, dishonest pack, who are constantly intangling the plantations business, as well as often ruining the best Negroes on the estate, both in body and mind". Lindsay was not looking for one of these but rather "a young gentleman (or supposing a married gentleman, his active wife might be very useful about a family) of *sobriety* and *industrious capacity*; who in a single glance of the estates books, to see into all its management by a happy ease and regularity in his form of accounts would guide a proprietor". Keeping the books would take not more than a couple of hours, and the young man would then be free "to perform many little devoirs, which a trusty person can do for the service of the house".[50]

Such a "young gentleman" – a character less refined than the "fine gentleman" of Lindsay's *Memoirs* – would ideally be also "a clergyman in English Orders and who as a missionary for the propagation of religion and virtue, would in his leisure hours be happy, to instruct the ignorant". Not only would he have time sufficient to perform his duties as chaplain and tutor, he might gradually learn the business of planting. With the assumption that "he shall be young, at least healthy; active; and has not *the fear of death before his eyes* (which if he hath, he has no business here)", he was to accompany his employer into the cane field and the sugar factory. Sufficiently informed, the young chaplain could act as "superintending attorney" in the absence of the proprietor. If he was educated in physic, all the better.[51]

With such a useful "missionary" in place, Lindsay saw the planter erecting a combined "school-house and chapel", located close to the plantation hospital so the sick might gain some benefit. The missionary was to read a short prayer in the morning, "beseeching grace for his pupils towards the improvement of the day, and to bless his own labours with success". On the other hand, to expect "the working gang in the field, to stand up and *say their prayers*, at the beginning of work, and at their leaving it" struck Lindsay as

PROSLAVERY PRIEST

ludicrous. In the evening, in the church, there might be "a full and extensive but short prayer" with "a warm amplification of *Gods greatness*, but also of his goodness and mercy, who in such greatness is allways gently ready to grant us his unworthy creatures, what he knows is best for us". As well as the hearing of catechisms, Lindsay "would then have my chaplin or minister to prelect, not by any sermon or written discourse . . . but extemporarily . . . on points most necessary for slaves to be well informd in" – by which he meant obedience and moral duty.[52]

Lindsay also proposed that the missionary should deliver "slightly premeditated harangues; in which he may have the general heads and scriptural proof, for the ease of his memory (such as we find in B. Beveredge Thesaurus Theologicus) committed to writing". Here Lindsay refers to the four-volume *Thesaurus Theologicus: or, A Complete System of Divinity; Summ'd up in Brief Notes upon Select Places of the Old and New Testament; Wherein the Sacred Text is Reduc'd under Proper Heads, Explain'd, and Illustrated with the Opinions and Authorities of the Ancient Fathers, &c.*, by William Beveridge, DD, published in 1710. Beveridge's method was to link a topic to a text (Genesis 17:1, for example), set out a question ("In what sense is God said to be almighty?"), discuss scriptural connections (John 19:11), quote saints such as Augustine (in Latin), draw out a series of observations ("He could create new worlds; make more stars of creatures"), and list implications and lessons (we must "submit to his will and pleasure"). It was no simple system in the manner of a catechism. Lindsay's more specific suggestions as to the content of his proposed "premeditated harangues" are somewhat different, designed to instil a knowledge of "the *constant presence of God*, and of his *dreadful judgement to come;* when he will reward the *righteous and consiencious* servant with the *joys of heaven*, and will punish the *lying, dishonest and undutiful* slave, with the *torments of the devil in hell, thro' all eternity*".[53]

In preaching the reality of hell and its torments, Lindsay was not afraid to apply the social control model, to argue that certain tenets might usefully be taught in order to instil fears in the ignorant that would help ensure stability, regardless of the preacher's own belief. The nature and location of hell worried many of Lindsay's contemporaries, some placing it in the heavens (the sun providing an appropriate fiery site) while others found hell on earth. The problem was closely associated with the idea of plural worlds, a concept with special appeal to deists and equally significant for those who held that life on earth was the best of all possible worlds. In contrast to his personal doubts about these matters, Lindsay threw overboard some of his prejudices in order to ensure the pragmatic value of teaching the terrors of hell and the devil. Here he concedes:

> let the private opinion of the master and his friends reguarding these popular points, be what they may – if he wishes that a good disposition and conscientious principle may be wrought upon his ignorant slave, he must with patience, sit in the utmost, at least the most seemingly full assent to every thing advanced; and be it ever such gargon and Methodistical cant, they must from policy itself, endeavour to have it believed by the ignorant infidel, that they are themselves thorough believers of all the preachers doctrines.

This was an ancient argument known as a theory of double truth, in which doubts were suppressed or kept secret because it seemed necessary to preach the reality of hell in order to prevent society collapsing into orgiastic anarchy. Only fear of eternal torment was thought to offer the ultimate deterrent to challenges to the social order.[54]

The theory of double truth was paralleled by the idea that whereas the thinking few might be allowed to toy with sceptical, freethinking and deist ideas, it was essential that society at large be held together by the preaching of religious orthodoxy. In accepting the possibility that these doctrines might come from the mouths of Methodists, Lindsay used what he saw as the most extreme outcome, knowing that the planter class shared with him a tremendous distaste for those of this persuasion. The Methodists of the United States had, after all, denounced slavery when they separated from the Anglican Church in 1784, and had threatened with expulsion any minister who did not free his slaves or any member who bought and sold people. Within a year, in the face of extreme hostility in the southern states, the American Methodists had made a pragmatic compromise, shifting their emphasis to preaching the duties and responsibilities of masters and slaves. Perhaps Lindsay had these recent developments in mind when he sought to demonstrate the theological depths to which it was necessary to sink in order to preserve social order.[55]

"The Revd Mr Ramsey of St Christopher"

Lindsay commenced the concluding chapter of the "Conjectural considerations" by declaring: "I shall not in the close of my work, think I have perform'd my task with satisfaction to myself, till I have taken notice of a few strictures that have drop'd from the Revd Mr Ramsey of St Christopher, on the subject now under consideration." He would end with Ramsay as he had begun. Condemning the emerging attacks on slavery and the slave trade as the products of "time servers", Lindsay observes: "Even Mr Ramsay of St Kitts, who has been much talk'd of – and has said so much on the subject – I declare has puzzled me . . . and considering the number of years he lived in the West Indeas, he ought to have understood the subject he wrote upon better, and wrote more to the purpose, than he seems to me to have done." However, although Lindsay notes that "God of his good pleasure, has been pleased to cast my lot too, on West Indean ground", he seems unaware of the close parallels in their two careers.[56]

PROSLAVERY PRIEST

James Ramsay (1733–89) lived at almost exactly the same time as John Lindsay (1729–88). They were both Scots; Ramsay was born at Fraserburgh, on the north-eastern tip of Aberdeenshire (figure 2.2). Although Ramsay's father was a ship's carpenter, his first hope was to train as a clergyman in the Church of Scotland. Lacking the funds to study, he apprenticed to a surgeon in Fraserburgh but soon found himself at the University of Aberdeen, at the feet of Thomas Reid, professor of moral philosophy. Ramsay moved to London in 1753 (the year Lindsay was ordained) and in 1757 qualified as a surgeon with the Royal Navy (in which service Lindsay was chaplain). He soon found himself cruising in the Atlantic, and in 1759 he had a transformative experience after boarding a slave ship on its way to Barbados, the people dying from dysentery. After a period in Antigua, Ramsay returned to England, where he was ordained by the Bishop of London in November 1761. The following year he was installed as a parish priest in St Kitts.[57]

Although Ramsay was said to be already committed to the cause of the enslaved, he married the daughter of a planter in St Kitts in 1763, just one year after Lindsay did the same thing in Jamaica. Also like Lindsay, Ramsay became a slave-owner. And he began publishing as well, not in the derring-do style of Lindsay but on matters of ethical concern, such as his *Essay on the Duty and Qualifications of a Sea Officer* (1765), which went through several editions and appeared also in translation. In 1770 Ramsay published in Basseterre his *Essay on Taxation*, which exposed the illegality of a scheme proposed by planters and earned him disapproval from the white population of St Kitts, who were already opposed to his efforts to include enslaved people in church services. He became a sea chaplain in 1778, serving in the West Indies, and published the first naval sermon to see the light of day since the beginning of the century. Ramsay made his final break with St Kitts in 1781, when he went to England with his wife and children (plate 16). Of the slaves he owned, Ramsay "freed such as he thought would make a proper use of it" and sold the others, except for one man, Nestor, who accompanied the family to England.[58]

In 1782, through the patronage of Sir Charles Middleton, Ramsay became a parish priest in the English county of Kent, where he lived near Middleton's estate, Barham Court. There and at his patron's London residence, Ramsay met many influential people, was sought out for advice on naval, medical and other matters, and was encouraged to write on slavery and the slave trade. It was an entrée Lindsay could only dream of. Ramsay talked not only to bishops but also to government ministers and members of the Clapham Sect, feeding information and ideas to Granville Sharp, Thomas Clarkson and William Wilberforce.[59] It was this influence at the heart of government that so perturbed Lindsay and ensured that his fire was directed specifically at Ramsay and his writings.

Published in 1784, Ramsay's major contribution to the attack on slavery is *An Essay on the Treatment and Conversion of African Slaves in the British Sugar Colonies*. Unlike Lindsay, Ramsay was not afraid to put his name to his work. He had begun the writing many years before and, in the wake of the American Revolution, edited out arguments about imperial government that he realized would make his message less palatable. It is a refined work. There are, however, significant similarities between Ramsay's *Essay* and Lindsay's "Conjectural considerations". Ramsay does not commence with the experience of enslaved people in St Kitts or refer to their testimony in the way that much later antislavery literature does; rather, like Lindsay, he sets out first to display his literary talents, classical learning and knowledge of world history.[60] The *Essay* is made up of five chapters. The first, "On the various ranks in social life", is chiefly devoted to a lengthy historical account of "master and slave". Chapters two and three are concerned with the social "advancement of slaves" and their religious instruction. Not until the fourth chapter does Ramsay consider the "natural capacity of African slaves" on the basis of philosophy, form and anatomy. The final chapter of the *Essay* proposes a "Plan for the improvement and conversion of African slaves" through clergy and police.

Ramsay defends the biblical account of monogenesis and explains human diversity by arguing: "at a period, when men had become numerous, profligate and daring, their Creator, to punish their rebellion, and . . . to make it instrumental in advancing society, and the more equal and speedy cultivation of the earth, divided them into families and languages, giving to each distinct features, and a separate speech". In discussing this second Creation, which is associated with the confusion of Babel, Ramsay refers to the common characteristics of the various "families or supposed races", which are in turn divided into "nations", but he hopes also for an "ultimate re-union of mankind" as part of God's revealed plan. He takes Kames to task for proposing that the Americans had a separate origin. Without naming him, Ramsay also criticizes Robertson for seeming to express the same opinion in his *History of America* but drawing back because it was an opinion contrary to Scripture. In view of "the scepticism of the age", Ramsay thought it essential that "the friends of virtue" avoid speculation, lest their opinions be taken up by infidels.[61]

PROSLAVERY PRIEST

Although he accepted, as did Lindsay, that God had established "a natural inequality, or diversity, which prevails among men that fits them for society, enables them to fill up all the different offices of polished life, and forms their varied abilities, nay, even their particular defects and wants, into a firm band of union", Ramsay believed that the relation of master and slave was "artificial, or unnatural" and therefore not part of "this law of nature, and of God". He argued that slavery could be ended without any loss of profit to the planter, assuming various conditions were met – some of them oppressive. His approach was in the short term ameliorationist, thus closing the gap between himself and the proslavery plantocracy. However, although Ramsay did not hanker for a utopian state of absolute freedom, he did look forward to a world without coerced labour. This was enough to induce a strong reaction.[62]

Ramsay's *Essay* was met by a great outpouring of letters and pamphlets from supporters of the West Indian interest. Some attacked the man, saying Ramsay was a charlatan, a Presbyterian who had switched to the Church of England for personal gain. Others attacked the truth of his account of slavery in the sugar islands. After completing his *Essay*, Ramsay spent the remainder of 1784 writing *An Inquiry into the Effects of Putting a Stop to the African Slave Trade, and of Granting Liberty to the Slaves in the British Sugar Colonies*, in which he argued that abolition would contribute to British economic growth. In 1785 he published a rebuttal to his opponents, *A Reply to the Personal Invectives and Objections Contained in Two Answers, Published by Certain Anonymous Persons*.[63] These works had a substantial role in advancing the cause of abolition, both with Clarkson, who spent a month as Ramsay's curate in 1787 (the year the Society for the Abolition of the Slave Trade was founded), and with William Pitt, who persuaded Wilberforce to take the issue to Parliament.

Early in 1788 Ramsay published *An Address on the Proposed Bill for the Abolition of the Slave Trade* and also *Objections to the Abolition of the Slave Trade, with Answers*. It is not known whether Lindsay read these later works. John Duke, a curate in Barbados, published a proslavery pamphlet in April 1788, but it is improbable that Lindsay made any use of it. Lindsay saw his task as much weightier, founded in philosophy and theology as much as practical experience. Thus his attack on Ramsay was directed particularly at the *Essay* of 1784. The first debate in the House of Commons did not happen until May 1789, however, when Lindsay was already dead. Ramsay died soon after, in July 1789, long before the final decision to abolish the slave trade in 1807.[64]

Lindsay opens his critique of the *Essay* with the Athenians and Ramsay's statement that "in the arbitrary relation of master and slave, no law restrains the one, no election or compact secures the other". He did not dispute the claim that in ancient Athens the law protected slaves from every injury caused by a citizen, but declared that in the West Indies it was impossible to have magistrates present everywhere to hear such complaints. Lindsay admitted that there were "domestic tyrants" (slave-owners), "void of all tender feelings", whose "parsimony, luxury, extravagance, caprice, passions and spite are eternally alive in a thousand distressing instances, to tease and torment the enslaved wretches every moment of their lives, sleeping or waking", but he believed such behaviour was hardly the rule and considered it checked by the "jurisdiction of our consciences, under the continual presence of a God of mercy and compassion". Making it personal, Lindsay declares: "we who are possessed of slaves, account for them as our children: and behave to them in the general as such – as far at least as patience and perverse provocation will permit".[65] There is a limit, he says, because

> there are Negroes, so very obstinate and refractory (I speak from my own experience) whom I have been obliged to correct, while my own heart, has bled as sore as their backs – when to others I have had inclination to give incouragement, to a degree perhaps further than the laws of prudence and the safety of the islands community would bear me through: and have often felt for good slaves, *whose honour* has been hurt and their *bodies* have been forceably abused, by some vicious rascal, whose skin was white, but whose heart was so black he did it, because he dared to do it.

Hoping that his probation scheme might promote advancement, Lindsay says that ultimately those who are "incorrigible . . . must as they deserve live and die in wretchedness – for it must lie with each individual slave, *of himself* – not of *his owner*, to better or advance his condition".[66]

Lindsay also opposed Ramsay's promotion of "marriage with religious ceremony among slaves", arguing not only that it would be cumbersome but also because "to bind indissolubly a man to a wife, who is already for life bound to a master – were rather hard". Further, the legal imperative for marriage was lacking, because "slaves having no property of their own, neither in progeny or freehold", had no need of the institution. There was no need to follow Ramsay's plan to bring marriage among slaves into "the intanglements of ecclesiastical law" until they had been freed and given "the *full privileges* granted to a *Christian denizon*". In the meantime, says Lindsay, "for mercies sake, wink at the weakness and ignorance of a poor slave, even though he has been made a Christian. As God himself in the full blaze of goodness and mercy, winked at the many improprieties, inconsistant with the law of nature in the antient nation of Israel."[67]

Although Lindsay claimed to hope that Ramsay's desire to bring religion to the enslaved would be rewarded, he asks, "What can be expected of the poor Negroe when we who call ourselves by the *name of Christ*, shew them *every example to irreligion and prophaneness*?" Noting that "our people of *colour and freedom* are ever ready and happy to imitate our customs and manners", Lindsay saw how vital it was "that no example of any thing vicious, immoral, or irreligious, be, by us, set before them". Speaking of his own experience in Spanish Town, Lindsay repeats his hope that the governors of Jamaica will again become regular members of the congregation and that it be "deem'd the greatest neglect, and the most likely to subject him to his sovereigns displeasure – that whatever their own private opinions be concerning religion, they shall shew themselves as head of the English church, and be attenders on that worship every Lords day in the royal pew prepar'd for their reception, at least once in the day". Here Lindsay finds support for his approach in the early history of Christianization, arguing, "it was not the good sense of the apostles doctrines – nor the *surprize* of gospel miracles, so much as the *good and examplary lives* and *patient sufferings* of its first martyrs and confessors, which so much work'd upon the minds of the heathen and infidel Jews amongst whom they lived".[68]

Occasionally Lindsay finds good things to say about his clerical counterpart. For example, he approves Ramsay's proposal for an improved slave law, saying, "The *Revd Mr Ramsay* has done his part – perhaps it has not pleased – let others continue to try the subject." Indeed, Lindsay claims a broader approval: "Well knowing the masters and owners of those people will be *very happy* at any mode which will make their *slaves happy* – because it will make *themselves the happier*." He also claims that Ramsay shares the view "that freedom if not brought about by slow degrees, would be no blessing to a slave".[69]

To this extent Ramsay and Lindsay were not so far apart. Where they differed was in their expectation of liberty and equality – however defined – in the longer term. Ramsay was hopeful, progressive on his terms. Although he considered that "[a] state of absolute freedom is indeed a revolution that we may rather wish for, than expect for some time to see", he believed that "doubtless it is within the plan of Providence, and of man's progressive advancement in society". Ramsay also believed that free people would be more productive than those who were enslaved, predicting that free field labourers would dig twice as many cane holes in a day. Lindsay, on the other hand, declares:

> I am not without my doubts, that after all that can be done in the cause of liberty (even through the help of religion) that it will go on but sluggishly: and will be given up at last, from a very serious and obvious consideration – viz that *Negroe men* (at least when free) *do seldom work*. To give up slavery therefore, in Mr Ramseys wild mode, I am affraid would in the end be, to give up the sugar colonies.

As proof, Lindsay points to the "five acre men of Barbadoes", the so-called Redlegs, descended from white indentured servants who had no slaves to work for them. He asks: "what sort of miserable looking, dead and alive, wretches are they?"[70]

Hume's Footnote M

Nearing the conclusion of "Conjectural considerations", Lindsay follows Ramsay along a path that leads straight to David Hume and "objections to African capacity", thus reconnecting with the first part of the text and the problem of human diversity. It is an unnecessary diversion, says Ramsay, for those "who, with Moses, believe that all men had one common parent, though for wise ends different families have since had distinguishing marks fixed on them". He then claims to quote Hume's essay "Of National Characters", to the effect that "mankind is composed of three or four different races; and that there never was a polished society, but of the white race, to which all others are naturally inferior". Ramsay also notes Hume's opinion "that there never arose a man of genius among negroes". These phrases were not in fact correctly copied from Hume, and it is interesting that Ramsay imposes *race* and *races* on Hume in place of the terms *species*, *kinds* and *breeds of men*. Lindsay did not criticize Ramsay for his gloss.[71]

Written in 1748, Hume's essay "Of National Characters" was directed at showing that "each nation has a peculiar set of manners, and that some particular qualities are more frequently to be met with among one people than among their neighbours". The Swiss were more honest than the Irish, for example, and the English more knowledgeable than the Danes. Hume noted that it was argued that such differences might stem from moral or physical causes, the first derived from institutions and the latter "qualities of the air and climate" that altered "the tone and habit of the body" and gave "a particular complexion". Although he dismissed "air, food or climate", Hume thought "that all the nations, which live beyond the polar circles or between the tropics, are inferior to the rest of the species, and are incapable of all the higher attainments of the human mind".[72]

It was at this point in the essay that in 1753 Hume inserted his infamous footnote M, which declares:

> I am apt to suspect the negroes, and in general all other species of men (for there are four or five different kinds) to be naturally inferior to the whites. There never was a civilized nation of any other complexion than white, nor even any individual eminent either in action or speculation. No ingenious manufactures amongst them, no arts, no sciences. On the other hand, the most rude and barbarous of the whites,

> such as the ancient Germans, the present Tartars, have still something eminent about them, in their valour, form of government, or some other particular. Such a uniform and constant difference could not happen, in so many countries and ages, if nature had not made an original distinction betwixt these breeds of men.[73]

A revised edition of 1777, published the year after Hume's death, amended the first sentence to read simply: "I am apt to suspect the negroes to be naturally inferior to the whites", deleting his reference to the four or five "species of men". Hume also weakened his claims that civilizations other than those of whites ever produced eminent individuals. In making these revisions, Hume both drew back from an implicit polygenesis and at the same time directed his argument exclusively at Africans.[74] Here, footnote M continues unrevised: "Not to mention our colonies, there are Negroe slaves dispersed all over Europe, of which none ever discovered any symptoms of ingenuity, tho' low people, without education, will start up amongst us, and distinguish themselves in every profession. In Jamaica, indeed, they talk of one negroe as a man of parts and learning; but 'tis likely he is admired for very slender accomplishments, like a parrot, who speaks a few words plainly."[75] Hume shows here that he has heard of the accomplishments of Francis Williams (plate 1). Neither Ramsay nor Lindsay seems to have been aware of Hume's revisions.

Referencing "Mr D. Hume in his National Characters (note M, vol. I, page 216)", Lindsay says:

> Mr Longs account of Black Williams, to whom Mr Hume in his note alludes, is true so far, as the picture taken of him, is in his best array, and when in his best days. My ingenious friend knew him in his best days, when he was admitted to the Governors levéé – in his tie-wig and sword. I knew him in his latter days, when reduced to keeping a Negroe school – nor did I ever hear much of the success of his labours in this line, unless a favourite scholar of his, named Brown – a fantastical blockhead, whose *chef d'oeuvre* was copying writings: and who made so honest and indiscreet a use of his pen, as to be a few years ago transported as a vagabond, for giving run-away Negroes, forged tickets of a masters leave of absence.

Lindsay goes on to describe blacks – particularly house slaves in towns, the people he knew best – as cunning and plausible liars in making their way through everyday life but rarely "capable of learning any thing that requires a *correct ingenuity*". Echoing Long, he says they are "seldom found clever in any useful performance – not even in the lowest parts of the mechanic arts", unable to cut with a saw, bore with a gimlet or auger, or even "drive a nail of an inch long in a streight or perpendicular direction". As to the supposed "sagacity of . . . house Negroes", says Lindsay, "I never or seldom at least knew a waiting boy who could be trusted of himself with even puting the cloath upon a table – one would forgive them in the art of placing the varieties of a table, as a mistress would approve – but the table itself, will be ever set awray in the hall or dineing room, and the cloath askew on the table, unless it be, by a mere chance, if you trust to them alone."[76]

Lindsay's enthusiasm for the infamous footnote was shared by other writers in the proslavery cause, but Hume was criticized by leading figures of the Scottish Enlightenment for what seemed idiosyncratic and contradictory to his own system of thought. It was a statement lacking empirical foundations and appeared fundamentally opposed to his essential scepticism. Yet Hume's repeated editing of footnote M demonstrates that it was not an offhand remark, exposing the often contradictory and ambiguous role of slavery and liberty in Enlightenment thought.[77]

The discussion of Hume's footnote M comes near the end of Lindsay's manuscript. He concludes his "Conjectural considerations" not with any broad issue but rather by approving Ramsay's proposal for the "trial of crimes amongst a gang of Negroes to be by a jury of themselves, in the face of the whole gathered together – two drivers being assistant judges with the overseer", adding only that he thinks it would better if the overseer was from a neighbouring plantation and that "punishments would have constantly to be given at the head of the corps, for the sake of examples, and in the most public manner". However, Lindsay considers that the granting of pardons should not be taken from the slave-owner and given to priests in the way proposed by Ramsay, saying:

> I declare myself no bigot to any religion – nor to the letter, or formula of any peculiar sect or body of men in Christendom: but do I adore the pure and simple spirit of the gospel – in which there is no appearance or latent sign of party, sect, or priest-craft whatsoever. I will never therefore agree with Mr Ramsay to give up my own *regal right* (for so I call it) of shewing mercy and granting respite, softening of punishments or giving pardon to criminals on my own estate or property, to gratifie or inhance the vanity of any priest whatever, whither of England or Moravia.[78]

Thus ends Lindsay's "Conjectural considerations".

CHAPTER TEN

Afterlife

JOHN LINDSAY DIED IN JAMAICA and was buried at his Spanish Town church on 3 November 1788. The church register identifies him as "Reverend John Lindsay D.D. Rector of the Parish of St. Catherine" and notes the cause of death as "bile", suggesting trouble in the digestive tract. A few years earlier, in 1783, he had been "on the verge of dropsy". His wife Grace, "gentlewoman and widow", died a year later of "consumption and gout".[1] It was not rebellion or war that took their lives, or even the dreaded climate, but simple breakdown of the body's internal workings, helped along by an indulgent lifestyle.

There is nothing to suggest that the Lindsays had living children to inherit the material things they left behind. In "Conjectural considerations", written in the last years of his life, John Lindsay made the tantalizing observation that his laundress washed for "a large and complicated family; of all colours and degrees – free and bond – white, black, and brown".[2] Who all these people were, how they lived together and what their kinship relations might have been can only be guessed at. Only the enslaved people are readily identified, and this because they were defined as "chattels", part of the personal property of the Lindsays. An inventory ordered in February 1790 by Richard Batty and William Mitchell, administrators of the estate, names and values twenty-six enslaved people living at the time of Grace Lindsay's death.[3] There are no clues in the inventory to support John Lindsay's claim to have been a planter; these people seem to have been attached to the Spanish Town rectory and its associated pen.

The names of the enslaved people included in the inventory suggest that ten were male and sixteen female. Mothers are linked to their children, at least six of them. Four were "left free": Grace Lindsay, Mary Grace Lindsay, Jenny Pusey and Peggy Johnston. These are the only slaves attributed surnames. Perhaps they took or were given their surnames at manumission, to emphasize their status, or perhaps the Lindsay and Pusey names indicate parentage. The former seems more likely, with Mary Grace Lindsay perhaps a daughter of Grace Lindsay, who was in turn named for her mistress. Apparently not freed was "Pinkey blind, left to Mary Grace Lindsay". Two of the men had classical names – Appollo and Cato – while Juba's was African, Duncan's Scottish, and York's English. Only Cato is attributed an occupation, that of cook. Jamaica was "very old".[4] The fact that Lindsay's household included a specialized cook as well as a butler and laundress does suggest a complex and carefully structured domestic unit: people moving busily through the halls and rooms of the rectory and spilling out into yard, street and market.

The only other clues to family and friends found in the inventory are that Mrs Lindsay desired that "16 pictures painted from Doctor Lindsay's designs" be given to Richard Batty, and that he should also have "a gold mourning ring for William Pusey [presumably Grace Lindsay's brother] with hair set round with diamonds . . . as a gift for remembrance". Batty also received a carriage horse named Ruby. Mrs Lindsay ordered that her clothes be given to Mrs Mary Pusey, along with table linen and sheeting, a set of blue enamelled tea china, and three family pictures. Mrs Penelope Williken Nevinson shared the table linen and sheeting.[5] Apart from this handful of bequests, the bulk of the goods left behind was sold at public auction.

Worldly Goods

Although John Lindsay's claims to plantership appear overblown, he died a wealthy man. All told, the inventoried estate was valued at £5,503, including a mortgage and bonds worth £3,000. The enslaved people were valued at £1,260. Even if the mortgage and bonds are excluded, the personalty of the Lindsays was above average for inventoried wealth holders in Jamaica around that time. The inventory covers only personalty; the rectory in which the Lindsays lived was, after all, parish property, not theirs to sell or bequeath.[6] The inventory does include a group of items "at the penn", which was a place to raise minor crops and livestock and to visit and stay at, but not a plantation. Perhaps this pen occupied the "sixty acres of rich pasture-land" close to Spanish Town allocated to the parish priest.[7] Probably some of the enslaved people spent most of their time there. At the pen were a bedstead and mattress, six "low backed yew chairs" (probably imported from Britain), two "mahogany chairs", a round dining table, a tea table and two old tables. The livestock comprised eighteen sheep and lambs, two rams, thirteen goats and three "old meagre steers".

More obvious signs of conspicuous consumption are found in the goods in the rectory. Not only did the Lindsays rule a larger domestic staff – some of them decked in fancy livery – than could be afforded by a typical contemporary British parish priest, they also possessed more material things. The inventory of 1790 lists these goods in minute detail, providing a much clearer picture of the domestic life of the Lindsays than can be constructed for any time while they were alive. The appraisers did not name the rooms of the rectory but followed a path that provides strong clues. Among the bedroom furniture was "a four post bedstead with net, matrasses, bolster, pillows etc" valued at £46; "a four post bedstead with net, two matrasses bolster pillows etc", £28; "a sopha with covers", £20 10s.; a wardrobe, £15; "a cabinet inlaid", £11; and "6 chamber chairs and 1 night chair with covers", £12; as well as (all under £10) "4 mahogany chamber chairs with covers 2 ditto stools", "a gouty chair and stool" (no doubt used by Grace Lindsay), "a mahogany chest upon chest", "swing glass with drawers" and "a swing glass and deal dressing table", a "basin stand with basin and pitcher", a tea table, a bidet, a tea chest, and "a chimney piece glass".

In what seems to have been a dining room was a buffet, three dining tables, a "sideboard table", a tea table, card tables, "7 low backed mahogany chairs and 3 high backed ditto", a clock, an urn and stand, candlesticks and a "globe lamp". Associated utensils included knives, forks, spoons, teaspoons, tongs, cruets, punchbowls, a coffeepot, a teapot, a sugar dish, china teacups and saucers, glasses, decanters, and two sets of Wedgwood tableware. In silver were castors, salts, a soup ladle and – of more local provenance – four "cocoa nut cups, silver mounted" and a plated coffee pot. Musical instruments included a harpsichord and a spinet.

Outside or near the back of the house was bulky cooking equipment – the tools of Cato's kitchen – including large iron pots, a grate, spits, a chafing dish, coffee and corn mills and a dripstone and frame. Supplies included "a cask and 3 dozen bottles of rum and four large case bottles, containing altogether 51 gallons" and sundry "old things in the butler's pantry". Probably put out after his death was "a trunk containing 4 doz. shirts and new and other cloths [clothes] of Doctor Lindsays". Another trunk contained new shoes, slippers and five new coloured handkerchiefs. Odds and ends, valued as a lot, included doeskin gloves, some "scarlet shag in liveries", remnants of shaloon, buckram, fustian, blue livery, livery lace and sheeting, as well as red and blue epaulettes and livery buttons. For looking after the clothing there was a clothes copper, plus several shoe brushes. For getting around there were two "chariot horses", "a chariot and pair of plated harness", and "a spare lining for the chariot".

Personal items that probably belonged to John Lindsay included a "silver tobacco box with burning glass", a pair of studs, a small gold seal, a "gold ring with Mrs Lindsay's picture" and a gold-headed cane. There was also "a pontipool case with scales and weights", which refers to a recently developed type of japanned metalware made in Pontypool, Wales. Probably the property of Grace Lindsay was "a tortoise shell box containing 4 gold rings set with diamonds and stones".[8] Items that marked out Lindsay's profession were confined to a plated cross and fourteen pairs of white burial gloves. The inventory makes no mention of books or manuscripts; these may have been disbursed previously, perhaps handed over to Dr Arthur Broughton.

"Holy Haggis"

No memorial was erected in Lindsay's honour, but this was no particular affront. He was not a governor or an admiral or a rich planter. Priests were public figures but ranked lower in the Jamaican scale of respect, which was based on wealth and power. As John Roby observes in the context of an inventory of the monuments of St Catherine parish church, collected in 1824, "It is somewhat remarkable that of the numerous Rectors of this parish there is not to be found a single memorial in the church or church-yard." Several governors who had died in the island were similarly missing. Roby's remark occurs in a footnote specifically referring to Lindsay. In this note Roby mentions that "Rev. John Lindsay, D.D. Rector" contributed two articles on waterspouts published in the *Gentleman's Magazine*, giving their full titles and dates (1781 and 1783), and records his date of death, but says he knows of no other claims to fame.[9]

Lindsay's name did survive on the walls of the cathedral church. In the north transept, a tablet erected in 1779, headed "Benefactors to the Poor", recorded that in 1765 Matthew Gregory, MD, had established a fund "to relieve any distressed object of this island coming to St. Jago de la Vega, to bind out poor children to trades, and to portion orphan girls at marriage". Lindsay was identified on the tablet as treasurer, a role that descended to him as rector. Lindsay's name also survived on a communion flagon refashioned in 1777 from old plate and inscribed "The Rev. John Lindsay, D.D. Rector".[10]

Recollections of Lindsay do not refer to his spiritual ministry but find significance in his life as a writer and a recorder of ideas and attitudes. This assessment is identifiable in the first notices of his death. In London, the *Gentleman's Magazine* of February 1789 describes him as "rector of the parish of

St. Catherine" and "author of the papers on water-spouts, and several other pieces in our Magazine; 'A Voyage to Senegal;' several novels; and a poem, called 'Sir John Tostle' ". An abbreviated version of this notice appeared in the *Scots Magazine* in the same month. Of these items, only the papers on waterspouts, *Voyage* and one novel have been found.[11] There is no mention of his unpublished works. Probably he kept "Conjectural considerations" to himself, and "Elegancies" had been forgotten. Sermons, published and unpublished, were two a penny.

Lindsay's contemporaries demonstrated little respect for the quality of his preaching. The June 1797 issue of the *Columbian Magazine*, the issue that published the *Critical Review*'s harsh judgement of Lindsay's *Memoirs*, includes an anonymous letter to the editor saying:

> You have of late been in the habit of giving some of the theological reveries of the late Rev. Mr. Lindsay, Rector of St. Jago de la Vega, *dec.*; a Gentleman who perhaps possessed the ambition, without the ability, to distinguish himself in the deluding walks of literature. As a substitute for those holy *Haggis*, I send for your insertion (and I rest assured you will not refuse them a place for insertion) two Funeral Sermons by a Rev. Gentleman of our island too; whose abilities are of the first class; and which, in the present instance, will be found to bear the strong attestation of men of confessed knowledge & judgement.

The editor acceded, publishing a funeral sermon given by Rev. Thomas Warren, "*Occasioned by the Death of the R.H. Countess of Effingham: Who was buried at St. Jago de la Vega, Nov. 2, 1791*". His text was drawn from I Corinthians 7:31: "For the fashion of this world passeth away."[12] Modern commentators have similarly ignored Lindsay's sermons and been little more enthusiastic about his other works. In 1982 Michael Craton called "Conjectural considerations" a "negrophobic tract" and described as "egregious" Lindsay's proposal for entrusting the Church of England with religious teaching of the enslaved. R.A. Minter, in 1990, described Lindsay's "Conjectural considerations" as "not distinguished by its objectivity" and "a wide-ranging attack on the Abolitionists".[13]

Rev. John Lindsay has sometimes been confused with the medical John Lindsay of Jamaica, introduced in chapter 7. In addition, several twentieth-century editions of the British *Dictionary of National Biography* conflated Lindsay with a better-known John Lindsay (1685/6–1768), a nonjuring Church of England clergyman and writer, the author of a history of England, biblical commentaries and anti-Catholic works. Recent editions of the *Dictionary* identify "John Lindsay (*fl.* 1758–59)" as a "naval chaplain and writer, who served as the chaplain in the *Forgueux* [*sic*] during Augustus Keppel's attack on Goree in September 1758", and indicate that these were two different men.[14] Several of Lindsay's publications are listed in this updated entry but there is no mention of his Jamaican career. Such disconnected encounters with the diverse facets of Lindsay's oeuvre encourage the idea that they must each belong to someone else.

Individually, perhaps the known elements of Lindsay's life and writing have limited interest for historians of the eighteenth century. Drawn together and attached to a single life, they become more significant, though it is impossible to construct a picture of Lindsay the man. It is not known whether he was short or tall, fat or thin, and indeed the only clues to the body he inhabited come in association with complaints. He tells us that before coming to Jamaica he had a persistent cough and poor bowel movements, and that these cleared up once he had settled in the island. In later life he probably wore spectacles and he may have shared his wife's gout. He died of "bile" a few years after coming close to succumbing to dropsy. These fragments do not add up to an attractive image, and they do little to build a notion of the character or personality of the man. He did not hide his distaste for many or most of his fellow human beings and he went out of his way to specifically denigrate and disparage Jews, Jesuits, Roman Catholics, enthusiastic Protestants, Methodists, Moravians, the French, blacks, (American) Indians, women and domestic servants. British white males were most to his liking, though he had no trouble venting his hostility at elements of this class.

Although the transatlantic life lived by Lindsay is not particularly remarkable in itself, he did rise high in the hierarchy of the Church of England within the constrained sphere of Jamaican slave society, and he did contribute to the intellectual world of the eighteenth-century Atlantic in an unusual combination of fields. Perhaps the elements did not always blend together in a coherent and consistent fashion, but, like a haggis, they were held together in a single skin.

"The Suburbs of Hell"

Sailing between Barbados and Puerto Rico on his way to Jamaica in 1778, Rev. William Jones labelled the West Indies "the suburbs of Hell".[15] The phrase had nothing to do with a harsh assessment of Jamaican slave society or the hellish lives lived by the enslaved people of the island; it referred rather to the precariousness of human existence in its exaggerated tropical version. The "suburbs of hell" appeared in dramatic literature from the early seventeenth century, where the phrase was used to mean the closeness of living human beings to the afterlife, with only "a dead wall between". It was in common use among preachers warning that human beings live always at the edge of death and the grave, bravely indifferent to their situation or perhaps overconfident about the certainty of their salvation.[16]

Lindsay was well aware of his mortality but chose not to think that living in Jamaica would make his end more imminent or more terrible. He lived among white people whose pervading fear of death was sufficient reason to wish to live in some better country, and he expressed a distaste for island society but not for the slavery that enabled them to live lives of leisure. For all his disparagement of blacks and his lack of missionary impulse, Lindsay seems not to have hankered for absenteeism but threw in his lot with the managers and governors of slave society, seeing in it his best chance of advancement and comfort. This was an attitude shared with whites who had lived apparently contentedly for generations in the island, along with long-term British-born settlers. As a priest it was easy enough to separate himself from those known best for their indulgence in food and drink, for their uncouth manners and preoccupation with making money. He aligned himself with the few – some of them existing paradoxically within the harshness of the plantation regime – who were possessed by a philosophical or scientific interest in the world around them. These free residents had one great advantage over the absentees: they lived within a tropical world that seemed strikingly different, full of interest and worthy of their curiosity.

Jamaica was still an exotic place at the forefront of scientific observation, offering both unknown species for description and classification and fertile sites for testing exotics from other parts of the tropical and temperate world. For those with the leisure and resources, there was much to discover and to delight in. Not only could they devote time to investigating the small island world in which they lived, but they could also afford to import the latest books, immersing themselves in the larger Atlantic Enlightenment world. These advantages gave Jamaica a prominent place within the British Empire, reflecting its relative wealth, though it was less important as a centre of Enlightenment literary culture than its rival neighbour, the French colony of Saint Domingue, with its larger and richer resident planter class and its larger slave population.[17]

The enslaved people of the sugar colonies lived within the same world and demonstrated a knowledge of many of its elements – particularly the vegetation and its potential medicinal applications – but they had little leisure and were severely limited in their mobility and access to technologies of communication. Documentary evidence of this knowledge, and how it related to the knowledge systems of the free leisured class, is hard to find and often reflects its exploitation by white writers. It is necessarily the surviving published and unpublished texts that offer access to this world, and few of them come directly from the enslaved. Only occasionally did white writers acknowledge that their scientific observations came to them from people whom they otherwise sought to deny and disparage. For the slaves there were often advantages to keeping knowledge concealed and secret.[18]

As noted above, Lindsay was one of those natural historians, reluctant to admit that he learned from those he loved to denigrate. He was more generous in earlier years, observing in his *Voyage* that in order for the naturalist to acquire knowledge in Africa it was essential "to cultivate in particular a good understanding with some of the more sensible and best skill'd of the natives". This was just one of the ways in which his attitudes hardened over the years. A few years later, in 1763, describing the tobacco plant in "Elegancies", Lindsay remarks that it is "pretty much planted by the Negroes for the use of the pipe; to which the Negroes are greatly inslaved", and notes that "they alledge that this alone is what make their other slavery the more tolerable".[19] Thus, in his youth and in Africa he appeared to have a relatively positive view of African people, but his years in the heart of the slave society of Jamaica, and his own participation in that oppressive system, produced a harsher perception of the people with whom he shared his daily life, and a growing willingness to commit his intellectual abilities to maintenance of that oppression. He had no ethnographic interest in observing those around him but devoted his energy to building a cosmology in which to locate the social hierarchy that ensured his prosperity.[20]

Lindsay was not alone in this reactionary retrogression. Individual theorists such as Buffon became progressively harsh in their disparagement of "degenerate" races. For Britons generally – who began to sing in 1740 that they never, never, never would be slaves – the liberty of living on top of slave society generated a taste for power and a lack of respect for others that was too often the quickest route to theological and scientific racism, an intellectual and social construct that left an indelible mark. Self-interest and personal fortune, together with the status and rank attributed to the supreme exploiters in slave society, combined to entrench conservative views of social structure and power relations. Even within this context there were both individuals who came reluctantly to more progressive views and, on the other hand, those who actively sought to hold back positive change by erecting intellectual systems consciously designed to justify wrong. Lindsay was one of the latter.[21]

The Enlightenment world of the eighteenth century was replete with contradictions between slavery and liberty, science and reason. Thus, although slave-owners might seem unlikely candidates for "enlightened" status, very often the ideas and attitudes of their European, even revolutionary, philosopher contemporaries were no more morally competent or progressive with respect to race and class theory. Liberty and equality were concepts that ushered in the modern world, but leading thinkers of the early Enlightenment had only a qualified understanding of those concepts. As Jonathan Israel argues, "The philosophies of Locke, Voltaire, Montesquieu, and Hume, in fact, could all be fairly readily utilized as devices of imperial legitimization owing to their stressing the divergent varieties of men", and "provided no real hindrance or opposition to the continuing prevalence of theological justifications for slavery".[22]

Only radical dissenting churches offered early theological arguments opposed to slavery, and these Lindsay happily dismissed as products of a lunatic fringe. Even Whitefield had followed the path of political expediency in the 1740s, finding it necessary to support the institution of slavery in South Carolina and its extension into Georgia, in order to evangelize the slave-owning community. The notion that Christian spiritual "freedom" had nothing to do with bodily freedom or human equality remained commonplace in Western Europe throughout Lindsay's lifetime. But the last ten or fifteen years of his life did place his ideas under pressure. Radical Enlightenment thinkers who declared slavery and colonialism to be fundamentally contrary to reason, justice and human equality became more common and more vocal.[23] Such arguments were, however, matched by alternative defensive voices, some of them simply reactionary but others rooted in Enlightenment literature and thought. They continued to develop and transmute long after Lindsay's passing in 1788. The attack on slavery was paralleled by the growth of a debilitating science of race and the professionalization of science and natural history, together with the development of optimistic readings of "slave society" which came to conceive of the institution as a positive good rather than a necessary evil. These views did not prevail in the long run but they contributed substantially to new narratives of colonialism.[24]

Lindsay died the year before the beginning of the French Revolution, with its calls for liberty, equality and fraternity – the revolution that boiled up in Jamaica's near neighbour the French colony of Saint Domingue, which was to become the republic of Haiti. He died twenty years before British abolition of the Atlantic slave trade and fifty years before the abolition of slavery. Although Lindsay struggled with such fundamentally radical ideas, he had barely begun the intellectual task of thinking out how to deal with them. His embrace of sceptical approaches to Scripture through exegesis and his preference for reason over mystery did not require him to throw overboard his most treasured political and cosmological models. Lindsay's Atlantic world was dominated by tradition, faith, theology and law, and by a hierarchical model of society directed by God and King.

Notes

Chapter 2

1. David Allan, *Scotland in the Eighteenth Century: Union and Enlightenment* (London: Longman, 2002); Callum G. Brown, *The Social History of Religion in Scotland since 1730* (London: Methuen, 1987); T.C. Smout, *A History of the Scottish People, 1560–1830* (London: Collins, 1970), 215; Linda Colley, *Britons: Forging the Nation, 1707–1837* (New Haven, Conn.: Yale University Press, 1992), 11–18.
2. Alexander Murdoch, *Scotland and America, c. 1600–c. 1800* (Basingstoke, UK: Palgrave Macmillan, 2010); Douglas J. Hamilton, *Scotland, the Caribbean and the Atlantic World, 1750–1820* (Manchester: Manchester University Press, 2005); T.M. Devine, *Scotland's Empire and the Shaping of the Americas, 1600–1815* (Washington, D.C.: Smithsonian Books, 2003); Alan L. Karras, *Sojourners in the Sun: Scottish Migrants in Jamaica and the Chesapeake, 1740–1800* (Ithaca, NY: Cornell University Press, 1992); Richard B. Sheridan, "The Role of the Scots in the Economy and Society of the West Indies", in *Comparative Perspectives on Slavery in New World Plantation Societies*, ed. Vera Rubin and Arthur Tuden, *Annals of the New York Academy of Sciences* 292 (1977): 95–96.
3. OPR Births, 473/0010 0016, Bothkennar, www.scotlandspeople.gov.uk; OPR Marriages, 685/001 0460 0332, Edinburgh, www.scotlandspeople.gov.uk; Hew Scott, *Fasti Ecclesiæ Scoticanæ: The Succession of Ministers in the Church of Scotland from the Reformation* (Edinburgh: Oliver and Boyd, 1923), 4:231.
4. Arthur Mitchell, ed., *Geographical Collections Relating to Scotland Made by Walter Macfarlane* (Edinburgh: Scottish History Society, 1906), 316–34; Sir John Sinclair, *The Statistical Account of Scotland, Drawn Up from the Communications of the Different Parishes* (Edinburgh: W. Creech, 1796), 17:295; T.M. Devine, *The Tobacco Lords: A Study of the Tobacco Merchants of Glasgow and Their Trading Activities c. 1740–90* (Edinburgh: John Donald, 1975); Philipp Robinson Rössner, *Scottish Trade in the Wake of Union (1700–1760): The Rise of a Warehouse Economy* (Stuttgart: Franz Steiner Verlag, 2008), 201; Hugh Kearney, *The British Isles: A History of Four Nations* (Cambridge: Cambridge University Press, 1989), 128–29; Allan, *Scotland in the Eighteenth Century*, 40–41; Stewart J. Brown, "Religion in Scotland", in *A Companion*

to Eighteenth-Century Britain, ed. H.T. Dickinson (Oxford: Blackwell Publishing, 2002), 260.

5. Stewart Brown, "Religion in Scotland", 265; Ian D.L. Clark, "From Protest to Reaction: The Moderate Regime in the Church of Scotland, 1752–1805", in *Scotland in the Age of Improvement: Essays in Scottish History in the Eighteenth Century,* ed. N.T. Phillipson and Rosalind Mitchison (Edinburgh: Edinburgh University Press, 1970), 202–26; Callum Brown, *Social History of Religion,* 28–29; Ian Hamilton, *The Erosion of Calvinist Orthodoxy: Seceders and Subscription in Scottish Presbyterianism* (Edinburgh: Rutherford House, 1990), 4; G.D. Henderson, *Religious Life in Seventeenth-Century Scotland* (Cambridge: Cambridge University Press, 1937), 2; J.H.S. Burleigh, *A Church History of Scotland* (London: Oxford University Press, 1960), 155; David Hempton, "Enlightenment and Faith", in *The Eighteenth Century, 1688–1815,* ed. Paul Langford (Oxford: Oxford University Press, 2002), 88.
6. William Mackelvie, *Annals and Statistics of the United Presbyterian Church* (Edinburgh: Oliphant and Company and Andrew Elliot, 1873), 8–9; Sinclair, *Statistical Account* 17:296; David C. Lachman, "Erskine, Ebenezer (1680–1754)", *Oxford Dictionary of National Biography* (Oxford: Oxford University Press, 2004); Richard B. Sher, *Church and University in the Scottish Enlightenment: The Moderate Literati of Edinburgh* (Princeton, NJ: Princeton University Press, 1985), 48–49; Martin Fitzpatrick, "The Enlightenment, Politics and Providence: Some Scottish and English Comparisons", in *Enlightenment and Religion: Rational Dissent in Eighteenth-Century Britain,* ed. Knud Haakonssen (Cambridge: Cambridge University Press, 1996), 73; Stewart Brown, "Religion in Scotland", 262–63.
7. Mackelvie, *Annals and Statistics,* 264.
8. Henry Lindsay, *The present state of the Church of Scotland, with the duty of the members thereof enquired into in a sermon at the opening of the synod of Perth and Stirling, October 9th 1733* (Edinburgh: printed by Tho. Lumisden and Jo. Robertson, 1733), 41, 43–48.
9. Ibid., 4, 51–52, 57–59.
10. Mackelvie, *Annals and Statistics,* 8–9; Callum Brown, *Social History of Religion,* 34–35; Allan, *Scotland in the Eighteenth Century,* 72–73; David C. Lachman, *The Marrow Controversy* (Edinburgh: Rutherford House, 1988), 1; Lachman, "Erskine, Ebenezer"; Margo Todd, *The Culture of Protestantism in Early Modern Scotland* (New Haven, Conn.: Yale University Press, 2002), 328; Kenneth B.E. Roxburgh, "Revival: An Aspect of Scottish Religious Identity", in *Religion and National Identity: Wales and Scotland c. 1700–2000,* ed. Robert Pope (Cardiff: University of Wales Press, 2001), 204–5; Richard Brown, *Church and State in Modern Britain, 1700–1850* (London: Routledge, 1991), 107–8.
11. Mackelvie, *Annals and Statistics,* 264; Donald Fraser, *The Life and Diary of the Reverend Ebenezer Erskine, A.M.: of Stirling, Father of the Secession Church* (Edinburgh: W. Oliphant, 1831), 394.
12. Fitzpatrick, "Enlightenment, Politics and Providence", 74–76.
13. John M'Kerrow, *History of the Secession Church* (Glasgow: A. Fullerton, 1841), 114–15; Mackelvie, *Annals and Statistics,* 182.
14. David Hempton, *Methodism: Empire of the Spirit* (New Haven, Conn.: Yale University Press, 2005), 17; Lachman, "Erskine, Ebenezer"; Markman Ellis, *The Politics of Sensibility: Race, Gender and Commerce in the Sentimental Novel* (Cambridge: Cambridge University Press, 1996), 147–55; T.C. Smout, "Born Again at Cambuslang:

New Evidence on Popular Religion and Literacy in Eighteenth-Century Scotland", *Past and Present* 97 (1982): 114–15.

15. Sinclair, *Statistical Account* 17:296; John Lindsay, *Memoirs of Sir Thomas Hughson and Mr Joseph Williams, with the remarkable history, travels, and distresses, of Telemachus Lovet: The whole calculated for the improvement of the mind and manners; and for a becoming and useful entertainment for the youth of both sexes* (London: L. Davis, T. Waller, T. Osborn, J. Shipton, A. Strahan, R. Griffiths, W. Fenner, J. Millan, Wilson and Durham, 1757), 1:xi; Register 38 ("Act Book"), Episcopal Register of Bishops Richard Reynolds and John Thomas, June 1723–October 1761 (Lincoln Archives, UK), www.theclergydatabase.org.uk (hereafter referred to as "Episcopal Register"); D.B. Horn, *A Short History of the University of Edinburgh, 1556–1889* (Edinburgh: University of Edinburgh Press, 1967), 43; Mark R.M. Towsey, *Reading the Scottish Enlightenment: Books and Their Readers in Provincial Scotland, 1750–1820* (Leiden: Brill, 2010), 122–31.

16. Douglas Guthrie, "The Influence of the Leyden School upon Scottish Medicine", *Medical History* 3 (1959): 108–22; Andrew Cunningham, "Medicine to Calm the Mind: Boerhaave's Medical System, and Why It Was Adopted in Edinburgh", in *The Medical Enlightenment of the Eighteenth Century*, ed. Andrew Cunningham and Roger French (Cambridge: Cambridge University Press, 1990), 65.
17. Jeremy J. Cater, "The Making of Principal Robertson: Politics and the University of Edinburgh in the Second Half of the Eighteenth Century", *Scottish Historical Review* 49 (1970): 60–84; Sher, *Church and University*, 120–41; R.A. Houston, *Social Change in the Age of Enlightenment: Edinburgh, 1660–1760* (Oxford: Clarendon Press, 1994), 164–67; Charles W.J. Withers, "Improvement and Enlightenment: Agriculture and Natural History in the Work of the Rev. Dr John Walker (1731–1803)", in *Philosophy and Science in the Scottish Enlightenment*, ed. Peter Jones (Edinburgh: John Donald, 1988), 102–16; Deborah C. Brunton, "The Transfer of Medical Education: Teaching at the Edinburgh and Philadelphia Medical Schools", in *Scotland and America in the Age of the Enlightenment*, ed. Richard B. Sher and Jeffrey R. Smitten (Edinburgh: Edinburgh University Press, 1990), 242–58; J.B. Morrell, "Medicine and Science in the Eighteenth Century", in *Four Centuries: Edinburgh University Life, 1583–1983*, ed. Gordon Donaldson (Edinburgh: University of Edinburgh, 1983), 38–39; Alexander Law, *Education in Edinburgh in the Eighteenth Century* (London: University of London Press, 1965), 22–23; Jerome S. Handler, *A Guide to Source Materials for the Study of Barbados History, 1627–1834* (Carbondale: Southern Illinois University Press, 1971), 57–73; D.J. Womersley, "The Historical Writings of William Robertson", *Journal of the History of Ideas* 47 (1986): 497–506.
18. Robert D. Anderson, Michael Lynch and Nicholas Phillipson, *The University of Edinburgh: An Illustrated History* (Edinburgh: Edinburgh University Press, 2003), 60–72; Horn, *Short History*, 40–47; Christine Shepherd, "University Life in the Seventeenth Century", in *Four Centuries: Edinburgh University Life, 1583–1983*, ed. Gordon Donaldson (Edinburgh: University of Edinburgh, 1983), 2–4; Jaroslav Pelikan, *Credo: Historical and Theological Guide to Creeds and Confessions of Faith in the Christian Tradition* (New Haven, Conn.: Yale University Press, 2003), 479.
19. Houston, *Social Change*, 2–3; A.J. Youngson, *The Making of Classical Edinburgh, 1750–1840* (Edinburgh: Edinburgh University Press, 1966), 1–15; Mary Cosh, *Edinburgh: The Golden Age* (Edinburgh: John Donald, 2003); Horn, *Short History*, 36–38;

Stephen Conway, *War, State, and Society in Mid-Eighteenth-Century Britain and Ireland* (Oxford: Oxford University Press, 2006), 260–61.

20. Lindsay, *Memoirs*, 2:134–36; Jeffrey R. Smitten, "Robertson, William (1721–1793)", *Oxford Dictionary of National Biography* (2004).
21. Lindsay, *Memoirs*, 1:xi. The teacher is identified as "the Rev[d] Mr P—k C—n, E.H. & S.S.T.P". This might be Patrick Cockburn (1678–1749), a Scottish Episcopal clergyman with an Edinburgh MA, resident in Aberdeen to 1739 and then Long Horsley to 1749, who was associated with the Scottish Episcopalian mystical tradition. See Rowan Strong, "Cockburn, Patrick (1678-1749)", *Oxford Dictionary of National Biography* (2004).
22. Lindsay, *Memoirs*, 1:xi. Cf. Ellis, *Politics of Sensibility*, 23–35.
23. Philip P. Boucher, *France and the American Tropics to 1700: Tropics of Discontent?* (Baltimore: Johns Hopkins University Press, 2008).
24. Allan I. Macinnes, *Union and Empire: The Making of the United Kingdom in 1707* (Cambridge: Cambridge University Press, 2007), 324–26; Colley, *Britons*, 11; Conway, *War, State, and Society*, 198–200; Iain Whyte, *Scotland and the Abolition of Black Slavery, 1756–1838* (Edinburgh: Edinburgh University Press, 2006), 56.
25. Richard Pares, *War and Trade in the West Indies, 1739–1763* (Oxford: Oxford University Press, 1936), 60–61; Jeremy Black, *Natural and Necessary Enemies: Anglo-French Relations in the Eighteenth Century* (London: Duckworth, 1986), 36; H.M. Scott, "Britain's Emergence as a European Power, 1688–1815", in *A Companion to Eighteenth-Century Britain*, ed. H.T. Dickinson (Oxford: Blackwell, 2002), 439; J.F.C. Fuller, *A Military History of the Western World* (New York: Da Capo Press, 1955), 2:154–55, 2:243–46. Cf. Colley, *Britons*, 25–28; Kathleen Wilson, "Empire, Trade and Popular Politics in Mid-Hanoverian Britain: The Case of Admiral Vernon", *Past and Present* 121 (1988): 74–109.
26. John Lindsay, "An Examination of the Hypothetical Doctrine of Water-spouts, in Opposition to the Ingenious Speculations of Dr. B. Franklin of Philadelphia, F.R.S.", *Gentleman's Magazine* 51 (1781): 559.
27. John Lindsay, "A few conjectural considerations upon the creation of the humane race; Occasioned by the present British Quixottical rage of setting the slaves from Africa at liberty", 102–3 (Long Mss, Add. 12439, British Library, London). Cited hereafter as "Conjectural considerations".
28. Lindsay, "Conjectural considerations", 125, 132. Cf. Carville V. Earle, "Environment, Disease, and Mortality in Early Virginia", in *The Chesapeake in the Seventeenth Century: Essays on Anglo-American Society*, ed. Thad W. Tate and David L. Ammerman (Chapel Hill: University of North Carolina Press, 1979), 113.
29. Lindsay, "Conjectural considerations", 121; Gordon Sayre, "Plotting the Natchez Massacre: Le Page du Pratz, Dumont de Montigny, Chateaubriand", *Early American Literature* 37 (2002): 385; John Oliphant, *Peace and War on the Anglo-Cherokee Frontier, 1756–63* (Baton Rouge: Louisiana State University Press, 2001), 23–25.
30. W. Stitt Robinson, ed., *Early American Indian Documents: Treaties and Laws, 1607–1789*, vol. 5, *Virginia Treaties, 1723–1775* (Frederick, Md.: University Publications of America, 1983), 113–17.
31. D.W. Meinig, *The Shaping of America: A Geographical Perspective on 500 Years of History*, vol. 1, *Atlantic America, 1492–1800* (New Haven, Conn.: Yale University Press, 1986), 153.

32. Kenneth P. Bailey, *The Ohio Company of Virginia and the Westward Movement, 1748–1792: A Chapter in the History of the Colonial Frontier* (Glendale, Calif.: Arthur H. Clark, 1939), 57–58; Alfred P. James, "The First English-Speaking Trans-Appalachian Frontier", *Mississippi Valley Historical Review* 17 (1930): 59; Alfred P. James, *The Ohio Company: Its Inner History* (Pittsburgh: University of Pittsburgh Press, 1959), 45–52; Corra Bacon-Foster, *Early Chapters in the Development of the Potomac Route to the West* (Washington, DC: Columbia Historical Society, 1912), 10; William M. Darlington, *Christopher Gist's Journals, with Historical, Geographical and Ethnological Notes and Biographies of His Contemporaries* (1893; reprint, New York: Argonaut Press, 1966).

33. James, *Ohio Company*, 53–54; Robinson, *Early American Indian Documents*, 129; William P. Palmer, ed., *Calendar of Virginia State Papers and Other Manuscripts, 1652–1781, Preserved in the Capitol at Richmond* (Richmond: Commonwealth ofVirginia, 1875), 1:245–47; R.A. Brock, ed., *The Official Records of Robert Dinwiddie, Lieutenant-Governor of the Colony of Virginia, 1751–1758, Now First Printed from the Manuscript in the Collections of the Virginia Historical Society* (Richmond: Virginia Historical Society, 1883), 6–10, 285, 473; Louis Knott Koontz, *Robert Dinwiddie: His Career in American Colonial Government and Westward Expansion* (Glendale, Calif.: Arthur H. Clark, 1941), 133; Amy C. Schutt, *Peoples of the River Valleys: The Odyssey of the Delaware Indians* (Philadelphia: University of Pennsylvania Press, 2007), 149.
34. John Richard Alden, *Robert Dinwiddie: Servant of the Crown* (Charlottesville: University Press ofVirginia, 1973), 3, 7–10, 33; Koontz, *Robert Dinwiddie*, 153–55; Brock, *Official Records of Robert Dinwiddie*, ix; Kenneth Morgan, "Robert Dinwiddie's Reports on the British American Colonies", *William and Mary Quarterly* 65 (2008): 305–46.
35. Alden, *Robert Dinwiddie*, 14–15, 42; Brock, *Official Records of Robert Dinwiddie*, 17–19; Bacon-Foster, *Early Chapters*, 9; Charles Royster, *The Fabulous History of the Dismal Swamp Company: A Story of George Washington's Times* (New York: Alfred A. Knopf, 1999), 52–55; James Thomas Flexner, *George Washington: The Forge of Experience (1732–1775)* (Boston: Little, Brown, 1965), 54; William R. Nester, *The Great Frontier War: Britain, France, and the Imperial Struggle for North America, 1607–1755* (Westport, Conn.: Praeger, 2000), 35–36.
36. Robinson, *Early American Indian Documents*, 116, 402n17; James, *Ohio Company*, 57.
37. Lois Mulkearn, ed., *George Mercer Papers: Relating to the Ohio Company of Virginia* (Pittsburgh: University of Pittsburgh Press, 1954), 273–84; Nester, *Great Frontier War*, 37; Robinson, *Early American Indian Documents*, xx, 137–39. Cf. Timothy D. Willig, *Restoring the Chain of Friendship: British Policy and the Indians of the Great Lakes, 1783–1815* (Lincoln: University of Nebraska Press, 2008), 66.
38. Robinson, *Early American Indian Documents*, 140–41; James, *Ohio Company*, 64–65; Schutt, *Peoples of the River Valleys*, 107; Royster, *Fabulous History*, 52–55; Nester, *Great Frontier War*, 37. Cf. Bacon-Foster, *Early Chapters*, 11.
39. Bailey, *Ohio Company*, 140; Mulkearn, *George Mercer Papers*, 286.
40. For example, Alfred T. Goodman, ed., *Journal of Captain William Trent from Logstown to Pickawillany, A.D. 1752* (Cincinnati: William Dodge, 1871), 83–92.
41. Lindsay, "Conjectural considerations", 131–32; John Lindsay, Letter on waterspouts, *Gentleman's Magazine* 53 (1783): 1027.

42. Lindsay, *Memoirs*, 1:237.
43. Bruce A. Ragsdale, "Young Washington's Virginia: Opportunity in the 'Golden Age' of a Planter Society", in *George Washington and the Virginia Backcountry*, ed. Warren R. Hofstra (Madison, Wisc.: Madison House, 1998), 47; John K. Nelson, *A Blessed Company: Parishes, Parsons, and Parishioners in Anglican Virginia, 1690–1776* (Chapel Hill: University of North Carolina, 2001), 94; Devine, *Tobacco Lords*, 55–61; Devine, *Scotland's Empire*, 77; Hamilton, *Scotland, the Caribbean and the Atlantic World*, 94.

44. Lindsay, *Memoirs*, 1:237–38.
45. Ibid., 1:238–39.
46. George Maclaren Brydon, *Virginia's Mother Church and the Political Conditions under Which It Grew* (Richmond: Virginia Historical Society, 1947), 1:235, 2:275; Nelson, *Blessed Company*, 138, 315, 407n53.
47. Lindsay, *Memoirs*, 3:261.
48. Robert Beverley ("A Native and Inhabitant of the Place"), *The History and Present State of Virginia, in Four Parts* (London: R. Parker, [1705], 3: 39–41. A similar account of "husquenawing" was given in 1720 by William Byrd; Kenneth A. Lockridge, *The Diary, and Life, of William Byrd II of Virginia, 1674–1744* (Chapel Hill: University of North Carolina Press, 1987), 107.
49. John C. Fitzpatrick, ed., *The Diaries of George Washington, 1748–1799* (Boston: Houghton Mifflin, 1925), 1:43–66; Flexner, *George Washington*, 49–56; Alden, *Robert Dinwiddie*, 44–47.
50. J. Frederick Fausz, " 'Engaged in Enterprises Pregnant with Terror': George Washington's Formative Years among the Indians", in *George Washington and the Virginia Backcountry*, ed. Warren R. Hofstra (Madison, Wisc.: Madison House, 1998), 124–27; Bailey, *Ohio Company*, 126; David Hackett Fischer and James C. Kelly, *Bound Away: Virginia and the Westward Movement* (Charlottesville: University Press of Virginia, 2000), 152–53; Royster, *Fabulous History*, 56–58.
51. This is the record of "John Lindsey" of Edinburgh University, ordained 23 December 1753, at the Prebendal Church, Buckden, Hunts. (now Cambridgeshire), in the Lincoln Diocese, in "Episcopal Register". R.A. Minter in *Episcopacy Without Episcopate: The Church of England in Jamaica before 1824* (Upton-upon-Severn, UK: Self Publishing Association, 1990), 177, says that John Lindsay "was priested at Lincoln in 1753". Frank Cundall, in *Historic Jamaica* (London: Institute of Jamaica, 1915), 95, claims that Lindsay was "ordained in December 1753 in Conduit Street Chapel, Hanover Square, London", but provides no source. On Dr John Thomas, formerly English chaplain at Hamburg, see Norman Sykes, *Church and State in England in the XVIIIth Century* (Cambridge: Cambridge University Press, 1934), 152.
52. John Walsh and Stephen Taylor, "The Church and Anglicanism in the 'Long' Eighteenth Century", in *The Church of England, c. 1689–c. 1833: From Toleration to Tractarianism*, ed. John Walsh, Colin Haydon and Stephen Taylor (Cambridge: Cambridge University Press, 1993), 51–57.
53. Sykes, *Church and State*, 96–101; Nelson, *Blessed Company*, 113; Alex D.D. Craik, "Geometry, Analysis, and the Baptism of Slaves: John West in Scotland and Jamaica", *Historia Mathematica* 25 (1998): 41; Tom Girtin, *Doctor with Two Aunts: A Biography of Peter Pindar* (London: Hutchinson, 1959), 46–47.
54. N.A.M. Rodger, "The Naval Chaplain in the Eighteenth Century", *British Journal*

for Eighteenth-Century Studies 18 (1995): 33–45; Gordon Taylor, *The Sea Chaplains: A History of the Chaplains of the Royal Navy* (Oxford: Oxford Illustrated Press, 1978), 504; A.G. Kealy, *Chaplains of the Royal Navy, 1626–1903* (Portsmouth: Wilkins and Son, [1912]), 61–62.

55. Rodger, "Naval Chaplain", 33–35; Kealy, *Chaplains of the Royal Navy*, 11, 20–22; Isobel G. Powell, "Naval Chaplains in the Early Stuart Period", *Mariner's Mirror* 8 (1922): 290–94.
56. ADM 36/6262, f. 8; ADM 51/628 (National Archives, Kew); Taylor, *Sea Chaplains*, 166; J.J. Colledge, *Ships of the Royal Navy* (Annapolis, Md.: Naval Institute Press, 1987), 141; N.A.M. Rodger, *The Wooden World: An Anatomy of the Georgian Navy* (New York: W.W. Norton, 1986), 159; Brian Lavery, *The Ship of the Line*, vol. 1, *The Development of the Battlefleet, 1650–1850* (London: Conway Maritime Press, 1983), 175.
57. Lindsay, "Oration", *Columbian Magazine* 2 (April 1797): 731n3.
58. ADM 51/628 (National Archives, Kew).
59. Ruddock Mackay and Michael Duffy, *Hawke, Nelson and British Naval Leadership, 1747–1805* (Woodbridge, UK: Boydell Press, 2009), 41–42; Ruddock F. Mackay, *Admiral Hawke* (Oxford: Clarendon Press, 1965), 10–12, 71–77; Black, *Natural and Necessary Enemies*, 50.
60. Mackay, *Admiral Hawke*, 114–15; William Laird Clowes, *The Royal Navy: A History, From the Earliest Times to the Present* (London: Sampson Low, Marston and Co., 1898), 3:142–45.
61. ADM 51/628 (National Archives, Kew); Mackay, *Admiral Hawke*, 129–33; Mackay and Duffy, *Hawke, Nelson and British Naval Leadership*, 42; David J. Starkey, *British Privateering Enterprise in the Eighteenth Century* (Exeter, UK: University of Exeter Press, 1990), 161–64.
62. ADM 51/628 (National Archives, Kew); Mackay, *Admiral Hawke*, 138–42; Ruddock F. Mackay, ed., *The Hawke Papers: A Selection, 1743–1771* (Aldershot, UK: Scolar Press, 1990), 129–33.
63. ADM 51/628 (National Archives, Kew); Mackay, *Hawke Papers*, 141–44.
64. ADM 51/4271 (National Archives, Kew); Clowes, *Royal Navy*, 3: 174–75, 188, 206; Lavery, *Ship of the Line*, 173–74; Frank McLynn, *1759: The Year Britain Became Master of the World* (New York: Grove Press, 2004), 186; W.E. May, "The *Panther* Affair", *Mariner's Mirror* 55 (1969): 402.
65. ADM 36/6264, f. 67 (National Archives, Kew).
66. Lindsay, *Voyage*, 11; Lindsay, *Memoirs*, 1:xiii–xiv; Clowes, *Royal Navy*, 3:167.

Chapter 3

1. *Columbian Magazine* (Kingston) 2 (February 1797): 582.
2. I thank James Robertson for sharing his discovery and alerting me to the Lindsay material in the *Columbian Magazine*. The copy of *Memoirs* used here is that in the Beinecke Collection at Yale University Library. See Robert Gayle Noyes, *The Thespian Mirror: Shakespeare in the Eighteenth-Century Novel* (Providence, RI: Brown University, 1953), 105–9. Neither Lindsay nor *Memoirs* appears in Robert Crawford, *Scotland's Books: A History of Scottish Literature* (Oxford: Oxford University

Press, 2009); Richard B. Sher, *The Enlightenment and the Book: Scottish Authors and Their Publishers in Eighteenth-Century Britain, Ireland, and America* (Chicago: University of Chicago Press, 2006); Douglas S. Mack, *Scottish Fiction and the British Empire* (Edinburgh: Edinburgh University Press, 2006); Samuel Halkett and John Laing, *Dictionary of Anonymous and Pseudonymous English Literature* (Edinburgh: Oliver and Boyd, 1926–62); or John Butt, *Oxford History of English Literature,* vol. 8, *The Mid-Eighteenth Century* (Oxford: Clarendon Press, 1979), 520–21.

3. Christopher Flint, "The Eighteenth-Century Novel and Print Culture: A Proposed Modesty", in *A Companion to the Eighteenth-Century English Novel and Culture*, ed. Paula R. Backscheider and Catherine Ingrassia (Oxford: Blackwell, 2005), 343–64; John Mullan, *Anonymity: A Secret History of English Literature* (London: Faber and Faber, 2007), 46.
4. Lindsay, *Memoirs*, 1:x, xii, xiv.
5. Jerry C. Beasley, *Novels of the 1740s* (Athens: University of Georgia Press, 1982), xi–xiv; Ruth Perry, *Novel Relations: The Transformation of Kinship in English Literature and Culture, 1748–1818* (Cambridge: Cambridge University Press, 2004), 6; Jill Campbell, *Natural Masques: Gender and Identity in Fielding's Plays and Novels* (Stanford, Calif.: Stanford University Press, 1995), 9; Ellis, *Politics of Sensibility*, 44; William Ray, *Story and History: Narrative Authority and Social Identity in the Eighteenth-Century French and English Novel* (Oxford: Basil Blackwell, 1990), 1–2.
6. Lindsay, *Memoirs*, 1:ix–x; Vic Gatrell, *City of Laughter: Sex and Satire in Eighteenth-Century London* (London: Atlantic Books, 2006), 306–8.
7. Liz Bellamy, *Commerce, Morality and the Eighteenth-Century Novel* (Cambridge: Cambridge University Press, 1998), 7.
8. Lindsay, *Memoirs*, 4:182–84; Sarah Fielding, *The Adventures of David Simple: Containing an Account of His Travels Through the Cities of London and Westminster in the Search of a Real Friend*, ed. Malcolm Kelsall (1744; reprint, London: Oxford University Press, 1969). *Memoirs* offers many precise dates, with dates and inclusive periods of years inserted in the margins. All are in the modern form, with the years beginning on 1 January. See Lindsay, *Memoirs*, 2:182–83.
9. Lindsay, *Memoirs*, 1:106–7; 3:61, 199–200.
10. Ibid., 1:xi–xii.
11. Ibid., 1:xiii–xiv; *Gentleman's Magazine* 27 (1757): 242.
12. *Gentleman's Magazine* 27 (1757): 242; Sher, *Enlightenment and the Book*, 267–70; H.R. Plomer, G.H. Bushnell and E.R. McC. Dix, eds., *A Dictionary of the Printers and Booksellers Who Were at Work in England, Scotland and Ireland from 1726 to 1775* (Oxford: Oxford University Press, 1932), 277–371.
13. Ibid., 72, 80, 92, 111–12, 170–71, 185–86, 254, 266; John Nichols, *Literary Anecdotes of the Eighteenth Century*, ed. Colin Clair (Carbondale: Southern Illinois University Press, 1967), 239–40, 264–67, 324–29; Peter Dixon, *Oliver Goldsmith Revisited* (Boston: Twayne, 1991), 75; Arthur Friedman, ed., *Collected Works of Oliver Goldsmith* (Oxford: Clarendon Press, 1966), 1:3.
14. *A New Catalogue of Lownds's Circulating Library, Consisting of about Ten Thousand Volumes* ([London]: Thomas Lownds, [1758]), 50; Mullan, *Anonymity*, 59–60; *T. Lowndes's Catalogue for 1778: Consisting of Books Collected in Different Parts of England* ([London]: Thomas Lownds, [1778]), 29–30; Howard Johnson, Introduction, in Edward Long, *The History of Jamaica* (Kingston: Ian Randle, 2002), 1:iv.

15. Dixon, *Oliver Goldsmith Revisited*, 1–3; John A. Dussinger, "Goldsmith, Oliver (1728?–1774)", *Oxford Dictionary of National Biography* (2004).
16. *Monthly Review* 16 (1757): 452; Friedman, *Collected Works of Oliver Goldsmith*, 1:16–17; Dixon, *Oliver Goldsmith Revisited*, 75.
17. *Monthly Review* 16 (1757): 452; Friedman, *Collected Works of Oliver Goldsmith*, 1:3, 15–50; Dixon, *Oliver Goldsmith Revisited*, 18.
18. Derek Roper, "Smollett's 'Four Gentlemen': The First Contributors to the *Critical Review*", *Review of English Studies* 10 (1959): 38–44; Sher, *Enlightenment and the Book*, 365–66; Mullan, *Anonymity*, 174.
19. S.D. Smith, *Slavery, Family, and Gentry Capitalism in the British Atlantic: The World of the Lascelles, 1648–1834* (Cambridge: Cambridge University Press, 2006), 183n18; Tobias Smollett, *The Adventures of Roderick Random* (1748; reprint, London: Everyman's Library, 1927), chapter 31, 35–36.
20. Henry Fielding, *Joseph Andrews*, ed. Martin C. Battestin (1742; reprint, Oxford: Clarendon Press, 1967), xxvii; Ian Simpson Ross, " 'More dull, but by no means so dangerous as that of Mr Hume': Smollett's 'Continuation' of *le bon David's History of England*", in *Tobias Smollett, Scotland's First Novelist: New Essays in Memory of Paul-Gabriel Boucé*, ed. O.M. Brack (Newark: University of Delaware Press, 2007), 217–18; Kenneth Simpson, "Smollett, Tobias George (1721–1771)", *Oxford Dictionary of National Biography* (2004).
21. *Critical Review; or, Annals of Literature* 3 (November 1757): 460–61; Roger D. Lund, "*A Tale of a Tub*, Swift's Apology, and the Trammels of Christian Wit", in *Augustan Subjects: Essays in Honour of Martin C. Battestin*, ed. Albert J. Rivero (Newark: University of Delaware Press, 1997), 93.
22. *Columbian Magazine* 3 (June 1797): 19–21.
23. Brian Vickers, ed., *Shakespeare: The Critical Heritage*, vol. 4, *1753–1765* (London: Routledge and Kegan Paul, 1976), 308; Margaret Anne Doody, *A Natural Passion: A Study of the Novels of Samuel Richardson* (Oxford: Clarendon Press, 1974), 15, 253.
24. Fielding, *Joseph Andrews*, 3. Cf. Eve Tavor, *Scepticism, Society and the Eighteenth-Century Novel* (London: Macmillan, 1987), 96–97.
25. Lindsay, *Memoirs*, 4:2; Tobias Smollett, *The Adventures of Ferdinand Count Fathom*, ed. Paul-Gabriel Boucé (London: Penguin, 1990), 16–18; Beasley, *Novels of the 1740s*, 76. Cf. Sarah F. Wood, "Transatlantic Cervantics: Don Quixote and the Fictions of American Enlightenment", in *The Atlantic Enlightenment*, ed. Susan Manning and Francis D. Cogliano (Aldershot, UK: Ashgate, 2008), 113–30.
26. Lindsay, *Memoirs*, 2:171–73. Cf. Mary V. Yates, "The Christian Rake in *Sir Charles Grandison*", *Studies in English Literature, 1500–1900* 24 (1984): 561; J. Paul Hunter, *Occasional Form: Henry Fielding and the Chains of Circumstance* (Baltimore: Johns Hopkins University Press, 1975), 4–5; Campbell, *Natural Masques*, 49–51.
27. Beasley, *Novels of the 1740s*, 82; Bellamy, *Commerce, Morality*, 39–40.
28. Lindsay, *Memoirs*, 1:5. Cf. Ellis, *Politics of Sensibility*, 23–26.
29. Lindsay, *Memoirs*, 3:248.
30. Homer, *The Odyssey*, trans. Robert Fagles (London: Penguin, 1996); Irad Malkin, *The Returns of Odysseus: Colonization and Ethnicity* (Berkeley: University of California Press, 1998), 126; Deborah Beck, "Speech Introductions and the Character Development of Telemachus", *Classical Journal* 94 (1999): 134–35.
31. Edith Hall, *The Return of Ulysses: A Cultural History of Homer's Odyssey* (London:

I.B. Tauris, 2008), 13, 51, 170–71; Hunter, *Occasional Form*, 134–35; Peter Hulme, "Polytropic Man: Tropes of Sexuality and Mobility in Early Colonial Discourse", in *Europe and Its Others*, ed. Francis Barker, Peter Hulme, Margaret Iversen and Diana Loxley (Colchester, UK: University of Essex, 1985), 1:20–23; Doody, *Natural Passion*, 20; Derek Walcott, *Omeros* (London: Faber, 1990).

32. Malkin, *Return of Odysseus*, 268–73; Hall, *Return of Ulysses*, 3–5, 63–64; Thomas Van Nortwick, *The Unknown Odysseus: Alternate Worlds in Homer's* Odyssey (Ann Arbor: University of Michigan Press, 2009), 75. Cf. William G. Thalmann, *The Swineherd and the Bow: Representations of Class in the* Odyssey (Ithaca, NY: Cornell University Press, 1998), 74; Pietro Pucci, *Oedipus and the Fabrication of the Father:* Oedipus Tyrannus *in Modern Criticism and Philosophy* (Baltimore: Johns Hopkins University Press, 1992), 203n29; Homer, *Odyssey*, 343–44; Susanne B. Kimball, "Fathers and Sons in Western Literature", *Germanic Notes and Reviews* 32 (2001): 165.
33. Lindsay, *Memoirs*, 1:217; 2:161–62; 4:80.
34. Thalmann, *Swineherd and the Bow*, 206–23; Sheila Murnaghan, "The Trials of Telemachus: Who Was the *Odyssey* Meant For?", *Arethusa* 35 (2002): 137–38.
35. Lindsay, *Memoirs*, 2:27. Cf. Tim Fulford, *Romantic Indians: Native Americans, British Literature, and Transatlantic Culture, 1756–1830* (Oxford: Oxford University Press, 2006), 17.
36. Lindsay, *Memoirs*, 2:74, 4:241.
37. Thomas R. Preston, "Biblical Criticism, Literature, and the Eighteenth-Century Reader", in *Books and Their Readers in Eighteenth-Century England*, ed. Isabel Rivers (Leicester, UK: Leicester University Press, 1982), 118–19.
38. François de Salignac de la Mothe Fénelon, *The Adventures of Telemachus, the Son of Ulysses* (third edition, 1720; reprint, New York: Garland, 1979); François de Fénelon, *Telemachus, Son of Ulysses*, ed. Patrick Bailey (Cambridge: Cambridge University Press, 1994); Hall, *Return of Ulysses*, 50; Edwin Wolf II, *The Book Culture of a Colonial American City: Philadelphia Books, Bookmen, and Booksellers* (Oxford: Clarendon Press, 1988), 53. Fénelon was also read in Jamaica; see April G. Shelford, "Pascal in Jamaica: or, The French Enlightenment in Translation", *Proceedings of the Western Society for French History* 36 (2008): 59–60.
39. Lindsay, *Memoirs*, 2:101, 141–42, 145; Hall, *Return of Ulysses*, 64.
40. Alden T. Vaughan, *Transatlantic Encounters: American Indians in Britain, 1500–1776* (Cambridge: Cambridge University Press, 2006), 113–19, 137–46.
41. Roberto Salinas Price, *Homeric Whispers: Imitations of Orthodoxy in the* Iliad *and* Odyssey (San Jerónimo Lídice, Mexico: Scylax Press, 2006), 137–39; Van Nortwick, *Unknown Odysseus*, 7–12; Hall, *Return of Ulysses*, 9–10.
42. In *Tom Jones*, Fielding often calls Tom's journey through life his "odyssey", his epic search for virtue and morality. See Hunter, *Occasional Form*, 131–39; M.C. Battestin, *The Moral Basis of Fielding's Art: A Study of* Joseph Andrews (Middletown, Conn.: Wesleyan University Press, 1959), 111; Ethel Margaret Thornbury, *Henry Fielding's Theory of the Comic Prose Epic* (1931; reprint, New York: Russell and Russell, 1966), 104; John Butt, *Fielding* (1954; reprint, London: Longmans, Green, 1968), 18.
43. M. Owen Lee, *Fathers and Sons in Virgil's* Aeneid: Tum Genitor Natum (Albany: State University of New York Press, 1979); Pucci, *Oedipus*; Maurice Daumas, *Le syndrome des grieux: La relation père/fils au XVIIIe siècle* (Paris: Éditions du Seuil,

1990); Kimball, "Fathers and Sons in Western Literature", 163–64; Hugh MacCallum, *Milton and the Sons of God: The Divine Image in Milton's Epic Poetry* (Toronto: University of Toronto Press, 1986); Christopher Hill, *Milton and the English Revolution* (London: Faber and Faber, 1979), 285; David Lee Miller, *Dreams of the Burning Child: Sacrificial Sons and the Father's Witness* (Ithaca, NY: Cornell University Press, 2003).

44. Elaine M. McGirr, *Eighteenth-Century Characters: A Guide to the Literature of the Age* (London: Palgrave Macmillan, 2007), 27–35; T.G.A. Nelson, *Children, Parents, and the Rise of the Novel* (Newark: University of Delaware Press, 1995), 128. Cf. Perry, *Novel Relations*, 77; Lawrence Stone, *The Family, Sex and Marriage in England, 1500–1800* (London: Weidenfeld and Nicolson, 1977), 452–56.

45. Rachel Weil, *Political Passions: Gender, the Family and Political Argument in England. 1680–1714* (Manchester: Manchester University Press, 1999), 32–37. Cf. Ignaz Maybaum, *Creation and Guilt: A Theological Assessment of Freud's Father–Son Conflict* (London: Vallentine, Mitchell, 1969); Avi Erlich, *Hamlet's Absent Father* (Princeton, NJ: Princeton University Press, 1977), 32–33.
46. Lindsay, *Memoirs*, 1:6–8. Cf. Patricia Brückmann, " 'Men, Women and Poles': Samuel Richardson and the Romance of a Stuart Princess", *Eighteenth-Century Life* 27 (2003): 41.
47. Lindsay, *Memoirs*, 1:8–9.
48. Ibid., 10–13.
49. Ibid., 13–14. See John Callow, *The Making of King James II: The Formative Years of a Fallen King* (Stroud, UK: Sutton, 2000), 282–84.
50. Lindsay, *Memoirs*, 1:14–17, 20, 26.
51. Ibid., 20. By contrast, Lord Chesterfield's immensely popular series of advice letters of 1739–52 was addressed directly to his son and not published as a book until 1774. See Christopher Mayo, "Manners and Manuscripts: The Editorial Manufacture of Lord Chesterfield in *Letters to His Son*", *Papers of the Bibliographical Society of America* 99 (2005): 37–38; Piers Dudgeon and Jonathan Jones, eds., *Dear Boy: Lord Chesterfield's Letters to His Son* (London: Bantam Press, 1989).
52. Lindsay, *Memoirs*, 1:22, 24.
53. Ibid., 1:26–28; 4:261–62.
54. Ibid., 1:102, 110–15, 163, 171–72; W.A. Speck, *Society and Literature in England 1700–60* (Dublin: Gill and Macmillan, 1983), 116–38.
55. Lindsay, *Memoirs*, 1:166, 170.
56. Ibid., 3:191; 4:255.
57. Ibid., 1:47–51, 153, 193–97. Cf. John A. Dussinger, "Love and Consanguinity in Richardson's Novels", *Studies in English Literature, 1500–1900* 24 (1984): 515–16.
58. Lindsay, *Memoirs*, 1:199. See Ralph Cudworth, *The True Intellectual System of the Universe: The First Part; wherein all the Reason and Philosophy of Atheism is Confuted; and Its Impossibility Demonstrated* (London: Richard Royston, 1678), 106–7; J.A. Passmore, *Ralph Cudworth: An Interpretation* (Cambridge: Cambridge University Press, 1951), 11, 69; John Redwood, *Reason, Ridicule and Religion: The Age of Enlightenment in England, 1660–1750* (London: Thames and Hudson, 1976), 50–56; Isabel Rivers, *Reason, Grace, and Sentiment: A Study of the Language of Religion and Ethics in England, 1660–1780*, vol. 2, *Shaftesbury to Hume* (Cambridge: Cambridge University Press, 2000), 130; J.G.A. Pocock, "Enthusiasm: The Antiself of Enlightenment", in *Enthusiasm and Enlightenment in Europe, 1650–1850*, ed. Lawrence E.

Klein and Anthony J. La Vopa (San Marino, Calif.: Huntington Library, 1998), 17–18.

59. Lindsay, *Memoirs*, 1:207.
60. Ibid., 214–16. Here he is called Thomson, but the spelling Tomson is soon established as the common form.
61. Ibid., 2:1–3.
62. Ibid., 3–5.
63. Ibid., 30–33.
64. Ibid., 164–65, 171–73. Cf. Campbell, *Natural Masques.*
65. Lindsay, *Memoirs*, 3:198, 205, 222, 248, 253–57.
66. Ibid., 4:3, 5–28, 36.
67. Ibid., 215–17, 222, 237.
68. Ibid., 1:214; 4:249–61. Cf. Fielding, *Joseph Andrews*, 335–39; Pucci, *Oedipus and the Fabrication of the Father.*
69. George Boulukos, *The Grateful Slave: The Emergence of Race in Eighteenth-Century British and American Culture* (Cambridge: Cambridge University Press, 2008), 2–3, 77, 154–55; Joseph Vogt, *Ancient Slavery and the Ideal of Man* (Oxford: Basil Blackwell, 1974), 129–45.
70. Lindsay, *Memoirs*, 2:2–3, 7.
71. Anthony J. Barker, *The African Link: British Attitudes to the Negro in the Era of the Atlantic Slave Trade, 1550–1807* (London: Frank Cass, 1978), 89; Derek Hughes, *Versions of Blackness: Key Texts on Slavery from the Seventeenth Century* (Cambridge: Cambridge University Press, 2007); Vernon Guy Dickson, "Truth, Wonder, and Exemplarity in Aphra Behn's *Oroonoko*", *Studies in English Literature, 1500–1900* 47 (2007): 584; Adam Sills, "Surveying 'The Map of Slavery' in Aphra Behn's *Oroonoko*", *JNT: Journal of Narrative Theory* 36 (2006): 314–40; Marta Figlerowicz, " 'Frightful Spectacles of a Mangled King': Aphra Behn's *Oroonoko* and Narration Through Theater", *New Literary History* 39 (2008): 321–34; Randy J. Sparks, *The Two Princes of Calabar: An Eighteenth-Century Atlantic Odyssey* (Cambridge: Harvard University Press, 2004), 119–20.
72. Joanna Lipking, " 'Others', Slaves, and Colonists in *Oroonoko*", in *The Cambridge Companion to Aphra Behn*, ed. Derek Hughes and Janet Todd (Cambridge: Cambridge University Press, 2004), 166–87; Wylie Sypher, "The African Prince in London", *Journal of the History of Ideas* 2 (1941): 239; Barker, *African Link*, 27–28; Laura Brown, *Fables of Modernity: Literature and Culture in the English Eighteenth Century* (Ithaca, NY: Cornell University Press, 2001), 177–94; *The Royal African: or, Memoirs of the Young Prince of Annamaboe. Comprehending a Distinct Account of His Country and Family; His Elder Brother's Voyage to France, and Reception There; the Manner in which Himself was Confided by His Father to the Captain Who Sold Him; His Condition while a Slave in Barbadoes; the True Cause of His Being Redeemed; His Voyage from Thence; and Reception Here in England* (London: W. Reeve, G. Woodfall and J. Barnes, [1754]), 37.
73. *Royal African*, ix–x, 55; Gerald Howson, *The Macaroni Parson: A Life of the Unfortunate Dr. Dodd* (London: Hutchinson, 1973), 51–55; Philip Rawlings, "Dodd, William (1729–1777)", *Oxford Dictionary of National Biography* (2004); Diana Jaher, "The Paradoxes of Slavery in Thomas Southerne's *Oroonoko*", *Comparative Drama* 42 (2008): 51.

74. Lindsay, *Memoirs*, 2:4–5.

75. Ibid., 10–11; Whyte, *Scotland and the Abolition*, 11–14.

76. Lindsay, *Memoirs*, 2:13–14; Steven M. Wise, *Though the Heavens May Fall: The Landmark Trial That Led to the End of Human Slavery* (London: Pimlico, 2006), 197–98; Christopher Leslie Brown, *Moral Capital: Foundations of British Abolitionism* (Chapel Hill: University of North Carolina Press, 2006), 96–98; Srividhya Swaminathan, "Developing the West Indian Proslavery Position after the Somerset Decision", *Slavery and Abolition* 24 (2003): 45–47; Whyte, *Scotland and the Abolition*, 10–11, 14–15, 32–33; Maurice Jackson, *Let This Voice Be Heard: Anthony Benezet, Father of American Abolitionism* (Philadelphia: University of Pennsylvania Press, 2009), 145–47.

77. Lindsay, *Memoirs*, 2:15–16.

78. Ibid., 225-26; Barker, *African Link*, 36-37; Roxann Wheeler, *The Complexion of Race: Categories of Difference in Eighteenth-Century British Culture* (Philadelphia: University of Pennsylvania Press, 2000), 139–41; Dror Wahrman, *The Making of the Modern Self: Identity and Culture in Eighteenth-Century England* (New Haven, Conn.: Yale University Press, 2004), 92–93.

79. Lindsay, *Memoirs*, 2:228–31. On some of these pages Sicco is called an Indian, but this is a temporary typographical lapse.

80. Ibid., 244–46.

81. Ibid., 247–49.

82. Ibid., 3:67–68, 125–28.

83. Ibid., 180–81, 214–15.

84. Ibid., 3:246–48, 252; 4:5, 35.

85. Ibid., 1:5.

86. Ibid., 7. See Ian Gentles, *The New Model Army in England, Ireland and Scotland, 1645–1653* (Oxford: Blackwell, 1992), 98, 102, 219, 310, 319, 361, 377, 381. Colonel John Hewson achieved considerable notoriety in his time. He was the subject of Hodg Turbervil [Edmund Gayton], "Chaplain to the Late Lord Hewson", *Walk Knaves, Walk: A Discourse Intended to Have Been Spoken at Court and Now Publish'd for the Satisfaction of All Those that have Participated in the Sweetness of Publike [Public] Employments* (London: 1659); a ballad, *The Cobblers Last Will and Testament; or, The Lord Hewson's Translation* (London: 1660); *Colonel Huson's (or the Cobler's) Confession: In a Fit of Despair, Taken in Short-Hand by the Pen of a Ready-Writer* (London: 1660); and a play, by "A True Friend to the Gentle Craft", *Hewson Reduc'd: or, the Shoomaker Return'd to His Trade; being a Show, Wherein is Represented the Honesty, Inoffensiveness, and Ingenuity of that Profession, when 'tis Kept Within its Own Bounds, and Goes Not Beyond the Last* (London: Austine Rice, 1661). Nearer to Lindsay's purpose was the ballad *The Traytors Downfall, or, A Brief Relation of that Phanatick Crew Who Traiterously Murthered the Late Kings Majesty of Blessed Memory: To the Tune of Fa la la, &c.* (London: Francis Coles, 1662), in which he appeared as "blind Hewson", keeper of a "coblers stall", 44. See also *The Humble Desires and Proposals of the Private Agitators of Colonel Hewsons Regiment to the Generall Agitators of the Army: To be Presented to His Excellency Sir Thomas Fairfax, and Communicated to Both Houses of Parliament* (London: I.C., 1647), 1.

87. Lindsay, *Memoirs*, 3:129–30; 4:82, 87–88, 95, 117; McGirr, *Eighteenth-Century Characters*, 39.

88. Lindsay, *Memoirs*, 4:109–15.
89. Ibid., 134–41.
90. Ibid., 145–46, 173–80.
91. Ibid., 153–61, 166, 179–85; W.A. Speck, *The Butcher: The Duke of Cumberland and the Suppression of the 45* (Oxford: Basil Blackwell, 1981), 201; Black, *Natural and Necessary Enemies*, 49–50.
92. Lindsay, *Memoirs*, 3:134–36, 139; Aline Mackenzie Taylor, *Next to Shakespeare: Otway's* Venice Preserv'd *and* The Orphan *and Their History on the London Stage* (Durham, NC: Duke University Press, 1950), 9–10; Richardson Wright, *Revels in Jamaica, 1682–1838* (New York: Dodd, Mead, 1937), 32, 112, 185.
93. Thomas Otway, *The Orphan: or, the Unhappy-Marriage: a Tragedy, as it is Acted at His Royal Highness the Duke's Theatre* (London: R. Bentley and M. Magnes, 1680); Samuel Richardson, *The History of Sir Charles Grandison*, ed. Jocelyn Harris (London: Oxford University Press, 1972), 2:539.
94. Lindsay, *Memoirs*, 3:137–42.
95. Ibid., 4:224-25. Cf. Battestin, *Moral Basis of Fielding's Art*, 130.
96. [Theophilus Lobb], *An Answer to that Important Question, Whether it is Lawful for the Professors of the Christian Religion to go to Plays?* (London: J. Buckland, 1757), 1–5, 30; Harry S. Stout, *The Divine Dramatist: George Whitefield and the Rise of Modern Evangelicalism* (Grand Rapids, Mich.: William B. Eerdmans, 1991), 237–48; [Adam Ferguson], *The Morality of Stage-Plays Seriously Considered* (Edinburgh: n.p., 1757), 3–5; Jeng-Guo S. Chen, "Providence and Progress: The Religious Dimension in Ferguson's Discussion of Civil Society", in *Adam Ferguson: History, Progress and Human Nature*, ed. Eugene Heath and Vincenzo Merolle (London: Pickering and Chatto, 2008), 181; Vanessa Cunningham, *Shakespeare and Garrick* (Cambridge: Cambridge University Press, 2008), 19–20.
97. Lindsay, *Memoirs*, 4:225; Noyes, *Thespian Mirror*, 105.
98. Lindsay, *Memoirs*, 4:228–33. Modern references to Lindsay's *Memoirs* are largely confined to the theatrical episodes. Telemachus's opinion of Garrick has been seen by one critic as offering an unusual example of "contemporary displeasure with Garrick's 'attitudes' – stage postures", but another equally dismisses it as "a completely unmemorable discussion". See Vickers, *Shakespeare*, 308; Graham Midgley, review of *Shakespeare: The Critical Heritage*, edited by Brian Vickers, *Notes and Queries* 223 (1978): 176. See also Cunningham, *Shakespeare and Garrick*, 66–75.
99. Lindsay, *Memoirs*, 1:1–3. Cf. Charles L. Griswold Jr, *Adam Smith and the Virtues of Enlightenment* (Cambridge: Cambridge University Press, 1999), 66–67.
100. Lindsay, *Memoirs*, 1:3; Michael Cordner, ed., *The Plays of Sir George Etherege* (Cambridge: Cambridge University Press, 1982), x, 219; Lisa Berglund, "The Language of the Libertines: Subversive Morality in *The Man of Mode*", *Studies in English Literature, 1500–1900* 30 (1990): 369, 374; Anne Barton, "Parks and Ardens", *Proceedings of the British Academy* 80 (1991): 62–64; John G. Hayman, "Dorimant and the Comedy of a Man of Mode", *Modern Language Quarterly* 30 (1969): 183–84; McGirr, *Eighteenth-Century Characters*, 28–30; Leslie H. Martin, "Past and Parody in *The Man of Mode*", *Studies in English Literature, 1500–1900* 16 (1976): 367–73; Dale Underwood, *Etherege and the Seventeenth-Century Comedy of Manners* (New Haven, Conn.: Yale University Press, 1957), 93.

101. Richard Steele, *The Spectator* 65 (15 May 1711), quoted in Hayman, "Dorimant", 183.
102. Lindsay, *Memoirs*, 1:3.
103. Cordner, *Plays of Sir George Etherege*, 6; Doody, *Natural Passion*, 135; Martin, "Past and Parody", 363; Richard Steele, *The Conscious Lovers*, ed. Shirley Strum Kenny (Lincoln: University of Nebraska Press, 1968), xix.
104. Lindsay, *Memoirs*, 1:3–4; Steele, *Conscious Lovers*, xix–xx.
105. Lindsay, *Memoirs*, 1:158, 209–12. Isabella Burchell (1734/5–1802) sang at the Vauxhall Pleasure Gardens in London throughout the 1750s, before the publication of *Memoirs*, and in the 1760s went on to perform at Garrick's Drury Lane Theatre. See Olive Baldwin and Thelma Wilson, "Vincent, Isabella (1734/5–1802)", *Oxford Dictionary of National Biography* (2004).
106. Lindsay, *Memoirs*, 2:210–11; A.E. Anton, " 'Handfasting' in Scotland", *Scottish Historical Review* 37 (1958): 89–102; Rosalind Mitchison and Leah Leneman, *Sexuality and Social Control: Scotland, 1660–1780* (Oxford: Basil Blackwell, 1989), 101–2; Stone, *Family, Sex and Marriage*, 31–35; Perry, *Novel Relations*, 31, 210, 277n63.
107. Lindsay, *Memoirs*, 4:262–64.

Chapter 4

1. Denise Gigante, ed., *The Great Age of the English Essay: An Anthology* (New Haven, Conn.: Yale University Press, 2008), 107–12.
2. Thornbury, *Henry Fielding's Theory*, 146; Robert Bittlestone, *Odysseus Unbound: The Search for Homer's Ithaca* (Cambridge: Cambridge University Press, 2005).
3. Lindsay, *Memoirs*, 1:5. Cf. J. Paul Hunter, "Protesting Fiction, Constructing History", in *The Historical Imagination in Early Modern Britain: History, Rhetoric, and Fiction, 1500–1800*, ed. Donald R. Kelley and David Harris Sacks (Cambridge: Cambridge University Press, 1997), 298–317; Everett Zimmerman, *The Boundaries of Fiction: History and the Eighteenth-Century British Novel* (Ithaca, NY: Cornell University Press, 1996), 1–4; Robert Mayer, *History and the Early English Novel: Matters of Fact from Bacon to Defoe* (Cambridge: Cambridge University Press, 1997), 227–33; Speck, *Society and Literature*, 167.
4. Alberto Manguel and Gianni Guadalupi, *The Dictionary of Imaginary Places* (London: Bloomsbury, 1999); Robert Markley, " 'I have now done with my island, and all manner of discourse about it': Crusoe's *Farther Adventures* and the Unwritten History of the Novel", in *A Companion to the Eighteenth-Century English Novel and Culture*, ed. Paula R. Backscheider and Catherine Ingrassia (Oxford: Blackwell, 2005), 25–32; John R. Gillis, "Taking History Offshore: Atlantic Islands in European Minds, 1400–1800", in *Islands in History and Representation*, ed. Rod Edmond and Vanessa Smith (London: Routledge, 2003), 26.
5. The map is at Lindsay, *Memoirs*, 3:172–73. Cf. Christian Jacob, *The Sovereign Map: Theoretical Approaches in Cartography Throughout History* (Chicago: University of Chicago Press, 2006), 281–84.
6. Lindsay, *Memoirs*, 3:177–78.
7. Ibid., 173–75.
8. Ibid., 178–79; John Speed, *A Prospect of the Most Famous Parts of the World* (1627; reprint, Amsterdam: Theatrum Orbis Terrarum, 1966), 1, 9.

9. Lindsay, *Memoirs*, 3:176; *Gentleman's Magazine* 27 (December 1757): 545.
10. Lindsay, *Memoirs*, 3:179–81.
11. Ibid., 181–82.
12. Ibid., 182–83.
13. Ibid., 184–86.
14. Ibid., 187–88.
15. Ibid., 258–61.
16. Ibid., 261–62.
17. Ibid., 262–67.
18. Ibid., 205–9.
19. Ibid., 226–28, 231–33, 239–42.
20. Ibid., 3:253–54; 4:3–5.
21. Ibid., 4:10–12, 20–34.
22. Ibid., 39–40.
23. Lindsay, "Oration", 731n3.
24. Janet L. Nelson, "Kingship and Empire in the Carolingian World", in *Carolingian Culture: Emulation and Innovation*, ed. Rosamond McKitterick (Cambridge: Cambridge University Press, 1994), 52–54.
25. Rosamond McKitterick, *Charlemagne: The Formation of European Identity* (Cambridge: Cambridge University Press, 2008), 24, 52–53, 96–103; Matthew Innes, "Charlemagne's Will: Piety, Politics and the Imperial Succession", *English Historical Review* 112 (1997): 835.
26. Lindsay, *Memoirs*, 4:40–41. See J.C.D. Clark, *English Society, 1660–1832: Religion, Ideology and Politics During the Ancien Régime* (Cambridge: Cambridge University Press, 2000), 115–19; Glenn Burgess, "England and Scotland", in *European Political Thought, 1450–1700: Religion, Law and Philosophy* (New Haven, Conn.: Yale University Press, 2007), 374.
27. Lindsay, *Memoirs*, 4:41–42.
28. Ibid., 42.
29. Ibid., 43–44.
30. Ibid., 44.
31. Ibid., 3:190.
32. Vogt, *Ancient Slavery*, 26–38.
33. Lindsay, *Memoirs*, 4:45–46.
34. Ibid., 47.
35. David Armitage, ed., *Bolingbroke: Political Writings* (Cambridge: Cambridge University Press, 1997); David Armitage, "A Patriot for Whom? The Afterlives of Bolingbroke's Patriot King", *Journal of British Studies* 36 (1997): 397–418; J. Steven Watson, *The Reign of George III, 1760–1815* (Oxford: Clarendon Press, 1960), 6; Lewis Namier, *England in the Age of the American Revolution* (1930; reprint, London: Macmillan, 1961), 83–93; William D. Liddle, " 'A Patriot King, or None': Lord Bolingbroke and the American Renunciation of George III", *Journal of American History* 65 (1979): 951–70; Doohwan Ahn, "The Politics of Royal Education: Xenophon's *Education of Cyrus* in Early Eighteenth-Century Europe", *Leadership Quarterly* 19 (2008): 439–52.
36. Lindsay, *Memoirs*, 4:47.
37. Ibid., 3:205–6.

38. Ibid., 4:48.
39. See Callow, *Making of King James II*, 282–97; Clark, *English Society*, 68–70; William Gibson, "The Limits of the Confessional State: Electoral Religion in the Reign of Charles II", *Historical Journal* 51 (2008): 27–29; Kearney, *British Isles*, 128–29; Nigel M. Kennell, *Spartans: A New History* (Chichester, UK: Wiley-Blackwell, 2010), 93–114; Paul Cartledge, *Ancient Greek Political Thought and Practice* (Cambridge: Cambridge University Press, 2009), 29–40; F.E. Adcock, *Roman Political Ideas and Practice* (Ann Arbor: University of Michigan Press, 1959), 42.
40. Lindsay, *Memoirs*, 4:49–50.
41. Ibid., 51, 54.
42. Ibid., 49–59, 63.
43. Adcock, *Roman Political Ideas*, 42; Victor Ehrenberg, *The Greek State* (London: Methuen, 1969), 59.
44. Lindsay, *Memoirs*, 4:74.
45. Ibid., 74–80.
46. Ibid., 75.
47. Ibid., 1:205–6.
48. Ibid., 206–7. Cf. David Hancock, *Citizens of the World: London Merchants and the Integration of the British Atlantic Community, 1735–1785* (Cambridge: Cambridge University Press, 1995), 20–21.

Chapter 5

1. Rodger, "Naval Chaplain", 34; Colledge, *Ships of the Royal Navy*, 141; Clowes, *Royal Navy*, 3:126–28, 140–41; Julian S. Corbett, *England in the Seven Years' War: A Study in Combined Strategy* (London: Longmans, Green, 1918), 1:53–55; Guy Frégault, *Canada: The War of the Conquest* (Toronto: Oxford University Press, 1969), 88–91; Nester, *Great Frontier War*, 220–22.
2. Andrew Hill Clark, *Acadia: The Geography of Early Nova Scotia to 1760* (Madison: University of Wisconsin Press, 1968), 271–72; Jeffers Lennox, "An Empire on Paper: The Founding of Halifax and Conceptions of Imperial Space, 1744–55", *Canadian Historical Review* 88 (2007): 399; John Robert McNeill, *Atlantic Empires of France and Spain: Louisbourg and Havana, 1700–1763* (Chapel Hill: University of North Carolina Press, 1985), 66; J.S. McLennan, *Louisbourg: From Its Foundation to Its Fall, 1713–1758* (Sydney, NS: Fortress Press, 1957), 182–83.
3. Clowes, *Royal Navy*, 3:141; McLennan, *Louisbourg*, 199–200, 205–6, 212; Rodger, *Wooden World*, 159; Lavery, *Ship of the Line*, 1:175; George Naish, "Naval Uniform", *Mariner's Mirror* 41 (1955): 95; *Gentleman's Magazine* 29 (January 1759): 44; *Gentleman's Magazine* 29 (March 1759): 137.
4. ADM 36/5616, *Fougueux* Muster, 34; ADM 33/559, *Fougueux* Pay Book; ADM 52/859, *Fougueux* Master's Log (National Archives, Kew).
5. John Entick, *The General History of the Late War: Containing It's Rise, Progress and Event, in Europe, Asia, Africa, and America* (1764; 4th ed., London: Edward and Charles Dilly, 1779), 2: 168; Mackay, *Admiral Hawke*, 155–58.
6. Smith, *Slavery, Family and Gentry Capitalism*, 51; Alden, *Robert Dinwiddie*, 12–13;

J.K. Laughton and Ruddock Mackay, "Holburne, Francis (1704–1771), naval officer", *Oxford Dictionary of National Biography* (2004); Mackay, *Admiral Hawke*, 96; McLennan, *Louisbourg*, 203n1.

7. *Gentleman's Magazine* 27 (May 1757): 235; ibid. (September 1757): 432; ADM 52/859, *Fougueux* Master's Log (National Archives, Kew); Clowes, *Royal Navy*, 3:167.
8. *Gentleman's Magazine* 27 (October 1757): 463; ibid. (November 1757): 528; ibid. (December 1757): 575; Clowes, *Royal Navy*, 3:167–69; Corbett, *England in the Seven Years' War*, 1:313–28; Frégault, *Canada*, 149–50; McNeill, *Atlantic Empires*, 66; A.J.B. Johnston, *Endgame 1758: The Promise, the Glory, and the Despair of Louisbourg's Last Decade* (Lincoln: University of Nebraska, 2007); Terry Crowley, *Louisbourg: Atlantic Fortress and Seaport*, Historical Booklet no. 48 (Ottawa: Canadian Historical Association, 1990), 3, 19–23; McLennan, *Louisbourg*, 203–5; Clark, *Acadia*, 273–74.
9. John Lindsay, *A Voyage to the Coast of Africa in 1758* (London: S. Paterson and W. Bristow, and York: C. Etherington, 1759), 11; Entick, *General History*, 2:390–94, 402–3.
10. Entick, *General History*, 3:189. Cf. *Gentleman's Magazine* 28 (August 1758): 397; Alexander William Crawford Lindsay (Lord Lindsay), *Lives of the Lindsays; or, a Memoir of the Houses of Crawford and Balcarres* (London: John Murray, 1849), 2:174n; Corbett, *England in the Seven Years' War*, 1:293–96; Jonathan Spain, "Kerr, William Henry, fourth marquess of Lothian (c. 1712–1775), army officer", *Oxford Dictionary of National Biography* (2004).
11. Payne's *Universal Weekly Chronicle*, reprinted in *Gentleman's Magazine* 28 (August 1758): 359–60; Conway, *War, State, and Society*, 147.
12. Entick, *General History*, 3:190–91. Cf. Corbett, *England in the Seven Years' War*, 1:293–96.
13. Lindsay, *Voyage*, 1–2. Cf. Lindsay, *Lives of the Lindsays*, 2:174n.
14. Lindsay, *Voyage*, 1–2, 7. Cf. Conway, *War, State, and Society*, 171–92.
15. Speck, *Butcher*, 136–37; Alden, *Robert Dinwiddie*, 14–15; Brock, *Official Records*, 208n135.
16. Lindsay, *Voyage*.
17. A.J. Marsh, "The Taking of Goree, 1758", *Mariner's Mirror* 51 (1965): 118.
18. Boubacar Barry, *Senegambia and the Atlantic Slave Trade* (Cambridge: Cambridge University Press, 1998), 44–59; Boubacar Barry, "Senegambia from the Sixteenth to the Eighteenth Century: Evolution of the Wolof, Sereer and 'Tukuloor' ", in *General History of Africa*, vol. 5, *Africa from the Sixteenth to the Eighteenth Century*, ed. B.A. Ogot (Paris: UNESCO, 1992), 262–65.
19. James L.A. Webb Jr, "The Mid-Eighteenth Century Gum Arabic Trade and the British Conquest of Saint-Louis du Sénégal, 1758", *Journal of Imperial and Commonwealth History* 25 (1997): 43; C.W. Fagg and G.E. Allison, *Acacia senegal and the Gum Arabic Trade*, Tropical Forestry Papers no. 42 (Oxford: Oxford Forestry Institute, 2004), 44–47; Barry, "Senegambia", 269; Paul E. Lovejoy, *Transformations in Slavery: A History of Slavery in Africa* (Cambridge: Cambridge University Press, 1983), 128–29; Barry, *Senegambia and the Atlantic Slave Trade*, 76; James F. Searing, *West African Slavery and Atlantic Commerce: The Senegal River Valley, 1700–1860* (Cambridge: Cambridge University Press, 1993), 94–95; George E. Brooks Jr, "The *Signares* of Saint-Louis and Gorée: Women Entrepreneurs in Eighteenth-

Century Senegal", in *Women in Africa: Studies in Social and Economic Change*, ed. Nancy J. Hafkin and Edna G. Bay (Stanford, Calif.: Stanford University Press, 1976), 21.

20. Michel Adanson, *A Voyage to Senegal, the Island of Goree, and the River Gambia* (London: J. Nourse and W. Johnston, 1759), 159–61; Webb, "Mid-Eighteenth Century Gum Arabic Trade", 46; Philip D. Curtin, *Economic Change in Precolonial Africa: Senegambia in the Era of the Slave Trade* (Madison: University of Wisconsin Press, 1975), 109–10; Barry, *Senegambia and the Atlantic Slave Trade*, 110–12; Searing, *West African Slavery*, 132–44.
21. Thomas Keppel, *The Life of Augustus Viscount Keppel, Admiral of the White, and First Lord of the Admiralty in 1782–83* (London: Henry Colburn, 1842), 1:268; Frank McLynn, *1759*, 99–100; Webb, "Mid-Eighteenth Century Gum Arabic Trade", 47–50; Marsh, "Taking of Goree", 117–19.
22. Lindsay, *Voyage*, 1; Keppel, *Life of Augustus Viscount Keppel*, 1:269.
23. ADM 51/351, Master's log, *Fougueux* (National Archives, Kew); Lindsay, *Voyage*, 13.
24. Lindsay, *Voyage*, 13–14; Marsh, "Taking of Goree", 121; Rodger, "Naval Chaplain", 37.
25. ADM 51/351, Master's log, *Fougueux* (National Archives, Kew); Keppel, *Life of Augustus Viscount Keppel*, 1:271.
26. ADM 51/351, Master's log, *Fougueux* (National Archives, Kew); Keppel, *Life of Augustus Viscount Keppel*, 1:273; *Gentleman's Magazine* 29 (January 1759): 43–44; Marsh, "Taking of Goree", 122–23; Rodger, *Wooden World*, 48.
27. Lindsay, *Voyage*, 26, 34; *Gentleman's Magazine* 29 (January 1759): 43; Entick, *General History*, 3:272–77; Marsh, "Taking of Goree", 125–26.
28. Lindsay, *Voyage*, 50, 84n. Cf. Joyce E. Chaplin, "Knowing the Ocean: Benjamin Franklin and the Circulation of Atlantic Knowledge", in *Science and Empire in the Atlantic World*, ed. James Delbourgo and Nicholas Dew (New York: Routledge, 2008), 86.
29. Lindsay, *Voyage*, 49, 52–59.
30. Ibid., 56–57.
31. Adanson, *Histoire naturelle du Sénégal*, reviewed under the title *An Account of the Isle of Senegal, on the Coast of Africa, lately taken by his Majesty's Ships*, *Gentleman's Magazine* 28 (June 1758): 262–63.
32. Adanson, *Voyage to Senegal*, iv–v, 2. Cf. *Gentleman's Magazine* 29 (March 1759): 134; Frans A. Stafleu, *Linnaeus and the Linnaeans: The Spreading of Their Ideas in Systematic Botany, 1735–1789* (Utrecht, Netherlands: International Association for Plant Taxonomy, 1971), 313–20; John S. Wilkins, *Species: A History of the Idea* (Berkeley: University of California Press, 2009), 79–81.
33. Adanson, *Voyage to Senegal*, 39–40. See also Londa Schiebinger, "Scientific Exchange in the Eighteenth-Century Atlantic World", in *Soundings in Atlantic History: Latent Structures and Intellectual Currents, 1500–1830*, ed. Bernard Bailyn and Patricia L. Denault (Cambridge, Mass: Harvard University Press, 2009), 305.
34. Lindsay, *Voyage*, 55, 59. Cf. Adanson, *Voyage to Senegal*, 214.
35. Lindsay, *Voyage*, 61–63.
36. Adanson, *Voyage to Senegal*, 166; Searing, *West African Slavery*, 61–62, 89; John S. Mbiti, *African Religions and Philosophy* (London: Heinemann, 1969), 244–45; Gwendolyn Midlo Hall, *Africans in Colonial Louisiana: The Development of Afro-Creole*

Culture in the Eighteenth Century (Baton Rouge: Louisiana State University Press, 1992), 34–36, 44–45.

37. Lindsay, *Voyage*, 83; Searing, *West African Slavery*, 106. See also Brooks, "*Signares*", 21; Curtin, *Economic Change*, 112–15; Barry, *Senegambia and the Atlantic Slave Trade*, 74–76; Margaret Priestley, *West African Trade and Coast Society: A Family Study* (London: Oxford University Press, 1969).
38. Lindsay, *Voyage*, 70, 93; Entick, *General History*, 3:277; Keppel, *Life of Augustus Viscount Keppel*, 1:278; Curtin, *Economic Change*, 125–26.
39. Lindsay, *Voyage*, 70–71.
40. Ibid., 71–72.
41. Ibid., 72–73. See John K. Thornton, *Warfare in Atlantic Africa, 1500–1800* (London: Routledge, 2004), 44.
42. Lindsay, *Voyage*, 73–74; Curtin, *Economic Change*, 109n2.
43. Lindsay, *Voyage*, 74.
44. Ibid., 76–78. Cf. Brooks, "*Signares*", 26; Philip D. Morgan, "British Encounters with Africans and African-Americans, circa 1600–1780", in *Strangers Within the Realm: Cultural Margins of the First British Empire*, ed. Bernard Bailyn and Philip D. Morgan (Chapel Hill: University of North Carolina Press, 1991), 214.
45. Lindsay, *Voyage*, 78; Searing, *West African Slavery*, 93–94; Adanson, *Voyage to Senegal*, 39–40.
46. Cf. Taylor, *Sea Chaplains*, 167.
47. William Smith, *A New Voyage to Guinea* (London: John Nourse, 1744), 213–14; Long, *History of Jamaica*, 2:379, attributing the story to Bosman.
48. Lindsay, *Voyage*, 75.
49. Ibid., 75.
50. Ibid., 76.
51. Ibid., 68–69, 80. Cf. Adanson, *Voyage to Senegal*, 209–11.
52. Lindsay, *Voyage*, 81.
53. Smith, *New Voyage to Guinea*, 21; Dena J. Epstein, *Sinful Tunes and Spirituals: Black Folk Music to the Civil* War (Urbana: University of Illinois Press, 1977), 55.
54. A.M. Jones, *Africa and Indonesia: The Evidence of the Xylophone and Other Musical and Cultural Factors* (Leiden: E.J. Brill, 1971), 2; Richard Cullen Rath, "African Music in Seventeenth-Century Jamaica: Cultural Transit and Transition", *William and Mary Quarterly* 50 (1993): 716–20; J.H. Kwabema Nketia, "Tradition and Innovation in African Music", *Jamaica Journal* 11, no. 3/4 (March 1978): 2–9; F.G. Cassidy and R.B. Le Page, eds., *Dictionary of Jamaican English* (1967; reprint, Cambridge: Cambridge University Press, 1980), 21; Epstein, *Sinful Tunes and Spirituals*, 57–58.
55. Lindsay, *Voyage*, 81–82.
56. Ibid., 82. Cf. Smith, *New Voyage to Guinea*, 215.
57. Lindsay, *Voyage*, 73, 77; Hall, *Africans in Colonial Louisiana*, 51, 163; Cassidy and Le Page, *Dictionary of Jamaican English*, 210.
58. Lindsay, *Voyage*, 86, 94–95.
59. Ibid., 77. Cf. Thornton, *Warfare in Atlantic Africa*, 43–44.
60. Lindsay, *Voyage*, 86–88; Curtin, *Economic Change*, 126. Cf. Taylor, *Sea Chaplains*, 167.
61. Lindsay, *Voyage*, 88, 94, 97, 99–100.
62. Ibid., 97–99.
63. Ibid., 97, 102, 106.

64. Ibid., 105–6.
65. Ibid., 78.
66. Ibid., 99–101.
67. Ibid., 104.
68. Ibid., 104–5; Lindsay, "Conjectural considerations", 158.
69. Keppel, *Life of Augustus Viscount Keppel*, 1:277n, quoting *Gentleman's Magazine* (1762): 440; Marshall Smelser, *The Campaign for the Sugar Islands, 1759: A Study of Amphibious Warfare* (Chapel Hill: University of North Carolina Press, 1955), 104.
70. Entick, *General History*, 3:269. Cf. Keppel, *Life of Augustus Viscount Keppel*, 1:277.
71. Corbett, *England in the Seven Years' War*, 1:337; 2:82; Marsh, "Taking of Goree", 117.
72. Lindsay, *Voyage*, 107–10; Colledge, *Ships of the Royal Navy*, 141.
73. *Gentleman's Magazine* 29 (October 1759): 447. The review is not mentioned in Boswell's *Life of Johnson*. Marshall Waingrow, ed., *The Correspondence and Other Papers of James Boswell Relating to the Making of the* Life of Johnson (New Haven, Conn.: Yale University Press, 2001), 6 and n34.
74. *Gentleman's Magazine* 29 (October 1759): 448–49. Cf. Lindsay, *Voyage*, 63, 67.
75. *Gentleman's Magazine* 29 (October 1759): 450.
76. Curtin, *Economic Change*, 126; Marsh, "Taking of Goree", 122; Webb, "Mid-Eighteenth Century Gum Arabic Trade", 57n56.
77. Barker, *African Link*, 18.
78. McLynn, *1759*, 366–88; Mackay and Duffy, *Hawke, Nelson and British Naval Leadership*, 45–88; Smelser, *Campaign for the Sugar Islands*, 14; Fuller, *Military History*, 2:268.
79. Taylor, *Sea Chaplains*, 166–67; Mackay, *Admiral Hawke*, 250–51; Lavery, *Ship of the Line*, 1:176.

Chapter 6

1. Lindsay, *Voyage*, 1:1; T.G. Burnard, " 'Prodigious Riches': The Wealth of Jamaica before the American Revolution", *Economic History Review* 54 (2001): 520. Cf. Alfred Spencer, ed., *Memoirs of William Hickey* (London: Hurst and Blackett, 1918), 2:20; Devine, *Scotland's Empire*, 242.
2. Lindsay, *Memoirs*, 1:240. Cf. Devine, *Tobacco Lords*, 62.
3. Lindsay, *Memoirs*, 3:30–31.
4. Ibid., 32. Cf. Candace Ward, "Sensibility, Tropical Disease, and the Eighteenth-Century Sentimental Novel", in *Discourses of Slavery and Abolition: Britain and its Colonies, 1760–1838*, ed. Brycchan Carey, Markman Ellis and Sara Salih (Basingstoke, UK: Palgrave Macmillan, 2004), 63–77.
5. Lindsay, *Memoirs*, 3:33, 35, 38–44, 169.
6. Karras, *Sojourners in the Sun*, 22, 64; Trevor Burnard, " 'The Countrie Continues Sicklie': White Mortality in Jamaica, 1655–1780", *Social History of Medicine* 12 (1999): 67–70; Vincent Brown, *The Reaper's Garden: Death and Power in the World of Atlantic Slavery* (Cambridge, Mass.: Harvard University Press, 2008), 1–5.
7. *Columbian Magazine* 2 (February 1797): 581; Robert Mowbray Howard, ed., *Records and Letters of the Family of the Longs of Longville, Jamaica, and Hampton Lodge, Surrey*

(London: Simpkin, Marshall, Hamilton, Kent, 1925), 1:184–86; Joseph S. Tiedemann, "Moore, Sir Henry, first baronet (1713–1769)", *Oxford Dictionary of National Biography* (2004); George Metcalf, *Royal Government and Political Conflict in Jamaica, 1729–1783* (London: Longmans, 1965), 138–49; Philip Wright, *Monumental Inscriptions of Jamaica* (London: Society of Genealogists, 1966), 61.

8. Metcalf, *Royal Government*, 144–49.
9. Ibid.; K.E. Ingram, *Sources of Jamaican History, 1655–1838* (Zug, Switzerland: Inter Documentation, 1976), 1:333; Jack P. Greene, " 'Of Liberty and of the Colonies': A Case Study of Constitutional Conflict in the Mid-Eighteenth-Century British American Empire", in *Liberty and American Experience in the Eighteenth Century*, ed. David Womersley (Indianapolis, Ind.: Liberty Fund, 2006), 90–92; William J. Meggs, "Epidemics of Mold Poisoning Past and Present", *Toxicology and Industrial Health* 25 (2009): 572–73.
10. Philip C. Ritterbush, "John Lindsay and the Sensitive Plant", *Annals of Science* 18 (1962): 233–35; Carla Gardina Pestana, *The English Atlantic in an Age of Revolution, 1640–1661* (Cambridge, Mass.: Harvard University Press, 2004), 177–81.
11. Francis J. Osborne, *History of the Catholic Church in Jamaica* (Chicago: Loyola University Press, 1988), 140–41; Long, *History of Jamaica*, 2:235; Frank Wesley Pitman, *The Development of the British West Indies, 1700–1763* (1917; reprint, London: Frank Cass, 1967), 29; Metcalf, *Royal Government*, 7.
12. Long, *History of Jamaica*, 2:235–37; Charles Leslie, *A New and Exact Account of Jamaica, wherein the Antient and Present State of that Colony, Its Importance to Great Britain, Laws, Trade, Manners and Religion, together with the most remarkable and curious Animals, Plants, Trees, &c. are described: With a particular Account of the Sacrifices, Libations, &c. at this Day in Use among the Negroes* (Edinburgh: R. Fleming, 1740), 198–200; J.B. Ellis, *The Diocese of Jamaica: A Short Account of its History, Growth and Organisation* (London: Society for Promoting Christian Knowledge, 1913), 44–45; Arthur Charles Dayfoot, *The Shaping of the West Indian Church, 1492–1962* (Kingston: University of the West Indies Press, 1999), 103-7; Edward Brathwaite, *The Development of Creole Society in Jamaica, 1770–1820* (Oxford: Clarendon Press, 1971), 20-25. Cf. William H. Seiler, "The Anglican Parish in Virginia", in *Seventeenth-Century America: Essays in Colonial History*, ed. James Morton Smith (Chapel Hill: University of North Carolina Press, 1959), 119–42; Charles F. Irons, *The Origins of Proslavery Christianity: White and Black Evangelicals in Colonial and Antebellum Virginia* (Chapel Hill: University of North Carolina Press, 2008), 26; Sykes, *Church and State*, 149–50, 208–15; Metcalf, *Royal Government*, 8.
13. Hans Cnattingius, *Bishops and Societies: A Study of Anglican Colonial and Missionary Expansion, 1698–1850* (London: Society for Promoting Christian Knowledge, 1952), 7–8; Ellis, *Diocese of Jamaica*, 40–41; J.H. Proctor, "Scottish Missionaries and Jamaican Slaveholders", *Slavery and Abolition* 25 (2004): 51; Hamilton, *Scotland, the Caribbean and the Atlantic World*, 49. Cf. Rowan Strong, *Anglicanism and the British Empire c. 1700–1850* (Oxford: Oxford University Press, 2007), 6, 13–15, 84–111; Jon Butler, *Awash in a Sea of Faith: Christianizing the American People* (Cambridge, Mass.: Harvard University Press, 1990), 99–105.
14. Mary Turner, *Slaves and Missionaries: The Disintegration of Jamaican Slave Society, 1787–1834* (Urbana: University of Illinois Press, 1982), 11; Shirley C. Gordon, *God Almighty Make Me Free: Christianity in Preemancipation Jamaica* (Bloomington: Indi-

ana University Press, 1996), 4–5; Richard S. Dunn, *Moravian Missionaries at Work in a Jamaican Slave Community, 1754–1835* ([Minneapolis, Minn.]: Associates of the James Ford Bell Library, University of Minnesota, 1994), 7; A. Caldecott, *The Church in the West Indies* (1898; reprint, London: Frank Cass, 1970), 72–76; Dayfoot, *Shaping of the West Indian Church*, 128–31; M.J. Steel, "A Philosophy of Fear: The World View of the Jamaican Plantocracy in a Comparative Perspective", *Journal of Caribbean History* 27 (1993): 11; Jon F. Sensbach, *A Separate Canaan: The Making of an Afro-Moravian World in North Carolina, 1763–1840* (Chapel Hill: University of North Carolina Press, 1998); Butler, *Awash in a Sea of Faith*, 164–65; O.F. Christie, ed., *The Diary of the Rev. William Jones, 1777–1821: Curate and Vicar of Broxbourne and the Hamlet of Hoddesdon, 1781–1821* (London: Brentano's, 1929), 35.

15. George W. Roberts, *The Population of Jamaica* (Cambridge: Cambridge University Press, 1957), 33–36; Robert V. Wells, *The Population of the British Colonies in America before 1776* (Princeton, NJ: Princeton University Press, 1975), 196; Nicholas M. Beasley, *Christian Ritual and the Creation of British Slave Societies, 1650–1780* (Athens: University of Georgia Press, 2009), 33; Richard B. Sheridan, *Sugar and Slavery: An Economic History of the British West Indies, 1623–1775* (Barbados: Caribbean Universities Press, 1974), 222–33; Brathwaite, *Development of Creole Society*, 24.
16. Lindsay, "Conjectural considerations", 191; Minter, *Episcopacy*, 306–9. Cf. Cundall, *Historic Jamaica*, 385.
17. Louis Nelson, "Building 'Cross-Wise': Reconstructing Jamaica's Eighteenth-Century Anglican Churches", *Jamaican Historical Review* 22 (2002): 14–15; Spencer, *Memoirs of William Hickey*, 2:46; James Robertson, *Gone Is the Ancient Glory: Spanish Town, Jamaica, 1534–2000* (Kingston: Ian Randle, 2005), 69–71.
18. Robertson, *Gone Is the Ancient Glory*, 116–17; Pitman, *Development of the British West Indies*, 29; Long, *History of Jamaica*, 2:6.
19. Robertson, *Gone Is the Ancient Glory*, 91, 116–17; Pitman, *Development of the British West Indies*, 27–29; Metcalf, *Royal Government*, 8.
20. Long, *History of Jamaica*, 2:33; Metcalf, *Royal Government*, 9; Nicholas M. Beasley, "Ritual Time in British Plantation Colonies, 1650–1780", *Church History* 76 (2007): 546; Kathleen Wilson, *The Island Race: Englishness, Empire and Gender in the Eighteenth Century* (London: Routledge, 2003), 161–67.
21. Wilson, *Island Race*, 161, 166; Errol Hill, *The Jamaican Stage, 1655–1900: Profile of a Colonial Theatre* (Amherst: University of Massachusetts Press, 1992), 216–23, 230–31.
22. Robertson, *Gone Is the Ancient Glory*, 68–82; Brathwaite, *Development of Creole Society*, 31, 269; Giles Barber, "Books from the Old World for the New: The British International Trade in Books in the Eighteenth Century", *Studies on Voltaire and the Eighteenth Century* 151–55 (1976): 198–200, 224; Wolf, *Book Culture*, 29–34; Roderick Cave, *Printing and the Book Trade in the West Indies* (London: Pindar Press, 1987), 227–28; Shelford, "Pascal in Jamaica", 53–74.
23. Lindsay, "Conjectural considerations", 196; Long, *History of Jamaica*, 2:40–41, 475–85; John Gilmore, "Williams, Francis (c. 1690–1762)", *Oxford Dictionary of National Biography* (2004); Vincent Carretta, "Who Was Francis Williams?" *Early American Literature* 38 (2003): 221; Michele Valerie Ronnick, "Francis Williams: An Eighteenth-Century Tertium Quid", *Negro History Bulletin* 61 (1998): 22–23; Metcalf, *Royal Government*, 9; Robertson, *Gone Is the Ancient Glory*, 74–76. The catalogue of

the Victoria and Albert Museum attributes the painting of Williams to England, c. 1745; Robertson contends that it was painted in Jamaica, c. 1734.

24. Nelson, *Blessed Company*, 201–4; Sykes, *Church and State*, 256; Ann Matheson, *Theories of Rhetoric in the 18th-Century Scottish Sermon* (Lewiston, NY: Edwin Mellen Press, 1995), 190.
25. *Columbian Magazine* 1 (December 1796): 433; Leslie, *New and Exact Account*, 306–7; Beasley, "Ritual Time", 565; Beasley, *Christian Ritual*, 49–50.
26. *Columbian Magazine* 2 (January 1797): 503–4; ibid. (February 1797): 582; Minter, *Episcopacy*, 306–7.
27. *Columbian Magazine* 1 (December 1796): 433.
28. Ibid., 434.
29. *Columbian Magazine* 2 (January 1797): 498.
30. *Columbian Magazine* 1 (December 1796): 439n.
31. *Columbian Magazine* 2 (January 1797): 499–500.
32. Ibid., 500.
33. Ibid., 500–501; *Jamaica Act*, 1789, cap. 13, "An act to prevent the burying of the dead in the churches of this island; and to enable the justices and vestry of certain parishes to purchase lands for burial-grounds". Cf. Christie, *Diary of the Rev. William Jones*, 40.
34. *Columbian Magazine* 2 (January 1797): 501–2.
35. Ibid., 504–5; *Gentleman's Magazine* 30 (June 1760): 294; ibid. (July 1760): 307; ibid. (August 1760): 392; Craton, *Testing the Chains*, 124–39; Diana Paton, "Punishment, Crime, and the Bodies of Slaves in Eighteenth-Century Jamaica", *Journal of Social History* 34 (2001): 939–42.
36. *Columbian Magazine* 2 (January 1797): 505.
37. Ibid., 505–6.
38. Cf. Robertson, *Gone Is the Ancient Glory*, 72.
39. Nelson, "Building 'Cross-Wise' ", 18–19; Long, *History of Jamaica*, 2:69.
40. Register of Baptisms, Burials and Marriages, Clarendon, Vere, vol. 2 (no folio number), 1B/11/8, 4 (Jamaica Archives, Spanish Town); Long, *History of Jamaica*, 2:74; Howard, *Records and Letters*, 1:14, 122–23.
41. Ingram, *Sources of Jamaican History*, 1:563; Wright, *Monumental Inscriptions*, 146.
42. Lindsay, Drawings, vol. 7 ("on Leather coat [fish]"); Lindsay, "Elegancies of Jamaica", 176–77.
43. Wright, *Monumental Inscriptions*, 145, 148; Cundall, *Historic Jamaica*, 389; Ingram, *Sources of Jamaican History*, 1:563.
44. Register of Baptisms, Burials and Marriages, Clarendon, Vere, vol. 2, List of Rectors, 1B/11/8, 4 (Jamaica Archives, Spanish Town); Lindsay, "Conjectural considerations", 191; Minter, *Episcopacy*, 306–9; Long, *History of Jamaica*, 2:59. Cf. Cundall, *Historic Jamaica*, 385.
45. *Columbian Magazine* 2 (February 1797): 580.
46. Watson, *Reign of George III*, 85.
47. *Columbian Magazine* 2 (February 1797): 580–81; Tiedemann, "Moore, Sir Henry"; Metcalf, *Royal Government*, 138–49.
48. *Columbian Magazine* 2 (February 1797): 581.
49. Ibid., 582; Graydon Beeks, "Handel's Sacred Music", in *The Cambridge Companion to Handel*, ed. Donald Burrows (Cambridge: Cambridge University Press, 1997),

177; Jeremy Black, *George III: America's Last King* (New Haven, Conn.: Yale University Press, 2006), 48, 173.

50. *Columbian Magazine* 2 (February 1797): 582.
51. Ibid., 582–83.
52. Ibid., 583–84.
53. Ibid. (March 1797): 635–36; ibid. (April 1797): 727–29; Greene, " 'Of Liberty and of the Colonies' ", 102.
54. *Columbian Magazine* 2 (February 1797): 584–86.
55. Ibid. (March 1797): 644.
56. Ibid., 635; ibid. (April 1797): 729, 732.
57. Lindsay, "Hypothetical Doctrine of Water-spouts", 615; *A Catalogue of the Graduates in the Faculties of Arts, Divinity and Law of the University of Edinburgh Since the Foundation* (compiled 1858), 12 January 1773, cited in Ritterbush, "John Lindsay and the Sensitive Plant", 235. Cf. David Dobson, *Scots in the West Indies, 1707–1857* (Baltimore: Clearfield, 2006), 2:61.
58. Horn, *Short History of the University of Edinburgh*, 43.
59. Ibid., 76, 78.
60. Fulham Papers, 18:239 (Lambeth Palace, London).
61. Alexander Lindsay, *Lives of the Lindsays*, 1:443; John Lindsay, "Conjectural considerations", 178–79; Scott, *Fasti Ecclesiæ*, 4:231; Robertson, *Gone Is the Ancient Glory*, 178.
62. Long, *History of Jamaica*, 2:5–6; Wright, *Revels in Jamaica*, 69–72; Hill, *Jamaican Stage*, 21; John Roby, *Monuments of the Cathedral-Church and Parish of St. Catharine* (Montego Bay, Jamaica: Alex. Holmes, 1831), 7; Beasley, *Christian Ritual*, 29.
63. Lindsay to Robertson, 3 May 1776, Robertson-Macdonald Papers, ff. 216–18, ms. 3942 (National Library of Scotland). I am indebted to James Robertson for his transcript of this letter. Cf. Ingram, *Sources of Jamaican History*, 1:352.
64. Lindsay to Robertson, 6 August 1776, Robertson-Macdonald Papers, ff. 259–60, ms. 3942 (National Library of Scotland). I am indebted to James Robertson for his transcript of this letter. Sections of it are quoted in Richard B. Sheridan, "The Jamaican Slave Insurrection Scare of 1776 and the American Revolution", *Journal of Negro History* 61 (1976): 300–301; Andrew Jackson O'Shaughnessy, *An Empire Divided: The American Revolution and the British Caribbean* (Philadelphia: University of Pennsylvania Press, 2000), 153; and Michael Craton, *Testing the Chains: Resistance to Slavery in the British West Indies* (Ithaca, NY: Cornell University Press, 1982), 172–74.
65. Lindsay to Robertson, 6 August 1776, Robertson-Macdonald Papers, ff. 260–63.
66. Lesley Lewis, "English Commemorative Sculpture in Jamaica", *Jamaican Historical Review*, 9 (1972): 53–56; Joan Coutu, *Persuasion and Propaganda: Monuments and the Eighteenth-Century British Empire* (Montreal: McGill-Queen's University Press, 2006), 237–41.
67. John Lindsay, *A Sermon Preached at the Funeral of His Excellency Sir Basil Keith, Knt. Governour of Jamaica* (London: John Donaldson, 1780); Christie, *Diary of the Rev. William Jones*, 68. Cf. Minter, *Episcopacy Without Episcopate*, 177-78.
68. Lindsay, *Sermon*, v–vi; Robert Harrison, "Dick, Sir Archibald, third baronet (1703–1785)", *Oxford Dictionary of National Biography* (2004); Jeffrey Smitten, "Robertson's Letters and the Life of Writing", in *William Robertson and the Expansion of*

Empire, ed. Stewart J. Brown (Cambridge: Cambridge University Press, 1997), 45–46.

69. Lindsay, *Sermon*, vi–viii, 11, 40. Cf. Lindsay, "Conjectural considerations", 192; Metcalf, *Royal Government*, 182–98.
70. Lindsay, *Sermon*, 9.
71. Ibid., 12–13.
72. Ibid., 14–18, 20, 27. Cf. Harro Höpfl, *The Christian Polity of John Calvin* (Cambridge: Cambridge University Press, 1982), 74.
73. Lindsay, *Sermon*, 20–21.
74. Ibid., 37, 40, 42–46.
75. Ibid., 48–49.
76. Lindsay, "Conjectural considerations", 192.
77. Sykes, *Church and State*, 3–6, 189–90; Caldecott, *Church in the West Indies*, 46–60; Ellis, *Diocese of Jamaica*, 41–42; Karras, *Sojourners in the Sun*, 64n52; Beasley, *Christian Ritual*, 24, 87–92.
78. *Columbian Magazine* 1 (December 1796): 439n.
79. Beasley, *Christian Ritual*, 24; Beasley, "Ritual Time", 550, 561; Spencer, *Memoirs of William Hickey*, 2:46. Cf. Sykes, *Church and State*, 231–39; Patricia U. Bonomi and Peter R. Eisenstadt, "Church Adherence in the Eighteenth-Century British American Colonies", *William and Mary Quarterly* 39 (1982): 246–86.
80. Peter Marsden, *An Account of the Island of Jamaica* (Newcastle, UK: 1788), 41; Robert Worthington Smith, "Slavery and Christianity in the British West Indies", *Church History* 19 (1950): 173; Beasley, "Ritual Time", 556; Christie, *Diary of the Rev. William Jones*, 17.
81. Fulham Papers, 29:129–33. Cf. Ingram, *Sources of Jamaican History*, 1:483.
82. Christie, *Diary of the Rev. William Jones*, 46.
83. Long, *History of Jamaica*, 2:238. Cf. W.J. Gardner, *A History of Jamaica* (1873; reprint, London: Frank Cass, 1971), 193–96; Orlando Patterson, *The Sociology of Slavery: An Analysis of the Origins, Development and Structure of Negro Slave Society in Jamaica* (London: MacGibbon and Kee, 1967), 40; Steel, "Philosophy of Fear", 11.
84. Lindsay, "Conjectural considerations", 191.
85. Ibid., 154, 191–92; Beasley, *Christian Ritual*, 78; Robertson, *Gone Is the Ancient Glory*, 133–34.
86. Lindsay, "Conjectural considerations", 192; David Buisseret, "Charles Boucher of Jamaica and the Establishment of Greenwich Longitude", *Imago Mundi* 62 (2010): 239; Dava Sobel and William J.H. Andrewes, *The Illustrated Longitude* (London: Fourth Estate, 1998), 142–43. Cf. Metcalf, *Royal Government*, 152–81.
87. Lindsay, "Conjectural considerations", 192. Cf. Metcalf, *Royal Government*, 181–82.
88. Lindsay, "Conjectural considerations", 192. Cf. Metcalf, *Royal Government*, 182–98.
89. Lindsay, "Conjectural considerations", 192–93; Metcalf, *Royal Government*, 199–217; O'Shaughnessy, *Empire Divided*, 189.
90. Lindsay, "Conjectural considerations", 193; Metcalf, *Royal Government*, 220–26.
91. Lindsay, "Conjectural considerations", 193.
92. Ibid., 192–93.
93. Lindsay, *Memoirs*, 1:20–23.
94. Hempton, "Enlightenment and Faith", 84; Emma Rothschild, "The Atlantic Worlds of David Hume", in *Soundings in Atlantic History: Latent Structures and Intellectual*

Currents, 1500–1830, ed. Bernard Bailyn and Patricia L. Denault (Cambridge, Mass.: Harvard University Press, 2009), 405–48; John Robertson, *The Case for the Enlightenment: Scotland and Naples, 1680–1760* (Cambridge: Cambridge University Press, 2005), 289; Roy Porter, *Enlightenment: Britain and the Creation of the Modern World* (London: Penguin, 2001), 128–29.

95. R.H. Popkin, "Scepticism in the Enlightenment", in *Scepticism in the Enlightenment*, ed. Richard H. Popkin, Ezequiel de Olaso and Giorgio Tonelli (Dordrecht: Kluwer Academic, 1997), 9–10; James K. Cameron, "Theological Controversy: A Factor in the Origins of the Scottish Enlightenment", in *The Origins and Nature of the Scottish Enlightenment*, ed. R.H. Campbell and Andrew S. Skinner (Edinburgh: John Donald, 1982), 116–30; Robertson, *Case for the Enlightenment*, 261, 314–15.

96. *Gentleman's Magazine* 30 (November 1760): 505; ibid. (October 1760): 469; W.M. Jacob, "John Wesley and the Church of England", *Bulletin of the John Rylands University Library of Manchester* 85 (2003): 57; R.A. Knox, *Enthusiasm: A Chapter in the History of Religion, with Special Reference to the XVII and XVIII Centuries* (Oxford: Clarendon Press, 1950), 449–54; Bernard Semmel, *The Methodist Revolution* (London: Heinemann, 1974), 13-19; Hempton, *Methodism*, 33–43.

97. Henning Graf Reventlow, *The Authority of the Bible and the Rise of the Modern World* (London: SCM Press, 1984), 289–90; Preston, "Biblical Criticism", 121.

98. J.A.I. Champion, *The Pillars of Priestcraft Shaken: The Church of England and Its Enemies, 1660–1730* (Cambridge: Cambridge University Press, 1992), 121–22; Roland N. Stromberg, *Religious Liberalism in Eighteenth-Century England* (Oxford: Oxford University Press, 1954), 52–69; Reventlow, *Authority of the Bible*, 357.

99. Jonathan Israel, *Enlightenment Contested: Philosophy, Modernity, and the Emancipation of Man, 1670–1752* (Oxford: Oxford University Press, 2006), 116–17; Rivers, *Reason, Grace, and Sentiment*, 9–10, 23; Hill, *Milton and the English Revolution*, 285–305; Pocock, "Enthusiasm", 11; Thomas J. Schlereth, *The Cosmopolitan Ideal in Enlightenment Thought: Its Form and Function in the Ideas of Franklin, Hume, and Voltaire, 1694–1790* (Notre Dame, Ind.: University of Notre Dame Press, 1977), 74–75; Diego Lucci, *Scripture and Deism: The Biblical Criticism of the Eighteenth-Century British Deists* (Bern: Peter Lang, 2008), 17–18.

100. James A. Herrick, *The Radical Rhetoric of the English Deists: The Discourse of Skepticism, 1680–1750* (Columbia: University of South Carolina Press, 1997), 161–62; Schlereth, *Cosmopolitan Ideal*, 73, 81; Robertson, *Case for the Enlightenment*, 256–61; Joyce E. Chaplin, *The First Scientific American: Benjamin Franklin and the Pursuit of Genius* (New York: Basic Books, 2006), 51.

101. Fitzpatrick, "Enlightenment, Politics and Providence", 64; Champion, *Pillars of Priestcraft*, 231–32; Hill, *Milton and the English Revolution*, 251, 285; Reventlow, *Authority of the Bible*, 411; Stromberg, *Religious Liberalism*, x–xi; Richard Brown, *Church and State*, 97–101; E.J. Dijksterhuis, *The Mechanization of the World Picture: Pythagoras to Newton* (1950; reprint, Princeton, NJ: Princeton University Press, 1986), 491.

102. Girtin, *Doctor with Two Aunts*, 33, 42–50, 196; Robert L. Vales, *Peter Pindar (John Wolcot)* (New York: Twayne, 1973), 14–23; William R. Jones, "Wolcot, John (bap. 1738, d. 1819)", *Oxford Dictionary of National Biography* (2004). Cf. Gardner, *History of Jamaica*, 196.

103. *Columbian Magazine* 2 (January 1797): 497.

104. *Columbian Magazine* 1 (December 1796): 439n. Cf. Hill, *Milton and the English Revolution*, 251; Dijksterhuis, *Mechanization*, 491.
105. *Columbian Magazine* 1 (December 1796): 438.
106. Ibid., 435–36. Cf. Basil Willey, *The Eighteenth Century Background: Studies on the Idea of Nature in the Thought of the Period* (1940; reprint, London: Chatto and Windus, 1957), 65–67; Peter Byrne, *Natural Religion and the Nature of Religion: The Legacy of Deism* (London: Routledge, 1989), 1–10; Lucci, *Scripture and Deism*, 19.
107. Lindsay, *Memoirs*, 1:114–15; Lindsay, *Sermon*, 22; A.D. Nuttall, *Pope's "Essay on Man"* (London: George Allen and Unwin, 1984), 131; Pat Rogers, *Pope and the Destiny of the Stuarts: History, Politics, and Mythology in the Age of Queen Anne* (Oxford: Oxford University Press, 2005), 3; Willey, *Eighteenth Century Background*, 110–18.
108. Lindsay, *Memoirs*, 1:62–65; Andrew Cambers, " 'But Where Shall My Soul Repose?': Nonconformity, Science and the Geography of the Afterlife, c. 1660–1720", in *The Church, the Afterlife and the Fate of the* Soul, ed. Peter Clarke and Tony Claydon (Woodbridge, UK: Boydell Press, 2009), 268–69.
109. R. Elliot, "A Summary of Gospel Doctrine Taught by Mr Whitefield" (1770), in *Select Sermons of George Whitefield* (London: Banner of Truth Trust, 1964), 52–60; Stout, *Divine Dramatist*, 38–39; Frank Lambert, *"Pedlar in Divinity": George Whitefield and the Transatlantic Revivals, 1737–1770* (Princeton, NJ: Princeton University Press, 1994), 20–25; Kenneth J. Collins, "Rethinking the Systematic Nature of John Wesley's Theology", *Bulletin of the John Rylands University Library of Manchester* 85 (2003): 313–15; Ted A. Campbell, "John Wesley and the Legacy of Methodist Theology", *Bulletin of the John Rylands University Library of Manchester* 85 (2003): 407–9.
110. Lindsay, *Present state of the Church of Scotland*, 34–37. Cf. Matheson, *Theories of Rhetoric*, 190.
111. Henry Lindsay, *Christ's advocateship, practically discoursed from I. John, Chap. II. Ver. 1, 2. on the Monday after the celebration of the Lord's Supper, in the Talbooth Church of Edinburgh* (Edinburgh: printed by Alexander Alison for John Trail, 1734), 10; Burleigh, *Church History*, 292.
112. Henry Lindsay, *An essay upon 1 Corinth. Chap. i. vers. 21. against the infidelity of the age; and wherein is especially consider'd the wisdom of God, as to the time of Christianity, its being published to the world* (Edinburgh: "printed for Messrs Davidson and Trail and sold at their shop", 1736), 3, 6, 12–14, 35, 63–64. Henry Lindsay also published *A letter to the learned author of the Queries, being a detection of several errors and heresies contain'd in a pamphlet, entitled, Answer to the queries* (Edinburgh, 1737) and *The clergy's plea of conscience considereed: in an address to the author of a pamphlet, intituled, the letter to the learned author of the Queries unmasked* (Edinburgh, 1737). Cf. Scott, *Fasti Ecclesiæ*, 4:231.

Chapter 7

1. Long, *History of Jamaica*, 2:53–59, 67–74.
2. *Columbian Magazine* 2 (February 1797): 581; Lindsay, "Conjectural considerations", 189.
3. G.S. Rousseau, "Science Books and Their Readers in the Eighteenth Century", in *Books and Their Readers in Eighteenth-Century England*, ed. Isabel Rivers (Leices-

ter, UK: Leicester University Press, 1982), 224–25; P.B. Wood, "The Natural History of Man in the Scottish Enlightenment", *History of Science* 28 (1990): 89.

4. *Journals of the Assembly of Jamaica*, 11 December 1770, VI, 313.
5. *Journals of the Assembly of Jamaica*, 11 and 13 December 1770, VI, 313 and 317. Cf. *Gleaner*, 21 December 1929, 31.
6. Lindsay, "Hypothetical Doctrine of Water-spouts", 615; Ingram, *Sources of Jamaican History*, 1:67; 2:941; M.D. Crane, "Arthur Broughton, a Late Eighteenth Century Botanist in Bristol and Jamaica", *Archives of Natural History* 10 (1981): 320.
7. The "Elegancies" volume has the most ancient of the bindings, the others having been rebound sometime late in the twentieth century. Cf. Crane, "Arthur Broughton", 320; K.E. Ingram, *Manuscript Sources for the History of the West Indies* (Kingston: University of the West Indies Press, 2000), 345.
8. Lindsay, "Elegancies", 87–88. Plant identification by Nick Wray, Superintendent, University of Bristol Botanic Garden, 1998.
9. Quoted in Crane, "Arthur Broughton", 321, 328; Broughton Papers (Bristol Museum and Art Gallery); Kenneth Morgan, ed., *The Bright-Meyler Papers: A Bristol–West India Connection, 1732–1837* (Oxford: Oxford University Press/British Academy, 2007), 63–69.
10. In 1871 the Bristol Library Society merged with the Bristol Institution for the Advancement of Science, Literature and the Arts, creating the Bristol Museum and Library Association. Lindsay's volumes, along with the other elements of the Broughton bequest, were incorporated into the museum collections and remained with them when the museum was taken over by the City of Bristol and the library was separated. See Crane, "Arthur Broughton", 321–22; Ritterbush, "John Lindsay and the Sensitive Plant", 235; Minter, *Episcopacy Without Episcopate*, 178.
11. Rather than being lost, it appears that the volumes had been on long-term loan and, when finally returned, given to the library rather than the museum or sent to the library in error. In the second volume to be published of the seven-volume *Flora of Jamaica*, prepared by William Fawcett and Alfred Barton Rendle for the Natural History Section of the British Museum, Rendle's preface, dated November 1914, notes that since publication of the initial volume in 1910 they had "ascertained the existence in the Bristol Museum of an interesting collection made in Jamaica by Dr. Arthur Broughton between the years 1783 and 1796, together with a series of drawings (1761–69) by the Rev. John Lindsay, and we are indebted to the Bristol Museum for the loan of these". Fawcett and Rendle printed up labels on which they wrote their plant identifications and these labels were pasted on the bottom of many of the sheets of Lindsay's drawings. A cover page of volume 7 bears the stamp "AVON COUNTY LIBRARY, 11 SEP 1974" and declares the volume a "GIFT FROM MUSEUM", but all of this is over-stamped "WITHDRAWN", along with the note "Returned to Museum 15.6.78". A further volume of Lindsay's work may still survive in a location to be identified, and another may indeed have been destroyed in the Second World War. See William Fawcett and Alfred Barton Rendle, *Flora of Jamaica: Containing Descriptions of the Flowering Plants Known from the Island* (London: British Museum, 1914), 3:v; Cundall, *Historic Jamaica*, 95; Ingram, *Sources of Jamaican History*, 1:67–68; Ingram, *Manuscript Sources*, 345–46.
12. A gap of three to four years seems to be common. The "Elegancies" volume is paginated (in pencil) but the others are not. Some sheets bear the watermark of

the papermaker J. Whatman but are apparently undated, suggesting that the paper was made and used before 1794, when dates became a legal requirement. Cf. Thomas Balston, *James Whatman, Father and Son* (London: Methuen, 1957).

13. Lindsay, "Elegancies", 42. Reproduced in B.W. Higman, *Jamaican Food: History, Biology, Culture* (Kingston: University of the West Indies Press, 2008), 260.
14. Lindsay, "Elegancies", 63, 66, 77. The Guinea corn is reproduced in Higman, *Jamaican Food*, 212–13. Cf. Angela Lakwete, *Inventing the Cotton Gin: Machine and Myth in Antebellum America* (Baltimore: Johns Hopkins University Press, 2003), 32–34; Kay Dian Kriz, *Slavery, Sugar, and the Culture of Refinement: Picturing the British West Indies, 1700–1840* (New Haven, Conn.: Yale University Press, 2008), 29–30.
15. Lindsay, Drawings, vol. 6; *Columbian Magazine* 2 (January 1797): 497; Dijksterhuis, *Mechanization of the World Picture*, 491.
16. Lindsay, Drawings, vol. 6; Clement Ellis, *The Scripture Catechist: or, The Whole Religion of a Christian: Being a Full Explanation of the Church Catechism; Containing, a Comprehensive Body of Practical Divinity* (London: C. Rivington and J. Hutton, 1738).
17. Lindsay, Drawings, vol. 7 (turbutt [turbot]; reproduced in Higman, *Jamaican Food*, 261); Lindsay, "Elegancies", 187 (granadilla; reproduced in Higman, *Jamaican Food*, 173); Lindsay, Drawings, vol. 7 (parrot fish). The macaw has been identified by Ivan Goodbody.
18. Lindsay, Drawings, vol. 6, 2; ibid., vol. 7 (grunt; reproduced in Higman, *Jamaican Food*, 260–61).
19. Lindsay, Drawings, vol. 7 (flying fish, turtle and "sea lizzard"); Lindsay, "Elegancies", 84 (July-flower); Lindsay, Drawings, vol. 6 (spider). The turtle is reproduced in Higman, *Jamaican Food*, 260–61.
20. Lindsay, Drawings, vol. 7 ("blue grooper", Medusa's head and stadholder); Long, *History of Jamaica*, 2:72.
21. Ingram, *Sources of Jamaican History*, 1:202; Ritterbush, "John Lindsay and the Sensitive Plant", 235n12; T.D.A. Cockerell, "A Little Known Jamaican Naturalist, Dr. Anthony Robinson", *American Naturalist* 28 (1894): 775.
22. Lindsay, "Elegancies", 96; Lindsay, Drawings, vol. 6 (flying insects); ibid., vol. 7 (leather coat, hind fish, angel fish, ten pounder, mud unicorn and cutlass fish; reproduced in Higman, *Jamaican Food*, 309). Cf. Lindsay, Drawings, vol. 7 (mullet).
23. Lindsay, Drawings, vol. 7 (ten pounder, cone fish, leather coat and Medusa's head); Lindsay, "Elegancies", 48–57; William Hughes, *The American Physitian; or, a Treatise of the Roots, Plants, Trees, Shrubs, Fruit, Herbs, &c. Growing in the English Plantations in America* (London: William Crook, 1672); Higman, *Jamaican Food*, 172–73, 191–93.
24. Lindsay, Drawings, vol. 6. *Papilio* is the oldest generic name applied to butterflies and was applied by Linnaeus to all varieties known to him in 1758. See F. Martin Brown and Bernard Heineman, *Jamaica and Its Butterflies* (London: E.W. Classey, 1972), 322, 339; Kriz, *Slavery, Sugar*, 13–14; Therese O'Malley and Amy R.W. Meyers, eds., *The Art of Natural History: Illustrated Treatises and Botanical Paintings, 1400–1850* (Washington, DC: National Gallery of Art, 2008).
25. Arthur MacGregor, *Curiosity and Enlightenment: Collectors and Collections from the Sixteenth to the Nineteenth Century* (New Haven, Conn.: Yale University Press, 2007), 140–49.
26. Ibid., 120–22. See also Arthur MacGregor, ed., *Sir Hans Sloane: Collector, Scientist, Antiquary, Founding Father of the British Museum* (London: British Museum Press,

1994); Carl von Linné, *Flora Jamaicensis* (Uppsala: 1759); Gabriel Elmgren, *Plantarum Jamaicensium Pugillus* (Uppsala: 1759), a thesis supervised by Linnaeus.

27. Lindsay, Drawings, vol. 6. On naming practices, see Londa Schiebinger, *Plants and Empire: Colonial Bioprospecting in the Atlantic World* (Cambridge, Mass.: Harvard University Press, 2004), 219–24.
28. Long, *History of Jamaica*, 2:134–37.
29. Long Mss, Add. 22678, f. 17 (British Library, London); Dancer to Long, 6 April 1788, Long Mss, Add. 22678, f. 3; Dancer, "A brief account of the culture and uses of the cinnamon tree", Long Mss, Add. 22678, ff. 19–27.
30. "Abstract of an oration deliver'd at a Board of Directors under the new Act (1789) respecting the Bath and the Botanic Garden in Jamaica by T. Dancer M.D., Island Botanist, 1 March 1790", Long Mss, Add. 22678, f. 35. For Kew, see Richard Drayton, *Nature's Government: Science, Imperial Britain, and the "Improvement" of the World* (New Haven, Conn.: Yale University Press, 2000).
31. Long Mss, Add. 22678, ff. 36–41. Cf. Douglas Hall, "Botanical and Horticultural Enterprise in Eighteenth-Century Jamaica", in *West Indies Accounts: Essays on the History of the British Caribbean and the Atlantic Economy in Honour of Richard Sheridan*, ed. Roderick A. McDonald (Kingston: University of the West Indies Press, 1996), 101–25.
32. Crane, "Arthur Broughton", 317–19; G. Munro Smith, *A History of the Bristol Royal Infirmary* (Bristol: J.W. Arrowsmith, 1917), 133.
33. A.B. Rendle, "Three Early Jamaican Botanists", *Journal of Botany* 53 (1915): 104; William Fawcett, "Notes on Jamaica Plants", *Journal of Botany* 55 (1917): 37–38; Crane, "Arthur Broughton", 321.
34. Ray Desmond, *Dictionary of British and Irish Botanists and Horticulturists* (London: Taylor and Francis, 1977), 38; Crane, "Arthur Broughton", 326–27n31; John Lunan, *Hortus Jamaicensis, or a Botanical Description, (According to the Linnean System) and an Account of the Virtues, &c. of its Indigenous Plants Hitherto Unknown, as also of the Most Useful Exotics* (Spanish Town: St Jago de la Vega Gazette, 1814), iii.
35. Dancer to Long, 28 December 1790, Long Mss, Add. 22678, f. 57 (British Library, London); Henry Barham, *Hortus Americanus: Containing an Account of the Trees, Shrubs, and Other Vegetable Productions, of South-America and the West-India Islands, and Particularly of the Island of Jamaica* (Kingston: Alexander Aikman, 1794), 5–7.
36. Patrick Browne, *The Civil and Natural History of Jamaica* (London: T. Osborne and J. Shipton, 1756), iv, vii, lxx [70], ccclxxix [379]; Stafleu, *Linnaeus and the Linnaeans*, 202–3; Raymond Phineas Stearns, *Science in the British Colonies of America* (Urbana: University of Illinois Press, 1970), 376–78; Fawcett and Rendle, *Flora of Jamaica*, 4: xv.
37. Stafleu, *Linnaeus and the Linnaeans*, 203; Fawcett and Rendle, *Flora of Jamaica*, 4:xv.
38. Ingram, *Sources of Jamaican History*, 1:202; 2:927–30; Cockerell, "Little Known Jamaican Naturalist", 775.
39. Anthony Robinson, "Birds of Jamaica", vol. 1, ms 178 (National Library of Jamaica, Kingston). Lunan used these; see *Hortus Jamaicensis*, i. Philip Henry Gosse saw more of Robinson's work in the 1840s, referring, for example, to his observations of the manatee and the cane-piece rat. Philip Henry Gosse, *A Naturalist's Sojourn in Jamaica* (London: Longman, Brown, Green, and Longmans, 1851), 348, 445; Philip Henry Gosse, *The Birds of Jamaica* (London: John van Voorst, 1847).

40. Dr John Lindsay, "Account of the Germination and Raising of Ferns from the Seed", *Transactions of the Linnean Society* (London), 2 (1794): 93–100; Crane, "Arthur Broughton", 321; Philip C. Ritterbush, *Overtures to Biology: The Speculations of Eighteenth-Century Naturalists* (New Haven, Conn.: Yale University Press, 1964), 148, 192–93, plate 6; Ritterbush, "John Lindsay and the Sensitive Plant", 233–36. Ritterbush contends that the original 1788 manuscript was in fact written by Rev. John Lindsay, but there is no basis to this argument. Cf. Ingram, *Sources of Jamaican History*, 2:941; *Memoir of the Late William Wright, M.D., Fellow of the Royal Societies of London and Edinburgh, etc. with Extracts from His Correspondence, and a Selection of His Papers on Medical and Botanical Subjects* (Edinburgh: William Blackwood, 1828), 200; Ingram, *Sources of Jamaican History*, 1:68.

41. Ingram, *Sources of Jamaican History*, 2:938–39; Rendle, "Three Early Jamaican Botanists", 106; Trevor Burnard, *Mastery, Tyranny, and Desire: Thomas Thistlewood and His Slaves in the Anglo-Jamaican World* (Chapel Hill: University of North Carolina Press, 2004), 119; Ritterbush, "John Lindsay and the Sensitive Plant", 234; Lorraine Daston and Katharine Park, *Wonders and the Order of Nature, 1150–1750* (New York: Zone Books, 1998), 316–28.
42. *Memoir of the Late William Wright*, 1–3, 11; Norris D. Saakwa- Mante, "William Wright (1735–1819), Military Physician and Naturalist", *Oxford Dictionary of National Biography* (2004).
43. *Memoir of the Late William Wright*, 27–29, 33–34, 44; William Fawcett, "William Wright, a Jamaican Botanist (1735–1819)", *Journal of Botany* 60 (1922): 330–31.
44. William Wright, Edinburgh, to Chaloner Archdeckine, London, 1 March 1788, Vanneck-Arcedeckne Papers, 3G/3 (Cambridge University Library); *Memoir of the Late William Wright*, 15–16, 88. Cf. Ward, "Sensibility, Tropical Disease", 70.
45. Saakwa-Mante, "William Wright"; Fawcett, "William Wright", 333; Wright to Banks, 12 July 1783, Papers of Sir Joseph Banks, www.sl.nsw.gov.au/Banks/. Cf. *Memoir of the Late William Wright*, 246.
46. Lindsay, "Conjectural considerations", 121; Charles W.J. Withers, "Improvement and Enlightenment: Agriculture and Natural History in the Work of the Rev. Dr. John Walker (1731–1803)", in *Philosophy and Science in the Scottish Enlightenment*, ed. Peter Jones (Edinburgh: John Donald, 1988), 105–6. Cf. Brian W. Ogilvie, *The Science of Describing: Natural History in Renaissance Europe* (Chicago: University of Chicago Press, 2006), 268–71; Harold J. Cook, *Matters of Exchange: Commerce, Medicine, and Science in the Dutch Golden Age* (New Haven, Conn.: Yale University Press, 2007), 411.
47. Minter, *Episcopacy Without Episcopate*, 55, 131, 177, 181, 309.
48. Craik, "Geometry, Analysis", 41–51; Minter, *Episcopacy Without Episcopate*, 61–62, 179, 309.
49. Jan Golinski, *British Weather and the Climate of Enlightenment* (Chicago: University of Chicago Press, 2007), 193–95; Willey, *Eighteenth Century Background*, 111; Minter, *Episcopacy Without Episcopate*, 178.
50. Benjamin Franklin, *Experiments and Observations on Electricity, Made at Philadelphia in America* (London: David Henry, 1769), 216–33; Lindsay, "Conjectural considerations", 132; Chaplin, *First Scientific American*, 19; Stout, *Divine Dramatist*, 220–33; Lambert, *"Pedlar in Divinity"*, 63, 110–13; Schlereth, *Cosmopolitan Ideal*, 73, 81;

I. Bernard Cohen, *Benjamin Franklin's Science* (Cambridge, Mass.: Harvard University Press, 1990), 30; Robertson, *Case for the Enlightenment*, 256–61.

51. Lindsay, "Hypothetical Doctrine of Water-spouts", 559.
52. [Robert Dixon], "An authentic account of a water spout, which mostly fell upon Brackenthwaite in the County of Cumberland, on Sept. 19, 1760; by an Eye-witness", *Gentleman's Magazine* 30 (November 1760): 520–22; Lindsay, "Hypothetical Doctrine of Water-spouts", 560n, 616n. Cf. Marie Peters, "Early Hanoverian Consciousness: Empire or Europe?" *English Historical Review* 122 (2007): 646–50.
53. Lindsay, "Hypothetical Doctrine of Water-spouts", 559.
54. Ibid., 559.
55. Ibid., 559–60.
56. Ibid., 560.
57. Franklin, *Experiments and Observations*, 221; Lindsay, "Hypothetical Doctrine of Water-spouts", 560; W.E. Knowles Middleton, *A History of Theories of Rain and Other Forms of Precipitation* (New York: Franklin Watts, 1966), 60.
58. Edward Aguado and James E. Burt, *Understanding Weather and Climate* (Upper Saddle River, NJ: Pearson Education, 2004), 350–51; Michalis V. Sioutas and Alexander G. Keul, "Waterspouts of the Adriatic, Ionian and Aegean Sea and Their Meteorological Environment", *Atmospheric Research* 83 (2007): 543–44.
59. Lindsay, "Hypothetical Doctrine of Water-spouts", 615; Chaplin, *First Scientific American*, 148; Chaplin, "Knowing the Ocean", 84–86.
60. Lindsay, Letter on waterspouts, 1027–28; Chaplin, "Knowing the Ocean", 86.
61. Lindsay, "Hypothetical Doctrine of Water-spouts", 616; Smith, *New Voyage to Guinea*, 55–56; Leslie, *New and Exact Account*, 6; R.M.N., "Charms against Waterspouts", *Mariner's Mirror* 6 (1920): 160; G.C. Wallis, "The Custom of 'Cutting a Waterspout' ", *Mariner's Mirror* 63 (1977): 106; Henning Henningsen, "Superstitions about Waterspouts", *Mariner's Mirror* 63 (1977): 193–94.
62. Lindsay, Letter on waterspouts, 1025–26. Cf. Middleton, *History of Theories of Rain*, 23–36.
63. Lindsay, Letter on waterspouts, 1026–27; Daston and Park, *Wonders and the Order of Nature*, 324–28.
64. John Lindsey [*sic*], Letter on whirlwinds, *Gentleman's Magazine* 55, no. 2 (1785): 594.
65. Ibid., 594–95.
66. Ibid., 595; José Carlos Millás, *Hurricanes of the Caribbean and Adjacent Regions, 1492–1800* (Miami: Academy of the Arts and Sciences of the Americas, 1968), 220–81; Michael Chenoweth, *The 18th Century Climate of Jamaica: Derived from the Journals of Thomas Thistlewood, 1750–1786* (Philadelphia: American Philosophical Society, 2003), 5–8, 110.
67. Lindsey, Letter on whirlwinds, 597.
68. Ibid., 598. In 1788 Lindsay ("Conjectural considerations", 132) mentions Franklin's "Letter to Mr. Nairne, of London, from Dr. Franklin, Proposing a Slowly Sensible Hygrometer for Certain Purposes", *Transactions of the American Philosophical Society*, 2 (1786): 51–56.

Chapter 8

1. Lindsay, "Conjectural considerations". The manuscript was presented to the British Museum by C.E. Long on 8 March 1842.
2. Lindsay to Long, Long Mss, Add. 18959, 18 (British Library, London); Folarin Shyllon, *James Ramsay: The Unknown Abolitionist* (Edinburgh: Canongate, 1977), 131.
3. Lindsay, "Conjectural considerations", 9, 25.
4. Ibid., 102, 127.
5. Lindsay to Long, Long Mss., Add. 18959, 18; James Ramsay, *An Essay on the Treatment and Conversion of African Slaves in the British Sugar Colonies* (Dublin: T. Walker, C. Jenkin, R. Marchbank, L. White, R. Burton and P. Byrne, 1784); James Ramsay, *An Inquiry into the Effects of Putting a Stop to the African Slave Trade, and of Granting Liberty to the Slaves in the British Sugar Colonies* (London: James Phillips, 1784).
6. Miguel Cervantes Saavedra, *Don Quixote of La Mancha*, trans. and ed. Walter Starkie (London: Macmillan, 1954), 118–28, 188–90.
7. Thomas Clarkson, *An Essay on the Slavery and Commerce of the Human Species, Particularly the African* (1788; reprint, New York: AMS Press, 1972); Roger Anstey, *The Atlantic Slave Trade and British Abolition, 1760–1810* (London: Macmillan, 1975), 248–50; Shyllon, *James Ramsay*, 1–3.
8. Lindsay, "Conjectural considerations", 9; Lindsay to Long, Long Mss, Add. 18959, 18.
9. Anstey, *Atlantic Slave Trade*, 267–70; Shyllon, *James Ramsay*, 87–91.
10. Lindsay to Long, Long Mss, Add. 18959, 18.
11. Edward Long, *Candid Reflections upon the Judgement Lately Awarded by the Court of King's Bench, in Westminster-Hall, on what is Commonly Called the Negro-Cause, by a Planter* (London: T. Lowndes, 1772); Samuel Estwick, *Considerations on the Negroe Cause Commonly so Called, Addressed to the Right Honourable Lord Mansfield, Lord Chief Justice of the Court of King's Bench, &c.* (London: J. Dodsley, 1773); James Tobin ("Friend to the West India Colonies and Their Inhabitants"), *Cursory Remarks upon the Reverend Mr Ramsay's Essay on the Treatment and Conversion of African Slaves in the Sugar Colonies* (London: G. and T. Wilkie, 1785); David L. Crosby, "Anthony Benezet's Transformation of Anti-Slavery Rhetoric", *Slavery and Abolition* 23 (2002): 39–41; Christopher Brown, *Moral Capital*, 96–98, 364–75, 396–98; Swaminathan, "Developing the West Indian Proslavery Position", 46–50; Shyllon, *James Ramsay*, 42–74, 98–99; Vincent Carretta, *Equiano, the African: Biography of a Self-Made Man* (New York: Penguin, 2006), 257–60.
12. Lindsay, "Conjectural considerations", 25, 108.
13. Lindsay to Long, Long Mss, Add. 18959, 18. Long added occasional short sentences and a longer passage extracted from Gibbon's *Decline and Fall* of 1776. Lindsay, "Conjectural considerations", 80–82. Cf. Ritterbush, "John Lindsay and the Sensitive Plant", 235–36.
14. Lindsay, "Conjectural considerations", 8; Mayo, "Manners and Manuscripts", 67–68.
15. Lindsay to Long, Long Mss, Add. 18959, 18.
16. Ibid., 18.
17. Ibid., 18; Howard, *Records and Letters*, 1:43.
18. Long Mss, Add. 12438, 1. All of this was intended to contribute, *inter alia*, to the

proposed new edition of his *History of Jamaica*. Dancer to Long, 28 December 1790, Long Mss, Add. 22678, 57; Long Mss, Add. 12429.

19. Lindsay, "Conjectural considerations", 3, 40.
20. Ibid., 29–30. Cf. James Hervey, *Remarks on Lord Bolingbroke's Letters on the Study and Use of History: So Far as They Relate to the History of the Old Testament; and Especially to the Case of Noah, Denouncing a Curse upon Canaan* (London: J. and J. Rivington, 1752); Mr de P**** [Cornélius de Pauw], *Recherches philosophiques sur les Américains, ou, Mémoires intéressants pour servir à l'histoire de l'espece humaine* (London: 1770), 1:176.
21. Lindsay, "Conjectural considerations", 30.
22. Ibid., 30.
23. Ibid., 31. Cf. Sankar Muthu, *Enlightenment Against Empire* (Princeton, NJ: Princeton University Press, 2003), 183–85; Robert Wokler, "Apes and Races in the Scottish Enlightenment: Monboddo and Kames on the Nature of Man", in *Philosophy and Science in the Scottish Enlightenment*, ed. Peter Jones (Edinburgh: John Donald, 1988), 156; Clarence J. Glacken, *Traces on the Rhodian Shore: Nature and Culture in Western Thought from Ancient Times to the End of the Eighteenth Century* (Berkeley: University of California Press, 1967), 608.
24. Lindsay, "Conjectural considerations", 25.
25. Ibid., 57.
26. Ibid., 143.
27. Ibid., 17–20; Peter Jimack, ed., *A History of the Two Indies: A Translated Selection of Writings from Raynal's* Histoire philosophique et politique des établissements des Européens dans les deux Indes (Alderhsot, UK: Ashgate, 2006), ix–xiii; Muthu, *Enlightenment Against Empire*, 72; Roger Mercier, "L'Amérique et les Américains dans *l'Histoire des deux Indes* de l'abbé Raynal", *Revue Française Histoire Outre-Mer* 65 (1978): 308–24.
28. Robert Wokler, "Anthropology and Conjectural History in the Enlightenment", in *Inventing Human Science: Eighteenth-Century Domains*, ed. Christopher Fox, Roy Porter and Robert Wokler (Berkeley: University of California Press, 1995), 34–35; David Allan, *Virtue, Learning and the Scottish Enlightenment: Ideas of Scholarship in Early Modern History* (Edinburgh: Edinburgh University Press, 1993), 151–54; Nicholas Hudson, *Writing and European Thought, 1600–1830* (Cambridge: Cambridge University Press, 1994), 56–75; Dugald Stewart, "Account of the Life and Writings of Adam Smith, LL.D.", ed. I.S. Ross, in *Adam Smith: Essays on Philosophical Subjects*, ed. W.P.D. Wightman and J.C. Bryce (Oxford: Clarendon Press, 1980), 292; Griswold, *Adam Smith*, 163.
29. Stewart, "Account of the Life and Writings of Adam Smith", 293. See also Wood, "Natural History of Man", 111–15; Larry Wolff and Marco Cipollini, eds., *The Anthropology of the Enlightenment* (Stanford, Calif.: Stanford University Press, 2007); Aaron Garrett, "Anthropology: The 'Original' of Human Nature", in *The Cambridge Companion to the Scottish Enlightenment*, ed. Alexander Broadie (Cambridge: Cambridge University Press, 2003), 79–80.
30. Adam Ferguson, *An Essay on the History of Civil Society*, ed. Fania Oz-Salzberger (Cambridge: Cambridge University Press, 1995), 1, 8, 247; Annette Meyer, "Ferguson's 'Appropriate Stile' in Combining History and Science: The History of Historiography Revisited", in *Adam Ferguson: History, Progress and Human Nature*, ed.

Eugene Heath and Vincenzo Merolle (London: Pickering and Chatto, 2008), 134–45.

31. Immanuel Kant, *Essays and Treatises on Moral, Political, and Various Philosophical Subjects* vol. 1 (London: William Richardson, 1798), 317–36. Cf. Wilkins, *Species*, 85–89; Muthu, *Enlightenment Against Empire*, 126, 184–85; Ivan Hannaford, *Race: The History of an Idea in the West* (Baltimore: Johns Hopkins University Press, 1996), 218–24; Lois Whitney, *Primitivism and the Idea of Progress in English Popular Literature of the Eighteenth Century* (Baltimore: Johns Hopkins University Press, 1934), 145–54; Naomi Zack, *Philosophy of Science and Race* (New York: Routledge, 2002), 18–24; Chen, "Providence and Progress", 174–76.
32. Lindsay, "Conjectural considerations", 9, 12, 56, 80.
33. Wahrman, *Making of the Modern Self*, 112; Nicholas Hudson, "From 'Nation' to 'Race': The Origin of Racial Classification in Eighteenth-Century Thought", *Eighteenth-Century Studies* 29 (1996): 247–48; Bruce Dain, *A Hideous Monster of the Mind: American Race Theory in the Early Republic* (Cambridge, Mass.: Harvard University Press, 2002), 6–8.
34. Long, *History of Jamaica*, 2:353; Pestana, *English Atlantic*, 180; Hudson, "From 'Nation' to 'Race' ", 248; Stewart J. Brown, "An Eighteenth-Century Historian on the Amerindians: Culture, Colonialism and Christianity in William Robertson's *History of America*", *Studies in World Christianity* 2 (1996): 204–22; Jeffrey Smitten, "Impartiality in Robertson's *History of America*", *Eighteenth-Century Studies* 19 (1985): 58–62; Jeffrey Smitten, "Moderatism and History: William Robertson's Unfinished History of British America", in *Scotland and America in the Age of the Enlightenment*, ed. Richard B. Sher and Jeffrey R. Smitten (Edinburgh: Edinburgh University Press, 1990), 174; D.J. Womersley, "Historical Writings of William Robertson", 497–506.
35. Zack, *Philosophy of Science and Race*, 1–2; Hudson, "From 'Nation' to 'Race' ", 251; Ann Thomson, *Bodies of Thought: Science, Religion, and the Soul in the Early Enlightenment* (Oxford: Oxford University Press, 2008), 239.
36. Lisbet Koerner, *Linnaeus: Nature and Nation* (Cambridge, Mass.: Harvard University Press, 1999), 57, 87–88; Wilkins, *Species*, 70–74; Gladys Bryson, *Man and Society: The Scottish Inquiry of the Eighteenth Century* (Princeton, NJ: Princeton University Press, 1945), 74; Colin Kidd, *The Forging of Races: Race and Scripture in the Protestant Atlantic World, 1600–2000* (Cambridge: Cambridge University Press, 2006), 9; Dain, *Hideous Monster*, 9–13; Hudson, "From 'Nation' to 'Race' ", 253; Felicity A. Nussbaum, *The Limits of the Human: Fictions of Anomaly, Race, and Gender in the Long Eighteenth Century* (Cambridge: Cambridge University Press, 2003), 11.
37. Sarah A. Tishkoff et al., "The Genetic Structure and History of Africans and African Americans", *Science* 324 (22 May 2009): 1035; Joshua Glasgow, *A Theory of Race* (New York: Routledge, 2009); Ricki Lewis, *Human Genetics: Concepts and Applications* (Boston: McGraw-Hill, 2008); Lorena Madrigal and Guido Barbujani, "Partitioning of Genetic Variation in Human Populations and the Concept of Race", in *Anthropological Genetics: Theory, Methods and Applications*, ed. Michael H. Crawford (Cambridge: Cambridge University Press, 2007), 20; Stephen Molnar, *Human Variation: Races, Types, and Ethnic Groups* (Upper Saddle River, NJ: Prentice Hall, 2002), 1–30; Peter Beurton, Raphael Falk and Hans-Jörg Rheinberger, eds., *The Concept of the Gene in Development and Evolution: Historical and Epistemological Per-*

spectives (Cambridge: Cambridge University Press, 2000); Miriam Eliav-Feldon, Benjamin Isaac and Joseph Ziegler, eds., *The Origins of Racism in the West* (Cambridge: Cambridge University Press, 2009).

38. Alden T. Vaughan, "From White Man to Redskin: Changing Anglo-American Perceptions of the American Indian", *American Historical Review* 87 (1982): 918.
39. Lindsay, "Conjectural considerations", 37, 156; Arthur O. Lovejoy, *The Great Chain of Being: A Study of the History of an Idea* (1936; reprint, Cambridge, Mass: Harvard University Press, 1964), 186–89.
40. Lindsay, "Conjectural considerations", 36–37; Wheeler, *Complexion of Race*, 178–81.
41. Lindsay, "Conjectural considerations", 156.
42. Ibid., 36–37.
43. Lovejoy, *Great Chain of Being*, 189–90; Wilkins, *Species*, 50–53; James Daly, *Cosmic Harmony and Political Thinking in Early Stuart England* (Philadelphia: American Philosophical Society, 1979), 3.
44. Lindsay, "Conjectural considerations", 10, 25; Bryson, *Man and Society*, 66–74; Wokler, "Apes and Races", 161–63; David N. Livingstone, *Adam's Ancestors: Race, Religion, and the Politics of Human Origins* (Baltimore: Johns Hopkins University Press, 2008), 69–73.
45. Christie, *Diary of the Rev. William Jones*, 25–26.
46. Long, *History of Jamaica*, 2:371; Livingstone, *Adam's Ancestors*, 69. Cf. Thomson, *Bodies of Thought*, 77–79, 243; Wokler, "Apes and Races", 161–63; Wheeler, *Complexion of Race*, 213–14.
47. Long, *History of Jamaica*, 2:372; Koerner, *Linnaeus*, 57, 87–88; Hudson, "From 'Nation' to 'Race' ", 253; Nussbaum, *Limits of the Human*, 11; Livingstone, *Adam's Ancestors*, 68; Wokler, "Anthropology and Conjectural History", 34–36. Cf. Wheeler, *Complexion of Race*, 232.
48. Lindsay, "Conjectural considerations", 10.
49. Ibid., 12. On Wheatley and Sancho, see Ellis, *Politics of Sensibility*, 55–67, 79–86; Helen Thomas, *Romanticism and Slave Narratives: Transatlantic Testimonies* (Cambridge: Cambridge University Press, 2000), 201–8; Maurice Jackson, "Diasporan Voices of the African Past: James Albert Ukawsaw Gronniosaw, Quobna Ottobah Cugoano, Olaoudah Equiano, and Ignatius Sancho as Sources of African History", in *The Changing Worlds of Atlantic Africa: Essays in Honor of Robin Law*, ed. Toyin Falola and Matt D. Childs (Durham, NC: Carolina Academic Press, 2009), 366–69; Brycchan Carey, *British Abolitionism and the Rhetoric of Sensibility: Writing, Sentiment, and Slavery, 1760–1807* (Houndmills, UK: Palgrave Macmillan, 2005), 57–63. For Burns, see Robert Crawford, "Burns, Robert (1759–1796)", *Oxford Dictionary of National Biography* (2004).
50. Lindsay, "Conjectural considerations", 27.
51. Ibid., 27, 32–34, 46, 49.
52. Ibid., 41, 44.
53. Ibid., 39.
54. Ibid., 40–41, 49–50, 52, 55.
55. Ibid., 41; Nicholas Hudson, " 'Oral Tradition': The Evolution of an Eighteenth-Century Concept", in *Tradition in Transition: Women Writers, Marginal Texts, and the Eighteenth-Century Canon* (Oxford: Clarendon Press, 1996), 161–67.

56. Lindsay, "Conjectural considerations", 25.
57. Ibid., 56–57.
58. Ibid., 57–59. Cf. Keith Thomson, *Before Darwin: Reconciling God and Nature* (New Haven, Conn.: Yale University Press, 2005), 187–93.
59. Lindsay, "Conjectural considerations", 59; Livingstone, *Adam's Ancestors*; Philip Almond, "Adam, Pre-Adamites, and Extra-Terrestrial Beings in Early Modern Europe", *Journal of Religious History* 30 (2006): 174; Howard Eilberg-Schwartz, *The Savage in Judaism: An Anthropology of Israelite Religion and Ancient Judaism* (Bloomington: Indiana University Press, 1990), 39–41; Kidd, *Forging of Races*, 34; Nussbaum, *Limits of the Human*, 11.
60. Lindsay, "Conjectural considerations", 29, 56. Cf. Kidd, *Forging of Races*, 33–35.
61. Lindsay, "Conjectural considerations", 71; William McKee Evans, "From the Land of Canaan to the Land of Guinea: The Strange Odyssey of the 'Sons of Ham' ", *American Historical Review* 85 (1980): 17; Stephen R. Haynes, *Noah's Curse: The Biblical Justification of American Slavery* (Oxford: Oxford University Press, 2002), 6–8; Irons, *Origins of Proslavery Christianity*, 25; Kidd, *Forging of Races*, 39–41; Vaughan, "From White Man to Redskin", 920. Cf. Peter Rowley-Conwy, *From Genesis to Prehistory: The Archaeological Three Age System and Its Contested Reception in Denmark, Britain, and Ireland* (Oxford: Oxford University Press, 2007), 8–9.
62. Lindsay, "Conjectural considerations", 51, 63; William Dodd, *The Wisdom and Goodness of God, in the Vegetable Creation: A Sermon Preached at St. Martin's Church, Ludgate, on September the 20th, 1759, Before the Worshipful Company of Apothecaries* (London: L. Davis, C. Reymers and W. Bristow, 1760), 2–4; William Dodd, *A Commentary on the Books of the Old and New Testament* (London: R. Davis, L. Davis, T. Carnan and F. Newbery, 1770), 1: Genesis 3; Rawlings, "Dodd, William"; O.M. Brack Jr, *The Macaroni Parson and the Concentrated Mind: Samuel Johnson's Writings for the Reverend William Dodd* (n.p.: Samuel Johnson Society of Southern California, 2004), 1–4.
63. Dodd, *Commentary*, 1: Genesis 9:22–25. Cf. David M. Whitford, *The Curse of Ham in the Early Modern Era: The Bible and the Justifications for Slavery* (Farnham, UK: Ashgate, 2009), 1–17; Bill T. Arnold, *Genesis* (Cambridge: Cambridge University Press, 2009), 112–17.
64. Lindsay, "Conjectural considerations", 71. Cf. de Pauw, *Recherches philosophiques*, 1:176; Kidd, *Forging of Races*, 41–43.
65. Ian Simpson Ross, *Lord Kames and the Scotland of His Day* (Oxford: Clarendon Press, 1972); Alastair J. Durie and Stuart Handley, "Home, Henry, Lord Kames (1696–1782)", *Oxford Dictionary of National Biography* (2004).
66. Lindsay, "Conjectural considerations", 83–85; Henry Home, Lord Kames, *Sketches of the History of Man* (Edinburgh: W. Creech, W. Strahan and T. Cadell, 1774), 1:38–39; Glacken, *Traces on the Rhodian Shore*, 595–96; Bryson, *Man and Society*, 64–65.
67. Lindsay, "Conjectural considerations", 67.
68. Ibid., 66–67.
69. Ibid., 107.
70. Ross, *Lord Kames*, 333–48; Bryson, *Man and Society*, 64–66; Glacken, *Traces on the Rhodian Shore*, 596; Kimihiro Koyanagi, "Civilization and History in Lord Kames and William Robertson", in *The Rise of Political Economy in the Scottish Enlighten-*

ment, ed. Tatsuya Sakamoto and Hideo Tanaka (London: Routledge, 2003), 160; Kidd, *Forging of Races*, 95–100.

71. Wokler, "Apes and Races", 162; Glacken, *Traces on the Rhodian Shore*, 565; Andrew Curran, "Rethinking Race History: The Role of the Albino in the French Enlightenment Life Sciences", *History and Theory* 48 (2009): 172–74.
72. Kames, *Sketches*, 1:4; Lindsay, "Conjectural considerations", 79–80.
73. Lindsay, "Conjectural considerations", 81; Kames, *Sketches*, 1:15, 37.
74. Lindsay, "Conjectural considerations", 89, 107; [Georges-Louis Leclerc], Count de Buffon, *The Natural History of Animals, Vegetables, and Minerals; with the Theory of the Earth in General* (London: T. Bell, 1775), 1:171; Curran, "Rethinking Race History", 162–71.
75. Buffon, *Natural History*, 1:270; Hudson, "From 'Nation' to 'Race' ", 253–54; Dain, *Hideous Monster*, 14–18; Glacken, *Traces on the Rhodian Shore*, 588–89; Nussbaum, *Limits of the Human*, 11; Wilkins, *Species*, 75–79; Phillip Sloan, "The Gaze of Natural History", in *Inventing Human Science: Eighteenth-Century Domains*, ed. Christopher Fox, Roy Porter and Robert Wokler (Berkeley: University of California Press, 1995), 134–39; Tzvetan Todorov, *On Human Diversity: Nationalism, Racism, and Exoticism in French Thought* (Cambridge, Mass.: Harvard University Press, 1993), 96–106.
76. Lindsay, "Conjectural considerations", 89–91.
77. Ibid., 91, 93, 104–6.
78. Ibid., 114, 117–19, 121, 123; Long, *History of Jamaica*, 2:351–63; de Pauw, *Recherches philosophiques*; Curran, "Rethinking Race History", 178.
79. Lindsay, "Conjectural considerations", 125, 127. Cf. de Pauw, *Recherches philosophiques*, 1:57; 2:153.
80. Lindsay, "Conjectural considerations", 148–49; Pernety, *Dissertation*, in de Pauw, *Recherches philosophiques*, vol. 2; Antonello Gerbi, *The Dispute of the New World: The History of a Polemic, 1750–1900* (Pittsburgh: University of Pittsburgh Press, 1973), 240–43; Wokler, "Apes and Races", 159–60; Sean X. Goudie, *Creole America: The West Indies and the Formation of Literature and Culture in the New Republic* (Philadelphia: University of Pennsylvania Press, 2006), 7.
81. Lindsay, "Conjectural considerations", 151–54; Susan Scott Parrish, *American Curiosity: Cultures of Natural History in the Colonial British Atlantic World* (Chapel Hill: University of North Carolina Press, 2006), 238–39.
82. Lindsay, "Conjectural considerations", 154; Charles E. Ronan, *Francisco Javier Clavigero, S.J. (1731–1787), Figure of the Mexican Enlightenment: His Life and Works* (Rome: Institutum Historicum S.I., 1977), 246–52.
83. D. Francesco Saverio Clavigero, *The History of Mexico: Collected from Spanish and Mexican Historians, from Manuscripts, and Ancient Paintings of the Indians; Illustrated by Charts, and other Copper Plates; To which are added, Critical Dissertations on the Land, the Animals, and Inhabitants of Mexico* (London: G.G.J. and J. Robinson, 1787); *Critical Review* 63 (1787): 410–17; D.A. Brading, *The First America: The Spanish Monarchy, Creole Patriots, and the Liberal State, 1492–1867* (Cambridge: Cambridge University Press, 1991), 450–52.
84. Lindsay, "Conjectural considerations", 153; Clavigero, *History of Mexico*, 1:78–82; *Critical Review* 63 (1787): 415; Jeffrey R. Smitten, "Moderatism and History", 167–68.

85. Ronan, *Francisco Javier Clavigero*, 254; Brading, *First America*, 453; *Critical Review* 63 (1787): 413.
86. Lindsay, "Conjectural considerations", 79; Thomson, *Bodies of Thought*, 241; Rivers, *Reason, Grace*, 257–58; Nussbaum, *Limits of the Human*, 12.
87. Lindsay, "Conjectural considerations", 151; Patrick Wyse Jackson, *The Chronologers' Quest: Episodes in the Search for the Age of the Earth* (Cambridge: Cambridge University Press, 2006), 19–27; John McManners, ed., *The Oxford History of Christianity* (Oxford: Oxford University Press, 1993), 4; Tishkoff, "Genetic Structure", 1035.
88. Pascal Richet, *A Natural History of Time* (Chicago: University of Chicago Press, 2007), 122–36; Jackson, *Chronologers' Quest*, 111–18; Claude C. Albritton Jr, *The Abyss of Time: Changing Conceptions of the Earth's Antiquity after the Sixteenth Century* (San Francisco: Freeman, Cooper, 1980), 84–86; Claude C. Albritton Jr, *Catastrophic Episodes in Earth History* (London: Chapman and Hall, 1989), 20–23; Rhoda Rappaport, *When Geologists Were Historians, 1665–1750* (Ithaca, NY: Cornell University Press, 1997), 254; Glacken, *Traces on the Rhodian Shore*, 407, 666; Richard J. Chorley, Antony J. Dunn and Robert P. Beckinsale, *The History of the Study of Landforms or the Development of Geomorphology* (London: Methuen, 1964), 1:13.
89. Lindsay, "Conjectural considerations", 33, 81; Kames, *Sketches*, 1:26, 38–43; Garrett, "Anthropology", 88–89.
90. Lindsay, "Conjectural considerations", 80, 83; Long Mss, Add. 12438, 1–2, 12. Cf. Sloan, "Gaze of Natural History", 137; Wheeler, *Complexion of Race*, 220–25.
91. Lindsay, "Conjectural considerations", 80–81.
92. Ibid., 110, 143; as agreed with by Leslie, *New and Exact Account*, 328–29. Cf. Long Mss, Add. 12438, 1–2, 12.
93. Lindsay, "Conjectural considerations", 109–12. Cf. Long, *History of Jamaica*, 2:350; Curran, "Rethinking Race History", 173–74.
94. Lindsay, "Conjectural considerations", 100–102, 138–40. Cf. de Pauw, *Recherches philosophiques*, 1:131, 241–81.
95. Lindsay, "Conjectural considerations", 141, 154–56. Cf. de Pauw, *Recherches philosophiques*, 1:281–326.
96. Lindsay, "Conjectural considerations", 95–96.
97. Ibid., 98.
98. Thomson, *Bodies of Thought*, 239–40; Bryson, *Man and Society*, 57; Goldsmith, *History of the Earth*, 1:381; Buffon, *Natural History*, 1:178.
99. Lindsay, "Conjectural considerations", 112.
100. Ibid., 123.
101. Ibid., 29, 141; Glacken, *Traces on the Rhodian Shore*, 609–10.
102. Lindsay, "Conjectural considerations", 31.
103. *Columbian Magazine* 1 (December 1796): 436–38. Cf. Lindsay, *Sermon*, 22.
104. Lindsay, "Conjectural considerations", 138.
105. Ibid., 156.
106. Michael J. Crowe, *The Extraterrestrial Life Debate, 1750–1900: The Idea of a Plurality of Worlds from Kant to Lowell* (Cambridge: Cambridge University Press, 1986), 37; Rowan Strong, "Rescuing the Perishing Heathen: The British Empire versus the Empire of Satan in Anglican Theology, 1701–1721", in *The Church, the Afterlife and the Fate of the* Soul, ed. Peter Clarke and Tony Claydon (Woodbridge, UK: Boydell Press, 2009), 332–35.

Chapter 9

1. Lindsay to Long, Long Mss, Add. 18959, f. 18 (British Library, London); Lindsay, "Conjectural considerations", 115.
2. Lindsay, "Conjectural considerations", 76–78. Cf. Smith, "Slavery and Christianity", 185; Carolyn Steedman, *Labours Lost: Domestic Service and the Making of Modern England* (Cambridge: Cambridge University Press, 2009), 60–64.
3. Lindsay, "Conjectural considerations", 10.
4. Ibid., 9, 19–21.
5. P.A. Brunt, *Studies in Greek History and Thought* (Oxford: Clarendon Press, 1986), 345; Giuseppe Cambiano, "Aristotle and the Anonymous Opponents of Slavery", *Slavery and Abolition* 8 (1987): 22–41; Peter Garnsey, *Ideas of Slavery from Aristotle to Augustine* (Cambridge: Cambridge University Press, 1996), 38, 126–27; Evans, "From the Land of Canaan", 39; Hughes, *Versions of Blackness*, xii–xiii.
6. Dale B. Martin, *Slavery as Salvation: The Metaphor of Slavery in Pauline Christianity* (New Haven, Conn.: Yale University Press, 1990), 147–49; Vogt, *Ancient Slavery*, 143–45; Garnsey, *Ideas of Slavery*, 218–19, 242–43.
7. Lindsay, "Conjectural considerations", 175. Cf. Eric Foner, *The Story of American Freedom* (New York: W.W. Norton, 1998), 4–5; Duncan J. MacLeod, *Slavery, Race and the American Revolution* (Cambridge: Cambridge University Press, 1974), 17–26; Höpfl, *Christian Polity of John Calvin*, 74.
8. Lindsay, "Conjectural considerations", 11; Peter Garnsey, *Thinking about Property: From Antiquity to the Age of Revolution* (Cambridge: Cambridge University Press, 2007), 210; James Robertson, "A 1748 'Petition of Negro Slaves' and the Local Politics of Slavery in Jamaica", *William and Mary Quarterly* 67 (2010): 319–46; William A. Pettigrew, "Free to Enslave: Politics and the Escalation of Britain's Transatlantic Slave Trade, 1688–1714", *William and Mary Quarterly* 64 (2007): 34–35; Greene, " 'Of Liberty and of the Colonies' ", 21–102; Jack P. Greene, " 'A Plain and Natural Right to Life and Liberty': An Early Natural Rights Attack on the Excesses of the Slave System in Colonial British America", *William and Mary Quarterly* 57 (2000): 793–808; Jack P. Greene, "Liberty, Slavery and the Transformation of British Identity in the Eighteenth-Century West Indies", *Slavery and Abolition* 21 (2000): 11–23; Jack P. Greene, "The Jamaica Privilege Controversy, 1764–66: An Episode in the Process of Constitutional Definition in the Early Modern British Empire", *Journal of Imperial and Commonwealth History* 22 (1994): 16–53; Alan Houston, *Benjamin Franklin and the Politics of Improvement* (New Haven, Conn.: Yale University Press, 2008), 200–203.
9. Lindsay, "Conjectural considerations", 15.
10. Ibid., 15–17.
11. Ibid., 157–58.
12. Ibid., 12, 146, 157–60.
13. Ibid., 13. Cf. Alvin O. Thompson, " 'Happy – Happy Slaves!': Slavery as a Superior State to Freedom", *Journal of Caribbean History* 29 (1995): 93–119.
14. Lindsay, "Conjectural considerations", 108–9, 147. Cf. Kames, *Sketches*, 1:32.
15. Lindsay, "Conjectural considerations", 196.
16. Ibid., 13.

17. Ibid., 13–15, 189. On "refuse Negroes", see *Columbian Magazine* 2 (April 1797): 701; Shyllon, *James Ramsay*, 15–16.
18. Lindsay, "Conjectural considerations", 196.
19. Ibid., 114. On early versions of "amelioration", see J.R. Ward, *British West Indian Slavery, 1750–1834: The Process of Amelioration* (Oxford: Clarendon Press, 1988), 215–32; Paton, "Punishment, Crime", 924.
20. Lindsay, "Conjectural considerations", 115.
21. Ibid., 115–16. Cf. Vincent Brown, *Reaper's Garden*, 164–68.
22. Lindsay, "Conjectural considerations", 162.
23. Ibid., 9, 78.
24. Ibid., 162–65.
25. Ibid., 165.
26. Lindsay, *Sermon*, 45.
27. Lindsay, "Conjectural considerations", 166.
28. Ibid., 166–68.
29. Ibid., 168.
30. Ibid., 168.
31. Ibid., 170.
32. Ibid., 165, 170.
33. Ibid., 170.
34. Ibid., 171; K.R. Bradley, *Slaves and Masters in the Roman Empire: A Study in Social Control* (New York: Oxford University Press, 1987), 81.
35. Lindsay, "Conjectural considerations", 171–72.
36. Ibid., 172.
37. Ibid., 172.
38. Ibid., 172–73. Cf. Henrice Altink, "Deviant and Dangerous: Pro-slavery Representations of Jamaican Slave Women's Sexuality, c. 1780–1834", *Slavery and Abolition* 26 (2005): 272–75.
39. Lindsay, "Conjectural considerations", 173.
40. Ibid., 173–74.
41. Ibid., 174.
42. Ibid., 174.
43. Ibid., 174.
44. Lindsay, *Memoirs*, 1:21–22; Lindsay, "Conjectural considerations", 174–75.
45. Lindsay, "Conjectural considerations", 175.
46. Ibid., 175.
47. Dean Tucker, *Reflections on the Present Matters in Dispute between Great Britain and Ireland* (1785), quoted in Shyllon, *James Ramsay*, 77.
48. Boulukos, *Grateful Slave*, 138–40. Cf. William Snelgrave, *A New Account of some Parts of Guinea, and the Slave-Trade* (London: James, John and Paul Knapton, 1734), 46.
49. N.A.T. Hall, "Some Aspects of the Deficiency Question in Jamaica in the Eighteenth Century", *Jamaica Journal* 7, nos. 1–2 (March–June 1973): 36–41.
50. Lindsay, "Conjectural considerations", 177.
51. Ibid., 177, 183. Cf. Steel, "Philosophy of Fear", 11.
52. Lindsay, "Conjectural considerations", 179–80.
53. Ibid., 180–81; William Beveridge, *Thesaurus Theologicus: or, A Complete System of*

Divinity; Summ'd up in Brief Notes upon Select Places of the Old and New Testament; Wherein the Sacred Text is Reduc'd under Proper Heads, Explain'd, and Illustrated with the Opinions and Authorities of the Ancient Fathers, &c. (London: Richard Smith, 1710), 100–103.

54. *Columbian Magazine* 1 (December 1796): 435; Lindsay, "Conjectural considerations", 181; Lindsay, *Memoirs*, 1:62–65. Cf. Hempton, *Methodism*, 132–34; D.P. Walker, *The Decline of Hell: Seventeenth-Century Discussions of Eternal Torment* (London: Routledge and Kegan Paul, 1964), 4–6; Philip C. Almond, *Heaven and Hell in Enlightenment England* (Cambridge: Cambridge University Press, 1994), 158–61; Ronald Paulson, "Henry Fielding and the Problem of Deism", in *The Margins of Orthodoxy: Heterodox Writing and Cultural Response, 1660–1750,* ed. Roger D. Lund (Cambridge: Cambridge University Press, 1995), 262–63; Crowe, *Extraterrestrial Life Debate*, 26–36; Cambers, " 'But Where Shall My Soul Repose?' ", 268–69.

55. Lindsay, "Conjectural considerations", 181; Lacy K. Ford, *Deliver Us from Evil: The Slavery Question in the Old South* (Oxford: Oxford University Press, 2009), 25–26.
56. Lindsay, "Conjectural considerations" 13, 184.
57. Shyllon, *James Ramsay*, 1–5, 14; James Watt, "James Ramsay, 1733–1789: Naval Surgeon, Naval Chaplain and Morning Star of the Anti-slavery Movement", *Mariner's Mirror* 81 (1995): 156–58.
58. Rodger, "Naval Chaplain", 34, 37; Shyllon, *James Ramsay*, 12–13, 52–55.
59. Shyllon, *James Ramsay*, 82–87.
60. Ramsay, *Essay*, 25. On the history of the drafts, see Christopher Brown, *Moral Capital*, 244–53; Shyllon, *James Ramsay*, 18–41.
61. Ramsay, *Essay*, 174–77.
62. Ibid., 1–3, 108–9; David Brion Davis, *The Problem of Slavery in the Age of Revolution, 1770–1823* (Ithaca, NY: Cornell University Press, 1975), 377–78; Christopher Brown, *Moral Capital*, 245, 325–26; Steedman, *Labours Lost*, 91–94.
63. Ramsay, *Inquiry*; James Ramsay, *A Reply to the Personal Invectives and Objections Contained in Two Answers, Published by Certain Anonymous Persons, to An Essay on the Treatment and Conversion of African Slaves, in the British Colonies* (London: James Phillips, 1785); Christopher Brown, *Moral Capital*, 325; Carey, *British Abolitionism*, 119–24.
64. Shyllon, *James Ramsay*, 94–98; Whyte, *Scotland and the Abolition*, 70; James Ramsay, *An Address on the Proposed Bill for the Abolition of the Slave Trade: Humbly Submitted to the Consideration of the Legislature* (London: James Phillips, 1788); James Ramsay, *Objections to the Abolition of the Slave Trade, with Answers: To which are Prefixed, Strictures on a Late Publication, Intitled, "Considerations on the Emancipation of Negroes, and the Abolition of the Slave Trade, by a West India Planter"* (London: James Phillips, 1788); David Barry Gaspar, *Bondmen and Rebels: A Study of Master-Slave Relations in Antigua* (Baltimore: Johns Hopkins University Press, 1985), 78, 217; Jerome S. Handler, "A Rare Eighteenth-Century Tract in Defense of Slavery in Barbados: The Thoughts of the Rev. John Duke, Curate of S. Michael", *Journal of the Barbados Museum and Historical Society* 51 (2005): 58–65.
65. Ramsay, *Essay*, 13, 19; Lindsay, "Conjectural considerations", 184–86. Cf. Yvon Garlan, *Slavery in Ancient Greece* (1982; reprint, Ithaca, NY: Cornell University Press, 1988), 40–45.
66. Lindsay, "Conjectural considerations", 186–89.

67. Ibid., 189–91.
68. Ibid., 191, 193. Cf. Ramsay, *Essay*, 126; Ramsay MacMullen, *Christianizing the Roman Empire (A.D. 100–400)* (New Haven, Conn.: Yale University Press, 1984), 25–42.
69. Lindsay, "Conjectural considerations", 160, 194; Ramsay, *Essay*, 101. Cf. Larry E. Tise, *Proslavery: A History of the Defense of Slavery in America, 1701–1840* (Athens: University of Georgia Press, 1987), 83–84; Thompson, " 'Happy – Happy Slaves!' ", 93–119.
70. Ramsay, *Essay*, 102–3, 109; Lindsay, "Conjectural considerations", 194.
71. Ramsay, *Essay*, 168–69; John Immerwahr, "Hume's Revised Racism", *Journal of the History of Ideas* 53 (1992): 485; Kidd, *Forging of Races*, 94.
72. David Hume, *Essays and Treatises on Several Subjects* (London: T. Cadell, C. Elliot and T. Kay and Co., 1788), 1: 177-85. Cf. Glacken, *Traces on the Rhodian Shore*, 585-87.
73. Hume, *Essays and Treatises*, 1:472; Kidd, *Forging of Races*, 93–94; Wheeler, *Complexion of Race*, 185; Immerwahr, "Hume's Revised Racism", 481–82; Emmanuel C. Eze, "Hume, Race, and Human Nature", *Journal of the History of Ideas* 61 (2000): 691–92.
74. Immerwahr, "Hume's Revised Racism", 482–83; Kidd, *Forging of Races*, 94. Cf. Zack, *Philosophy of Science and Race*, 13–18.
75. Hume, *Essays and Treatises*, 1:472. Cf. Ellis, *Politics of Sensibility*, 52–54; Wise, *Though the Heavens May Fall*, 14–15.
76. Lindsay, "Conjectural considerations", 194–96.
77. Estwick, *Considerations*, 77–79; Rothschild, "Atlantic Worlds", 422–29; Garrett, "Anthropology", 88. Cf. Ward, *British West Indian Slavery*, 3–4.
78. Lindsay, "Conjectural considerations", 196–98.

Chapter 10

1. Original Register of St Catherine, 1764–1808: Baptisms, Marriages and Burials, no folio number, 1B/11/8/3, 48 (Jamaica Archives, Spanish Town). The record of John Lindsay's burial was made by the curate, James Steel. Grace Lindsay was buried on 15 October 1789, as recorded by the new rector, Alexander Cumine. The dropsy is mentioned in William Wright to Banks, 12 July 1783, Papers of Sir Joseph Banks, www.sl.nsw.gov.au/Banks/.
2. Lindsay, "Conjectural considerations", 13–15, 143, 189.
3. Inventories, liber 75, 131–35 (Jamaica Archives, Spanish Town).
4. Ibid., 134.
5. Ibid., 132.
6. Ibid., 131–35; Burnard, " 'Prodigious Riches' ", 514–15.
7. Long, *History of Jamaica*, 2:5–6.
8. Inventories, liber 75, 132.
9. Roby, *Monuments*, 43n68, 65n103.
10. Ibid., 43n68. Cf. Wright, *Monumental Inscriptions*, 100; S. Purcell Hendrick, *A Sketch of the History of the Cathedral Church of St Jago de la Vega, Spanish Town, in the Parish of St Catherine, Jamaica* (Kingston: Jamaica Times, 1911), 12; Beasley, *Christian Ritual*, 100.

11. *Gentleman's Magazine* 59, no. 1 (February 1789), 178; *Scots Magazine*, February 1789, 101. If Lindsay did produce a plurality of novels, it is probable the others were, like *Memoirs*, published anonymously. One candidate might be *The West Indian; or Memoirs of Fredric Charlton*, published in two volumes in 1788 and called by one reviewer "an imitation of Roderick Random". *The West Indian* was available from at least one contemporary circulating library, but no copy is known to have survived. See Edward Jacobs and Antonia Fraser, " 'Lost Books' and Publishing History: Two Annotated Lists of Imprints for the Fiction Titles Listed in the Circulating Library Catalogs of Thomas Lowndes (1766) and M. Heavisides (1790), of Which No Known Copies Survive", *Bibliographical Society of America, Papers* 89 (1995): 292.

12. *Columbian Magazine* 3 (June 1797): 21.
13. Craton, *Testing the Chains*, 172, 247; Minter, *Episcopacy Without Episcopate*, 179.
14. Alexander Du Toit, "Lindsay, John (1685/6–1768), nonjuring Church of England clergyman and writer", *Oxford Dictionary of National Biography* (2004.) See also Desmond, *Dictionary of British and Irish Botanists*, 386–87.
15. Christie, *Diary of the Rev. William Jones*, 14, 245.
16. David Gunby, David Carnegie and Antony Hammond, eds., *The Works of John Webster: An Old-Spelling Critical Edition* (Cambridge: Cambridge University Press, 1995), 1:565, 666.
17. James E. McClellan III, *Colonialism and Science: Saint Domingue in the Old Regime* (Baltimore: Johns Hopkins University Press, 1992); Brunton, "Transfer of Medical Education", 242–58; Shelford, "Pascal in Jamaica", 58; Nicholas Canny, "Atlantic History and Global History", in *Atlantic History: A Critical Appraisal*, ed. Jack P. Greene and Philip D. Morgan (Oxford: Oxford University Press, 2009), 328–29.
18. Susan Scott Parrish, "Diasporic African Sources of Enlightenment Knowledge", in *Science and Empire in the Atlantic World*, ed. James Delbourgo and Nicholas Dew (New York: Routledge, 2008), 293–94; Parrish, *American Curiosity*, 1–8; Schiebinger, "Scientific Exchange", 302–5; Schiebinger, *Plants and Empire*, 44–46; Jackson, "Diasporan Voices", 369–70; Neil Safier, *Measuring the New World: Enlightenment Science and South America* (Chicago: University of Chicago Press, 2008), 97–98.
19. Lindsay, *Voyage*, 56–57, Lindsay, "Elegancies", 143. For a clear account of the unequal exchange of knowledge, see John Southall, *A Treatise of Buggs* (London: J. Roberts, 1730).
20. Cf. "Characteristic Traits of the Creolian and African Negroes in this Island, &c. &c.", *Columbian Magazine* 3 (June 1797): 3–5.
21. Morgan, "British Encounters", 214–15. Cf. Paul Finkelman, *Slavery and the Founders: Race and Liberty in the Age of Jefferson* (New York: M.E. Sharpe, 2001), 190–94; Kirsten McKenzie, *The Making of an English Slave-Owner: Samuel Eusebius Hudson at the Cape of Good Hope, 1796–1807* (Cape Town: UCT Press, 1993), 62–64.
22. Israel, *Enlightenment Contested*, 593, 606; Whyte, *Scotland and the Abolition*, 65–66; Laurent Dubois, "An Enslaved Enlightenment: Rethinking the Intellectual History of the French Atlantic", *Social History* 31 (2006): 1–14; Louis Sala-Molins, *Dark Side of the Light: Slavery and the French Enlightenment* (Minneapolis: University of Minnesota Press, 2006); Muthu, *Enlightenment Against Empire*, 183.
23. Alan Gallay, "The Great Sellout: George Whitefield and Slavery", in *Looking South:*

Chapters in the Story of an American Region, ed. Winfred B. Moore Jr and Joseph F. Tripp (New York: Greenwood Press, 1989), 27; Israel, *Enlightenment Contested*, 607–8; Muthu, *Enlightenment Against Empire*, 282; Dubois, "Enslaved Enlightenment", 1–14. For the contrasting trajectories of George Whitefield and John Wesley, see Lambert, *"Pedlar in Divinity"*, 204–5; Brycchan Carey, "John Wesley's *Thoughts upon Slavery* and the Language of the Heart", *Bulletin of the John Rylands University Library of Manchester* 85 (2003): 269–84; Carey, *British Abolitionism*, 88–92.

24. Gaspar, *Bondmen and Rebels*, 217; Keith A. Sandiford, *The Cultural Politics of Sugar: Caribbean Slavery and Narratives of Colonialism* (Cambridge: Cambridge University Press, 2000); Elizabeth A. Bohls, "The Planter Picturesque: Matthew Lewis's *Journal of a West India Proprietor*", *European Romantic Review* 13 (2002): 63–76; Chad Vanderford, "Proslavery Professors: Classic Natural Right and the Positive Good Argument in Antebellum Virginia", *Civil War History* 55 (2009): 5–30; Ford, *Deliver Us from Evil*, 143–47.

Bibliography

Manuscripts

Bristol Museum and Art Gallery

Broughton Papers.

Lindsay, John. Drawings.

———. "Elegancies of Jamaica".

Long, Robert. "A Supplement attempted or Appendix and Addendum to Sir Hans Sloane and Dr. Pat. Brown in Notes and Observations *Natural* and Moral on the Native Blacks, the Quadrupeds, Reptiles, Insects Plants Birds Fishes Air and Clime &c. of Jamaica by Rt. L'g, – Being occasional Remarks and observations from 1752 to 1762, inclusive".

British Library, London

Lindsay, John. "A few conjectural considerations upon the creation of the humane race; Occasioned by the present British Quixottical rage of setting the slaves from Africa at liberty". Long Mss, Add. 12439.

Long Mss, Add. 12429, 12438, 12439, 18959, 22678.

Cambridge University Library, Cambridge

Vanneck-Arcedeckne Papers.

Jamaica Archives, Spanish Town

Inventories.

Original Register of St Catherine, 1764–1808: Baptisms, Marriages and Burials, 1B/11/8/3.

Register of Baptisms, Burials and Marriages, Clarendon, Vere. Vol. 2, 1B/11/8.

Lambeth Palace, London

Fulham Papers.

National Archives, Kew

ADM 33/559, *Fougueux* Pay Book.
ADM 36/5616, *Fougueux* Muster.
ADM 36/6262.
ADM 36/6264.
ADM 51/628.
ADM 51/4271.
ADM 52/859, *Fougueux* Master's Log.

National Library of Jamaica, Kingston

Robinson, Anthony. "Birds of Jamaica". Vol. 1, Ms 178.

National Library of Scotland, Edinburgh

Robertson-Macdonald Papers, Ms 3942.

Websites

Clergy of the Church of England Database. www.theclergydatabase.org.uk.
General Register Office for Scotland, National Archives of Scotland and Court of the Lord Lyon. ScotlandsPeople. www.scotlandspeople.gov.uk.
Oxford Dictionary of National Biography. www.oxforddnb.com.
Science. ScienceXpress. www.sciencexpress.org.
State Library of New South Wales. Papers of Sir Joseph Banks. www2.sl.nsw.gov.au/Banks.

Newspapers and Periodicals

Columbian Magazine (Kingston). Vols. 2–3 (1797).
Critical Review; or, Annals of Literature (London).
Gentleman's Magazine (London).
Journals of the Assembly of Jamaica (Spanish Town).
Monthly Review (London).
Scots Magazine (Edinburgh).
Town and Country Magazine (London).

Books and Articles First Published before 1900

Adanson, Michel *Histoire naturelle du Sénégal: Coquillages avec la relation abrégee d'unvoyage fait en ce pays, pendant les années 1749, 50, 51, 52 et 53*. Paris: C.-J.-B. Bauche, 1757.

———. *A Voyage to Senegal, the Island of Goree, and the River Gambia*. London: J. Nourse and W. Johnston, 1759.

Barham, Henry. *Hortus Americanus: Containing an Account of the Trees, Shrubs, and Other Vegetable Productions, of South-America and the West-India Islands, and Particularly of the Island of Jamaica*. Kingston: Alexander Aikman, 1794.

Beveridge, William. *Thesaurus Theologicus: or, A Complete System of Divinity; Summ'd up in Brief Notes upon Select Places of the Old and New Testament; Wherein the Sacred Text is Reduc'd under Proper Heads, Explain'd, and Illustrated with the Opinions and Authorities of the Ancient Fathers, &c.* London: Richard Smith, 1710.

Beverley, Robert ("A Native and Inhabitant of the Place"). *The History and Present State of Virginia, in Four Parts*. London: R. Parker, 1705.

Brock. R.A., ed. *The Official Records of Robert Dinwiddie, Lieutenant-Governor of the Colony Of Virginia, 1751–1758, Now First Printed from the Manuscript in the Collections of the Virginia Historical Society*. Richmond: Virginia Historical Society, 1883.

Browne, Patrick. *The Civil and Natural History of Jamaica*. London: T. Osborne and J. Shipton, 1756.

Buffon, Count de [Georges-Louis Leclerc]. *The Natural History of Animals, Vegetables, and Minerals; with the Theory of the Earth in General*. London: T. Bell, 1775.

Caldecott, A. *The Church in the West Indies*. 1898. Reprint, London: Frank Cass, 1970.

A Catalogue of the Graduates in the Faculties of Arts, Divinity and Law of the University of Edinburgh since the Foundation. Edinburgh, 1858.

"Characteristic Traits of the Creolian and African Negroes in this Island, &c. &c.". *Columbian Magazine* (Kingston) 2 (April 1797): 699–704; 2 (May 1797): 765–68; 3 (June 1797): 3–8; 3 (July 1797): 107–10; 3 (August 1797): 166–72; 3 (September 1797): 249–53; 3 (October 1797): 287–89.

Clarkson, Thomas. *An Essay on the Slavery and Commerce of the Human Species, Particularly the African*. 1788. Reprint, New York: AMS Press, 1972.

Clavigero, D. Francesco Saverio. *The History of Mexico: Collected from Spanish and Mexican Historians, from Manuscripts, and Ancient Paintings of the Indians; Illustrated by Charts, and other Copper Plates; To which are added, Critical Dissertations on the Land, the Animals, and Inhabitants of Mexico*. London: G.G.J. and J. Robinson, 1787.

Clowes, William Laird. *The Royal Navy: A History, From the Earliest Times to the Present*. London: Sampson Low, Marston and Co., 1898.

The Cobblers Last Will and Testament, or, The Lord Hewson's Translation. London, 1660.

Cockerell, T.D.A. "A Little Known Jamaican Naturalist, Dr. Anthony Robinson". *American Naturalist* 28 (1894): 775–80.

Colonel Huson's (or the Cobler's) Confession: In a Fit of Despair, Taken in Short-Hand by the Pen of a Ready-Writer. London, 1660.

Cudworth, Ralph. *The True Intellectual System of the Universe: The First Part; wherein all the Reason and Philosophy of Atheism is Confuted; and Its Impossibility Demonstrated*. London: Richard Royston, 1678.

Darlington, William M. *Christopher Gist's Journals with Historical, Geographical and Ethnological Notes and Biographies of His Contemporaries*. 1893. Reprint, New York: Argonaut Press, 1966.

[de Pauw, Cornélius] "Mr. de P****". *Recherches philosophiques sur les Américains, ou, Mémoires intéressants pour servir à l'histoire de l'espece humaine*. London. 1770.

[Dixon, Robert]. "An authentic account of a water spout; which mostly fell upon Brackenthwaite in the County of Cumberland, on Sept. 19, 1760; by an Eye-witness". *Gentleman's Magazine* 30 (November 1760): 520–22.

Dodd, William. *A Commentary on the Books of the Old and New Testament*. London: R. Davis, L. Davis, T. Carnan and F. Newbery, 1770.

———. *The Wisdom and Goodness of God, in the Vegetable Creation: A Sermon Preached at St. Martin's Church, Ludgate, on September the 20th, 1759, Before the Worshipful Company of Apothecaries*. London: L. Davis, C. Reymers and W. Bristow, 1760.

Elliot, R. "A Summary of Gospel Doctrine Taught by Mr Whitefield" [1770]. In *Select Sermons of George Whitefield*, 51–71. London: Banner of Truth Trust, 1964.

Ellis, Clement. *The Scripture Catechist: or, The Whole Religion of a Christian: Being a Full Explanation of the Church Catechism; Containing, a Comprehensive Body of Practical Divinity*. London: C. Rivington and J. Hutton, 1738.

Elmgren, Gabriel. *Plantarum Jamaicensium Pugillus*. Uppsala, 1759.

Entick, John. *The General History of the Late War: Containing It's Rise, Progress and Event, in Europe, Asia, Africa, and America* [1764]. 4th ed. London: Edward and Charles Dilly, 1779.

Estwick, Samuel. *Considerations on the Negroe Cause Commonly so Called, Addressed to the Right Honourable Lord Mansfield, Lord Chief Justice of the Court of King's Bench, &c.* London: J. Dodsley, 1773.

Fénelon, François de Salignac de la Mothe. *The Adventures of Telemachus, the Son of Ulysses*. 3rd ed. 1720. Reprint, New York: Garland, 1979.

———. *Telemachus, Son of Ulysses*. Edited by Patrick Bailey. Cambridge: Cambridge University Press, 1994.

[Ferguson, Adam]. *The Morality of Stage-Plays Seriously Considered*. Edinburgh, 1757.

———. *An Essay on the History of Civil Society* [1767]. Edited by Fania Oz-Salzberger. Cambridge: Cambridge University Press, 1995.

Fielding, Henry. *Joseph Andrews* [1742]. Edited by Martin C. Battestin. Oxford: Clarendon Press, 1967.

Fielding, Sarah. *The Adventures of David Simple: Containing an Account of His Travels Through the Cities of London and Westminster in the Search of a Real Friend* [1744]. Edited by Malcolm Kelsall. London: Oxford University Press, 1969.

Franklin, Benjamin. *Experiments and Observations on Electricity, Made at Philadelphia in America*. London: David Henry, 1769.

———. "Letter to Mr. Nairne, of London, from Dr. Franklin, Proposing a Slowly Sensible Hygrometer for Certain Purposes". *Transactions of the American Philosophical Society* 2 (1786): 51–56.

Fraser, Donald. *The Life and Diary of the Reverend Ebenezer Erskine, A.M.: of Stirling, Father of the Secession Church*. Edinburgh: W. Oliphant, 1831.

Gardner, W.J. *A History of Jamaica*. 1873. Reprint, London: Frank Cass, 1971.

Goldsmith, Oliver. *An History of the Earth, and Animated Nature*. London: J. Nourse, 1774.

Goodman, Alfred T., ed. *Journal of Captain William Trent from Logstown to Pickawillany, A.D. 1752*. Cincinnati: William Dodge, 1871.

Gosse, Philip Henry. *The Birds of Jamaica*. London: John van Voorst, 1847.

———. *A Naturalist's Sojourn in Jamaica*. London: Longman, Brown, Green, and Longmans, 1851.

Hervey, James. *Remarks on Lord Bolingbroke's Letters on the Study and Use of History: So Far as They Relate to the History of the Old Testament; and Especially to the Case of Noah, Denouncing a Curse upon Canaan*. London: J. and J. Rivington, 1752.

Hickeringill, Edmund. *Jamaica Viewed*. London: John Williams, 1661.

Home, Henry [Lord Kames]. *Sketches of the History of Man*. Edinburgh: W. Creech, W. Strahan and T. Cadell, 1774.

Homer. *The Odyssey*. Translated by Robert Fagles. London: Penguin Books, 1996.

Hughes, William. *The American Physitian; or, a Treatise of the Roots, Plants, Trees, Shrubs, Fruit, Herbs, &c. Growing in the English Plantations in America*. London: William Crook, 1672.

The Humble Desires and Proposals of the Private Agitators of Colonel Hewsons Regiment to the Generall Agitators of the Army: To be Presented to His Excellency Sir Thomas Fairfax, and Communicated to Both Houses of Parliament. London: I.C., 1647.

Hume, David. *Essays and Treatises on Several Subjects*. London: T. Cadell, C. Elliot and T. Kay, 1788.

Kant, Immanuel. *Essays and Treatises on Moral, Political, and Various Philosophical Subjects*. London: William Richardson, 1798.

Keppel, Thomas. *The Life of Augustus Viscount Keppel, Admiral of the White, and First Lord of the Admiralty in 1782–8*. London: Henry Colburn, 1842.

Leslie, Charles. *A New and Exact Account of Jamaica, wherein the Antient and Present State of that Colony, Its Importance to Great Britain, Laws, Trade, Manners and Religion, together with the most remarkable and curious Animals, Plants, Trees, &c. are described: With a particular Account of the Sacrifices, Libations, &c. at this Day in Use among the Negroes*. Edinburgh: R. Fleming, 1740.

Lindsay, Alexander William Crawford [Lord Lindsay]. *Lives of the Lindsays; or, a Memoir of the Houses of Crawford and Balcarres*. London: John Murray, 1849.

Lindsay, Henry. *Christ's advocateship, practically discoursed from I. John, Chap. II. Ver. 1, 2. on the Monday after the celebration of the Lord's Supper, in the Talbooth Church of Edinburgh*. Edinburgh: John Trail, 1734.

———. *The clergy's plea of conscience considered: in an address to the author of a pamphlet, intituled, the letter to the learned author of the Queries unmasked*. Edinburgh, 1737.

———. *An essay upon 1 Corinth. Chap. i. vers. 21. against the infidelity of the age; and wherein is especially consider'd the wisdom of God, as to the time of Christianity, its being published to the world*. Edinburgh: Davidson and Trail, 1736.

———. *A letter to the learned author of the Queries, being a detection of several errors and heresies contain'd in a pamphlet, entitled, Answer to the queries*. Edinburgh, 1737.

———. *The present state of the Church of Scotland, with the duty of the members thereof enquired into in a sermon at the opening of the synod of Perth and Stirling, October 9th 1733*. Edinburgh: Tho. Lumisden and Jo. Robertson, 1733.

Lindsay, John. "Account of the Germination and Raising of Ferns from the Seed". *Transactions of the Linnean Society* (London) 2 (1794): 93–100.

———. "An Examination of the Hypothetical Doctrine of Water-spouts, in Opposition to the Ingenious Speculations of Dr. B. Franklin of Philadelphia, F.R.S.". *Gentleman's Magazine* 51 (1781): 559–60 (plate opposite page 558), 615–16 (supplement).

———. Letter on waterspouts. *Gentleman's Magazine* 53 (1783): 1027.

——— [as John Lindsey]. Letter on Whirlwinds. *Gentleman's Magazine* 55, no. 2 (1785): 594–98.

———. *Memoirs of Sir Thomas Hughson and Mr Joseph Williams, with the remarkable history, travels, and distresses, of Telemachus Lovet: The whole calculated for the improvement of the mind and manners; and for a becoming and useful entertainment for the youth of both sexes.* London: L. Davis, T. Waller, T. Osborn, J. Shipton, A. Strahan, R. Griffiths, W. Fenner, J. Millan, Wilson and Durham, 1757.

———. "Oration", *Columbian Magazine* (Kingston) 2 (February 1797): 580–87; 2 (March 1797): 633–37; 2 (April 1797): 727–32.

———. *A Sermon Preached at the Funeral of His Excellency Sir Basil Keith, Knt. Governour of Jamaica.* London: John Donaldson, 1780.

———. *A Voyage to the Coast of Africa in 1758.* London: S. Paterson and W. Bristow, 1759.

Linné, Carl von. *Flora Jamaicensis.* Uppsala: 1759.

[Lobb, Theophilus]. *An Answer to that Important Question, Whether it is Lawful for the Professors of the Christian Religion to go to Plays?* London: J. Buckland, 1757.

Long, Edward. *Candid Reflections upon the Judgement Lately Awarded by the Court of King's Bench, in Westminster-Hall, on what is Commonly Called the Negro-Cause, by a Planter.* London: T. Lowndes, 1772.

———. *The History of Jamaica.* London: T. Lowndes, 1774.

Lowndes, Thomas. *T. Lowndes's Catalogue for 1778: Consisting of Books Collected in Different Parts of England.* [London]: Thomas Lownds, [1778].

Lunan, John. *Hortus Jamaicensis, or a Botanical Description, (According to the Linnean System) and an Account of the Virtues, &c. of its Indigenous Plants Hitherto Unknown, as also of the Most Useful Exotics.* Spanish Town: St Jago de la Vega Gazette, 1814.

Mackelvie, William. *Annals and Statistics of the United Presbyterian Church.* Edinburgh: Oliphant and Company and Andrew Elliot, 1873.

Marsden, Peter. *An Account of the Island of Jamaica.* Newcastle, 1788.

Memoir of the Late William Wright, M.D., Fellow of the Royal Societies of London and Edinburgh, etc. with Extracts from His Correspondence, and a Selection of His Papers on Medical and Botanical Subjects. Edinburgh: William Blackwood, 1828.

M'Kerrow, John. *History of the Secession Church.* Glasgow: A. Fullerton, 1841.

A New Catalogue of Lownds's Circulating Library, Consisting of about Ten Thousand Volumes. [London]: Thomas Lownds, [1758].

Otway, Thomas. *The Orphan: or, the Unhappy-Marriage: a Tragedy, as it is Acted at His Royal Highness the Duke's Theatre.* London: R. Bentley and M. Magnes, 1680.

Palmer, William P., ed. *Calendar of Virginia State Papers and Other Manuscripts, 1652–1781, Preserved in the Capitol at Richmond.* Richmond: Commonwealth of Virginia, 1875.

Ramsay, James. *An Address on the Proposed Bill for the Abolition of the Slave Trade: Humbly Submitted to the Consideration of the Legislature.* London: James Phillips, 1788.

———. *An Essay on the Treatment and Conversion of African Slaves in the British Sugar Colonies.* Dublin: T. Walker, C. Jenkin, R. Marchbank, L. White, R. Burton and P. Byrne, 1784.

———. *An Inquiry into the Effects of Putting a Stop to the African Slave Trade, and of Granting Liberty to the Slaves in the British Sugar Colonies.* London: James Phillips, 1784.

———. *Objections to the Abolition of the Slave Trade, with Answers: To which are Prefixed, Strictures on a Late Publication, Intitled, "Considerations on the Emancipation of Negroes, and the Abolition of the Slave Trade, by a West India Planter".* London: James Phillips, 1788.

———. *A Reply to the Personal Invectives and Objections Contained in Two Answers, Published by Certain Anonymous Persons, to An Essay on the Treatment and Conversion of African Slaves, in the British Colonies.* London: James Phillips, 1785.

Roby, John. *Monuments of the Cathedral-Church and Parish of St. Catharine.* Montego Bay: Alex. Holmes, 1831.

The Royal African: or, Memoirs of the Young Prince of Annamaboe. Comprehending a Distinct Account of His Country and Family; His Elder Brother's Voyage to France, and Reception There; the Manner in which Himself was Confided by His Father to the Captain Who Sold Him; His Condition while a Slave in Barbadoes; the True Cause of His Being Redeemed; His Voyage from Thence; and Reception Here in England. London: W. Reeve, G. Woodfall and J. Barnes, [1754].

Sinclair, John. *The Statistical Account of Scotland, drawn up from the Communications of the Different Parishes.* Edinburgh: W. Creech, 1791–99.

Smith, William. *A New Voyage to Guinea.* London: John Nourse, 1744.

Smollett, Tobias. *The Adventures of Ferdinand Count Fathom* [1753]. Edited by Paul-Gabriel Boucé. London: Penguin Books, 1990.

———. *The Adventures of Roderick Random.* 1748. Reprint, London: Everyman's Library, 1927.

Snelgrave, William. *A New Account of some Parts of Guinea, and the Slave-Trade.* London: James, John and Paul Knapton, 1734.

Southall, John. *A Treatise of Buggs.* London: J. Roberts, 1730.

Speed, John. *A Prospect of the Most Famous Parts of the World.* 1627. Reprint, Amsterdam: Theatrum Orbis Terrarum, 1966.

Tobin, James ("Friend to the West India Colonies and Their Inhabitants"). *Cursory Remarks upon the Reverend Mr Ramsay's Essay on the Treatment and Conversion of African Slaves in the Sugar Colonies.* London: G. and T. Wilkie, 1785.

The Traytors Downfall, or, A Brief Relation of that Phanatick Crew Who Traiterously Murthered the Late Kings Majesty of Blessed Memory: To the Tune of Fa la la, &c. London: Francis Coles, 1662.

"A True Friend to the Gentle Craft". *Hewson Reduc'd: or, the Shoomaker Return'd to His Trade; being a Show, Wherein is Represented the Honesty, Inoffensiveness, and Ingenuity of that Profession, when 'tis Kept Within its Own Bounds, and Goes Not Beyond the Last.* London: Austine Rice, 1661.

Turbervil, Hodg [Edmund Gayton] ("Chaplain to the Late Lord Hewson"). *Walk Knaves, Walk: A Discourse Intended to Have Been Spoken at Court and Now Publish'd for the Satisfaction of All Those that have Participated in the Sweetness of Publike Employments.* London, 1659.

Books and Articles First Published after 1900

Adcock, F.E. *Roman Political Ideas and Practice.* Ann Arbor: University of Michigan Press, 1959.

Aguado, Edward, and James E. Burt. *Understanding Weather and Climate.* Upper Saddle River, NJ: Pearson Education, 2004.

Ahn, Doohwan. "The Politics of Royal Education: Xenophon's *Education of Cyrus* in Early Eighteenth-Century Europe". *Leadership Quarterly* 19 (2008): 439–52.

Albritton, Claude C., Jr. *The Abyss of Time: Changing Conceptions of the Earth's Antiquity after the Sixteenth Century*. San Francisco: Freeman, Cooper, 1980.

Alden, John Richard. *Robert Dinwiddie: Servant of the Crown*. Charlottesville: University Press ofVirginia, 1973.

Allan, David. *Scotland in the Eighteenth Century: Union and Enlightenment*. London: Longman, 2002.

———. *Virtue, Learning and the Scottish Enlightenment: Ideas of Scholarship in Early Modern History*. Edinburgh: Edinburgh University Press, 1993.

Almond, Philip C. "Adam, Pre-Adamites, and Extra-Terrestrial Beings in Early Modern Europe". *Journal of Religious History* 30 (2006): 163–74.

———. *Heaven and Hell in Enlightenment England*. Cambridge: Cambridge University Press, 1994.

Altink, Henrice. "Deviant and Dangerous: Pro-Slavery Representations of Jamaican Slave Women's Sexuality, c. 1780–1834". *Slavery and Abolition* 26 (2005): 271–88.

Anderson, Robert D., Michael Lynch and Nicholas Phillipson. *The University of Edinburgh: An Illustrated History*. Edinburgh: Edinburgh University Press, 2003.

Anstey, Roger. *The Atlantic Slave Trade and British Abolition, 1760–1810*. London: Macmillan, 1975.

Anton, A.E. " 'Handfasting' in Scotland". *Scottish Historical Review* 37 (1958): 89–102.

Armitage, David, ed. *Bolingbroke: Political Writings*. Cambridge: Cambridge University Press, 1997.

———. "A Patriot for Whom? The Afterlives of Bolingbroke's Patriot King". *Journal of British Studies* 36 (1997): 397–418.

Arnold, Bill T. *Genesis*. Cambridge: Cambridge University Press, 2009.

Bacon-Foster, Corra. *Early Chapters in the Development of the Potomac Route to the West*. Washington, DC: Columbia Historical Society, 1912.

Bailey, Kenneth P. *The Ohio Company of Virginia and the Westward Movement, 1748–1792: A Chapter in the History of the Colonial Frontier*. Glendale, Calif.: Arthur H. Clark, 1939.

Bailyn, Bernard, and Patricia L. Denault, eds. *Soundings in Atlantic History: Latent Structures and Intellectual Currents, 1500–1830*. Cambridge, Mass.: Harvard University Press, 2009.

Baldwin, Olive, and Thelma Wilson. "Vincent, Isabella (1734/5–1802)". In *Oxford Dictionary of National Biography*. Oxford: Oxford University Press, 2004.

Balston, Thomas. *James Whatman, Father and Son*. London: Methuen, 1957.

Barber, Giles. "Books from the Old World for the New: The British International Trade in Books in the Eighteenth Century". *Studies on Voltaire and the Eighteenth Century* 151–55 (1976): 185–224.

Barker, Anthony J. *The African Link: British Attitudes to the Negro in the Era of the Atlantic Slave Trade, 1550–1807*. London: Frank Cass, 1978.

Barry, Boubacar. *Senegambia and the Atlantic Slave Trade*. Cambridge: Cambridge University Press, 1998.

———. "Senegambia from the Sixteenth to the Eighteenth Century: Evolution of the Wolof, Sereer and 'Tukuloor' ". In *General History of Africa*. Vol. 5, *Africa from the Sixteenth to the Eighteenth Century*, edited by B.A. Ogot, 262-99. Paris: UNESCO, 1992.

Barton, Anne. "Parks and Ardens". *Proceedings of the British Academy* 80 (1991): 49–71.

Battestin, M.C. *The Moral Basis of Fielding's Art: A Study of* Joseph Andrews. Middletown, Conn.: Wesleyan University Press, 1959.

Beasley, Jerry C. *Novels of the 1740s*. Athens: University of Georgia Press, 1982.

Beasley, Nicholas M. *Christian Ritual and the Creation of British Slave Societies, 1650–1780*. Athens: University of Georgia Press, 2009.

———. "Ritual Time in British Plantation Colonies, 1650–1780". *Church History* 76 (2007): 541–68.

Beck, Deborah. "Speech Introductions and the Character Development of Telemachus". *Classical Journal* 94 (1999): 121–41.

Beeks, Graydon. "Handel's Sacred Music". In *The Cambridge Companion to Handel*, edited by Donald Burrows, 164–81. Cambridge: Cambridge University Press, 1997.

Bellamy, Liz. *Commerce, Morality and the Eighteenth-Century Novel*. Cambridge: Cambridge University Press, 1998.

Berglund, Lisa. "The Language of the Libertines: Subversive Morality in *The Man of Mode*". *Studies in English Literature, 1500–1900* 30 (1990): 369–86.

Beurton, Peter, Raphael Falk and Hans-Jörg Rheinberger, eds. *The Concept of the Gene in Development and Evolution: Historical and Epistemological Perspectives*. Cambridge: Cambridge University Press, 2000.

Bittlestone, Robert. *Odysseus Unbound: The Search for Homer's Ithaca*. Cambridge: Cambridge University Press, 2005.

Black, Jeremy. *George III: America's Last King*. New Haven, Conn.: Yale University Press, 2006.

———. *Natural and Necessary Enemies: Anglo-French Relations in the Eighteenth Century*. London: Duckworth, 1986.

Bohls, Elizabeth A. "The Planter Picturesque: Matthew Lewis's *Journal of a West India Proprietor*". *European Romantic Review* 13 (2002): 63–76.

Bonomi, Patricia U., and Peter R. Eisenstadt. "Church Adherence in the Eighteenth-Century British American Colonies". *William and Mary Quarterly* 39 (1982): 246–86.

Boucher, Philip P. *France and the American Tropics to 1700: Tropics of Discontent?* Baltimore: Johns Hopkins University Press, 2008.

Boulukos, George. *The Grateful Slave: The Emergence of Race in Eighteenth-Century British and American Culture*. Cambridge: Cambridge University Press, 2008.

Brack, O.M., Jr. *The Macaroni Parson and the Concentrated Mind: Samuel Johnson's Writings for the Reverend William Dodd*. Samuel Johnson Society of Southern California, 2004.

Brading, D.A. *The First America: The Spanish Monarchy, Creole Patriots, and the Liberal State, 1492–1867*. Cambridge: Cambridge University Press, 1991.

Bradley, K.R. *Slaves and Masters in the Roman Empire: A Study in Social Control*. New York: Oxford University Press, 1987.

Brathwaite, Edward. *The Development of Creole Society in Jamaica, 1770–1820*. Oxford: Clarendon Press, 1971.

Breslaw, Elaine G. *Dr. Alexander Hamilton and Provincial America: Expanding the Orbit of Scottish Culture*. Baton Rouge: Louisiana State University Press, 2008.

Brooks, George E., Jr. "The *Signares* of Saint-Louis and Gorée: Women Entrepreneurs in Eighteenth-Century Senegal". In *Women in Africa: Studies in Social and Economic Change*, edited by Nancy J. Hafkin and Edna G. Bay, 18–44. Stanford, Calif.: Stanford University Press, 1976.

Brown, Callum G. *The Social History of Religion in Scotland since 1730*. London: Methuen, 1987.

Brown, Christopher Leslie. *Moral Capital: Foundations of British Abolitionism*. Chapel Hill: University of North Carolina Press, 2006.

Brown, F. Martin, and Bernard Heineman. *Jamaica and Its Butterflies*. London: E.W. Classey, 1972.

Brown, Laura. *Fables of Modernity: Literature and Culture in the English Eighteenth Century*. Ithaca, NY: Cornell University Press, 2001.

Brown, Richard. *Church and State in Modern Britain, 1700–1850*. London: Routledge, 1991.

Brown, Stewart J. "An Eighteenth-Century Historian on the Amerindians: Culture, Colonialism and Christianity in William Robertson's History of America". *Studies in World Christianity* 2 (1996): 204–22.

———. "Religion in Scotland". In *A Companion to Eighteenth-Century Britain*, edited by H.T. Dickinson, 260–70. Oxford: Blackwell, 2002.

——— (ed). *William Robertson and the Expansion of Empire*. Cambridge: Cambridge University Press, 1997.

Brown, Vincent. *The Reaper's Garden: Death and Power in the World of Atlantic Slavery*. Cambridge, Mass.: Harvard University Press, 2008.

Brückmann, Patricia. " 'Men, Women and Poles': Samuel Richardson and the Romance of a Stuart Princess". *Eighteenth-Century Life* 27 (2003): 31–52.

Brunt, P.A. *Studies in Greek History and Thought*. Oxford: Clarendon Press, 1986.

Brunton, Deborah C. "The Transfer of Medical Education: Teaching at the Edinburgh and Philadelphia Medical Schools". In *Scotland and America in the Age of the Enlightenment*, edited by Richard B. Sher and Jeffrey R. Smitten, 242–58. Edinburgh: Edinburgh University Press, 1990.

Brydon, George Maclaren. *Virginia's Mother Church and the Political Conditions under Which It Grew*. Richmond: Virginia Historical Society, 1947.

Bryson, Gladys. *Man and Society: The Scottish Inquiry of the Eighteenth Century*. Princeton, NJ: Princeton University Press, 1945.

Buisseret, David. "Charles Boucher of Jamaica and the Establishment of Greenwich Longitude". *Imago Mundi* 62 (2010): 239–47.

Burgess, Glenn. "England and Scotland". In *European Political Thought, 1450–1700: Religion, Law and Philosophy*, edited by Howell A. Lloyd, Glenn Burgess and Simon Hodson, 332–75. New Haven, Conn.: Yale University Press, 2007.

Burleigh, J.H.S. *A Church History of Scotland*. London: Oxford University Press, 1960.

Burnard, Trevor. " 'The Countrie Continues Sicklie': White Mortality in Jamaica, 1655–1780". *Social History of Medicine* 12 (1999): 67–70.

———. *Mastery, Tyranny, and Desire: Thomas Thistlewood and His Slaves in the Anglo-Jamaican World*. Chapel Hill: University of North Carolina Press, 2004.

———. " 'Prodigious Riches': The Wealth of Jamaica before the American Revolution". *Economic History Review* 54 (2001): 506–24.

Butler, Jon. *Awash in a Sea of Faith: Christianizing the American People*. Cambridge, Mass.: Harvard University Press, 1990.

Butt, John. *Fielding*. 1954. Reprint, London: Longmans, Green, 1968.

———. *The Oxford History of English Literature*. Vol. 8, *The Mid-Eighteenth Century*. Oxford: Clarendon Press, 1979.

Butterfield, William C. "John Wolcot (1738–1819)". *Journal of the American Medical Association* 216 (1971): 137–38.

Byrne, Peter. *Natural Religion and the Nature of Religion: The Legacy of Deism*. London: Routledge, 1989.

Callow, John. *The Making of King James II: The Formative Years of a Fallen King*. Stroud, UK: Sutton Publishing, 2000.

Cambers, Andrew. " 'But Where Shall My Soul Repose?': Nonconformity, Science and the Geography of the Afterlife, c. 1660–1720". In *The Church, the Afterlife and the Fate of the Soul*, edited by Peter Clarke and Tony Claydon, 268–79. Woodbridge, UK: Boydell Press, 2009.

Cambiano, Giuseppe. "Aristotle and the Anonymous Opponents of Slavery". *Slavery and Abolition* 8 (1987): 22–41.

Cameron, James K. "Theological Controversy: A Factor in the Origins of the Scottish Enlightenment". In *The Origins and Nature of the Scottish Enlightenment*, edited by R.H. Campbell and Andrew S. Skinner, 116–30. Edinburgh: John Donald, 1982.

Campbell, Jill. *Natural Masques: Gender and Identity in Fielding's Plays and Novels*. Stanford, Calif.: Stanford University Press, 1995.

Campbell, Ted A. "John Wesley and the Legacy of Methodist Theology". *Bulletin of the John Rylands University Library of Manchester* 85 (2003): 405–20.

Canny, Nicholas. "Atlantic History and Global History". In *Atlantic History: A Critical Appraisal*, edited by Jack P. Greene and Philip D. Morgan, 317–36. Oxford: Oxford University Press, 2009.

Carey, Brycchan. *British Abolitionism and the Rhetoric of Sensibility: Writing, Sentiment, and Slavery, 1760–1807*. Houndmills, UK: Palgrave Macmillan, 2005.

———. "John Wesley's *Thoughts upon Slavery* and the Language of the Heart". *Bulletin of the John Rylands University Library of Manchester* 85 (2003): 269–84.

Carretta, Vincent. *Equiano, the African: Biography of a Self-Made Man*. New York: Penguin, 2006.

———. "Who Was Francis Williams?" *Early American Literature* 38 (2003): 213–37.

Cartledge, Paul. *Ancient Greek Political Thought and Practice*. Cambridge: Cambridge University Press, 2009.

Cassidy, F.G., and R.B. Le Page, eds. *Dictionary of Jamaican English*. 1967. Reprint, Cambridge: Cambridge University Press, 1980.

Cater, Jeremy J. "The Making of Principal Robertson: Politics and the University of Edinburgh in the Second Half of the Eighteenth Century". *Scottish Historical Review* 49 (1970): 60–84.

Cave, Roderick. *Printing and the Book Trade in the West Indies*. London: Pindar Press, 1987.

Cervantes Saavedra, Miguel. *Don Quixote of La Mancha*. Translated and edited by Walter Starkie. London: Macmillan, 1954.

Champion, J.A.I. *The Pillars of Priestcraft Shaken: The Church of England and Its Enemies, 1660–1730*. Cambridge: Cambridge University Press, 1992.

Chaney, Edward. *The Evolution of the Grand Tour: Anglo-Italian Cultural Relations since the Renaissance*. London: Frank Cass, 1998.

Chaplin, Joyce E. *The First Scientific American: Benjamin Franklin and the Pursuit of Genius*. New York: Basic Books, 2006.

———. "Knowing the Ocean: Benjamin Franklin and the Circulation of Atlantic Knowledge". In *Science and Empire in the Atlantic World*, edited by James Delbourgo and Nicholas Dew, 73–96. New York: Routledge, 2008.

Chen, Jeng-Guo S. "Providence and Progress: The Religious Dimension in Ferguson's Discussion of Civil Society". In *Adam Ferguson: History, Progress and Human Nature*, edited by Eugene Heath and Vincenzo Merolle, 171–86. London: Pickering and Chatto, 2008.

Chenoweth, Michael. *The 18th Century Climate of Jamaica: Derived from the Journals of Thomas Thistlewood, 1750–1786*. Philadelphia: American Philosophical Society, 2003.

Chorley, Richard J., Antony J. Dunn and Robert P. Beckinsale. *The History of the Study of Landforms or the Development of Geomorphology*. London: Methuen, 1964.

Christie, O.F., ed. *The Diary of the Rev. William Jones, 1777–1821: Curate and Vicar of Broxbourne and the Hamlet of Hoddesdon, 1781–1821*. London: Brentano's, 1929.

Clark, Andrew Hill. *Acadia: The Geography of Early Nova Scotia to 1760*. Madison: University of Wisconsin Press, 1968.

Clark, Ian D.L. "From Protest to Reaction: The Moderate Regime in the Church of Scotland, 1752–1805". In *Scotland in the Age of Improvement: Essays in Scottish History in the Eighteenth Century*, edited by N.T. Phillipson and Rosalind Mitchison, 200–224. Edinburgh: Edinburgh University Press, 1970.

Clark, J.C.D. *English Society, 1660–1832: Religion, Ideology and Politics during the Ancien Régime*. Cambridge: Cambridge University Press, 2000.

Cnattingius, Hans. *Bishops and Societies: A Study of Anglican Colonial and Missionary Expansion, 1698–1850*. London: Society for Promoting Christian Knowledge, 1952.

Cohen, I. Bernard. *Benjamin Franklin's Science*. Cambridge, Mass.: Harvard University Press, 1990.

Colledge, J.J. *Ships of the Royal Navy*. Annapolis, Md.: Naval Institute Press, 1987.

Colley, Linda. *Britons: Forging the Nation, 1707–1837*. New Haven, Conn.: Yale University Press, 1992.

———. *The Ordeal of Elizabeth Marsh: A Woman in World History*. London: HarperCollins, 2007.

Collins, Kenneth J. "Rethinking the Systematic Nature of John Wesley's Theology". *Bulletin of the John Rylands University Library of Manchester* 85 (2003): 309–30.

Conway, Stephen. *War, State, and Society in Mid-Eighteenth-Century Britain and Ireland*. Oxford: Oxford University Press, 2006.

Cook, Harold J. *Matters of Exchange: Commerce, Medicine, and Science in the Dutch Golden Age*. New Haven, Conn.: Yale University Press, 2007.

Corbett, Julian S. *England in the Seven Years' War: A Study in Combined Strategy*. London: Longmans, Green, 1918.

Cordner, Michael, ed. *The Plays of Sir George Etherege*. Cambridge: Cambridge University Press, 1982.

Cosh, Mary. *Edinburgh: The Golden Age*. Edinburgh: John Donald, 2003.

Coutu, Joan. *Persuasion and Propaganda: Monuments and the Eighteenth-Century British Empire*. Montreal: McGill-Queen's University Press, 2006.

Cox, Jeffrey. *The British Missionary Enterprise since 1700*. New York: Routledge, 2008.

Craik, Alex D.D. "Geometry, Analysis, and the Baptism of Slaves: John West in Scotland and Jamaica". *Historia Mathematica* 25 (1998): 29–74.

Crane, M.D. "Arthur Broughton, a Late Eighteenth Century Botanist in Bristol and Jamaica". *Archives of Natural History* 10 (1981): 317–30.

Craton, Michael. *Testing the Chains: Resistance to Slavery in the British West Indies*. Ithaca, NY: Cornell University Press, 1982.

Crawford, Robert. "Burns, Robert (1759–1796)". *Oxford Dictionary of National Biography*. Oxford: Oxford University Press, 2004.

———. *Scotland's Books: A History of Scottish Literature.* Oxford: Oxford University Press, 2009.

Crosby, David L. "Anthony Benezet's Transformation of Anti- slavery Rhetoric". *Slavery and Abolition* 23 (2002): 39–58.

Crowe, Michael J. *The Extraterrestrial Life Debate, 1750–1900: The Idea of a Plurality of Worlds from Kant to Lowell.* Cambridge: Cambridge University Press, 1986.

Crowley, Terry. *Louisbourg: Atlantic Fortress and Seaport.* Historical Booklet no. 48. Ottawa: Canadian Historical Association, 1990.

Cundall, Frank. *Historic Jamaica.* London: Institute of Jamaica, 1915.

Cunningham, Andrew. "Medicine to Calm the Mind: Boerhaave's Medical System, and Why It Was Adopted in Edinburgh". In *The Medical Enlightenment of the Eighteenth Century*, edited by Andrew Cunningham and Roger French, 40–66. Cambridge: Cambridge University Press, 1990.

Cunningham, Andrew, and Roger French, eds. *The Medical Enlightenment of the Eighteenth Century.* Cambridge: Cambridge University Press, 1990.

Cunningham, Vanessa. *Shakespeare and Garrick.* Cambridge: Cambridge University Press, 2008.

Curran, Andrew. "Rethinking Race History: The Role of the Albino in the French Enlightenment Life Sciences". *History and Theory* 48 (2009): 151–79.

Curtin, Philip D. *Economic Change in Precolonial Africa: Senegambia in the Era of the Slave Trade.* Madison: University of Wisconsin Press, 1975.

Dain, Bruce. *A Hideous Monster of the Mind: American Race Theory in the Early Republic.* Cambridge, Mass.: Harvard University Press, 2002.

Daly, James. *Cosmic Harmony and Political Thinking in Early Stuart England.* Philadelphia: American Philosophical Society, 1979.

Daston, Lorraine, and Katharine Park. *Wonders and the Order of Nature, 1150–1750.* New York: Zone Books, 1998.

Daumas, Maurice. *Le syndrome des grieux: La relation père/fils au XVIIIe siècle.* Paris: Éditions du Seuil, 1990.

Davis, David Brion. *The Problem of Slavery in the Age of Revolution, 1770–1823.* Ithaca, NY: Cornell University Press, 1975.

Dayfoot, Arthur Charles. *The Shaping of the West Indian Church, 1492–1962.* Kingston: University of the West Indies Press, 1999.

Desmond, Ray. *Dictionary of British and Irish Botanists and Horticulturists.* London: Taylor and Francis, 1977.

Devine, T.M. *Scotland's Empire and the Shaping of the Americas, 1600–1815.* Washington, DC: Smithsonian Books, 2003.

———. *The Tobacco Lords: A Study of the Tobacco Merchants of Glasgow and Their Trading Activities, c. 1740–90.* Edinburgh: John Donald, 1975.

Dickson, Vernon Guy. "Truth, Wonder, and Exemplarity in Aphra Behn's *Oroonoko*". *Studies in English Literature, 1500–1900* 47 (2007): 573–94.

Dijksterhuis, E.J. *The Mechanization of the World Picture: Pythagoras to Newton.* 1950. Reprint, Princeton, NJ: Princeton University Press, 1986.

Dixon, Peter. *Oliver Goldsmith Revisited.* Boston: Twayne, 1991.

Dobson, David. *Scots in the West Indies, 1707–1857.* Baltimore: Clearfield, 2006.

Doody, Margaret Anne. *A Natural Passion: A Study of the Novels of Samuel Richardson.* Oxford: Clarendon Press, 1974.

Dox, Thurston J., ed. *American Oratorios and Cantatas: A Catalog of Works Written in the United States from Colonial Times to 1985*. Metuchen, NJ: Scarecrow Press, 1986.

Drayton, Richard. *Nature's Government: Science, Imperial Britain, and the "Improvement" of the World*. New Haven, Conn.: Yale University Press, 2000.

Dubois, Laurent. "An Enslaved Enlightenment: Rethinking the Intellectual History of the French Atlantic". *Social History* 31 (2006): 1–14.

Dudgeon, Piers, and Jonathan Jones, eds. *Dear Boy: Lord Chesterfield's Letters to His Son*. London: Bantam Press, 1989.

Dunn, Richard S. *Moravian Missionaries at Work in a Jamaican Slave Community, 1754–1835*. [Minneapolis]: Associates of the James Ford Bell Library, University of Minnesota, 1994.

Durie, Alastair J., and Stuart Handley. "Home, Henry, Lord Kames (1696–1782)". *Oxford Dictionary of National Biography*. Oxford: Oxford University Press, 2004.

Dussinger, John A. "Love and Consanguinity in Richardson's Novels". *Studies in English Literature, 1500–1900* 24 (1984): 513–26.

———. "Goldsmith, Oliver (1728?–1774)". *Oxford Dictionary of National Biography*. Oxford: Oxford University Press, 2004.

Du Toit, Alexander. "Lindsay, John (1685/6–1768), nonjuring Church of England clergyman and writer". *Oxford Dictionary of National Biography*. Oxford: Oxford University Press, 2004.

Earle, Carville V. "Environment, Disease, and Mortality in Early Virginia". In *The Chesapeake in the Seventeenth Century: Essays on Anglo-American Society*, edited by Thad W. Tate and David L. Ammerman, 96–125. Chapel Hill: University of North Carolina Press, 1979.

Ehrenberg, Victor. *The Greek State*. London: Methuen, 1969.

Eilberg-Schwartz, Howard. *The Savage in Judaism: An Anthropology of Israelite Religion and Ancient Judaism*. Bloomington: Indiana University Press, 1990.

Eliav-Feldon, Miriam, Benjamin Isaac and Joseph Ziegler, eds. *The Origins of Racism in the West*. Cambridge: Cambridge University Press, 2009.

Ellis, J.B. *The Diocese of Jamaica: A Short Account of its History, Growth and Organisation*. London: Society for Promoting Christian Knowledge, 1913.

Ellis, Markman. *The Politics of Sensibility: Race, Gender and Commerce in the Sentimental Novel*. Cambridge: Cambridge University Press, 1996.

Epstein, Dena J. *Sinful Tunes and Spirituals: Black Folk Music to the Civil War*. Urbana: University of Illinois Press, 1977.

Erlich, Avi. *Hamlet's Absent Father*. Princeton, NJ: Princeton University Press, 1977.

Evans, William McKee. "From the Land of Canaan to the Land of Guinea: The Strange Odyssey of the 'Sons of Ham' ". *American Historical Review* 85 (1980): 15–43.

Eze, Emmanuel C. "Hume, Race, and Human Nature". *Journal of the History of Ideas* 61 (2000): 691–98.

Fagg, C.W., and G.E. Allison. *Acacia Senegal and the Gum Arabic Trade*. Tropical Forestry Papers No. 42. Oxford: Oxford Forestry Institute, 2004.

Fausz, J. Frederick. " 'Engaged in Enterprises Pregnant with Terror': George Washington's Formative Years among the Indians". In *George Washington and the Virginia Backcountry*, edited by Warren R. Hofstra, 115–55. Madison, Wisc.: Madison House, 1998.

Fawcett, William. "Notes on Jamaica Plants". *Journal of Botany* 55 (1917): 35–38.

———. "William Wright, a Jamaican Botanist (1735–1819)". *Journal of Botany*, 60 (1922): 330–34.

Fawcett, William, and Alfred Barton Rendle. *Flora of Jamaica: Containing Descriptions of the Flowering Plants Known from the Island*. London: British Museum, 1914.

Figlerowicz, Marta. " 'Frightful Spectacles of a Mangled King': Aphra Behn's *Oroonoko* and Narration Through Theater". *New Literary History* 39 (2008): 321–34.

Finkelman, Paul. *Slavery and the Founders: Race and Liberty in the Age of Jefferson*. New York: M.E. Sharpe, 2001.

Fischer, David Hackett, and James C. Kelly. *Bound Away: Virginia and the Westward Movement*. Charlottesville: University Press of Virginia, 2000.

Fitzpatrick, John C., ed. *The Diaries of George Washington, 1748–1799*. Boston: Houghton Mifflin, 1925.

Fitzpatrick, Martin. "The Enlightenment, Politics and Providence: Some Scottish and English Comparisons". In *Enlightenment and Religion: Rational Dissent in Eighteenth-Century Britain*, edited by Knud Haakonssen, 64–98. Cambridge: Cambridge University Press, 1996.

Flexner, James Thomas. *George Washington: The Forge of Experience (1732–1775)*. Boston: Little, Brown, 1965.

Flint, Christopher. "The Eighteenth-Century Novel and Print Culture: A Proposed Modesty". In *A Companion to the Eighteenth-Century English Novel and Culture*, edited by Paula R. Backscheider and Catherine Ingrassia, 343–64. Oxford: Blackwell, 2005.

Foner, Eric. *The Story of American Freedom*. New York: W.W. Norton, 1998.

Ford, Lacy K. *Deliver Us from Evil: The Slavery Question in the Old South*. Oxford: Oxford University Press, 2009.

Frégault, Guy. *Canada: The War of the Conquest*. Toronto: Oxford University Press, 1969.

Friedman, Arthur, ed. *Collected Works of Oliver Goldsmith*. Oxford: Clarendon Press, 1966.

Fulford, Tim. *Romantic Indians: Native Americans, British Literature, and Transatlantic Culture, 1756–1830*. Oxford: Oxford University Press, 2006.

Fuller, J.F.C. *A Military History of the Western World*. New York: Da Capo Press, 1955.

Gallay, Alan. "The Great Sellout: George Whitefield and Slavery". In *Looking South: Chapters in the Story of an American Region*, edited by Winfred B. Moore Jr and Joseph F. Tripp, 17–30. New York: Greenwood Press, 1989.

Garlan, Yvon. *Slavery in Ancient Greece*. 1982. Reprint, Ithaca, NY: Cornell University Press, 1988.

Garnsey, Peter. *Ideas of Slavery from Aristotle to Augustine*. Cambridge: Cambridge University Press, 1996.

———. *Thinking about Property: From Antiquity to the Age of Revolution*. Cambridge: Cambridge University Press, 2007.

Garrett, Aaron. "Anthropology: The 'Original' of Human Nature". In *The Cambridge Companion to the Scottish Enlightenment*, edited by Alexander Broadie, 79–93. Cambridge: Cambridge University Press, 2003.

Gaspar, David Barry. *Bondmen and Rebels: A Study of Master–Slave Relations in Antigua*. Baltimore: Johns Hopkins University Press, 1985.

Gatrell, Vic. *City of Laughter: Sex and Satire in Eighteenth-Century London*. London: Atlantic Books, 2006.

Gentles, Ian. *The New Model Army in England, Ireland and Scotland, 1645–1653*. Oxford: Blackwell, 1992.

Gerbi, Antonello. *The Dispute of the New World: The History of a Polemic, 1750–1900.* Pittsburgh: University of Pittsburgh Press, 1973.

Gibson, William. "The Limits of the Confessional State: Electoral Religion in the Reign of Charles II". *Historical Journal* 51 (2008): 27–47.

Gigante, Denise, ed. *The Great Age of the English Essay: An Anthology.* New Haven, Conn.: Yale University Press, 2008.

Gillis, John R. "Taking History Offshore: Atlantic Islands in European Minds, 1400–1800". In *Islands in History and Representation*, edited by Rod Edmond and Vanessa Smith, 19–31. London: Routledge, 2003.

Gilmore, John. "Williams, Francis (c. 1690–1762)". *Oxford Dictionary of National Biography.* Oxford: Oxford University Press, 2004.

Girtin, Tom. *Doctor with Two Aunts: A Biography of Peter Pindar.* London: Hutchinson, 1959.

Glacken, Clarence J. *Traces on the Rhodian Shore: Nature and Culture in Western Thought from Ancient Times to the End of the Eighteenth Century.* Berkeley: University of California Press, 1967.

Glasgow, Joshua. *A Theory of Race.* New York: Routledge, 2009.

Gloudon, A., and C. Tobisch. *Orchids of Jamaica.* Kingston: University of the West Indies Press, 1995.

Golinski, Jan. *British Weather and the Climate of Enlightenment.* Chicago: University of Chicago Press, 2007.

Gordon, Shirley C. *God Almighty Make Me Free: Christianity in Preemancipation Jamaica.* Bloomington: Indiana University Press, 1996.

Goudie, Sean X. *Creole America: The West Indies and the Formation of Literature and Culture in the New Republic.* Philadelphia: University of Pennsylvania Press, 2006.

Greene, Jack P. "The Jamaica Privilege Controversy, 1764–66: An Episode in the Process of Constitutional Definition in the Early Modern British Empire". *Journal of Imperial and Commonwealth History* 22 (1994): 16–53.

———. "Liberty, Slavery and the Transformation of British Identity in the Eighteenth-Century West Indies". *Slavery and Abolition* 21 (2000): 1–31.

———. " 'Of Liberty and of the Colonies': A Case Study of Constitutional Conflict in the Mid-Eighteenth-Century British American Empire". In *Liberty and American Experience in the Eighteenth Century*, edited by David Womersley, 21–102. Indianapolis, Ind.: Liberty Fund, 2006.

———. " 'A Plain and Natural Right to Life and Liberty': An Early Natural Rights Attack on the Excesses of the Slave System in Colonial British America". *William and Mary Quarterly* 57 (2000): 793–808.

Griswold, Charles L., Jr. *Adam Smith and the Virtues of Enlightenment.* Cambridge: Cambridge University Press, 1999.

Gunby, David, David Carnegie and Antony Hammond, eds. *The Works of John Webster: An Old-Spelling Critical Edition.* Cambridge: Cambridge University Press, 1995.

Guthrie, Douglas. "The Influence of the Leyden School upon Scottish Medicine". *Medical History* 3 (1959): 108–22.

Halkett, Samuel, and John Laing. *Dictionary of Anonymous and Pseudonymous English Literature.* Edinburgh: Oliver and Boyd, 1926–62.

Hall, Douglas. "Botanical and Horticultural Enterprise in Eighteenth-Century Jamaica". In *West Indies Accounts: Essays on the History of the British Caribbean and the Atlantic*

Economy in Honour of Richard Sheridan, edited by Roderick A. McDonald, 101–25. Kingston: University of the West Indies Press, 1996.

Hall, Edith. *The Return of Ulysses: A Cultural History of Homer's Odyssey*. London: I.B. Tauris, 2008.

Hall, Gwendolyn Midlo. *Africans in Colonial Louisiana: The Development of Afro-Creole Culture in the Eighteenth Century*. Baton Rouge: Louisiana State University Press, 1992.

Hall, N.A.T. "Some Aspects of the Deficiency Question in Jamaica in the Eighteenth Century". *Jamaica Journal* 7, nos. 1–2 (March–June 1973): 36–41.

Hamilton, Douglas J. *Scotland, the Caribbean and the Atlantic World, 1750–1820*. Manchester: Manchester University Press, 2005.

Hamilton, Ian. *The Erosion of Calvinist Orthodoxy: Seceders and Subscription in Scottish Presbyterianism*. Edinburgh: Rutherford House Books, 1990.

Hancock, David. *Citizens of the World: London Merchants and the Integration of the British Atlantic Community, 1735–1785*. Cambridge: Cambridge University Press, 1995.

Handler, Jerome S. *A Guide to Source Materials for the Study of Barbados History, 1627–1834*. Carbondale: Southern Illinois University Press, 1971.

———. "A Rare Eighteenth-Century Tract in Defense of Slavery in Barbados: The Thoughts of the Rev. John Duke, Curate of S. Michael". *Journal of the Barbados Museum and Historical Society* 51 (2005): 58–65.

Hannaford, Ivan. *Race: The History of an Idea in the West*. Baltimore: Johns Hopkins University Press, 1996.

Harrison, Robert. "Dick, Sir Archibald, third baronet (1703–1785)". *Oxford Dictionary of National Biography*. Oxford: Oxford University Press, 2004.

Hayman, John G. "Dorimant and the Comedy of *A Man of Mode*". *Modern Language Quarterly* 30 (1969): 183–97.

Haynes, Stephen R. *Noah's Curse: The Biblical Justification of American Slavery*. Oxford: Oxford University Press, 2002.

Hempton, David. "Enlightenment and Faith". In *The Eighteenth Century, 1688–1815*, edited by Paul Langford, 71–100. Oxford: Oxford University Press, 2002.

———. *Methodism: Empire of the Spirit*. New Haven, Conn.: Yale University Press, 2005.

Henderson, G.D. *Religious Life in Seventeenth-Century Scotland*. Cambridge: Cambridge University Press, 1937.

Hendrick, S. Purcell. *A Sketch of the History of the Cathedral Church of St Jago de la Vega, Spanish Town, in the Parish of St Catherine, Jamaica*. Kingston: Jamaica Times, 1911.

Henningsen, Henning. "Superstitions about Waterspouts". *Mariner's Mirror* 63 (1977): 193–94.

Herman, Arthur. *The Scottish Enlightenment: The Scots' Invention of the Modern World*. London: Fourth Estate, 2001.

Herrick, James A. *The Radical Rhetoric of the English Deists: The Discourse of Skepticism, 1680–1750*. Columbia: University of South Carolina Press, 1997.

Higman, B.W. *Jamaican Food: History, Biology, Culture*. Kingston: University of the West Indies Press, 2008.

———. *Plantation Jamaica, 1750–1850: Capital and Control in a Colonial Economy*. Kingston: University of the West Indies Press, 2005.

Hill, Christopher. *Milton and the English Revolution*. London: Faber and Faber, 1979.

Hill, Errol. *The Jamaican Stage, 1655–1900: Profile of a Colonial Theatre.* Amherst: University of Massachusetts Press, 1992.

Höpfl, Harro. *The Christian Polity of John Calvin.* Cambridge: Cambridge University Press, 1982.

Horn, D.B. *A Short History of the University of Edinburgh, 1556–1889.* Edinburgh: University Press of Edinburgh, 1967.

Houston, Alan. *Benjamin Franklin and the Politics of Improvement.* New Haven, Conn.: Yale University Press, 2008.

Houston, R.A. *Social Change in the Age of Enlightenment: Edinburgh, 1660–1760.* Oxford: Clarendon Press, 1994.

Howard, Robert Mowbray, ed. *Records and Letters of the Family of the Longs of Longville, Jamaica, and Hampton Lodge, Surrey.* London: Simpkin, Marshall, Hamilton, Kent, 1925.

Howson, Gerald. *The Macaroni Parson: A Life of the Unfortunate Dr. Dodd.* London: Hutchinson, 1973.

Hudson, Nicholas. "From 'Nation' to 'Race': The Origin of Racial Classification in Eighteenth-Century Thought". *Eighteenth-Century Studies* 29 (1996): 247–64.

———. " 'Oral Tradition': The Evolution of an Eighteenth-Century Concept". In *Tradition in Transition: Women Writers, Marginal Texts, and the Eighteenth-Century Canon,* edited by Alvaro Ribeiro and James G. Basker, 161–76. Oxford: Clarendon Press, 1996.

———. *Writing and European Thought, 1600–1830.* Cambridge: Cambridge University Press, 1994.

Hughes, Derek. *Versions of Blackness: Key Texts on Slavery from the Seventeenth Century.* Cambridge: Cambridge University Press, 2007.

Hulme, Peter. "Polytropic Man: Tropes of Sexuality and Mobility in Early Colonial Discourse". In *Europe and Its Others,* edited by Francis Barker, Peter Hulme, Margaret Iversen and Diana Loxley. Vol. 1, 17–32. Colchester, UK: University of Essex, 1985.

Hunter, J. Paul. *Occasional Form: Henry Fielding and the Chains of Circumstance.* Baltimore: Johns Hopkins University Press, 1975.

———. "Protesting Fiction, Constructing History". In *The Historical Imagination in Early Modern Britain: History, Rhetoric, and Fiction, 1500–1800,* edited by Donald R. Kelley and David Harris Sacks, 298–317. Cambridge: Cambridge University Press, 1997.

Immerwahr, John. "Hume's Revised Racism". *Journal of the History of Ideas* 53 (1992): 481–86.

Ingram, K.E. *Manuscript Sources for the History of the West Indies.* Kingston: University of the West Indies Press, 2000.

———. *Sources of Jamaican History, 1655–1838.* Zug, Switzerland: Inter Documentation, 1976.

Innes, Matthew. "Charlemagne's Will: Piety, Politics and the Imperial Succession". *English Historical Review* 112 (1997): 833–55.

Irons, Charles F. *The Origins of Proslavery Christianity: White and Black Evangelicals in Colonial and Antebellum Virginia.* Chapel Hill: University of North Carolina Press, 2008.

Israel, Jonathan. *Enlightenment Contested: Philosophy, Modernity, and the Emancipation of Man, 1670–1752.* Oxford: Oxford University Press, 2006.

Jackson, Maurice. "Diasporan Voices of the African Past: James Albert Ukawsaw Gronniosaw, Quobna Ottobah Cugoano, Olaoudah Equiano, and Ignatius Sancho as Sources of African History". In *The Changing Worlds of Atlantic Africa: Essays in Honor of Robin Law*, edited by Toyin Falola and Matt D. Childs, 347–70. Durham, NC: Carolina Academic Press, 2009.

———. *Let This Voice Be Heard: Anthony Benezet, Father of American Abolitionism*. Philadelphia: University of Pennsylvania Press, 2009.

Jackson, Patrick Wyse. *The Chronologers' Quest: Episodes in the Search for the Age of the Earth*. Cambridge: Cambridge University Press, 2006.

Jacob, Christian. *The Sovereign Map: Theoretical Approaches in Cartography Throughout History*. Chicago: University of Chicago Press, 2006.

Jacob, W.M. "John Wesley and the Church of England". *Bulletin of the John Rylands University Library of Manchester* 85 (2003): 57–71.

Jacobs, Edward, and Antonia Fraser. " 'Lost Books' and Publishing History: Two Annotated Lists of Imprints for the Fiction Titles Listed in the Circulating Library Catalogs of Thomas Lowndes (1766) and M. Heavisides (1790), of Which No Known Copies Survive". *Bibliographical Society of America, Papers* 89 (1995): 260–97.

Jaher, Diana. "The Paradoxes of Slavery in Thomas Southerne's *Oroonoko*". *Comparative Drama* 42 (2008): 51–71.

James, Alfred P. "The First English-Speaking Trans-Appalachian Frontier". *Mississippi Valley Historical Review* 17 (1930): 55–71.

———. *The Ohio Company: Its Inner History*. Pittsburgh: University of Pittsburgh Press, 1959.

Jimack, Peter, ed. *A History of the Two Indies: A Translated Selection of Writings from Raynal's* Histoire philosophique et politique des établissements des Européens dans les deux Indes. Aldershot, UK: Ashgate, 2006.

Johnson, Howard. Introduction to *The History of Jamaica*, by Edward Long. Vol. 1, i–xxv. Kingston: Ian Randle, 2002.

Johnston, A.J.B. *Endgame 1758: The Promise, the Glory, and the Despair of Louisbourg's Last Decade*. Lincoln: University of Nebraska, 2007.

Jones, A.M. *Africa and Indonesia: The Evidence of the Xylophone and Other Musical and Cultural Factors*. Leiden: E.J. Brill, 1971.

Jones, William R. "Wolcot, John (bap. 1738, d. 1819)". *Oxford Dictionary of National Biography*. Oxford: Oxford University Press, 2004.

Karras, Alan L. *Sojourners in the Sun: Scottish Migrants in Jamaica and the Chesapeake, 1740–1800*. Ithaca, NY: Cornell University Press, 1992.

Kealy, A.G. *Chaplains of the Royal Navy, 1626–1903*. Portsmouth: Wilkins and Son, [1912].

Kearney, Hugh. *The British Isles: A History of Four Nations*. Cambridge: Cambridge University Press, 1989.

Kennell, Nigel M. *Spartans: A New History*. Chichester, UK: Wiley- Blackwell, 2010.

Kidd, Colin. *The Forging of Races: Race and Scripture in the Protestant Atlantic World, 1600–2000*. Cambridge: Cambridge University Press, 2006.

Kimball, Susanne B. "Fathers and Sons in Western Literature". *Germanic Notes and Reviews* 32 (2001): 163–70.

Knox, R.A. *Enthusiasm: A Chapter in the History of Religion, with Special Reference to the XVII and XVIII Centuries*. Oxford: Clarendon Press, 1950.

Koerner, Lisbet. *Linnaeus: Nature and Nation*. Cambridge, Mass.: Harvard University Press, 1999.

Koontz, Louis Knott. *Robert Dinwiddie: His Career in American Colonial Government and Westward Expansion*. Glendale, Calif.: Arthur H. Clark, 1941.

Koyanagi, Kimihiro. "Civilization and History in Lord Kames and William Robertson". In *The Rise of Political Economy in the Scottish Enlightenment*, edited by Tatsuya Sakamoto and Hideo Tanaka, 150–62. London: Routledge, 2003.

Kriz, Kay Dian. *Slavery, Sugar, and the Culture of Refinement: Picturing the British West Indies, 1700–1840*. New Haven, Conn.: Yale University Press, 2008.

Lachman, David C. "Erskine, Ebenezer (1680–1754)". *Oxford Dictionary of National Biography*. Oxford: Oxford University Press, 2004.

———. *The Marrow Controversy*. Edinburgh: Rutherford House, 1988.

Lakwete, Angela. *Inventing the Cotton Gin: Machine and Myth in Antebellum America*. Baltimore: Johns Hopkins University Press, 2003.

Lambert, Frank. *"Pedlar in Divinity": George Whitefield and the Transatlantic Revivals, 1737–1770*. Princeton, NJ: Princeton University Press, 1994.

Laughton, J.K., and Ruddock Mackay. "Holburne, Francis (1704–1771), naval officer". *Oxford Dictionary of National Biography*. Oxford: Oxford University Press, 2004.

Lavery, Brian. *The Ship of the Line*. Vol. 1, *The Development of the Battlefleet, 1650–1850*. London: Conway Maritime Press, 1983.

Law, Alexander. *Education in Edinburgh in the Eighteenth Century*. London: University of London Press, 1965.

Lee, M. Owen. *Fathers and Sons in Virgil's* Aeneid: Tum Genitor Natum. Albany: State University of New York Press, 1979.

Lennox, Jeffers. "An Empire on Paper: The Founding of Halifax and Conceptions of Imperial Space, 1744–55". *Canadian Historical Review* 88 (2007): 373–412.

Lewis, Lesley. "English Commemorative Sculpture in Jamaica". *Jamaican Historical Review* 9 (1972): 9–140.

Lewis, Ricki. *Human Gentetics: Concepts and Applications*. Boston: McGraw-Hill, 2008.

Liddle, William D. " 'A Patriot King, or None': Lord Bolingbroke and the American Renunciation of George III". *Journal of American History* 65 (1979): 951–70.

Lipking, Joanna. " 'Others', Slaves, and Colonists in *Oroonoko*". In *The Cambridge Companion to Aphra Behn*, edited by Derek Hughes and Janet Todd, 166–87. Cambridge: Cambridge University Press, 2004.

Livingstone, David N. *Adam's Ancestors: Race, Religion, and the Politics of Human Origins*. Baltimore: Johns Hopkins University Press, 2008.

Lockridge, Kenneth A. *The Diary, and Life, of William Byrd II of Virginia, 1674–1744*. Chapel Hill: University of North Carolina Press, 1987.

Lovejoy, Arthur O. *The Great Chain of Being: A Study of the History of an Idea*. 1936. Reprint, Cambridge, Mass.: Harvard University Press, 1964.

Lovejoy, Paul E. *Transformations in Slavery: A History of Slavery in Africa*. Cambridge: Cambridge University Press, 1983.

Lucci, Diego. *Scripture and Deism: The Biblical Criticism of the Eighteenth-Century British Deists*. Bern: Peter Lang, 2008.

Lund, Roger D. "*A Tale of a Tub*, Swift's Apology, and the Trammels of Christian Wit". In *Augustan Subjects: Essays in Honour of Martin C. Battestin*, edited by Albert J. Rivero, 87–109. Newark: University of Delaware Press, 1997.

MacCallum, Hugh. *Milton and the Sons of God: The Divine Image in Milton's Epic Poetry*. Toronto: University of Toronto Press, 1986.

MacGregor, Arthur. *Curiosity and Enlightenment: Collectors and Collections from the Sixteenth to the Nineteenth Century*. New Haven, Conn.: Yale University Press, 2007.

———, ed. *Sir Hans Sloane: Collector, Scientist, Antiquary, Founding Father of the British Museum*. London: British Museum Press, 1994.

Macinnes, Allan I. *Union and Empire: The Making of the United Kingdom in 1707*. Cambridge: Cambridge University Press, 2007.

Mack, Douglas S. *Scottish Fiction and the British Empire*. Edinburgh: Edinburgh University Press, 2006.

Mackay, Ruddock F. *Admiral Hawke*. Oxford: Clarendon Press, 1965.

———, ed. *The Hawke Papers: A Selection, 1743–1771*. Aldershot, UK: Scolar Press, 1990.

Mackay, Ruddock, and Michael Duffy. *Hawke, Nelson and British Naval Leadership, 1747–1805*. Woodbridge, UK: Boydell Press, 2009.

MacLeod, Duncan J. *Slavery, Race and the American Revolution*. Cambridge: Cambridge University Press, 1974.

MacMullen, Ramsay. *Christianizing the Roman Empire (A.D. 100–400)*. New Haven, Conn.: Yale University Press, 1984.

Madrigal, Lorena, and Guido Barbujani. "Partitioning of Genetic Variation in Human Populations and the Concept of Race". In *Anthropological Genetics: Theory, Methods and Applications*, edited by Michael H. Crawford, 19–37. Cambridge: Cambridge University Press, 2007.

Malkin, Irad. *The Returns of Odysseus: Colonization and Ethnicity*. Berkeley: University of California Press, 1998.

Manguel, Alberto, and Gianni Guadalupi. *The Dictionary of Imaginary Places*. London: Bloomsbury, 1999.

Manning, Susan, and Francis D. Cogliano, eds. *The Atlantic Enlightenment*. Aldershot, UK: Ashgate, 2008.

Markley, Robert. " 'I have now done with my island, and all manner of discourse about it': Crusoe's *Farther Adventures* and the Unwritten History of the Novel". In *A Companion to the Eighteenth-Century English Novel and Culture*, edited by Paula R. Backscheider and Catherine Ingrassia, 25–47. Oxford: Blackwell, 2005.

Marks, Arthur S. "Benjamin West's *Jonah*: A Previously Overlooked Illustration for the Oratorio Composed in the New World". *American Art Journal* 28 (1997): 123–37.

Marsh, A.J. "The Taking of Goree, 1758". *Mariner's Mirror* 51 (1965): 117–30.

Martin, Dale B. *Slavery as Salvation: The Metaphor of Slavery in Pauline Christianity*. New Haven, Conn.: Yale University Press, 1990.

Martin, Leslie H. "Past and Parody in *The Man of Mode*". *Studies in English Literature, 1500–1900* 16 (1976): 363–76.

Matheson, Ann. *Theories of Rhetoric in the 18th-Century Scottish Sermon*. Lewiston, NY: Edwin Mellen Press, 1995.

May, W.E. "The *Panther* Affair". *Mariner's Mirror* 55 (1969): 401–10.

Maybaum, Ignaz. *Creation and Guilt: A Theological Assessment of Freud's Father–Son Conflict*. London: Vallentine, Mitchell, 1969.

Mayer, Robert. *History and the Early English Novel: Matters of Fact from Bacon to Defoe*. Cambridge: Cambridge University Press, 1997.

Mayo, Christopher. "Manners and Manuscripts: The Editorial Manufacture of Lord Chesterfield in *Letters to His Son*". *Papers of the Bibliographical Society of America* 99 (2005): 37–69.

Mbiti, John S. *African Religions and Philosophy*. London: Heinemann, 1969.

McClellan, James E., III. *Colonialism and Science: Saint Domingue in the Old Regime*. Baltimore: Johns Hopkins University Press, 1992.

McGirr, Elaine M. *Eighteenth-Century Characters: A Guide to the Literature of the Age*. London: Palgrave Macmillan, 2007.

McKenzie, Kirsten. *The Making of an English Slave-Owner: Samuel Eusebius Hudson at the Cape of Good Hope, 1796–1807*. Cape Town: UCT Press, 1993.

McKitterick, Rosamond. *Charlemagne: The Formation of European Identity*. Cambridge: Cambridge University Press, 2008.

McLennan, J.S. *Louisbourg: From Its Foundation to Its Fall, 1713–1758*. Sydney, NS: Fortress Press, 1957.

McLynn, Frank. *1759: The Year Britain Became Master of the World*. New York: Grove Press, 2004.

McManners, John, ed. *The Oxford History of Christianity*. Oxford: Oxford University Press, 1993.

McNeill, John Robert. *Atlantic Empires of France and Spain: Louisbourg and Havana, 1700–1763*. Chapel Hill: University of North Carolina Press, 1985.

Meggs, William J. "Epidemics of Mold Poisoning Past and Present". *Toxicology and Industrial Health* 25 (2009): 571–76.

Meinig, D.W. *The Shaping of America: A Geographical Perspective on 500 Years of History*. Vol. 1, *Atlantic America, 1492–1800*. New Haven, Conn.: Yale University Press, 1986.

Mercier, Roger. "L'Amérique et les Américains dans *l'Histoire des deux Indes* de l'abbé Raynal". *Revue française histoire outre-mer* 65 (1978): 308–24.

Metcalf, George. *Royal Government and Political Conflict in Jamaica, 1729–1783*. London: Longmans, 1965.

Meyer, Annette. "Ferguson's 'Appropriate Stile' in Combining History and Science: The History of Historiography Revisited". In *Adam Ferguson: History, Progress and Human Nature*, edited by Eugene Heath and Vincenzo Merolle, 131–45. London: Pickering and Chatto, 2008.

Middleton, W.E. Knowles. *A History of Theories of Rain and Other Forms of Precipitation*. New York: Franklin Watts, 1966.

Midgley, Graham. Review of *Shakespeare: The Critical Heritage*, edited by Brian Vickers. *Notes and Queries* 223 (1978): 175–77.

Millás, José Carlos. *Hurricanes of the Caribbean and Adjacent Regions, 1492–1800*. Miami: Academy of the Arts and Sciences of the Americas, 1968.

Miller, David Lee. *Dreams of the Burning Child: Sacrificial Sons and the Father's Witness*. Ithaca, NY: Cornell University Press, 2003.

Minter, R.A. *Episcopacy Without Episcopate: The Church of England in Jamaica before 1824*. Upton-upon-Severn, UK: Self Publishing Association, 1990.

Mitchell, Arthur, ed. *Geographical Collections Relating to Scotland Made by Walter Macfarlane*. Edinburgh: Scottish History Society, 1906.

Mitchison, Rosalind, and Leah Leneman. *Sexuality and Social Control: Scotland, 1660–1780*. Oxford: Basil Blackwell, 1989.

Molnar, Stephen. *Human Variation: Races, Types, and Ethnic Groups*. Upper Saddle River, NJ: Prentice Hall, 2002.

Morgan, Kenneth. "Robert Dinwiddie's Reports on the British American Colonies". *William and Mary Quarterly* 65 (2008): 305–46.

———, ed. *The Bright-Meyler Papers: A Bristol–West India Connection, 1732–1837*. Oxford: Oxford University Press/British Academy, 2007.

Morgan, Philip D. "British Encounters with Africans and African-Americans, circa 1600–1780". In *Strangers Within the Realm: Cultural Margins of the First British Empire*, edited by Bernard Bailyn and Philip D. Morgan, 157–219. Chapel Hill: University of North Carolina Press, 1991.

Morrell, J.B. "Medicine and Science in the Eighteenth Century". In *Four Centuries: Edinburgh University Life, 1583–1983*, edited by Gordon Donaldson, 38–52. Edinburgh: University of Edinburgh, 1983.

Mosse, George L. "Puritan Radicalism and the Enlightenment". *Church History* 29 (1960): 424–39.

Mulkearn, Lois, ed. *George Mercer Papers: Relating to the Ohio Company of Virginia*. Pittsburgh: University of Pittsburgh Press, 1954.

Mullan, John. *Anonymity: A Secret History of English Literature*. London: Faber and Faber, 2007.

Murdoch, Alexander. *Scotland and America, c. 1600–c. 1800*. Basingstoke, UK: Palgrave Macmillan, 2010.

Murnaghan, Sheila. "The Trials of Telemachus: Who Was the *Odyssey* Meant For?" *Arethusa* 35 (2002): 133–53.

Muthu, Sankar. *Enlightenment Against Empire*. Princeton, NJ: Princeton University Press, 2003.

Naish, George. "Naval Uniform". *Mariner's Mirror* 41 (1955): 91–114.

Namier, Lewis. *England in the Age of the American Revolution*. 1930. Reprint, London: Macmillan, 1961.

Nelson, Janet L. "Kingship and Empire in the Carolingian World". In *Carolingian Culture: Emulation and Innovation*, edited by Rosamond McKitterick, 52–87. Cambridge: Cambridge University Press, 1994.

Nelson, John K. *A Blessed Company: Parishes, Parsons, and Parishioners in Anglican Virginia, 1690–1776*. Chapel Hill: University of North Carolina, 2001.

Nelson, Louis. "Building 'Cross-Wise': Reconstructing Jamaica's Eighteenth-Century Anglican Churches". *Jamaican Historical Review* 22 (2002): 11–38.

Nelson, T.G.A. *Children, Parents, and the Rise of the Novel*. Newark: University of Delaware Press, 1995.

Nester, William R. *The Great Frontier War: Britain, France, and the Imperial Struggle for North America, 1607–1755*. Westport, Conn.: Praeger, 2000.

Nichols, John. *Literary Anecdotes of the Eighteenth Century*. Edited by Colin Clair. Carbondale: Southern Illinois University Press, 1967.

Nketia, J.H. Kwabema. "Tradition and Innovation in African Music". *Jamaica Journal* 11, nos. 3–4 (March 1978): 2–9.

Noyes, Robert Gayle. *The Thespian Mirror: Shakespeare in the Eighteenth-Century Novel*. Providence, RI: Brown University, 1953.

Nussbaum, Felicity A. *The Limits of the Human: Fictions of Anomaly, Race, and Gender in the Long Eighteenth Century*. Cambridge: Cambridge University Press, 2003.

Nuttall, A.D. *Pope's "Essay on Man"*. London: George Allen and Unwin, 1984.

Ober, William B. "John Wolcot, MD (1738–1819): Peter Pindar, the Satirist". *Journal of the American Medical Association* 208 (1969): 103–8.

Ogborn, Miles. *Global Lives: Britain and the World, 1550–1800*. Cambridge: Cambridge University Press, 2008.

Ogilvie, Brian W. *The Science of Describing: Natural History in Renaissance Europe*. Chicago: University of Chicago Press, 2006.

O'Gorman, Pamela. "An Eighteenth Century Jamaican Oratorio". *Jamaica Journal* 22, no. 4 (1989–90): 41–45; 23 (1990): 14–19.

Oliphant, John. *Peace and War on the Anglo-Cherokee Frontier, 1756–63*. Baton Rouge: Louisiana State University Press, 2001.

O'Malley, Therese, and Amy R.W. Meyers, eds. *The Art of Natural History: Illustrated Treatises and Botanical Paintings, 1400–1850*. Washington, DC: National Gallery of Art, 2008.

Osborne, Francis J. *History of the Catholic Church in Jamaica*. Chicago: Loyola University Press, 1988.

O'Shaughnessy, Andrew Jackson. *An Empire Divided: The American Revolution and the British Caribbean*. Philadelphia: University of Pennsylvania Press, 2000.

Pares, Richard. *War and Trade in the West Indies, 1739–1763*. Oxford: Oxford University Press, 1936.

Parrish, Susan Scott. *American Curiosity: Cultures of Natural History in the Colonial British Atlantic World*. Chapel Hill: University of North Carolina Press, 2006.

———. "Diasporic African Sources of Enlightenment Knowledge". In *Science and Empire in the Atlantic World*, edited by James Delbourgo and Nicholas Dew, 281–310. New York: Routledge, 2008.

Passmore, J.A. *Ralph Cudworth: An Interpretation*. Cambridge: Cambridge University Press, 1951.

Paton, Diana. "Punishment, Crime, and the Bodies of Slaves in Eighteenth-Century Jamaica". *Journal of Social History* 34 (2001): 923–54

Patterson, Orlando. *The Sociology of Slavery: An Analysis of the Origins, Development and Structure of Negro Slave Society in Jamaica*. London: MacGibbon and Kee, 1967.

Paulson, Ronald. "Henry Fielding and the Problem of Deism". In *The Margins of Orthodoxy: Heterodox Writing and Cultural Response, 1660–1750*, edited by Roger D. Lund, 240–70. Cambridge: Cambridge University Press, 1995.

Pelikan, Jaroslav. *Credo: Historical and Theological Guide to Creeds and Confessions of Faith in the Christian Tradition*. New Haven, Conn.: Yale University Press, 2003.

Perry, Ruth. *Novel Relations: The Transformation of Kinship in English Literature and Culture, 1748–1818*. Cambridge: Cambridge University Press, 2004.

Pestana, Carla Gardina. *The English Atlantic in an Age of Revolution, 1640–1661*. Cambridge, Mass.: Harvard University Press, 2004.

Peters, Marie. "Early Hanoverian Consciousness: Empire or Europe?" *English Historical Review* 122 (2007): 632–68.

Pettigrew, William A. "Free to Enslave: Politics and the Escalation of Britain's Transatlantic Slave Trade, 1688–1714". *William and Mary Quarterly* 64 (2007): 3–38.

Pitman, Frank Wesley. *The Development of the British West Indies, 1700–1763*. 1917. Reprint, London: Frank Cass, 1967.

Pitman, James Hall. *Goldsmith's Animated Nature: A Study of Goldsmith*. New Haven, Conn.: Yale University Press, 1924.

Plomer, H.R., G.H. Bushnell and E.R. McC. Dix, eds. *A Dictionary of the Printers and Booksellers Who Were at Work in England, Scotland and Ireland from 1726 to 1775*. Oxford: Oxford University Press, 1932.

Pocock, J.G.A. "Enthusiasm: The Antiself of Enlightenment". In *Enthusiasm and Enlightenment in Europe, 1650–1850*, edited by Lawrence E. Klein and Anthony J. La Vopa, 7–28. San Marino, Calif.: Huntington Library, 1998.

Popkin, R.H. "Scepticism in the Enlightenment". In *Scepticism in the Enlightenment*, edited by Richard H. Popkin, Ezequiel de Olaso and Giorgio Tonelli, 1–16. Dordrecht: Kluwer Academic, 1997.

Porter, Roy. *Enlightenment: Britain and the Creation of the Modern World*. London: Penguin, 2001.

Powell, Isobel G. "Naval Chaplains in the Early Stuart Period". *Mariner's Mirror* 8 (1922): 290–96.

Preston, Thomas R. "Biblical Criticism, Literature, and the Eighteenth-Century Reader". In *Books and Their Readers in Eighteenth-Century England*, edited by Isabel Rivers, 97–126. Leicester, UK: Leicester University Press, 1982.

Price, Roberto Salinas. *Homeric Whispers: Imitations of Orthodoxy in the* Iliad *and* Odyssey. San Jerónimo Lídice, Mexico: Scylax Press, 2006.

Priestley, Margaret. *West African Trade and Coast Society: A Family Study*. London: Oxford University Press, 1969.

Proctor, J.H. "Scottish Missionaries and Jamaican Slaveholders". *Slavery and Abolition* 25 (2004): 51–70.

Pucci, Pietro. *Oedipus and the Fabrication of the Father:* Oedipus Tyrannus *in Modern Criticism and Philosophy*. Baltimore: Johns Hopkins University Press, 1992.

Ragsdale, Bruce A. "Young Washington's Virginia: Opportunity in the 'Golden Age' of a Planter Society". In *George Washington and the Virginia Backcountry*, edited by Warren R. Hofstra, 35–60. Madison, Wisc.: Madison House, 1998.

Rappaport, Rhoda. *When Geologists Were Historians, 1665–1750*. Ithaca, NY: Cornell University Press, 1997.

Rath, Richard Cullen. "African Music in Seventeenth-Century Jamaica: Cultural Transit and Transition". *William and Mary Quarterly* 50 (1993): 700–726.

Rawlings, Philip. "Dodd, William (1729–1777)". *Oxford Dictionary of National Biography*. Oxford: Oxford University Press, 2004.

Ray, William. *Story and History: Narrative Authority and Social Identity in the Eighteenth-Century French and English Novel*. Oxford: Basil Blackwell, 1990.

Redwood, John. *Reason, Ridicule and Religion: The Age of Enlightenment in England, 1660–1750*. London: Thames and Hudson, 1976.

Rendle, A.B. "Three Early Jamaican Botanists". *Journal of Botany* 53 (1915): 104–7.

Reventlow, Henning. *The Authority of the Bible and the Rise of the Modern World*. London: SCM Press, 1984.

Richardson, John. *Slavery and Augustan Literature: Swift, Pope, Gay*. London: Routledge, 2004.

Richardson, Samuel. *The History of Sir Charles Grandison*. Edited by Jocelyn Harris. London: Oxford University Press, 1972.

Richet, Pascal. *A Natural History of Time*. Chicago: University of Chicago Press, 2007.

Ritterbush, Philip C. "John Lindsay and the Sensitive Plant". *Annals of Science* 18 (1962): 233–35.

———. *Overtures to Biology: The Speculations of Eighteenth-Century Naturalists*. New Haven, Conn.: Yale University Press, 1964.

Rivers, Isabel. *Reason, Grace, and Sentiment: A Study of the Language of Religion and Ethics in England, 1660–1780*. Vol. 2, *Shaftesbury to Hume*. Cambridge: Cambridge University Press, 2000.

"R.M.N." "Charms against Waterspouts". *Mariner's Mirror* 6 (1920): 160.

Roberts, George W. *The Population of Jamaica*. Cambridge: Cambridge University Press, 1957.

Robertson, James. "A 1748 'Petition of Negro Slaves' and the Local Politics of Slavery in Jamaica". *William and Mary Quarterly* 67 (2010): 319–46.

———. *Gone Is the Ancient Glory: Spanish Town, Jamaica, 1534–2000*. Kingston: Ian Randle, 2005.

Robertson, John. *The Case for the Enlightenment: Scotland and Naples, 1680–1760*. Cambridge: Cambridge University Press, 2005.

Robinson, W. Stitt, ed. *Early American Indian Documents: Treaties and Laws, 1607–1789*. Vol. 5, *Virginia Treaties, 1723–1775*. Frederick, Md.: University Publications of America, 1983.

Rodger, N.A.M. "The Naval Chaplain in the Eighteenth Century". *British Journal for Eighteenth-Century Studies* 18 (1995): 33–45.

———. *The Wooden World: An Anatomy of the Georgian Navy*. New York: W.W. Norton, 1986.

Rogers, Pat. *Pope and the Destiny of the Stuarts: History, Politics, and Mythology in the Age of Queen Anne*. Oxford: Oxford University Press, 2005.

Ronan, Charles E. *Francisco Javier Clavigero, S.J. (1731–1787), Figure of the Mexican Enlightenment: His Life and Works*. Rome: Institutum Historicum S.I., 1977.

Ronnick, Michele Valerie. "Francis Williams: An Eighteenth-Century Tertium Quid". *Negro History Bulletin* 61 (1998): 19–29.

Roper, Derek. "Smollett's 'Four Gentlemen': The First Contributors to the *Critical Review*". *Review of English Studies* 10 (1959): 38–44.

Ross, Ian Simpson. *Lord Kames and the Scotland of His Day*. Oxford: Clarendon Press, 1972.

———. " 'More dull, but by no means so dangerous as that of Mr Hume': Smollett's 'Continuation' of *le bon David's History of England*". In *Tobias Smollett, Scotland's First Novelist: New Essays in Memory of Paul-Gabriel Boucé*, edited by O.M. Brack, 217–39. Newark: University of Delaware Press, 2007.

Rössner, Philipp Robinson. *Scottish Trade in the Wake of Union (1700–1760): The Rise of a Warehouse Economy*. Stuttgart: Franz Steiner, 2008.

Rothschild, Emma. "The Atlantic Worlds of David Hume". In *Soundings in Atlantic History: Latent Structures and Intellectual Currents, 1500–1830*, edited by Bernard Bailyn and Patricia L. Denault, 405–48. Cambridge, Mass.: Harvard University Press, 2009.

Rousseau, G.S. "Science Books and Their Readers in the Eighteenth Century". In *Books and Their Readers in Eighteenth-Century England*, edited by Isabel Rivers, 197–255. Leicester, UK: Leicester University Press, 1982.

Rowell, Geoffrey. *Hell and the Victorians: A Study of the Nineteenth-Century Theological Controversies Concerning Eternal Punishment and the Future Life*. Oxford: Clarendon Press, 1974.

Rowley-Conwy, Peter. *From Genesis to Prehistory: The Archaeological Three Age System and Its Contested Reception in Denmark, Britain, and Ireland*. Oxford: Oxford University Press, 2007.

Roxburgh, Kenneth B.E. "Revival: An Aspect of Scottish Religious Identity". In *Religion and National Identity: Wales and Scotland, c. 1700–2000*, edited by Robert Pope, 200–220. Cardiff: University of Wales Press, 2001.

Royster, Charles. *The Fabulous History of the Dismal Swamp Company: A Story of George Washington's Times*. New York: Alfred A. Knopf, 1999.

Saakwa-Mante, Norris D. "William Wright (1735–1819), Military Physician and Naturalist". *Oxford Dictionary of National Biography*. Oxford: Oxford University Press, 2004.

Safier, Neil. *Measuring the New World: Enlightenment Science and South America*. Chicago: University of Chicago Press, 2008.

Sala-Molins, Louis. *Dark Side of the Light: Slavery and the French Enlightenment*. Minneapolis: University of Minnesota Press, 2006.

Sandiford, Keith A. *The Cultural Politics of Sugar: Caribbean Slavery and Narratives of Colonialism*. Cambridge: Cambridge University Press, 2000.

Sayre, Gordon. "Plotting the Natchez Massacre: Le Page du Pratz, Dumont de Montigny, Chateaubriand". *Early American Literature* 37 (2002): 381–413.

Schiebinger, Londa. *Plants and Empire: Colonial Bioprospecting in the Atlantic World*. Cambridge, Mass.: Harvard University Press, 2004.

———. "Scientific Exchange in the Eighteenth-Century Atlantic World". In *Soundings in Atlantic History: Latent Structures and Intellectual Currents, 1500–1830*, edited by Bernard Bailyn and Patricia L. Denault, 294–328. Cambridge, Mass.: Harvard University Press, 2009.

Schlereth, Thomas J. *The Cosmopolitan Ideal in Enlightenment Thought: Its Form and Function in the Ideas of Franklin, Hume, and Voltaire, 1694–1790*. Notre Dame, Ind.: University of Notre Dame Press, 1977.

Schutt, Amy C. *Peoples of the River Valleys: The Odyssey of the Delaware Indians*. Philadelphia: University of Pennsylvania Press, 2007.

Scott, Hew. *Fasti Ecclesiæ Scoticanæ: The Succession of Ministers in the Church of Scotland from the Reformation*. Edinburgh: Oliver and Boyd, 1923.

Scott, H.M. "Britain's Emergence as a European Power, 1688–1815". In *A Companion to Eighteenth-Century Britain*, edited by H.T. Dickinson, 431–46. Oxford: Blackwell, 2002.

Searing, James F. *West African Slavery and Atlantic Commerce: The Senegal River Valley, 1700–1860*. Cambridge: Cambridge University Press, 1993.

Seiler, William H. "The Anglican Parish in Virginia". In *Seventeenth-Century America: Essays in Colonial History*, edited by James Morton Smith, 119–42. Chapel Hill: University of North Carolina Press, 1959.

Semmel, Bernard. *The Methodist Revolution*. London: Heinemann, 1974.

Sensbach, John F. *Rebecca's Revival: Creating Black Christianity in the Atlantic World*. Cambridge, Mass.: Harvard University Press, 2005.

———. *A Separate Canaan: The Making of an Afro-Moravian World in North Carolina, 1763–1840*. Chapel Hill: University of North Carolina Press, 1998.

Shelford, April G. "Pascal in Jamaica: or, The French Enlightenment in Translation". *Proceedings of the Western Society for French History* 36 (2008): 53–74.

Shepherd, Christine. "University Life in the Seventeenth Century". In *Four Centuries: Edinburgh University Life, 1583–1983*, edited by Gordon Donaldson, 1–15. Edinburgh: University of Edinburgh, 1983.

Sher, Richard B. *Church and University in the Scottish Enlightenment: The Moderate Literati of Edinburgh*. Princeton, NJ: Princeton University Press, 1985.

———. *The Enlightenment and the Book: Scottish Authors and Their Publishers in Eighteenth-Century Britain, Ireland, and America.* Chicago: University of Chicago Press, 2006.

Sheridan, Richard B. "The Jamaican Slave Insurrection Scare of 1776 and the American Revolution". *Journal of Negro History* 61 (1976): 290–308.

———. "The Role of the Scots in the Economy and Society of the West Indies". In *Comparative Perspectives on Slavery in New World Plantation Societies*, edited by Vera Rubin and Arthur Tuden. *Annals of the New York Academy of Sciences* 292 (1977): 94–106.

———. *Sugar and Slavery: An Economic History of the British West Indies, 1623–1775.* Barbados: Caribbean Universities Press, 1974.

Shyllon, Folarin. *James Ramsay: The Unknown Abolitionist.* Edinburgh: Canongate, 1977.

Sills, Adam. "Surveying 'The Map of Slavery' in Aphra Behn's Oroonoko". *JNT: Journal of Narrative Theory* 36 (2006): 314–40.

Simpson, Kenneth. "Smollett, Tobias George (1721–1771)". *Oxford Dictionary of National Biography.* Oxford: Oxford University Press, 2004.

Sioutas, Michalis V., and Alexander G. Keul. "Waterspouts of the Adriatic, Ionian and Aegean Sea and Their Meteorological Environment". *Atmospheric Research* 83 (2007): 542–57.

Sloan, Phillip. "The Gaze of Natural History". In *Inventing Human Science: Eighteenth-Century Domains*, edited by Christopher Fox, Roy Porter and Robert Wokler, 112–51. Berkeley: University of California Press, 1995.

Smelser, Marshall. *The Campaign for the Sugar Islands, 1759: A Study of Amphibious Warfare.* Chapel Hill: University of North Carolina Press, 1955.

Smith, G. Munro. *A History of the Bristol Royal Infirmary.* Bristol, UK: J.W. Arrowsmith, 1917.

Smith, Robert Worthington. "Slavery and Christianity in the British West Indies". *Church History* 19 (1950): 171–86.

Smith, S.D. *Slavery, Family, and Gentry Capitalism in the British Atlantic: The World of the Lascelles, 1648–1834.* Cambridge: Cambridge University Press, 2006.

Smitten, Jeffrey. "Impartiality in Robertson's *History of America*". *Eighteenth-Century Studies* 19 (1985): 56–77.

———. "Moderatism and History: William Robertson's Unfinished History of British America". In *Scotland and America in the Age of the Enlightenment*, edited by Richard B. Sher and Jeffrey R. Smitten, 163–79. Edinburgh: Edinburgh University Press, 1990.

———. "Robertson, William (1721–1793)". *Oxford Dictionary of National Biography.* Oxford: Oxford University Press, 2004.

———. "Robertson's Letters and the Life of Writing". In *William Robertson and the Expansion of Empire*, edited by Stewart J. Brown, 36–54. Cambridge: Cambridge University Press, 1997.

Smout, T.C. "Born Again at Cambuslang: New Evidence on Popular Religion and Literacy in Eighteenth-Century Scotland". *Past and Present* 97 (1982): 114–27.

———. *A History of the Scottish People, 1560–1830.* London: Collins, 1970.

Sobel, Dava, and William J.H. Andrewes. *The Illustrated Longitude.* London: Fourth Estate, 1998.

Sorkin, David. *The Religious Enlightenment: Protestants, Jews, and Catholics from London to Vienna.* Princeton, NJ: Princeton University Press, 2008.

Spain, Jonathan. "Kerr, William Henry, fourth marquess of Lothian (c. 1712–1775), army officer". *Oxford Dictionary of National Biography*. Oxford: Oxford University Press, 2004.

Sparks, Randy J. *The Two Princes of Calabar: An Eighteenth-Century Atlantic Odyssey*. Cambridge, Mass.: Harvard University Press, 2004.

Speck, W.A. *The Butcher: The Duke of Cumberland and the Suppression of the 45*. Oxford: Basil Blackwell, 1981.

———. *Society and Literature in England, 1700–60*. Dublin: Gill and Macmillan, 1983.

Spencer, Alfred, ed. *Memoirs of William Hickey*. London: Hurst and Blackett, 1918.

Stafleu, Frans A. *Linnaeus and the Linnaeans: The Spreading of Their Ideas in Systematic Botany, 1735–1789*. Utrecht: International Association for Plant Taxonomy, 1971.

Starkey, David J. *British Privateering Enterprise in the Eighteenth Century*. Exeter, UK: University of Exeter Press, 1990.

Stearns, Raymond Phineas. *Science in the British Colonies of America*. Urbana: University of Illinois Press, 1970.

Steedman, Carolyn. *Labours Lost: Domestic Service and the Making of Modern England*. Cambridge: Cambridge University Press, 2009.

Steel, M.J. "A Philosophy of Fear: The World View of the Jamaican Plantocracy in a Comparative Perspective". *Journal of Caribbean History* 27 (1993): 1–20.

Steele, Richard. *The Conscious Lovers*. Edited by Shirley Strum Kenny. Lincoln: University of Nebraska Press, 1968.

Stewart, Dugald. "Account of the Life and Writings of Adam Smith, LL.D.". [1793]. Edited by I.S. Ross. In *Adam Smith: Essays on Philosophical Subjects*, edited by W.P.D. Wightman and J.C. Bryce 269–351. Oxford: Clarendon Press, 1980.

Stone, Lawrence. *The Family, Sex and Marriage in England, 1500–1800*. London: Weidenfeld and Nicolson, 1977.

Stout, Harry S. *The Divine Dramatist: George Whitefield and the Rise of Modern Evangelicalism*. Grand Rapids, Mich.: William B. Eerdmans, 1991.

Stromberg, Roland N. *Religious Liberalism in Eighteenth-Century England*. Oxford: Oxford University Press, 1954.

Strong, Rowan. *Anglicanism and the British Empire, c. 1700–1850*. Oxford: Oxford University Press, 2007.

———. "Cockburn, Patrick (1678–1749)". *Oxford Dictionary of National Biography*. Oxford: Oxford University Press, 2004.

———. "Rescuing the Perishing Heathen: The British Empire versus the Empire of Satan in Anglican Theology, 1701–1721". In *The Church, the Afterlife and the Fate of the* Soul, edited by Peter Clarke and Tony Claydon, 323–35. Woodbridge, UK: Boydell Press, 2009.

Swaminathan, Srividhya. "Developing the West Indian Proslavery Position after the Somerset Decision". *Slavery and Abolition* 24 (2003): 40–60.

Sykes, Norman. *Church and State in England in the XVIIIth Century*. Cambridge: Cambridge University Press, 1934.

Sypher, Wylie. "The African Prince in London". *Journal of the History of Ideas* 2 (1941): 237–47.

Tavor, Eve. *Scepticism, Society and the Eighteenth-Century Novel*. London: Macmillan, 1987.

Taylor, Aline Mackenzie. *Next to Shakespeare: Otway's* Venice Preserv'd *and* The Orphan *and Their History on the London Stage*. Durham, NC: Duke University Press, 1950.

Taylor, Gordon. *The Sea Chaplains: A History of the Chaplains of the Royal Navy*. Oxford: Oxford Illustrated Press, 1978.

Thalmann, William G. *The Swineherd and the Bow: Representations of Class in the* Odyssey. Ithaca, NY: Cornell University Press, 1998.

Thomas, Helen. *Romanticism and Slave Narratives: Transatlantic Testimonies*. Cambridge: Cambridge University Press, 2000.

Thompson, Alvin O. " 'Happy – Happy Slaves!': Slavery as a Superior State to Freedom". *Journal of Caribbean History* 29 (1995): 93–119.

Thomson, Ann. *Bodies of Thought: Science, Religion, and the Soul in the Early Enlightenment*. Oxford: Oxford University Press, 2008.

Thomson, Keith. *Before Darwin: Reconciling God and Nature*. New Haven, Conn.: Yale University Press, 2005.

Thornbury, Ethel Margaret. *Henry Fielding's Theory of the Comic Prose Epic*. 1931. Reprint, New York: Russell and Russell, 1966.

Thornton, John K. *Warfare in Atlantic Africa, 1500–1800*. London: Routledge, 2004.

Tiedemann, Joseph S. "Moore, Sir Henry, first baronet (1713–1769)". *Oxford Dictionary of National Biography*. Oxford: Oxford University Press, 2004.

Tise, Larry E. *Proslavery: A History of the Defense of Slavery in America, 1701–1840*. Athens: University of Georgia Press, 1987.

Tishkoff, Sarah A., et al. "The Genetic Structure and History of Africans and African Americans". *Science* 324 (22 May 2009): 1035–44.

Todd, Margo. *The Culture of Protestantism in Early Modern Scotland*. New Haven, Conn.: Yale University Press, 2002.

Todorov, Tzvetan. *On Human Diversity: Nationalism, Racism, and Exoticism in French Thought*. Cambridge, Mass.: Harvard University Press, 1993.

Towsey, Mark R.M. *Reading the Scottish Enlightenment: Books and their Readers in Provincial Scotland, 1750–1820*. Leiden: Brill, 2010.

Turner, Mary. *Slaves and Missionaries: The Disintegration of Jamaican Slave Society, 1787–1834*. Urbana: University of Illinois Press, 1982.

Underwood, Dale. *Etherege and the Seventeenth-Century Comedy of Manners*. New Haven, Conn.: Yale University Press, 1957.

Vales, Robert L. *Peter Pindar (John Wolcot)*. New York: Twayne, 1973.

Van Nortwick, Thomas. *The Unknown Odysseus: Alternate Worlds in Homer's* Odyssey. Ann Arbor: University of Michigan Press, 2009.

Vanderford, Chad. "Proslavery Professors: Classic Natural Right and the Positive Good Argument in Antebellum Virginia". *Civil War History* 55 (2009): 5–30.

Vaughan, Alden T. "From White Man to Redskin: Changing Anglo-American Perceptions of the American Indian". *American Historical Review* 87 (1982): 917–53.

———. *Transatlantic Encounters: American Indians in Britain, 1500–1776*. Cambridge: Cambridge University Press, 2006.

Vickers, Brian, ed. *Shakespeare: The Critical Heritage*. Vol. 4, *1753–1765*. London: Routledge and Kegan Paul, 1976.

Vogt, Joseph. *Ancient Slavery and the Ideal of Man*. Oxford: Basil Blackwell, 1974.

Wahrman, Dror. *The Making of the Modern Self: Identity and Culture in Eighteenth-Century England*. New Haven, Conn.: Yale University Press, 2004.

Waingrow, Marshall, ed. *The Correspondence and Other Papers of James Boswell Relating to the Making of the* Life of Johnson. New Haven, Conn.: Yale University Press, 2001.

Walcott, Derek. *Omeros*. London: Faber, 1990.

Walker, D.P. *The Decline of Hell: Seventeenth-Century Discussions of Eternal Torment*. London: Routledge and Kegan Paul, 1964.

Wallis, G.C. "The Custom of 'Cutting a Waterspout' ". *Mariner's Mirror* 63 (1977): 106.

Walsh, John, and Stephen Taylor. "The Church and Anglicanism in the 'Long' Eighteenth Century". In *The Church of England, c. 1689–c. 1833: From Toleration to Tractarianism*, edited by John Walsh, Colin Haydon and Stephen Taylor, 1–64. Cambridge: Cambridge University Press, 1993.

Walvin, James. *The Trader, the Owner, the Slave: Parallel Lives in the Age of Slavery*. London: Jonathan Cape, 2007.

Ward, Candace. "Sensibility, Tropical Disease, and the Eighteenth-Century Sentimental Novel". In *Discourses of Slavery and Abolition: Britain and Its Colonies, 1760–1838*, edited by Brycchan Carey, Markman Ellis and Sara Salih, 63–77. Basingstoke, UK: Palgrave Macmillan, 2004.

Ward, J.R. *British West Indian Slavery, 1750–1834: The Process of Amelioration*. Oxford: Clarendon Press, 1988.

Watson, J. Steven. *The Reign of George III, 1760–1815*. Oxford: Clarendon Press, 1960.

Watt, James. "James Ramsay, 1733–1789: Naval Surgeon, Naval Chaplain and Morning Star of the Anti-Slavery Movement". *Mariner's Mirror* 81 (1995): 156–70.

Webb, James L.A., Jr. "The Mid-Eighteenth Century Gum Arabic Trade and the British Conquest of Saint-Louis du Sénégal, 1758". *Journal of Imperial and Commonwealth History* 25 (1997): 37–58.

Weil, Rachel. *Political Passions: Gender, the Family and Political Argument in England, 1680–1714*. Manchester, UK: Manchester University Press, 1999.

Weinbrot, Howard D. *Eighteenth-Century Satire: Essays on Text and Context from Dryden to Peter Pindar*. Cambridge: Cambridge University Press, 1988.

Wells, Robert V. *The Population of the British Colonies in America before 1776*. Princeton, NJ: Princeton University Press, 1975.

Wheeler, Roxann. *The Complexion of Race: Categories of Difference in Eighteenth-Century British Culture*. Philadelphia: University of Pennsylvania Press, 2000.

Whitford, David M. *The Curse of Ham in the Early Modern Era: The Bible and the Justifications for Slavery*. Farnham, UK: Ashgate, 2009.

Whitney, Lois. *Primitivism and the Idea of Progress in English Popular Literature of the Eighteenth Century*. Baltimore: Johns Hopkins University Press, 1934.

Whyte, Iain. *Scotland and the Abolition of Black Slavery, 1756–1838*. Edinburgh: Edinburgh University Press, 2006.

Wightman, W.P.D., and J.C. Bryce, eds. *Adam Smith: Essays on Philosophical Subjects*. Oxford: Clarendon Press, 1980.

Wilkins, John S. *Species: A History of the Idea*. Berkeley: University of California Press, 2009.

Willey, Basil. *The Eighteenth Century Background: Studies on the Idea of Nature in the Thought of the Period*. 1940. Reprint, London: Chatto and Windus, 1957.

Willig, Timothy D. *Restoring the Chain of Friendship: British Policy and the Indians of the Great Lakes, 1783*–1815. Lincoln: University of Nebraska Press, 2008.

Wilson, Kathleen. "Empire, Trade and Popular Politics in Mid-Hanoverian Britain: The Case of Admiral Vernon". *Past and Present* 121 (1988): 74–109.

———. *The Island Race: Englishness, Empire and Gender in the Eighteenth Century*. London: Routledge, 2003.

Wise, Steven M. *Though the Heavens May Fall: The Landmark Trial That Led to the End of Human Slavery*. London: Pimlico, 2006.

Withers, Charles W.J. "Improvement and Enlightenment: Agriculture and Natural History in the Work of the Rev. Dr. John Walker (1731–1803)". In *Philosophy and Science in the Scottish Enlightenment*, edited by Peter Jones, 102–16. Edinburgh: John Donald, 1988.

———. *Placing the Enlightenment: Thinking Geographically about the Age of Reason*. Chicago: University of Chicago Press, 2007.

Wokler, Robert. "Anthropology and Conjectural History in the Enlightenment". In *Inventing Human Science: Eighteenth-Century Domains*, edited by Christopher Fox, Roy Porter and Robert Wokler, 31–52. Berkeley: University of California Press, 1995.

———. "Apes and Races in the Scottish Enlightenment: Monboddo and Kames on the Nature of Man". In *Philosophy and Science in the Scottish Enlightenment*, edited by Peter Jones, 145–68. Edinburgh: John Donald, 1988.

Wolf, Edwin, II. *The Book Culture of a Colonial American City: Philadelphia Books, Bookmen, and Booksellers*. Oxford: Clarendon Press, 1988.

Wolff, Larry, and Marco Cipollini, eds. *The Anthropology of the Enlightenment*. Stanford, Calif.: Stanford University Press, 2007.

Womersley, D.J. "The Historical Writings of William Robertson". *Journal of the History of Ideas* 47 (1986): 497–506.

Wood, P.B. "The Natural History of Man in the Scottish Enlightenment". *History of Science* 28 (1990): 89–123.

Wood, Sarah F. "Transatlantic Cervantics: Don Quixote and the Fictions of American Enlightenment". In *The Atlantic Enlightenment*, edited by Susan Manning and Francis D. Cogliano, 113–30. Aldershot, UK: Ashgate, 2008.

Wright, Philip. *Monumental Inscriptions of Jamaica*. London: Society of Genealogists, 1966.

Wright, Richardson. *Revels in Jamaica, 1682–1838*. New York: Dodd, Mead, 1937.

Yates, Mary V. "The Christian Rake in *Sir Charles Grandison*". *Studies in English Literature, 1500–1900* 24 (1984): 545–61.

Youngson, A.J. *The Making of Classical Edinburgh, 1750–1840*. Edinburgh: Edinburgh University Press, 1966.

Zack, Naomi. *Philosophy of Science and Race*. New York: Routledge, 2002.

Zimmerman, Everett. *The Boundaries of Fiction: History and the Eighteenth-Century British Novel*. Ithaca, NY: Cornell University Press, 1996.

Index